AF290122

A Broken Triangle

©2024. EDICO
Edition : JDH Éditions
77600 Bussy-Saint-Georges
Printed by Libri Plureos GmbH, Friedensallee 273, 22763 Hamburg, Germany

Cover making: Cynthia Skorupa

ISBN: 978-2-38127-409-6
Legal submission: May 2025

Patrick Pascal

Former Ambassador

A Broken Triangle

*Washington, Moscow, Beijing -
What place for Europe?*

JDH Éditions

Décryptages

This enterprise of universal monarchy, the greatest scourge with which the human race can be threatened, and the sure cause of eternal war'

(Germaine de Staël, *Dix années d'exil*)

'I am Cyrus who conquered this empire for the Persians. Do not envy me the tiny handful of earth that covers this soil.'

(Epitaph from the tomb of Cyrus at Pasargadae)

CONTENTS

Preface – A Broken Triangle? 11

1 – The new world and Hobbes' world 17

2 – Diplomacy and its tools 22
The outline of the reform of the Quai d'Orsay 22
Economic diplomacy 30
In praise of soft power 33

3 – An epidemic of international crises 38
Impasse in Ukraine 38
Damascus: lessons of a strike 44

4 – A moment of strategic change? 59
Dialectic of decision 59
Rebuilding the international system? 61

5 – The President and infra-nuclear thinking 70
Nuclear transgression 70
Faced with sub-nuclear crises: the invasion by Russia 72

6 – Metamorphosis of Russian power 79
Unrecognisable actors 79
From one putsch to another 85

7 – Russia's economic changeover 90
The ordeal and the way out of the crisis 94
Russia in search of a new stability 96

8 – Russian gas, a global issue 100
Nostalgia is not what it used to be 100
The trap of economic sanctions 105
A poorly conducted trial 109

9 – The nuclear complex 112
Nuclear renaissance 112
The Russian nuclear complex 117

10 – Russia-China: partnership and competition 122
The new Great Game 123
The dawn of Eurasia 129
Xi-Putin: the summit of fantasies 134

11 – The South, collective and specific 143
Secrets and treasures of Africa 143
India, a centre of multipolarity 151
Tradition of non-alignment and emerging power 152

For a Mediterranean Republic...153
Afghanistan, an adjustment variable................................160

12 – The old West and the new East 164
Cracks in the West, renewed anti-Americanism.....................164
At the crossroads of forgotten Europe..................................166
East/West: neglected convergences..171
A look back at the Cold War: tensions and search for stability
....175
Is China in NATO's sights?...177
A whiff of the Cold War..182

13 – An American in Paris... 187
Kamala Harris' moment? 187
The man/woman of his/her time 192
The verdict of the people and the world 198

14 – Facing permanent revolution in China 207
Xi, Sun, Chou, Deng and the others 207
From the Soong sisters to Xi Jinping....................................211

15 – Russia's Eurasian temptation 219
Enemies with unlimited friendship..219

16 – Western responsibility? Neutralising Ukraine? 225
The nagging question of NATO's westward expansion...............225
Buffer zone, ceasefire and neutralisation? 229

17 – The eternal question of politics and law....................... 239
Law and international relations...239
Law and society: the memory of Simone Veil and Ruth
Ginsburg...244

18 – Democracy in France 251
A reflection in the mind of Alexis de Tocqueville 251
Towards the end of the republican monarch? 257
Fifty shades of cohabitation...262
The sovereign Republic...266
Betting on instability?..270
A narrow path of ridges 271

19 – Spirituality without the Churches?.............................. 275
The spirit and the time of the Reformation 275
Woman, Life, Freedom, at the heart of Shiism........................281
Crossed spiritualities 286
Francis and the power of life 290

20 – Historical perspective 298

From Antiquity to the present day...298
From one war to another 306
21 – From one international system to another **314**
Crises and the international system...314
Does a system still exist today?..320
22 – Towards a new Washington, Moscou, Beijing triangle?..**332**
The new governance of the world 333
European nightmare..334
23 – Alexander's dream **342**
The world's centre of gravity 342
War and power...344
History, philosophy, spirituality...348
Epilogue – A baroque world half-grave, half-voluptuous....**354**
The essence of Baroque...354
Reformation and Counter-Reformation....................................355
The European crisis of conscience 356
The tip of the iceberg..357
Appendix **359**
Index **367**

Preface

A Broken Triangle?

The Cold War was characterised more by the existence of a duopoly, sometimes called a 'condominium', than by a triangular structure extended to a third power. The American-Soviet condominium reflected the ascendancy of the two nuclear superpowers. But R. Nixon conceived of a conflictual triangle as a way for the United States to take advantage of Sino-Soviet tensions. How has it evolved since then? Given the unstable nature of current international relations, we have to be rather cautious in our analysis and confine ourselves to formulating hypotheses.

Towards a world of revisionist powers?

The 'New International Order' was a concept formulated by George Bush Sr. in the early 1990s, when the Soviet Union was disintegrating and the United States had just won the Gulf War. The resulting world was characterised by American 'hyper-power', albeit mitigated by the maintenance of a degree of cooperation within the UN system. During this phase, powers such as China and, above all, Russia maintained their attachment to the UN Charter (*'the whole Charter, nothing but the Charter'*), which, in their view, could not be modified in any way; this applied in particular to the Security Council, whose membership could not be enlarged, let alone the veto mechanism called into question. These powers were described as 'anti-revisionists'.

We have now moved away from this system - which itself succeeded the opposition of the Cold War blocs - as a result of the emergence of a more multi-polar world and the now total paralysis of the Security Council mechanisms, due in particular to the war in Ukraine, which saw a permanent member flout the basic rules of international law contained in the Charter.

The arrival in power of D. Trump could well have heralded a new era. It is hard to imagine the United States promoting a multilateral system that it feels it can do without. Today's world, in its state of nature, is both one of large blocs and of force prevailing over law. Will Trump therefore eventually favour a three-way game with Moscow and Beijing? If so, the changes - introduced by powers that have become true revisionists of the system - would be considerable. Russia has been aspiring for over thirty years to regain its lost power and could live with this new status. For the United States, things are less clear-cut: the Washington-Moscow-Beijing triangle is no longer the Cold War triangle that allowed Nixon to open up to China in the early 1970s. Only China, closely linked to the USA in economic and commercial terms and to Russia for geo-strategic reasons, would be offered a certain - albeit delicate - room for manoeuvre. And what about Europe?

The Washington, Moscow, Beijing triangle

While the recent normalisation between Russia and the United States is proceeding apace - the further development of which will depend on how the war in Ukraine is resolved - China remained silent and lurking in the shadows. Voices in the West, which in the end are little more than speculation, are making China the backdrop to the rapprochement between Washington and Moscow and the ultimate objective - if not the main target - for the United States.

In recent years, the international system has undergone accelerated change, with the emergence of centres of power and a minimum of regulation within the framework of the UN. The emerging pattern is not necessarily a real division of the world between the most powerful, but rather that of a new three-way game, distinct by definition from the American-Soviet condominium of the Cold War, and even from the first Washington-Beijing-Moscow triangle of the same period. The opening towards China conceived by R. Nixon and implemented by H. Kissinger in the early 1970s was designed to drive a wedge between the two rival Communist powers of the day and to give the United States greater room for manoeuvre, particularly with a view to settling the Vietnam War. One of the effects of this wide-ranging policy - which led to the recognition of the People's Republic of China following the Shanghai communiqué of 1972 - was also to exert pressure on L. Brezhnev's Soviet Union and to promote major strategic arms control agreements, such as the ABM Treaty on anti-missile systems and SALT.

Does the new Republican administration in the United States have such a vision? Are we heading for a new 'Treaty of Tordesillas' to divide up the world, along the lines of the redefinition of relations between Spain and Portugal at the end of the 15th century? Will a minimum of multilateral cooperation within the framework of the United Nations - illustrated by the recent Security Council resolution on Ukraine - be restored? Will the major crises of nuclear proliferation, in North Korea and Iran for example, be brought under control? These are just some of the possible features and prospects for the new world that is taking shape.

The American fiasco

H. Kissinger's golden rule was *'never treat Russia and China in the same way, at the same time'*. At the start of his second term, D. Trump first embarked on a policy of appeasement with V. Putin's Russia against the backdrop of, if not complete normalisation, at least a settlement of the Ukraine affair. Given current relations between Russia and China - which it seems unrealistic to dissociate at this stage - one might have thought of the emergence of a new configuration substituting broad cooperation for the conflict triangle of the Cold War, or even a true division of the world keeping Europe on the sidelines. A world of powers revising the system of international relations that emerged from the Second World War would then have come into being, outside the framework of the United Nations.

The all-out tariff war, launched incoherently by the US President, quickly appeared to be aimed primarily at China, ruining any hopes that might have been raised. The first tug-of-war between Washington and Beijing has now turned to China's advantage. D. Trump has just made a pitiful retreat by exempting advanced technology products (NB: smartphones, computers, electronics) from Asia from tax; the Republican administration now seems keen to resume a trade dialogue with China, but it seems to be in a position of relative weakness. It will not be easy to find a way out of this crisis, and Xi Jinping will not be quick to forgive his American counterpart for having tried to publicly humiliate his country; it is even possible that no real dialogue will be resumed for the duration of Trump's term of office.

So the triangle of the greatest powers will therefore have lasted virtually a short time. Although the American President may have been credited with a desire to put an end to the war on the European continent, as he had announced, not without some rodomontades, he has just made his task more difficult by having lost his superbness. In addition to China, which no longer has the slightest illusion, the reliability of the United States as a partner in the Atlantic Alliance has been called into question; Russia, which has always wondered about the stability of American power and has no lasting memories of Trump's first term in office, will now be in a more reserved position. On the European continent, the military forces of its main nations could play a role in supporting the Ukrainian settlement; without breaking the transatlantic relationship, a re-examination of its energy relations with Russia and trade relations with China is also conceivable. Are we not then witnessing the emergence of a completely different triangle from the one we had envisaged, with the United States now on the sidelines? D. Trump may have forgotten that his President McKinley - to whom he referred in his inaugural speech - and his successor Theodore Roosevelt not only used the 'Big Stick', but that Roosevelt was also a great mediator in the Russo-Japanese war of 1904-1905.

A persistent case for diplomacy?

Despite the 'Imbalance of Terror' which today characterises the state of a world where nuclear deterrence no longer seems to guarantee relative stability in the international system, as it did during the Cold War; where war described as 'high intensity' has returned to the European continent for the first time since the Second World War; where the Near and Middle East are ablaze with unresolved historical conflicts and considerable regional ambitions; where the Straits of Formosa, the new 'blue line of the Vosges', the focus of superpower ambitions, is susceptible to extreme tensions; is there still a place for diplomacy in this more unstable universe at all ?

In a more multipolar world, as illustrated by the emergence of the BRICS, but where multilateralism, which could be defined as dialogue and international cooperation developed within the UN, '*the worst of systems, but the best of which had not been found*', had significantly regressed, what avenues should be explored in the aftermath of the war in Ukraine?

One way forward would be to finally complete a reform of the United Nations, envisaged more than twenty-five years ago, put on the drawing board but never completed. This transformation should aim, as a matter of priority, to ensure that the world organisation better reflects the real state of the world and responds to old, emerging and, in any case, legitimate ambitions. This should be reflected in an enlarged Security Council, whose decision-making mechanisms could also be adjusted.

But the global response cannot be limited to the question of institutional mechanisms. It will also, of course, have to take account of the international context as a whole. Apart from the question of the end of the war on the European continent - which seems to be affecting the system more than the conflicts in the Middle East, where Russia and a fortiori China have remained relatively aloof - what will be the policy of the new American administration? What will happen in the years to come to the Sino-American relationship, which will inevitably 'structure' the system on its own?

After an 'eclipse', diplomacy will find its time again. It has been defined by P. Renouvin and J.B. Duroselle, masters of international relations, as all '*relations between political communities organised within the framework of a territory*'. Diplomacy is therefore like a natural breath of air, dating back to time immemorial and known in Mesopotamia and among the Greek city-states, before being formalised in the Italian

Quattrocento. Diplomacy is, in the final analysis, eternal: with all due respect for inappropriate humour, it is also one of the 'oldest professions in the world', but it has to be constantly reinvented.

1

The new world and Hobbes' world

The war in Ukraine, which began on 24 February 2022, exploded like a thunderclap across the whole of Europe, a continent that had until then believed in a lasting peace that, despite its complexities and a problematic enlargement, had helped to build Europe. The tremor, of a telluric nature, spread like a shock wave that nothing could stem, producing at the very least global effects, if not raising fears of the prospect of a conflagration on a planetary scale.

Whatever the reasons, whatever the justifications, whatever the specific features of this major conflict compared with other crisis areas, because it directly involved a major nuclear power, a sovereign state with a population of some forty million was the object of a high-intensity war on the European continent; the scale of this war was unprecedented since the Second World War; the fundamental principles of the UN Charter were violated; Europe's problems were increased as a result; the economic consequences have been felt across the continents, including in the countries of the South, where food supplies have been disrupted by obstacles to the flow of supplies by sea across the Black Sea; force has taken precedence over law in a tumultuous manner, and the lasting effects are also likely, through knock-on effects and mimicry, to reverberate in other areas of tension, whether in the Near and Middle East or in the Taiwan Strait.

As a result, the international system built up since 1945, notably within the framework of the UN, appears disorganised, if not in tatters. The economic deregulation that has accompanied the globalisation of trade in recent decades - not all of which has been negative - has been followed by a questioning of the rules by which the international system operates, with law and diplomacy taking a back seat. The unstable nature of what we can now only hesitantly call 'international society' has even contaminated the military nuclear sphere. However, after the Cuban missile crisis in 1962, a balance of so-called 'terror' was established, guaranteeing predictability and a modicum of stability in relations between the major powers.

During the war in Ukraine, subliminal and sometimes much more explicit statements were repeatedly made about the possible use of nuclear weapons. Despite assurances of 'serious consequences', these threats were not countered by the West; the destruction of the Russian army or the Russian Black Sea fleet was sometimes mentioned. Is this not the beginning of the erosion of deterrence on the European continent? Indeed, in this theatre, there are those who announce what they might do and those who clearly state what they would not do in such and such a scenario.

Such departures from the 'grammar' of deterrence clearly show that the Ukraine we have supported is not one of our 'vital interests'. This is a far cry from General de Gaulle's words to a Soviet interlocutor: '*Well, Mr Ambassador, we'll die together.*'

We are no longer in the 'balance of terror' which, paradoxically, had brought stability to the international system, but rather in an 'imbalance' from the moment a nuclear state confronts a non-nuclear state. Russia's discourse - and its very practice of war since the start of the conflict - is, moreover, one of terror.

While we must always bet on the rationality of nuclear-armed actors - and it seems that the Americans and the Russians have never ceased their dialogue on these sensitive issues - the volatility of the current international situation can only lead us to think again of Dr Oppenheimer's mental tortures. No, Hiroshima and Nagasaki will not have given the guarantee of having been an ultimate moment, but sharing the nightmare of the American physicist is ultimately salutary and should bring us back to a more classical conception of deterrence.

This new 'Imbalance of Terror' is not limited to the world of military strategy. Insofar as many current positions are presented, albeit artificially and in the service of a certain narrative, as opposing groups (East-West), opposing systems (autocracies and democracies) at the end of the transformation of the Cold War blocs, the internal evolution of societies also deserves closer examination; this can be approached from the angle of historical legacies, the relationship between politics and law or the importance of the religious factor, which should not be confused with spirituality.

The Russian project in Ukraine was part of an imperial tradition aimed at restoring influence, if not at dominating new lands. If this was indeed the case, the use of force, as befits the Tsar, did not have the effect of internal repulsion that one might imagine, but on the contrary may have led to a strengthening of legitimacy. Internationally, it is clear that the Russian President prefers to be feared rather than seduced. This analysis of the mode of governance applied to an autocracy can also be transposed to Western societies, where there is of course great diversity. Not only is the phenomenon of populism the focus of our attention, but also, more generally, the evolution of democracies where, under the impact of the war after the pandemic, the discourse has become radicalised in order to contain, if necessary, increasingly centrifugal opposition. To the phenomenon of war and the internal tensions in certain societies, we need to add an analysis of the transnational threats that have already become very real perils, whether in the form of uncontrolled migratory flows, terrorism or even the attack on freedoms by unregulated new technologies.

Faced with these crises and problems, is there still an international system? This is the question being asked at a time when the UN Security Council is now paralysed. The Cold War world came to an end in 1990/1991 with the break-up of the Soviet Union and following the first Gulf War in January 1991; it gave rise to a 'New International Order', in reality dominated by the United States, but in which multilateral cooperation between the powers was not absent. Today we are witnessing the affirmation of a multipolar world, which should not be confused with multilateral practices.

The world today seems to have returned to a state of nature, as described by Thomas Hobbes in the seventeenth century *Leviathan*, where force prevails over law; the world is less unipolar than the one denounced by President Putin in his famous 2007 speech at the Munich *Wehrkunde*; for Europe, the concept of strategic autonomy is struggling to make headway, but circumstances could favour it; the opposition between East and West is not the reality that certain narratives would like to impose, because international relations have become more volatile and alliances are sectoral and ultimately 'à la carte'; it is therefore difficult to envisage real blocs.

But our new world - which ultimately resembles Hobbes's world - appears to be a system in the process of breaking down and also of recomposing itself. The nuclear threat, unthinkable during the Cold War, with the exception of the Cuban missile crisis in 1962, reveals a situation that can be characterised as 'infra-nuclear'. In Ukraine, we are not defending democracy or Western civilisation, but the law, the foundation of a minimum international order. As in Hobbes' time, we will have to restore a form of social contract for the whole mankind.

Whether it is the belligerents, those who assist them or more distant observers, the theme of war has become omnipresent, obsessive even, amplified by powerful media. Military chiefs come to speak, breaking the once intangible principle that the army should remain a 'great mute' in a republic and always remain subject to civilian authority. Historical comparisons flourish, the Donbas and the Sudetenland become entangled, and the mention of necessary negotiations leads to the denunciation of a suspicious pacifism, to the supreme insult of a reference to Munich in 1938, and even to the accusation of 'cowardice'; Nasser was once compared to Hitler by a war-mongering French head of government during the Suez crisis in 1956, and Putin has become the new Hitler of the nuclear age. Burdened by such a climate, even free peoples are left with no alternative but to send their children to 'ground troops', against the backdrop of an invasion of Europe and a possible Third World War.

This collective delirium obscures other threats on a global scale that require the cooperation of all, such as global warming, a veritable time bomb with an incomparable capacity for destruction, underdevelopment, uncontrolled migration and nuclear proliferation. So to talk about diplomacy without preconceptions and dialogue is not weakness, but the expression of a high sense of responsibility. This applies to Ukraine, as it does to all the world's conflicts.

Diplomacy can be developed in support of war, as Sergei Lavrov has shown with undeniable talent in his discreet but formidably effective mobilisation of a 'Global South', but it can also help to avoid the irreparable, as Secretary of State Antony Blinken tried to do for a time with his shuttles in the Middle East. But what would we do tomorrow faced with a nuclear Iran and a North Korea no longer under the dual tutelage of Russia and China? Who do we need now to ward off such perils?

These are the serious questions we must try to answer. And these questions require us to reflect on the state of the world without preconceptions, and to put things into perspective. We must strive to replace short-term analysis and knee-jerk reactions, which often prevail today, with an examination of longer sequences. These must be on the scale of history, as the survival of Hobbes's mental universe, several centuries later, is there to remind us.

2

Diplomacy and its tools

Is there still a place for diplomacy? Diplomacy is based on tangible realities and interests; it involves human lives. It is multidisciplinary and must bring together a large number of specialities: law, history, geography, economics, military strategy, technological subjects, foreign languages, etc. The list is not exhaustive. It proceeds from these components in a way that is sometimes even artisanal. This is the diplomat's added value. It must never forget, despite its sometimes limited visibility, because it is more generally discreet, if not secret, that it is only the 'superstructure' of a world that lives, survives, struggles, defends itself and more often than not suffers. The international system is by definition in a state of flux, and only stabilises, if at all, for limited periods of time throughout history. In 2025 and probably well beyond, diplomats will have to face up to the old challenges of the new world.

The outline of the reform of the Quai d'Orsay

Between the two rounds of the last French presidential election, the decree reforming by ordinance the recruitment of diplomats at the Quai d'Orsay was published in the *Journal Officiel* of the republic. Without in any way wishing to interfere in domestic political debates, it is important today to retrace the development of a great institution and to question this major reform.

The abolition of two of the Ministry's corps - that of plenipotentiary ministers and that of foreign affairs advisers - was part of an overall overhaul of the senior civil service sought by the Executive power. The demise of the diplomatic corps followed the disappearance of the corps of prefects and the transformation of the National High

School of Administration (ENA) into the *Institut national du service public*. Clearly, the reform of the Quai was determined by the desire for a common public administration, rapid changeover of civil servants and their interchangeability, all changes that were supposed to guarantee modernity.

In concrete terms, staff in the 'A' category, i.e. the top echelon - who represented around 700 people at the time - were to join the new *corps des Administrateurs de l'État* (State civil servants) by 2023. The announcement of these radical changes and the disappearance of all career prospects in the diplomatic service drew widespread criticism from politicians, who argued that 'competence' should be preserved and that 'appointments of convenience' should be avoided. Staff from all the unions announced a strike - the second since the 2003 strike over salary. But little has been heard from the leading figures at the Quai d'Orsay itself.

The main message of the reform seems to have been the need to 'adapt' instead of 'knowledge' and 'expertise'. But it is precisely the possession of these latter qualities that facilitates staff flexibility, if they are not even the *sine qua non* of it. Can you imagine an official from a *prefecture* (local administration) or tax administration being quickly and fully operational in a diplomatic or consular representation in Shanghai, St Petersburg or Riyadh?

The reform came at the end of a long, lean period, spanning several decades, during which staff numbers and resources were drastically reduced. We now need to look back at a parallel development, which is both the cause and consequence of a less streamlined diplomacy, affecting a diplomatic network that was the second largest in the world in terms of numbers, and then the third largest after the United States and China.

Corporatism or a specific institution of the Republic?

The expression 'diplomatic corps' is misleading because it implies a certain corporatism, a closing in of the corps to itself, a feeling reinforced by the relative ignorance of the work of diplomatic and consular agents, and even of their salaries and pensions. It is possible that the Quai d'Orsay, for not having communicated enough on these various aspects, bears some responsibility for this lack of awareness. All the same, given that clichés die hard, it is to be hoped that public opinion will no longer cling to the 'diplomacy of the cup of tea' or the brand-name chocolates served at ambassadorial receptions, as popularised by advertising.

In reality, diplomacy is not one job, but several very different jobs that Quai d'Orsay employees alternate between throughout their careers. There is in fact nothing in common between a posting to a bilateral post in East Berlin at the heart of the Cold War - where the main task, in a relatively confined environment, is to produce analyses for the 'Department', as it is known, i.e. the parent company - the exercise of public diplomacy in New York, at the United Nations, in the General Assembly and the Security Council, and the protection of French expatriate communities in countries at war or still threatened by seismic risks, in the Middle East, in Central Asia or today in Ukraine. Discovering the supposed need to adapt is like inventing gunpowder.

Diplomacy, which mainly consists of informing one's government, negotiating on its behalf and representing one's country, requires a 'cultural' approach that cannot be improvised. It has often become more technocratic, particularly in the multilateral forums of Brussels, New York, Geneva and Vienna, but it is not just that. The Quai d'Orsay, for example, could boast a corps of outstanding Arabists whose specialisation, particularly in languages, and long exposure to specific cultures and histories have often made all the difference. Let us not be afraid to say that, without the somewhat childish vanity of the first pupil in the class - for it is not rank that counts but what it enables us to achieve - French diplomacy in the Near and Middle East was incomparable. Aren't we sorely lacking such a tool at present?

If the aim today is to 'open up' the Quai d'Orsay to a wide range of profiles and backgrounds, it should be noted that this has been the case for a long time. The most visible aspect for public opinion is the appointment of outsiders as heads of post, which began with the election of François Mitterrand in 1981. A business leader was appointed to Washington, a media and cultural figure to Copenhagen, a Socialist Party leader to Rome and the list goes on. This change, which brought in a breath of fresh air, has generally proved positive and has not been strongly contested, since it has never reached the scale of the American-style spoil system. It's all a question of proportion and quality, and the process has continued despite political change.

The Quai d'Orsay used to be a rather welcoming place, and it was even less of an ivory tower in that its permanent staff could also leave it. They are encouraged to do so in order to enrich their careers for the greater benefit of the community. This is what is known as 'mobility', which takes the form of secondment (NB: assignment to another government department or public company), secondment financed by the original government department (e.g. to the *Institut du Monde Arabe* as Director of the Office of its President) or secondment - the legal maximum of which is ten years - to a private body or company, which then pays the employee's salary. Mobility in the private sector is implemented under the supervision of a specialised commission at *Bercy* (ministry of Finance), with regard to ethical issues. A civil servant may not be recruited by a private company of which he or she had prior knowledge in the performance of his or her duties in the service of the State. Similarly, the private sector activities of former heads of diplomatic posts are also 'regulated' for a period of three years after they retire from the civil service. In the same vein, the assets of serving ambassadors are subject to compulsory declaration to the High Authority for Transparency, as required by law.

In addition, it should be remembered that diplomats, and in particular ambassadors, represent not only the President of the Republic, who appoints them by decree of the Council of Ministers, but also the whole of the government and State administration. For some forty years now, delegations to the ordinary session of the UN General Assembly in New York have included members of parliament from various political parties as well as trade unionists.

Various government departments have representatives in the larger posts, starting with Bercy and Defence. For example, the weekly meetings of heads of department in London bring together dozens of people from all walks of life (cf. maritime attaché, tax attaché, judicial attaché, etc.). It's not now that Quai staff will be discovering administrative diversity.

Upward and downward spirals

In the end, the abolition of the diplomatic corps was not an invention from nothing but the culmination of an evolutionary process. As the world changes, it is only natural that the Quai d'Orsay should evolve too, and this is what it has done for many years. In addition to the technocratic evolution, the ministry has evolved in its sociological make-up. Recruitment through the ENA (Ecole Nationale d'Administration) following Michel Debré's reform was a clear improvement on the direct selection by co-option that had characterised previous republics.

The Quai's 'Oriental' competitive examinations, which require not only specific and 'rare' linguistic skills but also a mastery of general subjects - making this one of the longest competitive examinations in the civil service - have reinforced this sociological change in the diplomatic corps. While the ENA has ensured the republican unity of recruitment to the senior civil service, it has not done enough to promote modest social strata. At the *Institut des Langues Orientales -* INALCO (Institute for Oriental Languages), on the other hand, students from all walks of life with a passion for different languages and cultures were able to discover a vocation for foreign affairs and take the competitive entrance exams offered by this administration. Abolishing the Oriental competitive entrance examinations would lead to social regression.

Reform or no reform, in an increasingly complex world where states have become weaker, the result has also been a watering down of foreign policy discourse. The gradual shift towards Brussels of the centre of gravity of European nations has also played its part. Gone are the days when Maurice Couve de Murville, General de Gaulle's Foreign Minister, could say: '*France only speaks once*'. At the end of the

1970s, President Giscard d'Estaing was still giving a structured, wide-ranging speech on the subject at the UN special session on disarmament, which would serve as a diary for years to come for the diplomats at the Quai d'Orsay responsible for these issues. To put it simply, globalisation has come and gone and muddied many waters.

But we should not hide behind external factors alone, and the internal politics of states must also be taken into account. Basically, great foreign ministers have also worked alongside great presidents - in addition to their intrinsic merits, of course - and this is true in the United States even for Henry Kissinger and Richard Nixon. In addition to the aforementioned Couve de Murville, Michel Jobert comes to mind under the all-too-brief presidency of Georges Pompidou, and this list could of course be completed. But there were also, admittedly, more elusive profiles. Professor Zorgbibe has republished one of his works, giving it its original title: *Delcassé, l'inconnu du Quai d'Orsay* (The unknown minister at the Quai d'Orsay). If a book is devoted to an 'unknown', it is because his overall action was not negligible, whatever the external perception. In more recent times, the Quai has been headed by ministers who were not all bad managers or had neglected questions of internal organisation.

The institutions against the Republic or the Republic against its institutions?

An administration is at the service of the State, all the more so when the State is republican. It is therefore not a question of rejecting a reform a priori, which may have its merits (see above), but it would have been preferable for the question to have been debated beforehand. If it has not been debated beforehand, there is a strong risk that it will be debated afterwards, if only to finalise the implementation procedures because, as always, '*the devil is in the detail*'.

A Chief of Staff, spoiled by the Republic, has opposed the Head of State frontally and publicly, and it is out of the question to adopt a behaviour, all things considered, of a 'putschist' nature. Indeed, while an institution cannot call into question the republic that it must serve, it is also essential that the republic should not itself weaken the institutions on which it is based.

To put it bluntly, the Church in France has taken great risks by not having drawn the consequences of the Sauvé report until now. Education is a perpetual work in progress that seems difficult to order, and the political institutions themselves are being called into question with calls - not always unjustified by the way - for a new Republic that would, for example, be characterised by a strict separation of powers. What remains in this context? The Quai d'Orsay, which is small in size and often the object of jealousy, starting with Bercy, but which until now has functioned quite well and competently.

Do we want to throw it to the wolves, in the name of so-called egalitarianism and 'diversity', because it has little public support, and is unable to carry out other essential reforms? The great danger is that the reform, as announced, will lead to a Taylorism of the diplomatic function. This piecemeal approach, where overall vision and perspective are needed, would be tantamount to a self-destructive 'Ubérisation'.

The Hôtel du Quai d'Orsay, designed by Guizot under the July Monarchy and completed under the Second Empire, was the first building in Paris designed to house a ministry. This showcase of French excellence and influence is in danger of becoming the museum of a suicidal decline. Time would then stand still in the Salon de l'Horloge, the setting for so many historic moments, from the Congress of Paris at the end of the Crimean War to the Declaration by Robert Schuman in 1950, which laid one of the foundations of European integration.

The Quai d'Orsay is well worth a visit and deserves to be better known. We shouldn't be as jealous of it as Napoleon III, who, despite having wanted its magnificence, once said to the holder of the portfolio of Foreign Affairs, not without a touch of jealousy: '*But, my dear Minister, you are much better housed than I am!*' The Quai d'Orsay is not in the habit of complaining, let alone protesting, and despite these times of general budget shortages it has little reason to do so. It simply wants to be respected for what it really is, and allowed to continue serving the Republic and promoting France.

This was the Quai d'Orsay: Pierre Brochand

Pierre Brochand was an exceptional professional with unrivalled standards in diplomacy, particularly in his capacity as Deputy Permanent Representative of France to the UN Security Council in New York, where I had the privilege of working alongside him, under his authority, for four years. Not to mention our weekly jog around the 2.6 km reservoir in Central Park.

Pierre-Louis Blanc, a former collaborator of the General de Gaulle, then Ambassador to the United Nations (1987-1991) speaks of him in these terms in his book 'Valise diplomatique' (Diplomatic Pouch) in which he devotes a chapter to his mission in New York:

'We shared a deep admiration for de Gaulle, a real interest in sport in general and rugby in particular, and a strong attachment to Asia, which he knew much better than I did, having 'toured' there more than I did. Youthful in body and face, a marathon runner of quality, demanding a lot from others and even more from himself, with a razor-sharp intelligence, he didn't let anyone tell him what to do, excellent in negotiations, a hard worker under the appearance of a frail teenager. He was an excellent collaborator and a sort of younger brother to me. He will leave New York to become ambassador to Hungary, Israel and Portugal. He has just been appointed Director of External Security, which means that he will be in charge of our intelligence services, a delicate mission if ever there was one, and one that I am sure he will carry out wonderfully.'

One event, among many others in what was then a centre of world diplomacy, springs to mind. On Sunday 3 July 1988, on the eve of Independence Day, the US Navy mistakenly shot down an Iranian civilian Airbus over the Persian Gulf. The Security Council held an emergency meeting. In the absence of the ambassador, Pierre Brochand took the chair. The Iranians, who were boycotting the

Council at the time, seized the opportunity of this tragedy to return to the Council table.

In a way, it was the reverse image of the Italians leaving the League of Nations at the time of the Ethiopia affair. In his speech, Pierre Brochand suggested that Teheran should sublimate the tragedy in order to settle major issues concerning it. The Iranian Foreign Minister, Dr Velayati, standing next to him, watched him with rapt attention. Vice-President George Bush Sr. also came to the Council to express American compassion. Be that as it may, this dramatic event marked the beginning of a settlement of the Iran-Iraq war, along the lines set out by the French representative, between two countries in a state of exsanguination. The ceasefire was ratified on 20 August 1988 by Security Council Resolution 598.

Economic diplomacy

Compared with traditional diplomacy, which was based on political relations between states, economic diplomacy - which could also be said to have always existed in various forms - is nonetheless an innovation whose development has roughly coincided with globalisation. In a world where competition between economies and large companies is exacerbated, governments are now committed to supporting the latter, particularly in markets where economies are managed and where access to decision-makers is at the highest level. This does not mean, however, that small and medium-sized enterprises (SMEs) are being neglected when they boldly enter foreign markets, given their size and resources. Strategic sectors, which naturally include the weapons industry, but also transport, energy and space sectors, are at the heart of economic diplomacy, whatever the structure of the companies, whether the State is the majority shareholder or the companies are dependent on private shareholding. The following example of promoting the use of satellites in Central Asia, a relatively unknown region in the world, is an illustration of economic diplomacy.

The first Turkmen telecommunications satellite *TürkmenÄlem* 52°E (NB: meaning 'Turkmen world' or 'peace' like *Mir* in Russian;

geostationary position 52° East), built in Cannes by Thales Alenia Space, was successfully launched on 28 April 2015. The technical perfection of the launch and the excellent performance since then of the satellite - intended for television, broadcasting and the internet - were the culmination of a process of negotiation and technical development spanning more than five years.

Putting the deal together proved to be quite complex. In November 2011, the Turkmen Ministry of Communications signed a number of contracts with Thales Alenia Space for the manufacture and delivery of the satellite to the Turkmen state body NSSC (National System of Satellite Communications). In 2009, Space Systems International (SSI-Monaco) obtained a licence from the Monegasque government to use the 52° East orbital position. The Turkmen authorities have therefore also made a commitment to SSI for the use of this orbital position, reserving 12 of the 38 telecommunication channels of the future satellite for the Monegasque company's own use, with responsibility for marketing the others. This is why the Turkmen satellite was registered as both TürkmenÄlem 52° operated by Turkmenistan National Space Agency and MonacoSAT 1.

Turkmenistan has thus become a customer for *Spacebus* satellites produced by Thales Alenia Space. Spacebus is the name given to the family of platforms (NB: service modules designed to provide all the functions required by the satellite, whatever the specific mission payload, whether telecommunications, Earth observation, navigation or scientific). These geostationary telecommunications satellites were developed from the 1980s onwards by Aérospatiale, which became Alcatel Space, then Alcatel Alenia Space, and finally Thales Alenia Space in 2007. The name Spacebus was chosen in reference to the Airbus aeronautics programme. All products in the range have been exported.

In addition to the use of a generic platform, originally designed to adapt to the various missions and changes in launcher capabilities - which had the effect of lowering production costs - the choice was made for an 'ITAR-free' satellite from the Spacebus 4000 range (NB:

6th 4000C2 weighing more than 4 tonnes), i.e. without any components prohibited from export by US extraterritorial legislation. Thales, the project's prime contractor and the Turkmen state's main contractor, chose the Chinese *Long March* 3B (CZ-3B) launcher from a very wide range of options. Until then, the CZ-3B had been totally reliable and its price was attractive compared with Ariane 5.

The ITAR rule was finally tightened during the 2010 decade, bringing certain components under new bans, and pressure was brought to bear on Thales to end its ITAR-free range. Thales decided to terminate its contract with China Great Wall Industry Corp, which naturally entailed penalties. The Ariane 5 technical solution remained, but its cost would have cancelled out the commercial advantages gained from an initial contract that could no longer be renegotiated with the Turkmen authorities. Various launchers were examined, including the Russian *Proton*, but in the end the *Falcon* 9 rocket from the new Space X company was chosen. This was an extremely bold decision, given that at the time the contract was signed, the launcher only existed on the basis of its designers' plans.

The rest was not a smooth ride, as Thales, as prime contractor, had to contend with Turkmenistan's expectations and impatience for a project with a strong national dimension as well as regional prestige. The launch on 27 April from Cape Canaveral, followed in the middle of the Turkmen night from the Ashgabat control centre (NB: a back-up centre had been set up in the north of the country, not far from Uzbekistan, near the town of Dashoguz), had been preceded a few weeks earlier by a failed Falcon 9.

Years of negotiations and technical developments (ground infrastructure, staff training, etc.) have paid off. TürkmenÄlem 52°E now gives priority coverage to the Turkmenistan-Kazakhstan-Uzbekistan zone, so that its broadcasts can be received by small satellite dishes; the field of coverage has been extended to Russia, Scandinavia as far as north-west France and the south of the United Kingdom; the MENA (Middle East and North Africa) zone focuses on the Arabian Peninsula, with extensions to the south towards Sudan and Ethiopia. The satellite will have a lifetime of at least fifteen years.

The success of this first telecommunications satellite has also paved the way for a potential market for satellites extended to Earth observation (NB: optical and radar satellites), for both civilian and, where appropriate, military purposes in a border area, notably with Iran and Afghanistan. The President of Thales Alenia Space received a special welcome from Turkmen President Berdymuhamedov in June 2015. Generally speaking, bilateral relations between France and Turkmenistan have been strengthened, with Rashid Meredov, Turkmenistan's Minister of Foreign Affairs, being welcomed to Paris by his counterpart Laurent Fabius in July 2015. More than twenty years (1994) after President Mitterrand's visit, which benefited French interests in the country, plans were made for a French presidential visit in 2016, but this was never carried out. All in all, however, the TürkmenÄlem 52° E project was a highly successful example of what is known as 'economic diplomacy', involving state representatives and businesses throughout the process.

In praise of soft power

Soft power is also an instrument that can be used in the service of diplomacy. The Olympic Games are a case in point. Conceived for peaceful purposes exactly a century ago in the modern era, they are ultimately the sacred fire stolen from Zeus on Olympus, symbolised by a continuously burning cauldron and, this year, by an ingenious flaming hot-air balloon that was raised to the sky once again. It's a supreme Promethean undertaking where nothing is big enough or beautiful enough, where the athletes set themselves no other limit than gold, Olympic and world records, glory and a yearning for eternity.

When it comes to major world events, and even beyond sport, the Games represent a considerable, incomparable and hopefully lasting *soft powe*r for the host country or a multiplier of its influence. Paris 2024 was able to exploit this to the full, regardless of the relatively minor controversies, by ensuring the blockbuster status of its city, the Seine, its history and its myths.

And for the most successful athletes or those who have achieved one or more exceptional performances, they guarantee access to the Pantheon and remind us of the unique weight of individuals within the greatest constructions. Jesse Owens was stronger than Berlin. In return, the champion can magnify the community itself; in this respect, is the medal table, a somewhat notarial tally, so important? A single Olympic title is enough to put a country on the world map, at least for a while.

It is true, however, that the final hierarchy reflects, if not wealth, then the strength of the training and coaching structures, and a level of development sufficiently high to allow access to the elite of the sporting hierarchy; at Paris 2024, this diagnosis will have been confirmed: with the exception of China and, given the absence of Russia, the Top 10 - which may bring to mind a G7 enlarged at the margins - is made up exclusively of affluent, Western and European nations. Being close to this group, let alone joining it, confers an enviable status at a time when the world is breaking up.

Competitive rivalry

The term 'soft' power is partly misleading, even if Joseph Nye - a Harvard professor who served under Presidents Carter and Clinton, and later chaired the Trilateral Commission - coined the concept and, by transposing it to the world of international relations, sought to believe in the possibility of competitive rivalry between nations without major gaps.

This kind of thinking, tinged with irenicism and applied to situations of competition between powers - characterised by latent crises (e.g. Taiwan) or even confrontations between allies (e.g. today's Ukraine) - may seem like wishful thinking. It did, however, have the merit of theorising the importance for the United States of maximising soft power, i.e. profitable relations based on interdependence.

It has to be said that soft power has penetrated many areas of public life, starting with the cultural sphere. Could it be that culture, like geography, is also used to wage war, to paraphrase the geographer Yves Lacoste?

The disturbing concert in Palmyra

But we also need to be positive, and culture cannot be reduced to the pursuit of war by other means. We remember the Palmyra Concert conducted in 2015 by Valery Gergiev, against the backdrop of the war in Syria. The world-famous conductor of Ossetian origin, who heads the orchestra of the Mariinsky Theatre in St Petersburg, had organised the event somewhat hastily in the wake of the Russian military intervention in the country; in fact, there were more military uniforms than civilians in the stands and the Russian president himself took part by video conference to celebrate the rebirth of culture in these parts. But is it really so scandalous - despite the obvious propaganda intentions - that the images of a concert were substituted for those of the destruction of a thousand-year-old heritage and other abominations committed on the spot by Daesh, such as the execution in Palmyra itself of the Syrian Director of Antiquities?

Beyond catharsis

While it is far too early to draw up an assessment of the Paris 2024 Olympic Games, the collective enthusiasm has so far proved indisputable, well beyond even France's borders. France has astonished the world, and its own people have no doubt even surprised themselves by giving in to such enthusiasm, in the context of a delicate domestic political situation, to use a modest euphemism. Will France, which for a time sublimated negative passions, emerge transformed from the event? Will the Games be able to bring about beneficial internal changes?

We have to hope that the awareness of the need to carry out major projects and to innovate, to express positive passions, to show off and to benefit from an opening onto the world will set an example. But if we are not to play the Cassandra, this legacy will have to be nurtured if it is not to dissolve. The example of the London 2012 Games is worth looking at for a moment. In retrospect, similarities can be identified with the characteristics of the Paris Games, whether in terms of the quality of the organisation, the collective enthusiasm or the self-sacrifice of tens of thousands of volunteers.

Who then could have imagined, in contradiction to this atmosphere of unrestrained openness, a move towards Brexit that was naturally the result of complex factors?

Be that as it may, soft power has always been there. Wasn't it already the mainspring of Alexander the Great's conquests, thanks to the spread of Hellenistic civilisation? Closer to home, it was undoubtedly a peacetime weapon in the golden age of the United States in the Eisenhower years immediately after the Second World War. A power and a civilisation are only truly established over time through the seduction they exert. The Olympic Games can be an incomparable medium for this. We can only hope that Paris 2024 will have been both an outlet and a revelation of identity in a new modernity.

The new Marseillaise

Perhaps the most novel and surprising impression made on the French by the Olympic Games was produced by what they thought they knew best, that it was part of their collective expression and at the same time corresponded to their internalized image of the nation, amplified by sound: *La Marseillaise*.

Mezzo-soprano Axelle Saint-Cirel, braving the rain and the elements, set the tone from the top of the sumptuous rounded forms of the roofs of the Grand Palais, during the opening ceremony.

The *Divertimento* symphony orchestra from Seine-Saint-Denis, conducted by Zahia Ziouani for the closing ceremony, followed suit, delivering the anthem of a grandiose, cinematic project. But have the tones, which in their own way paint a vast historical picture, also become those of a new or rediscovered music, a kind of marching order for a more peaceful nation ? The evocative power of great past endeavours would then have been joined by the force of an intact and boundless universalism.

Music, including that sublimated by the admirable voice of a female singer, seems to have taken precedence over words. La Marseillaise has thus evolved, without necessarily repudiating it, from the revolutionary war song for the Army of the Rhine in 1792 to the Spanish Republic, the fighters of Mao's Long March and Salvador Allende's Chile.

The exaltation of the fight against foreign domination and the patriotic call for general mobilisation have merged into a song for freedom. The rhythm of the music has slowed down - as President Giscard d'Estaing had wished, in order to distance the anthem from a war song - and the tones have softened.

It was almost as if we were hearing La Marseillaise for the first time. The drum roll was overlaid by the piano; the musical phrases even seemed unfinished at times, like a destiny in suspension. The spectacle of the opening ceremony of the Games had ended with a few subtle, crystalline, almost feminine notes, barely perceptible, ginned up in the finale. The performance at the Stade de France spread them. It's up to everyone to listen to the new *Marseillaise*.

3

An epidemic of international crises

High-intensity warfare on the European continent, heightened tensions in the Near and Middle East against the backdrop of an Iran on the nuclear threshold, paralysis of the United Nations Security Council, a slow awakening in Europe, a multiplication of power poles and 'à la carte' alliances under the shadow of a China aspiring to the highest destinies, It is possible that the world is experiencing a moment of strategic change after a period which began in 1991 with the collapse of the Soviet Union, the first Gulf War and the assertion of American power in a *de facto* unipolar system.

The highly unstable nature of the international situation can best be illustrated by the current American hesitations in various major theatres of operation, in Ukraine and the Middle East, in relations with Russia and China, against the backdrop of presidential elections. The international system seems to be in tatters and will have to be rebuilt, even if the context is radically altered.

Impasse in Ukraine

The outlook for Ukraine is currently rather bleak, and President Zelensky has even envisaged defeat if US support were to cease. But the United States - paralysed for a long time in Congress over the renewal of its latest financial aid package to the tune of 60 billion dollars and with public opinion increasingly reticent - cannot allow a partial military collapse, let alone an even greater one, to take place in Ukraine.

Such a scenario would revive the 'Vietnam syndrome' of the abandonment of a country that had been strongly supported and then abandoned, and, without referring to South-East Asia, it is also Afghanistan that comes to mind, whose withdrawal - envisaged by the Trump presidency for May 2021 and finally carried out in August of the same year by President Biden - ended on 15 August with the return to power of the Taliban in Kabul.

Despite the considerable aid, both military and financial, initially provided by the United States to Ukraine, a fatal outcome for Kyiv would inevitably call into question Washington's reliability as a 'protector' and guarantor of European security. The image and credibility of the United States would be profoundly altered and the isolationist tendency in that country - in a cyclical process - would probably be reinforced.

In the situation of internal political deadlock that has long prevailed in Washington, the Democratic administration could only confirm that it has never considered sending ground troops to Ukraine, while reaffirming its determination to defend every inch of NATO territory (see President Biden's *not an inch...* formula). This was undoubtedly the main thrust of Secretary of State Antony Blinken's trips to Paris and Brussels.

The role of the European allies has indeed become more important for Washington in supporting Ukraine, but would they be in a position to take over from a paralysed administration, like an entangled Gulliver? Would a stronger commitment from France be sufficient?

In the absence of certainty, a freeze on the conflict, if not a rapid diplomatic settlement, could have been an avenue to explore in order to avert a political disaster, in the context of the American presidential campaign. President Biden would have reversed a negative spiral for himself and underlined a wisdom that would have given him the stature of a great peacemaker in the face of his rival. In the current impasse, with the presidential elections approaching, a relative status quo remains the best scenario for the Democratic administration. *Dying for Donbas?*

No one in Europe has ever wanted to die for Donbas, where responsibility for the war that started there in 2014 and for the failure of the parties to the conflict to implement the Minsk agreements has not been fully established. But Russia's aggression against Ukraine in February 2022 is no less unacceptable in terms of a nation's right to live in freedom, the violation of the principles of international law, the undermining of the functioning of the international system through the responsibility of a permanent member of the UN Security Council and the considerable disruption to Europe's development, not to mention the economic consequences for many countries around the world.

The stalemate has resulted not only in the virtual freezing of military positions on a front line more than 1,000 km long, but also in continuing destruction and considerable loss of life. Kiev still fears that it will gradually run out of ammunition and manpower, and even that it will partially collapse or even collapse on a larger scale. This is all the more true given that American aid will not be renewable for ever, and that Europe - despite its talk of a 'war economy' - will not be able to make up for this shortfall in the short to medium term.

The words of the Pope, which sometimes caused offence (see '*the courage of the white flag*'), and those of Elon Musk more recently ('*The longer the conflict goes on, the more territory Russia will gain*'), finally converged on the prospect of a future that could be even crueller in military terms for Ukraine. Russia, which is in a rather strong position overall, has no a priori interest in negotiating, even if war is just as destructive for it and because it can be satisfied with the blurred borders (see frozen conflicts) inherent in its imperial vision. But a de facto or formal ceasefire could prove to be a survival measure for Ukraine while it waits for better days. With President Zelensky having lowered the conscription age to 25, are young Ukrainians themselves still willing to die, at best, for a few 'acres of land' in the Donbas?
Ukraine: after the war, diplomacy?

The facts of the war in Ukraine have not fundamentally changed since 2023; it is important to recall them as the war in Ukraine has been relegated to the background on our radar screens, while public opinion has focused on the Near and Middle East.

At the time, it was claimed that military scenarios would determine the way out of the crisis. The war of aggression, whatever its motives, had naturally led to a reaction from Kyiv; the UN Charter had been violated and the international system had been disrupted; a high-intensity war on the European continent could not fail to handicap Europe's prosperity and development.

But the context had already changed, more than a year after the start of the conflict: if the Ukrainians had been unable to reach the end of the negotiations, *with a gun to their heads* (see Istanbul talks, March 2023), a counter-offensive on their part did not augur well; the powerful Russian artillery and Russia's control of the skies had to be taken into account; public opinion was becoming weary (war fatigue) in the United States and Europe; the cost of the war, as well as the foreseeable cost of reconstruction, were beginning to appear as unbearable burdens for Kyiv's supporters.

Diplomatic initiatives were emerging here and there (e.g. China, Africa) which, taken together, raised hopes of achieving a result. The G7 debates in Hiroshima had confirmed that the United States had set itself limits that could not be exceeded; on the Russian side, the question of Crimea was an implicit red line, revealed by more than subliminal statements on the possible use of tactical nuclear weapons. France, which had endeavoured to maintain channels of communication with Moscow in the run-up to the crisis, had perhaps envisaged negotiations prematurely and no longer really got involved when it should have in order to avoid stalemate or, worse still, escalation. Are we now returning to a diplomatic path, now that a first international conference has just been held in Switzerland? The war in Ukraine has profoundly affected Europe's prosperity and disrupted its mechanisms, even beyond the Treaties that govern it.

This is untenable. The 'NATOisation' of Europe - after the contrary diagnosis of *'brain-dead'* - with the accession of Finland and Sweden in particular, can only ruin plans for European strategic autonomy in the long term, which would not be limited to military issues, but would also encompass high technology. The revision of the international system, if not its overhaul, will also have to take account of the new poles of power: they see the conflict in Ukraine as just another war and have their own interests.

Exiting the war: buffer zone or neutralisation?

At a time when tensions are running high, particularly between France and Russia, it may seem out of place to think about a way out of the crisis in Ukraine, or at least about ways of easing tensions. Indeed, were French-style efforts at 'conventional deterrence' (NB: the hypothesis of ground troops in the context of greater strategic ambiguity) credible in isolation? Is a classic deterrent (NB: the France-Ukraine security agreement refers to an 'active deterrent') not an adventurous approach?

Given the Ukrainian military impasse (see the relative failure of the United States, inadequate armaments, recruitment problems), we cannot rule out the possibility that Russia may also be looking for a way out. V. Putin's relatively recent reference to a 'buffer zone' is not necessarily a simple reference to a de facto ceasefire (see frozen conflict) or a formalised ceasefire (see Panmunjom in Korea). We can also imagine that, in the minds of Russian officials, the buffer zone would be equivalent to a form of 'neutralisation' on the scale of the whole of Ukraine. At this stage, this objective would not inevitably require broad negotiations on European security. In the absence of a formal settlement, the dividing line between Russia and Ukraine would remain blurred, the conflict could flare up again and Kyiv's inclusion in an alliance such as NATO would be prevented. This could be yet another reason for V. Putin not to negotiate. Preconceived ideas about neutrality need to be corrected by distinguishing between states that have a policy of neutrality and those that opt for permanent neutrality. The former demonstrate a desire to remain outside blocs and alliances, as was the case with Finland and Sweden before they joined NATO. Permanent neutrality, on the other hand, entails international rights and obligations established by treaty. It is a commitment not to use force, except to defend its independence and territorial integrity; neutrality is therefore not synonymous with disarmament. This commitment is recognised symmetrically by other States, which guarantee to use force against those who breach the status of neutrality. This status has a long history: the legal basis for Swiss neutrality dates back to 1815; the 1955 Austrian State Treaty involved the USSR, France, the United Kingdom and the United States. The failure to comply with the Budapest 'Protocol' of 1994 is not an argument in its favour, but it was not a real treaty, and the transposition of permanent neutrality to Ukraine would concern the entire international community.

Between Paris and Moscow, comedy and bitterness

The ultimately frosty Scottish shower inflicted on France - according to the information available - during a telephone conversation between the French Defence Minister and his Russian counterpart at the time, Sergei Shoigu, was the result of a combination of calculated political posturing and less controlled feelings.

In provocatively questioning the possible involvement of the French secret services in the recent Moscow attack claimed by the Islamic State - at a time when France had indicated a willingness to cooperate more closely in the fight against terrorism - Minister Choigu pointed out that relations with Russia were always based on a balance of power. Moreover, it was logical that, after constantly denouncing the 'collective' West over recent months and years, Moscow could not have an exchange with France without showing itself to be extremely rigid. In this respect, the press release on the telephone conversation issued by the Russian side was also intended for domestic opinion. All in all, the shocking remarks incriminating France could have led us to say of the Russian authorities, as Pope Pius VII would have described Napoleon, who even imprisoned him: '*Comediante ! Tragediante !*'

This Russian reaction must also be seen as the expression of a deep-seated bitterness on the part of Russia - especially after the recent stance taken by the President of the French Republic - which has always considered France to be a partner apart from the rest of the Western community. There is an element of repressed feelings in this bitterness, which Paris has also noted in other times with Saddam Hussein or Bashar El-Assad, who, despite their turpitudes, thought they could preserve the friendships of yesteryear.

But the totally justified French initiative to re-establish a channel of political communication is not necessarily stillborn. It needs to be put into perspective. Experience shows that normalisation processes between states often begin with security cooperation. Even in the 'balmy days' of Franco-Soviet cooperation, invective could erupt face-to-face. The difference this time is that things have been made public, in the age of the communication war.

Damascus: lessons of a strike

In another theatre of operations, the strike on the Iranian Consulate in Damascus, attributed to Israel, which killed senior members of the Iranian Al Quds unit, which specialises in external operations, was a twofold feat. The precision of the strike: the operation was apparently carried out using F-35 aircraft and missiles, but it may just as well have been carried out from the nearby Golan Heights, held by Israel; although the Mezze district, where the Iranian diplomatic base is located, is off-centre and less densely populated than the heart of the capital, collateral victims appear to have been avoided. The second feat was the extremely high quality of the intelligence that enabled the presence of the targets to be identified and the strikes to be carried out in real time. Such 'feats' have since been repeated, as shown by the war between Israel and Hezbollah.

If Israel is indeed the perpetrator, the message also appeared to be twofold: Israel retains the ability to intervene at any time and in any place (see eliminations in Iran itself of scientists involved in the nuclear programme, in the heart of Hezbollah's stronghold in Beirut and again in Syria at Aleppo and Damascus airports); by striking the

Iranian embassy in Syria - because the Consulate is an integral part of it - Israel was not necessarily seeking escalation but was speaking directly to Tehran to dissuade it from undertaking large-scale military operations through Hezbollah and from widening a second front after that of 7 October/Gaza.

Deafening silence from Moscow

Apart from Israel's predictable silence, the initial reactions of the states concerned are worth noting. Unsurprisingly, the strongest reaction came from Tehran. Moscow's reaction was rather measured.

Absorbed by Ukraine, Russia is in fact relatively inaudible in general about developments in the Middle East. This silence, which may seem surprising for a country with a military presence in Syria - with the port of Tartus and an air base since the intervention in 2015 - can also be explained by reasons other than the war in Ukraine.

In this context, there is also a tendency to over-interpret the relationship between Moscow and Tehran. The recent meeting in Turkmenistan between V. Putin and the new Iranian President Massoud Pezeskhian is a case in point. The purpose of the Russian President's visit was in fact to take part in a regular meeting of the countries bordering the Caspian Sea.

It is clear that Russia and Iran are both hostile to the West. Relations between the two countries have intensified, notably as a result of the war in Ukraine, with Tehran supplying equipment for military use, such as Shahed-136 drones; there is also talk of Russian deliveries of Sukhoi Su-35 fighter jets, but so far only Yak-130 training aircraft have been made available to Iranian fighter pilots.

But such a rapprochement in no way implies a form of alliance. If we put the relationship in perspective since the mullahs' revolution, we can only observe a relative caution - even fear - towards the Shiite regime's proselytism. Moscow demonstrated such an attitude in the construction of the civilian Busher nuclear power plant and great responsibility in the multilateral discussions that led to the agreement of 14 July 2015 on Iran's nuclear programme; it was not Russia that withdrew from the treaty guaranteeing IAEA controls. It would not be in Moscow's interests to do so, and the same applies to North Korea.

In the acute crisis with Hezbollah, i.e. Iran, Moscow was heard very little or not at all. This was also the case during the strikes attributed to Israel on the Iranian Consulate in Damascus last April. The facts of the matter were as follows: Russia and Iran were already perceived as close allies, but Moscow, which has control of the Syrian skies, has always allowed Israel to carry out its strikes on Syria over the past few years; its policy towards the Arab and Islamic world is complex, and it was not its intention to fall out with the Sunni world, even though the Middle East region has been a battleground for Sunni and Shiite powers for several decades now, through their allies.

Russia cannot but be concerned now about the Iranian retreat in the Middle East; the collapse of Hezbollah and the Pasdaran in Syria could prove damaging to its own presence in the region. This is what matters to Moscow. Its silence therefore deserves to be better deciphered.

As for the Syrian regime itself, which owes its survival to Moscow and Teheran, its Basist, i.e. secular, basis is diametrically opposed to Iran's theocratic proselytism. It should also be remembered that Israel and Syria have not faced each other since the Golan Heights disengagement agreement of 1974, and were ultimately the best partners and adversaries. Can we be sure that Assad's war against Islamist forces such as Daesh and Al-Qaeda was not basically favoured by Tel Aviv? Has the West been equally clear-headed on this point? Whatever the case today, the war in Gaza is also being waged through Tehran. Shouldn't we have started there?

Palestinians, Israel and Iran

We can have well-founded sympathy for the Palestinians, having known them around the world, particularly in Syria where they were treated well. The Palestinians have been the victims of almost everyone, including Hamas today.

Several opportunities to establish a Palestinian state have been missed, notably by Yasser Arafat, following the Camp David II talks, under the aegis of President Clinton, with Prime Minister Ehud Barak. But wasn't this already the case with the 1947 Partition Plan? Who is now genuinely committed to a Palestinian state? High-profile and respectable figures have sometimes been mentioned, but have they had any real impact? Did President Obama's speech in Cairo not go down well? UN Secretary-General Boutros Ghali paid for his commitment, particularly after the tragedy at Qana in southern Lebanon in 1996, by not being reappointed.

The moment now seemed paroxysmal and Iran, the 'mastermind' of much of the violence in the region through its 'proxies', set itself up, out of ambition for power, as the defender of the Palestinians against Israel, whose existence it denies; the risk for Teheran was that it would end up becoming the main target. President Biden warned of the risk of a 'massive attack' by Iran on Israel. This public announcement initially had some merits for him (e.g. easing tensions within his Democratic Party; seeking a dissuasive effect on Iran; diverting attention from Washington's paralysis over Ukraine). Tehran has since renewed a massive attack on its designated enemy with over 200 missiles that could not go unanswered.

Today, the question of a Palestinian state requires the neutralisation of Iran, which is what many people in the Arab world and beyond actually want. This could prove tragic for so many remarkable Iranians. Is the alleged 'normalisation' between Tehran and Riyadh credible after decades of opposition in the 'Shiite arc' of the Middle East? Hasn't Riyadh's enemy become Iran rather than Israel?
Whatever the case, everyone needs to be clear in an increasingly 'complicated' and dangerous East: no, the Jews are not an external population to the region in question; yes, Israel must first and foremost concern itself with its security, which can be based on the creation of a Palestinian state; no, the Palestinians' supporters cannot continue to put forward certain unrealistic demands, such as

the return of all the refugees since 1948. That would mean the end of Israel. The prospect of two states requires an end to the half-truths and fantasies that can only postpone an absolutely essential political settlement.

Reshaping the Middle East

This objective was mentioned by certain Israeli officials, particularly after 7 October 2023 and the clashes that followed that tragedy in Gaza, Lebanon and with the Houthis in Yemen. But the backdrop is Iran, the sponsor of Islamist movements operating in these countries, which has long been predicted to be on the 'nuclear threshold'. Tel Aviv's hesitation over military scenarios with Tehran, eager to re-establish its own deterrent capacity in the region, reveals the scale of the target and the consequences that a major undertaking could provoke.

In the context of the Israeli army (IDF) operation undertaken in southern Lebanon, UNIFIL (United Nations Interim Force) has been at the heart of the controversy, notably between the UN Secretariat itself and the governments of some of the main troop contributors to the Force - in particular Italy, as well as Spain and France - and the Israeli government. UNIFIL was mandated by Security Council Resolution 1701 of 2006 to accompany, in liaison with the Lebanese army, the demilitarisation of the area between the Litani River and the Israeli border. It has never been able to fulfil its mission, particularly as regards the disarmament of Hezbollah, also provided for by previous resolutions; the 10. With the Force's 10,000 men still on the ground, Hezbollah elements are able to use them as a kind of 'shield', which clearly hampers IDF operations. Both the UN and the States contributing to the Force have every right to be concerned about the safety of the contingents; but it can also be argued that UNIFIL, which has been unable to accomplish its mission, is also providing a kind of de facto protection for Hezbollah that has no basis in international law, while Resolution 1701 is being rewritten.

The clashes in southern Lebanon are just one aspect of the decomposition of Lebanon, whose state structures were already weakened and where the blows dealt to Hezbollah could lead to communities that fought each other ferociously during the civil war from 1975 to 1990 coming face to face once again.

Such a scenario, in a substantially different context, cannot be ruled out in Syria if Hezbollah is destroyed and the Iranian Pasdaran eliminated. The question of Russia's role in the country, if not its presence, could then be raised in new terms. Would Bashar al-Assad then be in a position to avoid inter-communal clashes in the areas he regained control of during the last phase of the war that began in 2011? Should the Western powers not then reconsider their policy towards this country and the region as a whole?

History accelerating

The lightning advance of Islamist forces in Syria (and since then their victory), from the north-east of the country, and the threats it poses to the very survival of Bashar al-Assad's regime, heralded major changes in the Middle East. This is also a turning point for France, which cannot analyse the possible fall of power in Damascus by forgetting history.

The Alawite community - currently 10-12% of the Syrian population - is often considered to be a sect of Shi'ism, and some even doubt whether it really belongs to Islam. It was persecuted by the Sunnis, in particular by the Ottomans from the 16th century onwards. Recluse in the mountains that form the hinterland of the port of Latakia (NB: *Jebel Ansariyé*), it was France that brought it out of its state of subjugated backwardness to ensure its promotion, starting with gradual integration into the army at the Homs Cadet School. In 1922, the French mandate over Syria and Lebanon even granted autonomous status to an Alawite state. France's policy of supporting minorities (see the Maronites in Lebanon) was also followed by the Assad regime, which protected them, starting with the Christians. What will happen now and in the future, despite the initial ecumenical declarations by the leader of the rebellion, a former leader of *Al Nosra*, which was linked to Al Qaeda? The question also arises for the Kurdish community, especially in the north-west of the country (see the duck's beak), insofar as the Islamist wave is clearly supported by Turkey.

Every 11 November, a ceremony was held at the French military cemetery in Dmeir on the road to Palmyra, near Damascus, in the presence of the authorities from both countries. The aim was to honour the victims of the war in Cilicia in 1920-1921, the operations in Jebel Druze and in Damascus itself in 1924-1925 and the fighting in the Second World War, in a place containing 4,000 graves, some of them in a Muslim 'plot'. From 2005 onwards, and especially during the war that began in 2011, France distanced itself from the fervour that bound it to Syria. In so doing, it lost all capacity for influence in a region where it was the dominant external power, as developments in Lebanon over the last few years have shown. One day we may well regret the Syrian Arab Republic.

It was President Chirac who brought Bashar al-Assad into the fold. He was also the only Western head of state to attend Hafez el-Assad's funeral in June 2000. Before him, President Mitterrand had made his mark by being the first French head of state to visit Syria in 1984 since the country's independence in 1943.

Uncertainties over the future

The Syrian Golan, is one example of the bones of contention. With the exception of a few isolated incidents with uncontrolled groups during the war in Syria that followed the Arab Spring, the Golan remained calm for almost fifty years. The Six Day War in 1967 and the Yom Kippur War in 1973 caused Hafez el-Assad's troops to lose part of the Golan Heights, in particular the strategic heights that overlook both Israeli and Syrian territory. The result for the Alawite power in Damascus was a wound that has never healed; since then, Bashar al-Assad, who succeeded his father, has never ceased to reaffirm Syria's claim to the Golan, which is indissolubly linked to the identity of the Basque regime. However, the 1974 disengagement agreement and UN Security Council Resolution 350

- under which the UNDOF observation force was deployed in no-man's-land between the parties - have always been fully respected. Bashar al-Assad, despite his militant rhetoric, has shown himself to be Israel's best partner and adversary in the Golan Heights affair. The Syrian head of state has used his territorial claims to justify his regime's harshness at home; Israel has used Syria's supposed dangerousness in an attempt to get recognition of its occupation of the Golan, which is not recognised by the international community.

The penetration of the Israeli army - whatever the political changes in Syria - into the region of Quneitra in Syria - a city left untouched by the destruction of the past war and visited by Pope John Paul II - in the no-man's-land controlled by the UN observation force, where no incident has occurred with the Assad regime since the disengagement agreement of 1974, is unacceptable. There is no security justification for such a military move for Israel, which already occupies the Golan Heights. And international law must be remembered once again: the Golan is Syrian and has been occupied for 50 years. The recent declarations by the Israeli Prime Minister that the Golan Heights belong to Israel once and for all will do nothing to change this. This explains why France and Russia - for the first time in a long time - have just spoken out along the same lines, warning Israel. There are limits to chaos and predation, and we must not give arguments to a new Syrian power who is already causing concern.

But if we are talking about the Golan Heights, we should also mention the Kurdish problem. Turkey's obvious support for Syrian Islamist forces is obviously not unrelated to this issue. With the West supporting the Kurds spread over several countries (NB: Turkey, Iraq and Syria), President Erdogan's policy will come up against major difficulties, not to mention the policies of powers such as Saudi Arabia and Qatar, which are less visible at present behind the new masters of Damascus, but whose agendas are specific. The future of Syria is therefore far from already written, and by the same token that of the region as a whole.

The road to Damascus

Forgetting its historical responsibilities inherited from the mandate given to it by the League of Nations at the San Remo Conference in 1920, and the role of guarantor of regional peace and stability that such proximity to the Levant conferred on it, France effectively abandoned Syria some twenty years ago. It did so out of blindness and faint-heartedness: After its opposition in the UN Security Council to an American intervention in Iraq in 2003, Paris gave in - in order to re-establish a badly damaged transatlantic relationship - to American neo-conservative policy, which in the Near and Middle East was reflected in a desire to break up states; In so doing, France has sold off a historic asset, gradually faded from the region, may be partly responsible for the uncontrolled development of the war in Syria in the wake of the Arab Spring, and is still paying the price of its lost influence - Lebanon knows all about it - for this short-sighted, disruptive policy.

It will be appropriate for historians to look into this period, and for the French to be told the truth one day after too long a *'omertà'*. The marked weakening of French diplomacy in recent years, which went hand in hand with a sort of dismemberment of the Quai d'Orsay under the effect of an incoherent and incomprehensible reform, was not responsible for everything. With the benefit of hindsight, the break that occurred in the early years of the 2000s seems all the more incomprehensible given that the period that preceded it had been marked by great continuity. President Mitterrand, the first French Head of State to visit Syria in 1984 since the country's independence in 1943, summed up France's fundamental position when he said that *'nothing could be achieved in the Middle East without Syria's help'*. Years later, President Chirac followed in his footsteps by coming to Damascus to *'renew the threads of an old friendship'*. Indeed, in the early 2000s, France embarked on a policy of cooperation with the Syrian regime, aimed primarily at reforming and modernising the country.

The lesson of these errors is not just a historical curiosity; it must be learned for today, when important diplomatic manoeuvres are unfolding within the framework of a deregulated international system from which the great powers are thinking of freeing themselves. Diplomacy is not just a matter of pure, quantifiable power, only worthy of admiration and respect. France, admittedly weakened in many respects, is well placed to know this. Its contemporary history bears witness to this. At a time when large groups are dominating the world, this will also be a moment of truth for Europe.

The journey to Damascus by the French Foreign Minister and his German colleague - a short time after the new authorities took over - should not give rise to controversy. The road to Damascus is not one of conversion - like Paul's - it is quite simply one of recognition of realities and the role that diplomacy can play. France, which had already hoisted the flag on its buildings a few days ago - including the Residence de France, the former residence of the Ottoman governor of the city and the short-lived home of King Farouk - did not have to formally recognise the new authorities. Its traditional doctrine is to recognise states, not governments. Places that were closed at the start of the war, mainly for security reasons, have now been reopened.

France and Germany are not the only countries to establish contacts with the new Syrian authorities; they have complementary interests. For France, it is above all a question of historical continuity in the Levant, where it exercised a mandate over Syria and Lebanon under the League of Nations. Paris has never had any real economic or commercial ambitions in the country; its interests have coincided with any policy aimed at stabilising a key country in the region and a neighbour on the Mediterranean. France owes this, as well as the objective of development, to all the Syrians who have traditionally looked to it and who, in their millions, have suffered the most severe suffering, forced displacement and exile. Germany, which has been home to a sizeable Syrian community for several years, is also concerned. Migration and security issues are central to the concerns of both countries, as they are to those of all European countries.

The path taken by Syria and ourselves in our relations with it remains fragile - as the French minister acknowledged - so many challenges remain after more than ten years of ferocious war. The country is not completely at peace, with pockets still controlled by the most radical Islamist groups; long-standing problems, such as the Kurdish question in the north-east of the country, remain. From this point of view, dialogue with Turkey, which is also important for Germany, will be a particularly sensitive issue. The Sunni powers in the region, which have finally supplanted a retreating Iran, will also have a key role to play overall.

The list of dimensions of the Syrian crisis, which has clearly not been completely overcome, is not exhaustive. It confirms the extreme attention paid by France since President Mitterrand and President Chirac. Syria should now be a matter of consensus in France, and the responsiveness of European diplomacy can for once only be applauded.

The Kurdish myth

In a surprising convergence, a former President of the French Republic and a former Prime Minister, have gone somewhat astray in a joint Tribune aimed at committing France to defending the Kurdish community on Syrian territory with military means.

Every community in Syria, including the Alawites from whom the deposed President Assad came, deserves respect and protection. This is also the policy of the new government in Damascus. While the Kurds have fought the Islamic State, the latter is now also the enemy of Syria's new masters. Irrespective of the fact that the authors of the Tribune highlight the current situation of the Kurds - somewhat surprisingly in view of this last consideration -, it should be pointed out that the deployment of French forces in Kurdish areas would constitute an attack on the sovereignty of the Syrian state, towards which France has made a positive approach by reopening its embassy in Damascus on the occasion of the visit of its Minister of Foreign Affairs.
While the beginnings of a re-establishment of Franco-Syrian relations remain subject to inventory, depending on the evolution of the new power in Syria, it is in our interest that the latter respects its initial

commitments. If it is necessary for it to inspire lasting confidence in us, let's not destroy that confidence from the outset.

It should be remembered that there was no real Kurdish problem under Assad. The Kurds enjoyed a fairly large degree of autonomy in the north-east of the country (NB: the towns of Hassake and Qamishli).
The war has effectively changed the situation and the Kurds, who are spread across several countries (in addition to Syria, Iraq, Iran and Turkey), have once again been encouraged to fight for a state to which they have long aspired, albeit in a rather unrealistic way. They have probably been promised this by the West in gratitude for their commitment to their side during the war in Syria.

There is a tendency to idealise the Kurds in France, especially since Mrs. Mitterrand, whose media campaign was assisted by former French doctor activist and minister of Foreign affairs B. Kouchner. It is all the easier to exploit this capital to some extent today because the myth lives on.
It is often forgotten - and hardly ever mentioned - that the Kurds were the ferocious executors of the policy of exterminating the Armenians at the end of the Ottoman Empire. As for Turkey, which often has a heavy hand against Kurdish militants, it is also a recurrent victim of large-scale PKK terrorism.

The co-signatories should have learned more about the subject before delivering us a rough and not very coherent text. It is true that the former President has never got over not having been able to strike Syria in 2013 - which would undoubtedly have brought Daesh to power in Damascus - while the other co-author is not far off the mark in terms of demagoguery.
On 7 October renewed

Almost on the sly, shamefully, Hamas is expected to return new bodies of Israeli hostages, including that of the youngest hostage in history. These returns, which have been taking place over months and even years, add to the initial monstrosity of 7 October. If this last date had only been the moment of a barbaric blunder, there should not have been this subsequent policy of bartering horror.

If we want to respect the victims, and in these circumstances the murder of absolute innocence, we must never forget these events. Collective punishment is not the preserve of developed societies, but the Palestinian cause will inevitably have regressed. How can the dogma of two states living side by side still offer a realistic solution?

The Israeli withdrawal from Gaza and the return of international aid for reconstruction will once again only benefit the worst extremists, in this case the jailers united by a Hamas that has not been eradicated in a strip of land that will quickly become an open-air prison again; this will once again result in a major security problem for Israel on its southern flank. The West Bank, which has become a 'leopard skin' with the continuation of colonisation, will not offer an alternative for the creation of a Palestinian state; the reputation of the Palestinian Authority, increasingly challenged by more radical forces, is well established and offers no guarantees.

The rejection of proposals for a Palestinian state has been repeated since the rejection of the Partition Plan of 1947. The basis of this attitude was in fact the rejection of the legitimacy of Israel, whatever the arguments put forward, including the unrealistic demand for the return of all the refugees. Camp David II in 2000 was perhaps the final missed opportunity that could not be revived in 2002 by the peace initiative of Crown Prince Abdullah of Saudi Arabia. History holds many unexpected twists and turns. But the tragedy of 7 October may lead one to think that it is now very late.

Letter to a friend from the Arab world

'Dear friend of this Orient that is both near and far,

I have lived among you, worked alongside you, and the closeness remains, dictated to us by history, culture, religion and above all the Mediterranean Sea. This prompts me to write to you in such troubled times when communication, despite its uncontrollable proliferation, is in reality poor and so difficult.

In Greek tragedy, the fatal outcome is immediately apparent and the essence of tragedy lies in the convulsions taking place before our eyes, without the slightest escape. Today, faced with so many dramas that you are experiencing and that we are sharing, we are no longer even sure what tomorrow will bring and how far the catastrophe will go.

War has not been eradicated anywhere, and the European continent is a sad illustration of this, but the conflicts taking place in your country seem even more anachronistic and violent than those we thought had been consigned to antiquity and the darkest pages of the sacred texts that sometimes tell their story.

Violence begets violence and ends up killing all humanity, as shown by the suffering endured by civilian populations and, closer to home, the paroxysm of child martyrs, as well as annihilating all individual reflection. The real revolt should be against this apparent inevitability. How is it possible that in this area of immense civilisations, this cradle of three great monotheistic religions, the beginnings of a virtuous transformation are not taking place at the bottom of the abyss?

Social and political conformism must be combated, the sense of a community and solidarity that transcends borders must not prove oppressive; above all, spirituality should be retained from religions; mental barriers must be abolished. What is important above all is that a perception of the sacred be preserved, a perception that can even be accessed without the idea of God, sometimes even outside of churches when they hinder it and aspire only to be a power.

I have experienced the metaphysical breadth of landscapes in the Nejd region of the Arabian Peninsula, as well as calls of the muezzins setting the shores of the Red Sea ablaze with the setting sun and reverberating off the mountainous barrier near the Hejaz. I would get up in Damascus before dawn so as not to miss the illumination of the dawn by countless green lanterns above the city's religious buildings; it was near the place of conversion of Paul of Tarsus and also near the Umayyad Mosque that one could be drawn into the dizzying whirl of Sufi dances inside old palaces.

At the end of the ancient Roman Via Recta, next to the Christian quarter, was the Jewish quarter, which has been depopulated, especially since the Six Days and the Yom Kippur Wars, but of which the synagogue and some perfectly preserved houses remain, awaiting a 'return'. The so-called 'limestone plateau' in the Idlib region is also the site of 'dead cities', which contain a treasure trove of countless 5th-century churches, well predating the Christian buildings that we strive to renovate and sometimes even save from destruction.

In the National Museum of Damascus, among the most beautiful pieces are figurative frescoes from the 2nd and 3rd centuries, still unique to this day, from one of the oldest known ancient synagogues. This considerable edifice, deeply buried underground - which protected it for so many centuries - along the ramparts of Dura Europos on the Euphrates, the 'Pompeii of the Orient', was exhumed in 1930 and restored under the French mandate.

The Alawites of Jebel Ansariye, near the Mediterranean coast, were able to coexist with other minorities, such as the Druze of the agricultural region of Hauran near Jordan and Beiteddine in the Lebanese Chouf. The Shiites, whose beliefs could not be assimilated to those of the Alawites, came in large numbers on pilgrimage to the suburbs of Damascus, including from Iran, to honour the mausoleum of Sayyida Zeinab, dedicated to a granddaughter of the prophet.

This incomparable wealth, experienced as an offering, often unsuspected from the outside and even forgotten from the inside, cannot be reduced to a shapeless mass. On the contrary, it is a unique matrix that is not intended to lead to the forging of weapons but to trace the paths of liberation, starting with that of consciousness.

'Pain is the greatest of prophets,' wrote Germaine de Staël after the death of her father Necker. Who can understand this better, dear friend, than your suffering East, which is thus closer to us than ever?'

4

A moment of strategic change?

President Biden could not have committed himself lightly by announcing a 'massive' attack by Iran on Israel for purely domestic purposes. Such a move would ultimately have damaged the credibility of the President's words and the United States.

The concerns were based on real threats, fomented in Tehran and carried out by 'allies', be they the Houthis, Hezbollah or Hamas. A significant escalation took place, the first signs of which were the firing from southern Lebanon, then the boarding of a ship supposedly 'linked' to Israel, and finally salvos fired from Iranian territory. So the American President had not overestimated the danger.

Dialectic of decision

It is in this type of situation that the dialectic of centre and periphery in strategic decision-making comes into play. The *Essence of Decision* was analysed by Graham Allison in his famous book on the Cuban missile crisis in 1962, but this is something quite different. The Middle East can only be dealt with at the highest political level. But the ultimate decision is increasingly the result of a considerable amount of information gathered on the ground by the military and intelligence services, sorted by the bureaucracy and then passed on to the highest level, in the case of the United States the Oval Office.

Such is the dialectic that can sometimes lead subordinates - in a reversal of the order of the chain of command - to influence, unintentionally, the centre of power. The conversion of all the data becomes complex, as if it were a question of translating several languages into a single, clear, operational line. Given the overabundance of data captured, where is the threshold for triggering widespread preventive action, or even a massive response?

The situation described here is not without precedent, despite the evolution of the international system and technological means: the invasion of Kuwait in August 1990 led the Security Council to meet continuously until the Gulf War in 1991 and to adopt a series of highly technical resolutions, culminating in Resolution 678 authorising the use of force to liberate Kuwait. The specific nature of the UN's procedures, which were hermetic for many politicians, meant that the periphery was able to influence the centre. Later, in 2003, when Colin Powell displayed a vial of anthrax to denounce the risk posed by Iraq's supposed weapons of mass destruction, was he lying or mistaken on the basis of technical data he had not mastered? Be that as it may, there was a war with Operation *Desert Storm*. The opposite example is Ukraine, where Western intelligence was reliable, but was not taken into account - or insufficiently so - by the political powers in Kiev before 24 February 2022.

Is the periphery about to rule the centre? Will technology dominate political thinking in the age of artificial intelligence? Times seem to have changed, but John F. Kennedy, drawing on his own experience in 1962, concluded that *'the essence of the ultimate decision remains impenetrable to the observer and often, in truth, to the decision-maker himself...'*.

The madman's diagonal

International relations are primarily based on interests. In a world of collective, immediate and epidermal emotions, which now often take precedence over cold analysis, shouldn't this basic principle be re-examined in the light of a few contemporary crises?

Khrushchev was dismissed from office in 1964 by the Praesidium of the Central Committee of the CPSU, which denounced his 'adventurism'. The criticism was clearly aimed at the Cuban rocket crisis, which was seen as a humiliation in the USSR. The withdrawal of the American Jupiter rockets from Turkey, which Washington did not publicly announce, reinforced the perception that Moscow was backing down. But why were the missiles actually installed on the island, despite clear warnings from Washington? Was it to improve the USSR's first-strike capability, which was bound to provoke a vigorous reaction from Kennedy? Where was the logic?

The Brezhnev period reflected greater Soviet rationality, but isn't the war in Ukraine being waged by Russia, the successor state to the USSR, the result of initial miscalculations and the spasms of an outdated imperial project? Whatever the military outcome, wasn't an anachronistic war lost on 24 February 2022 to the soldiers of Valmy, the embodiment of the fight for freedom?

Iran's attack on Israel was presented by the Islamic Republic as the expression of the 'apogee' of Iranian power. Another interpretation would be to point to Tehran's technological inferiority - with the exception of its nuclear programme - when 99% of its delivery systems failed to reach their target. What's more, Iran will have succeeded above all in strengthening solidarity with Tel Aviv, which has been undermined by developments in Gaza. Ubris is an old story, dating back to Antiquity, which has played many tricks on Persia in particular.

After the 13 days of the Cuban crisis, there were the 12 days of the 1972 Christmas bombings, to bring the North Vietnamese regime to heel. In his book Kissinger, Professor Charles Zorgbibe developed the 'madman theory' of the tandem with Nixon. Kissinger had studied *the political uses of madness* at Harvard. So is there an unconscious madness that is suffered and a simulated madness that acts as a deterrent? Hasn't an Iranian regime official just said: *'We are crazier than you imagine'* ?

Rebuilding the international system?

To the extent that a permanent member of the Security Council has broken away from the fundamental principles of the United Nations Charter, the international system based on the UN has been more than weakened and, in reality, blocked and powerless. Apart from the Council, which is the only body with decision-making powers if the permanent members agree, what are the other main bodies of the Organisation, starting with the Secretary-General?

There have been great UN Secretaries-General: the Swede Dag Hammarskjöld, who died in a plane crash while on mission in Africa in 1961; the Egyptian Boutros Boutros-Ghali, who knew how to stand his ground in Middle East affairs and paid for it with his post; the Ghanaian Kofi Annan, a man of synthesis and supreme balance between the Western world and emerging or developing countries. No woman has yet been Secretary-General, but several could have been, including Kristalina Georgieva, now head of the IMF, and Mary Robinson, former President of Ireland and United Nations High Commissioner for Human Rights. This brief list is by no means exhaustive.

The fact that Kofi Annan had long held management positions far removed from the more visible activities of the Security Council and the General Assembly had contributed to the relative anonymity of the candidate. He had also been somewhat hastily lumped into the category of UN officials who were a priori open to the radical conception of reform that prevailed in Washington. It could also be argued that such suspicion was not only hurtful, but ignored the difficulty for an international civil servant worthy of the name to hold the balance equally between the permanent members, to be neither obliged to them nor to oppose them head-on.

The record of the Secretary General's two terms is well known: the trauma of Rwanda, when he was not yet Secretary General, left its mark on him and Bosnia for ever; NATO's bombing of Yugoslavia in March 1999, without the backing of the Security Council; the 2003 operation in Iraq, which he described as 'illegal' ; and the attack that same year on the Argentine diplomat Sergio Viera de Mello, whom he had delegated to Baghdad; but also the relentless and ongoing battle against AIDS; the 2000 Agenda for the UN (*We the Peoples: The Role of the United Nations in the 21st Century*); the Nobel Peace Prize in 2001, but still the marginalisation of the UN after 11 September.

During his eight years as Secretary General, Kofi Annan met the great and the good of the world and so many anonymous human beings from all five continents. Most importantly, Kofi Annan was the noble embodiment of the international community, and we will always keep alive his message at the end of his Memoirs (*Interventions*): '*A United Nations that serves not just States, but also peoples, and becomes the forum where governments are held accountable for their behaviour towards their own citizens, will earn its place in the 21st century*'.

The inevitable enlargement of the Security Council

There is no formal text setting out the criteria by which a Member State may join the Council as a permanent member. However, the criterion of participation in UN peacekeeping operations is considered relevant. In addition, it is generally accepted that the size of countries, their economic weight and their political influence are the benchmarks that must be met. France has long publicly supported the candidacies of Germany, Japan, India and a '*major African country*'.

The Council could have been enlarged at the end of the 1990s. At the time there was talk of the 'Razali Plan', named after the Malaysian ambassador to the UN, who had been very active on these issues. But it was the nuclear experiments in India and Pakistan in 1998 that arguably blocked the process. France, which spoke of '*minimum deterrence*' at the time, never publicly criticised New Delhi. But the process was hampered, because 'proliferating' countries could not be rewarded (NB: the Permanent Five are all nuclear-weapon states, but none of them were, including the United States, when the San Francisco Charter was adopted in June 1945).

In any case, according to commonly accepted criteria, the enlargement of the Council should be based on a dual requirement: to better reflect the state of the world and to preserve the Council's effectiveness. This means that the Council must not, beyond a certain number, become a second General Assembly with a purely deliberative role. Enlargement would not be a reform per se that would radically change the mechanisms of the system, but it would better reflect the real state of the world. We may be sceptical about the feasibility of such a transformation, in the context of the current extreme tensions. But we must look ahead to the end of the crisis and never forget that the League of Nations was born out of the First World War, just as the UN in 1945 was born out of the Second.

A Security Council at a standstill: the current situation in the UN Security Council is a key indicator of the state of the international system. The Council has gone through phases of deadlock and paralysis, particularly during the Cold War. Depending on the outcome of the war in Ukraine, the system could even be radically overhauled. But above all, in a form of apparent regression, we are witnessing the return of powers, power relations and war, where we thought they had disappeared for good. In this context, is there still a place for diplomacy?

UN bashing is currently enjoying its heyday. It is convenient to systematically blame the United Nations in times of unresolved crises, as if it were a supranational entity that had failed in its responsibilities. If Louis XIV said: *'L'État, c'est moi'* (the State is me), we need to remind large sections of uninformed public opinion that *'The UN is us'*.

The UN is in fact at the service of its Member States, who run it, in particular the Security Council and a fortiori its permanent members, who govern it. The General Assembly has only a consultative role, and its resolutions are not binding. As for the Secretary General of the Organisation, he is the head of the administration, but remains in the hands of the Security Council, as his title emphasises; he cannot be at the service of a State, even the most powerful, but he also cannot oppose it head-on, without risk (NB : The Secretary-General, on the other hand, while endowed with courage and moral authority, can rely on one article of the Charter - just one - Article 99, under which he can *'draw the attention of the Council to any situation which may endanger international peace and security'*.

The Security Council is now paralysed because a permanent member has 'violated' the UN Charter by invading Ukraine. This is what Secretary-General António Guterres immediately said in these very terms, and was then powerless to do anything about it for the reasons given above. On the other hand, Guterres, fully in his role, was very involved in the Gaza crisis, particularly in its humanitarian aspects.

The international system, dominated by the UN, is therefore currently at a standstill and even worse, in a state of dislocation, when, for example, there is no longer a consensus among the permanent members to sanction North Korea because of its continued nuclear proliferation. Russia, which has favoured the use of force over the rule of law, is largely responsible for this; Ukraine is no less harsh towards the Organisation, in an understandable but unrealistic way, when voices are heard calling for Russia's exclusion from the UN or calling into question its seat as a permanent member, maintained in favour of Moscow at the time of the succession of the Soviet state. The current rules do not allow for this.

The UN, *the worst of systems, but no better has ever been found*, as the saying goes, will have to be reformed. This may seem unrealistic today, but it was at the end of the First World War that the League of Nations was created and in 1945 that the UN was founded. At the very least, the Council will have to be enlarged to better reflect the state of the world. This will happen if we really want it to, because it is us and it is for all of us.

Genesis of the Atlantic alliance

The genesis of the Atlantic Alliance is well known, but a reminder sheds us of its identity at a time of possible transformation. It was the break with the USSR from 1947 onwards that led the West to look for a new alliance system, and the 1948 Berlin blockade, which lasted almost a year, can be seen as the beginning of the Cold War. The idea of a defensive pact, in the form of automatic assistance in the event of aggression - on unspecified terms - then emerged; it was translated into the famous Article 5 of the Charter. The then Secretary-General of the United Nations initially expressed some reservations about regional alliances, which could have developed to the detriment of collective security (NB: even though Article 52 of the UN Charter recognises the existence of regional agreements or organisations, Article 53 specifies that no 'coercive action' shall be taken at the regional level without the authorisation of the Security Council).

On 4 April 1949, an Atlantic Pact limited by definition to a specific area was signed in Washington at the State Department (N.B.: the first departure from the 'Atlantic' nature of the Alliance - and the issue was debated at the time - came with the admission of Greece and Turkey in 1952). General Eisenhower was the first Supreme Commander in Europe. SHAPE (Superior Headquarter of Allied Powers in Europe) was established at Roquencourt, near Versailles.
In September of the same year, the first atomic explosion in the USSR was detected. But 1948 had already seen the extension of the Soviet zone of influence in Eastern Europe, while in the Far East the positions of the Chinese nationalists led by Chiang Kai-shek had deteriorated. The USSR immediately recognised the People's Republic of China as soon as it was proclaimed in September-October 1949; it was followed in early 1950 by India and Pakistan, and also by Great Britain - which is sometimes forgotten - which no doubt wished to preserve important commercial interests in China.

An extension of the geographical scope? NATO member states, including France, intervened in Afghanistan, in support of the United States, after the attacks on the World Trade Center; this was the only time in the Alliance's history that Article 5 of its Charter was applied. This important development did not, however, imply a formal extension of the geographical scope of the Organisation's intervention. More recently, NATO has been qualified by the President of the French Republic as *brain-dead*.
East/West: Forgotten and unanckoxledged convergences

Bitterness was felt in Moscow after 11 September. It is too often forgotten that V. Putin was the first leader to express his solidarity with the United States and its President George Bush Jr after the attacks on the World Trade Center in New York and the Pentagon in Washington. This was not just rhetoric limited to feelings of compassion for the victims and a vague solidarity whose contours were never precisely defined. Russia immediately took action and offered the United States facilities to transfer troops and military equipment to Afghanistan, which had been the US administration's preferred target for its response to 11 September. Nor should we forget the role that Moscow played with certain Central Asian states, such as Tajikistan, where Russian border guards were stationed on the border with Afghanistan.

In a way, Russia behaved as if it had been a member of the Atlantic Alliance and had made use of Article 5 of its Charter (NB: for the first and only time in the history of the Alliance). This very special moment of rapprochement with the West did not last and Russia felt that it had not been 'rewarded' in return, for example in 2004 with the first wave of enlargement of NATO to include six countries that had formerly belonged to the USSR (NB: after Poland, Hungary and the Czech Republic in 1999), at the Alliance Summit in Bucharest in 2008 - where the question arose for Ukraine and Georgia - and under President Obama (2009-2017) with the Maidan 'revolution' in Kyiv.

Large-scale Islamist terrorism erupted in Moscow in a concert hall in March 2024, with the attack claimed by the Islamic State of Khorasan. Attacks on Orthodox churches and a synagogue, which were also claimed by the Islamic State, took place a month later in Dagestan - an entity of the Russian Federation - in June 2024. The modus operandi of the first event, the location and the number of victims, brought back memories of the Bataclan and the Paris attacks in November 2015, prompting expressions of compassion and even a willingness to cooperate in the fight against terrorism.

In 1981, between the rounds of the presidential election in France, a leading French figure came to East Berlin to work in the industrial sector and met the highest East German leaders. The Euromissiles crisis (i.e. the threat of American cruise missiles and Pershing II rockets in response to Soviet SS-20 aimed at Europe) was then in full swing. Nevertheless, the message was one of cooperation and restoring balance to the international system. In a vision that could have been premonitory, the personality in question developed the prospect of eventual convergence between the powers of the northern hemisphere, which were then opposed to each other in the face of the problems of common interest which they would have to deal with in a preponderant manner.

Realism in Geopolitics

With his incomparable teaching talent, Thierry de Montbrial, the founder and chairman of the IFRI (French Institute of International Relations) delivers a remarkable summary of the geopolitical issues of the moment, which he places in historical perspective. The war underway on the European continent forms the backdrop to his analysis.

In his view, realism means conducting a clinical analysis, free from any political ulterior motive, and avoiding a Manichean view based on notions of good and evil. Conflicts are not always resolved on the basis of justice

This understanding naturally applies to Ukraine, where the '*deep forces*', as Pierre Renouvin and Jean-Baptiste Duroselle, the great masters of international relations analysis, would have said, must be taken into account. These do not boil down exclusively to material factors, but include a non-quantitative dimension which may be nationalism or patriotism, and which for convenience may be called 'soft power'.

Thierry de Montbrial, who has just published *L'Ère des affrontements* (The Era of Confrontation), after many other reference works, published a *Journal de Russie* (Diary of Russia) in 2012. He was also a member of the 'Valdaï Group' of international experts, and in this capacity frequented Russia and its leaders. This close relationship with the subject gives him the right to talk about the notion of empire, which he considers to be *'consubstantial'* with this singular country that includes so many peoples; its expansion has taken place according to a geographical contiguity that is foreign to overseas adventures. The intervention in Afghanistan in 1979, in Georgia in 2008 and today in the Donbas, and more generally the problems in Ukraine since 2004 - and more globally the torments of the post-Soviet period - must be seen in this historical perspective, where the notion of security, even in the form of an obsidional complex, is paramount.

In this respect, Thierry de Montbrial is critical of the European Union, *'an association of nation states, each with its own vision'*, and calls for a *'proper understanding of the threat'*, whereas in his view many leaders and 'elites' often lack a *'historical culture'*.

5

The President and infra-nuclear thinking

Whatever the domestic dimension of the President of French the Republic's stance on the question of war and peace - due to poor polling and a worrying outlook for the European elections on 9 June 2024 - the repeated statements on *'ground troops'* in Ukraine and the consideration given, at a later stage, to the *'pooling'* of French nuclear armaments on a European scale, were undoubtedly also intended to be part of a logic of deterrence.

Nuclear transgression

During the Cold War, nuclear power paradoxically guaranteed a certain stability in the international system. This is no longer the case today. Whereas nuclear power guaranteed peace, with the notable exception of the 1962 Cuban rocket crisis when the world was on the brink of collapse, it now enables and even encourages war. A major nuclear power relies on a redundant arsenal - through veiled or more explicit declarations - to confront a non-nuclear state. This scenario could well become a reference model, and we would then have well and truly entered the era of the 'infra-nuclear', i.e. a period of erosion of traditional deterrence. For example, would the nuclear weapons carried by French *Rafales* - which are pre-strategic *'last warning'* weapons - eventually become tactical weapons for potential use on the battlefield?

The debate is undoubtedly somewhat premature as long as the United States guarantees many European countries a nuclear 'umbrella'. We might even think that - even in the event of a Trump victory - they will not leave NATO, which offers them many advantages.

For France, having tactical nuclear weapons again would mean the theoretical acceptance of a limited nuclear war on the European continent. If we consider that its strategic nuclear weapons would then be de facto '*decoupled*' in a way from its other nuclear means, this would mean a major change in its doctrine. General de Gaulle, if I am not mistaken, once had similar thoughts about American tactical weapons in Europe, which he saw as decoupling them from the central system in Washington.

Can we really believe in the possibility of using nuclear weapons on the European continent? After all, isn't our nuclear energy reserved for the threat that could be posed by new nuclear powers, deemed irrational on the face of it?

Appeasement and nuclear threshold

The spectre of Munich continues to haunt us and, curiously and paradoxically - while contemporary international crises are very different from the Sudetenland crisis of 1938 (NB: we are not negotiating until now on behalf of the Ukrainians, for example, as we did with Czechoslovakia) - we tend to be lulled, if not to succumb, to the soothing music of *appeasement*.

Israel's failure to react to Iran's swarms of drones and missiles was hoped for by many in the name of necessary restraint, which could also be called cowardly relief. This language is clearly being repeated today - at a time when Israel has just sent a message to Tehran by targeting a military site near Isfahan - in official statements. For example, the President of the European Commission strangely referred to the stability that prevailed in the region before this latest development (see '*It is absolutely necessary that the region remain stable...*'). Or France, which declared that it was '*working towards de-escalation*'.

But beyond the confrontation between Tehran and Tel Aviv, there remains the nagging question of Iran's military nuclear programme. If Iran were to cross the nuclear threshold, it would mean more than a regional upheaval; it would actually affect world order (or disorder).

During his state visit to the United States in 2018, during his first term as President, the President of the French Republic solemnly declared before Congress that Iran should never be a nuclear power (NB: '*Neither today, nor in five years, nor in ten years*'; '*never, never*', he repeated). It is vital that we stick firmly to this line. Israel, with Washington's *nihil obstat*, has undoubtedly sent Iran - after the first wave of missiles and drones - a final warning. Although Tel Aviv, through the voice of its Prime Minister, has stated that it will not bow to pressure and will defend its vital interests, the latter - in this case - are also ours.

Faced with sub-nuclear crises: the invasion by Russia

There was no Olympic truce between Russia, many of whose sportsmen and women were excluded from the Games or reduced to taking part under a neutral banner, and Ukraine. The high-intensity war continued unabated on the European continent - at a rate of considerable daily loss of life (NB: the Ukrainians put forward the figure of 1,000 Russian victims per day) - while the focus was on the Near and Middle East. The audacious Ukrainian penetration of Russian territory in the region around the town of Kursk, from 6 August 2024, was a further demonstration of this, which could change the course of the conflict.

Pascal's gamble in Kyiv

The surprise Ukrainian incursion - (NB: it involved a border strip around 40 km wide and 30 km deep; the Ukrainian Defence Minister has spoken of 1,000 km2) - was the first spectacular advance by Kyiv's forces since the liberation of Kharkiv at the end of 2022; it was the first military operation to demonstrate Ukraine's capacity to react, having done nothing but suffer since the failure of the 'counter-offensive' last autumn.

The Ukrainian gamble may have been as follows: the audacity of the undertaking consisted first of all in clearing other eastern fronts for the purposes of this specific attack and pushing Moscow to do the same; the operation was carried out on Russian territory itself, which had not been invaded since 1941, and no longer on entities of the Donbas that Russia had annexed by authority. Naturally, Ukraine does not have the capacity to occupy part of Russian territory over the long term, but in so doing it exposed Russia's vulnerability along its endless borders. Moreover, the objective was undoubtedly also political in that it aimed to demonstrate the inability of the central power in Moscow to ensure the safety of its population throughout the country (NB: more than 120,000 Russian civilians have already fled the border zone or have been displaced). This twofold weakness has the potential to undermine the solidity of the regime.

Other explanations have also been put forward to explain this unexpected campaign: psychological factors (NB: the aim would have been to boost the morale of the Ukrainian population, who saw no light at the end of the tunnel of two and a half years of war; on the other hand, the Russian narrative of invincibility was affected, even though Kursk is also the tragic and still traumatic reference to the disappearance at sea, in August 2000, of the submarine of the same name); the desire to make it clear to Western supporters that helping Ukraine is not like throwing into a bottomless pit, but can produce military results (NB: it should be noted that the Ukrainian intervention in Russia also relied on military equipment, including armoured vehicles and anti-aircraft defences, supplied by the West).

It was a daring gamble that could also provoke a backlash. If the operation were to be sustained, it would also have a military and human cost for Kyiv that could alter its defence capabilities in the future. If the aim was to 'take pledges' for an exchange of territories as part of future negotiations for a comprehensive settlement, there is no guarantee that Russia would go along with it. But the main danger lies in the scenario of military escalation to unprecedented levels; here we are talking about the risk of using tactical nuclear weapons.

A final warning to Zaporijjia?

While the Ukrainian offensive seems to have taken several Western chancelleries by surprise, it should be remembered that the rhetoric of Kyiv's arms suppliers had evolved over time towards greater understanding of the use of these weapons on Russian territory, a prospect that had long been clearly ruled out.

President Putin was quick to denounce this development in martial declarations in line with his constant denunciation of a confrontation with the West through Ukrainians (see '*the West is waging war on us using Ukrainians*'; '*the enemy will certainly receive the response it deserves and all our objectives, without a shadow of a doubt, will be achieved*').

It is worth returning here to the fire that occurred almost simultaneously at the Zaporijjia nuclear power station in Ukraine, currently controlled by Russian forces. After an exchange of anathemas between the two belligerents over who was responsible for the incident, it seems that the occupying forces in the area may have been responsible for the fire that broke out in one of the plant's cooling towers. At no time did the fire threaten the nuclear reactors themselves, several hundred metres away, or the used radioactive waste stored nearby but protected in concrete and steel. Russia was quick to announce that the problem - which was spectacular, with columns of smoke rising high into the sky - was under control. But one wonders whether Moscow's message to Kyiv was not that the site could be destroyed, leading to a major nuclear accident affecting the whole of Ukraine and causing widespread radiation. What's more, a Chernobyl-type nuclear power station is in operation near Kursk, which would have issued an additional warning (NB: the Russian regional authorities are in the process of evacuating a large number of civilians living near the town of Kursk). If a distinction must be made between civil and military nuclear power, is this not a case of the 'grammar' of deterrence?

Another manifestation of a policy of terror?

The Cold War was characterised by a balance of terror, based mainly - and paradoxically - on '*mutually assured destruction*' (MAD), itself based on the possession of strategic nuclear weapons. This is no longer the case, in a world where power is dispersed in place of the American-Soviet condominium, where the international system is breaking down, where alliances are à la carte and, in short, where there is great volatility. The use of nuclear weapons, mentioned more than subliminally - but not officially - during the war in Ukraine, which pits a 'nuclear-armed' state against a conventional military power, would allow us to speak of an *imbalance of terror*.

Leaks a few months ago - organised by Moscow? - of classified Russian documents from 2008 to 2014 revealed that the thresholds for the use of tactical nuclear weapons were lower than previously thought. An enemy attack on Russian territory or the annihilation of border units were among the criteria used to decide whether to use the weapon. About a year ago, President Putin himself reiterated the basic principles of the Russian nuclear doctrine: first respond to a nuclear attack (see first nuclear strike); threat to the existence of the Russian state even from the use of conventional weapons.

Finally, a distinction must be made between the doctrine as it is stated and the doctrine as it actually is. All the nuclear-weapon states maintain a lack of clarity about the theoretical conditions for the use of nuclear weapons; this is the case with the French concept of *'vital interests'*. In Russia, as elsewhere, strategic thinking is characterised by constant evolution and adaptation aimed at offering decision-makers different credible options; this process of reflection is necessary and naturally finds its limits in the decisions that only political power at the highest level is called upon to take.

A difficult but necessary decision?

In this respect, it is worth paying attention to the relatively recent analyses by Russian specialists in international and strategic issues, who are reputed to be close to the Kremlin. This is the case of Sergei Karaganov, honorary president of the Council on Foreign Defense Policy, who published in June 2023 a highly acclaimed article entitled '*A Difficult but Necessary Decision*'.

S. Karaganov goes well beyond the war in Ukraine, where he sees no good exit scenarios for Russia: whether it is a partial victory (NB: the liberation of four entities in the Donbas) or a crushing one, the cost will be high, and Russia will remain mobilised against the West. The question for him is how to put a lasting end to the West's policy of support for Kyiv, which only weakens Russia.

This is followed by a lengthy description of the weakening of the Western world (see *'five centuries during which the riches of the world have been exploited'*) and, at the same time, its renewed aggressiveness towards the world beyond its control. Faced with the West, a new group is emerging, dubbed the *'world majority'*, whose economic engines are China and, to some extent, India, and whose *'military-strategic pillar'* is Russia.

In his view, Russia had failed to understand the inevitability of a major confrontation with a hostile world for which Ukraine was a field of manoeuvre. This error of perception had resulted in the nuclear threshold being set too high. What's more, for more than 75 years of relative peace on a global scale, the reality of the horrors of war had been forgotten. Fear, the guarantor of relative peace, had to be reactivated to break the West's tendency towards aggression. Without forgetting the European sources of its history and culture, Russia had to refocus on Eurasia. This is what the Russian Ministry of Foreign Affairs (MID) had theorised with the concept of the *'State-Civilisation'*.

As S. Karaganov says, referring to statements by Russian officials on the nuclear threat, *'the enemy must know that a pre-emptive strike is possible in response to aggression'*. The ladder had to be climbed quickly towards deterrence-escalation, and S. Karaganov asserts that no American retaliation would then intervene in favour of the Europeans. He admits that Russia's main partners, starting with China, which he describes as *'weak'* in nuclear matters, would not be satisfied with raising the confrontation to a nuclear level, but would appreciate the status of the United States being shaken. In conclusion, the *'nuclear taboo'* had to end.

These thoughts do not necessarily apply to the situation around Kursk, but they even go beyond it by advocating the almost pedagogical value of the use of nuclear weapons. At the Valdai Forum in Sochi, Sergei Karaganov publicly questioned V. Putin on the question of nuclear weapons. Putin on the question of lowering the nuclear threshold. The Russian President remained coy and confined himself to setting out a completely conventional view, as already expressed. But over and above the purely military issues at stake, can the Russian government now allow its authority to be undermined by a process that contradicts its desire for power, with the risk that this also entails for the country's internal stability?

French nuclear umbrella and European strategic autonomy

The question of Europe's nuclear protection needs to be considered at a time when the future commitment of the United States to the continent and the durability of the American nuclear umbrella are being called into question. For his part, the President of the French Republic has opened a public debate on the possible *'mutualisation'* of French nuclear weapons.

France's current deterrence doctrine in no way envisages this prospect. It merely refers to France's *'vital interests'*, which could, if necessary - but nothing is clearly specified - be extended to the European geographical area.

Pooling the French deterrent makes absolutely no sense if the American nuclear umbrella is maintained, and the European countries that have it will not exchange one umbrella for another; it is no secret that a country like Germany, for example, will always prefer to be under American rather than French protection. Before embarking on the debate on *'mutualisation'*, the status of the Atlantic Alliance and the doctrines for the use of nuclear weapons by the French would have to change significantly.

Furthermore, from a technical point of view, the French arsenal is not adapted to provide a guarantee to our European partners. Unlike American tactical nuclear weapons on European soil, carried in particular by American aircraft (NB: this requires the purchase of F-35 aircraft by the United States' allies), French nuclear weapons carried by Rafale aircraft are not tactical weapons; they are very powerful pre-strategic weapons, known as *'last warning'* weapons before the nuclear apocalypse.

While the French President is undoubtedly looking to the very distant future of European strategic autonomy - which is not limited to the defence sector - there are still many steps to be taken. For the time being, France has no plans to share the nuclear co-decision process. France's deterrence doctrine remains focused on vital national interests. At the time, General de Gaulle clearly understood that American tactical nuclear weapons were a means of 'disengaging' from Washington's central systems. In a sense, this meant accepting the prospect of a nuclear confrontation with the Soviet Union but limited to Europe. For France, which has abandoned its Hades tactical weapons, the situation is different.

Any existential threat to France implies the potential use of strategic weapons. The French President's evocations therefore appear dangerous and unrealistic. Could we run the risk of having our strategic missiles carried by submarines because of the Donbas? A little seriousness and a sense of responsibility: deterrence is not a toy to be waved around for fun.

6

Metamorphosis of Russian power

The coup-style military operation launched by militia leader Wagner on 24 June 2023 in south-west Russia against the central government in Moscow confirmed the emergence in Russian political life of a category of actors that had been forgotten for over 30 years - since the August 1991 putsch against Gorbachev - that of the warlords/putchists.

In the wake of the war in Ukraine, the slag from which fell on the country that had started it, Russia was clearly destabilised internally. These events marked the failure, for a time at least, of Vladimir Putin, whose programme was perceived by the Russian people as dominated by the objectives of rebuilding the state, guaranteeing domestic stability and improving living standards.

Even before the crisis triggered by the putsch, the behaviour of the Russian leaders, who had been in power for many years, seemed unrecognisable. From predictable partners/adversaries, they had become incomprehensible actors. The attack on Ukraine itself, with considerable resources and in ways unseen on the European continent since the Second World War, had generally not been foreseen - with the exception of certain intelligence services - because of its irrational dimension and the consequences it would entail.

Unrecognisable actors

Let's take a few examples: Sergei Lavrov, who gave a perfectly legalistic speech at the UN, where he was ambassador for ten years, became inaudible after the annexation of Crimea in 2014. Margarita Simonian, who had created *Russia Today*, a media that was intended

79

to be modern and meet Western standards, abruptly evolved to adopt the most provocative style, exclusively at the service of propaganda. Dimitri Medvedev was an open-minded president, advocating economic diversification and working to develop a kind of Moscow Silicon Valley at Skolkovo, but he seemed shipwrecked, making extreme threats. Specialists in international relations and great connoisseurs of Western strategic thinking, such as Sergei Karaganov and Fyodor Loukianov - respectively head of the Council for Foreign and Defence Policy and editor-in-chief of the magazine *Russia in Global Affairs* - and Dimitri Trenin, former director of the Carnegie Foundation in Moscow, are now considering the possibility of using tactical nuclear weapons. Only Dmitri Peskov, the Kremlin spokesman who held the same position ten years ago, is keeping up appearances given his position, but he obviously cannot deviate from the official line.

The Russian Talleyrand

The case of Sergei Lavrov deserves a closer look, as he is the most surprising embodiment of the radical changes in attitude that have taken place in recent years. The Russian Foreign Minister has limited his public appearances. This in no way means that he has remained inactive, because mobilising countries that are not a priori insensitive to Russia's narrative, particularly in what is now known as the *'Global South'* where he has made many visits, is an important part of President Putin's strategy to make the conflict appear as a confrontation with the West.

Sergei Lavrov has sometimes been dubbed the *'Russian Talleyrand'* because of the position he has held at the head of his country's diplomacy for the past twenty years, but he has probably been misnamed because his manner has always been more direct - at the risk of sometimes being considered rough - than the convoluted contortions and backroom manoeuvres of his illustrious predecessor. Instead, he should be seen as a sort of *'Russian Chou En-lai'*, minus the patrician air, in other words, a patriot and a staunch defender of the State in all circumstances.

Sergei Lavrov, the irremovable one, has held positions of responsibility for some thirty years, starting in 1992 as Deputy Minister and Head of the Department of the United Nations and International Organisations at the Russian Ministry of Foreign Affairs (MID); he has been an interlocutor of the greatest, and has above all enjoyed his relationship as a partner-adversary of the United States. In this role, he was fully in tune with Russia's aspirations to maintain - or rather to try to regain - the level achieved in the good old days of the American-Soviet condominium.

The experience he gained during his time in New York, first as an embassy counsellor and then as his country's permanent representative on the UN Security Council, and his command of the English language after a decade as an expatriate in the United States, made his task easier.

The year 2013 was something of a high point in the Minister's career and international profile, as he dealt with both Ukrainian affairs and the Syrian dossier with his American counterpart, Secretary of State John Kerry. I remember a working lunch in London in April 2013, as part of the G8 foreign ministers' meeting. The only item on the agenda was the Near and Middle East. John Kerry, who had just returned from a tour of the region, had given a brilliant report to his colleagues, and only Sergei Lavrov took the floor to comment on it and assert his positions.

Sergei Lavrov has always shown consideration for France. On the sidelines of the same G8 ministerial meeting under the British Presidency, French Foreign Minister Laurent Fabius was the only person with whom he agreed to hold in-depth bilateral discussions, despite very limited time slots in a particularly busy schedule. Here again, Sergei Lavrov followed a tradition of constant Franco-Russian dialogue, whatever the differences; did his father's Armenian origins give him a particular sensitivity and thus influence his general approach to bilateral relations?

Low profile of diplomacy

2014 was something of *annus horribilis* for Russian diplomacy. Indeed, the annexation of Crimea in contravention of international rules immediately rendered the Russian minister's ever-legalistic discourse inaudible. It was largely this rigour that had been the strength of Sergei Lavrov's speech at the United Nations, in particular at the Security Council. At the time, Russia's anti-revisionist position on an international system under the aegis of the UN could be summed up as follows: the whole Charter, nothing but the Charter.

The influential minister - and President Putin's famous Munich speech in 2007 denouncing the trend towards a unipolar world can be seen as 'Lavrovian' in inspiration - and his entire administration, which had been reinvigorated by Evgeny Primakov before Sergei Lavrov replaced Primakov as head of the Ministry of Foreign Affairs (MID), stepped aside in favour of the Russian president, who became the country's undisputed leader, both at home and abroad.

The notorious Security Council meeting in Moscow on the eve of the attack on Ukraine was undoubtedly a difficult moment for the Foreign Minister, who appeared somewhat stunned, judging by the images made public. But the Minister did escape the humiliation suffered by other participants, from Security Council Secretary Nikolai Patrushev to Head of Foreign Intelligence Sergei Narychkin and former President and Prime Minister Dmitry Medvedev.

If war is simply the extension of politics by other means, as Clausewitz famously put it, then it is clear that the invasion of Ukraine left Russian diplomacy no option but to echo the narrative established at the top of the state about the '*the genocidaires and neo-Nazis in Kyiv*'. It is in this general context that Sergei Lavrov's media performances should be placed.

The Lavrov indicator

It is clear that, as he rarely spoke, Minister Lavrov rarely appeared in the spotlight during the conflict; when he did, no detail of the speech was overlooked, even to the point of staging the event. This was the case on French television on 29 May 2022, where, quite unusually, the setting for the speech was not the usual impersonal press room at the MID, but a comfortable lounge in the Ministry or its private hotel (*Osobniak*) designed to receive distinguished visitors. It was as if, in a world awash with images and declarations of war, there was a need to recreate, albeit artificially, the new-found atmosphere of a certain normality and desired appeasement.

The choice of a French media outlet was not indifferent either. Despite a few sharp comments on France's role in supporting Ukraine (see '*France feeds Ukrainian nationalism... it supplies offensive weapons*'), Sergei Lavrov emphasised the long-standing and constant dialogue between the French President and his Russian counterpart.

On the substance, the Minister appeared combative and true to his reputation. He referred, as expected, to Moscow's doctrine (see the protection of the Russian people and language; NATO's continuing move closer to Russia's borders; the questioning of the United States as '*sovereign of the world*' and of Ukraine as '*an instrument of a unipolar world*') and repeated ad nauseam the speech on the need to "denazify' Ukraine. But the overall tone of the interview actually corrected this apparent intransigence.

Sergei Lavrov did not assign his country any war objective other than the self-proclaimed entities of Donbas (see '*the absolute priority is the liberation of Donetsk and Lugansk*'). He acknowledged France's efforts, while stressing its isolation in Europe, to promote a '*new European security architecture*' and '*strategic autonomy*'. While he did not give the impression that his country was in a position to make demands (see he repeated on several occasions: '*We are not imposing ourselves*'), he in no way closed the door on Franco-Russian dialogue at the highest level.

The issue of sanctions was only touched upon; Sergei Lavrov described them as '*hysterical, indicative of impotence, and prepared a long time ago to prevent Russia's development*'. He was pessimistic about the prospects for lifting them, even though the issue is undoubtedly a priority for Moscow. The indiscriminate use of the Ukrainian grain blockade, which has had global repercussions, could prove to be a double-edged sword for Russia. Apart from the risk of further damaging its image in developing countries open to its views, the long-term economic consequences could prove disastrous. Equally affected, Europe has endeavoured to redirect its energy supplies to Europe, for example by organising the transit via Romania and Poland of the 25 million tonnes of cereals that were blocked for a time. This overall situation may explain the relative openness shown by President Putin on this issue with the French President and Chancellor Scholz.

The exegesis of the Russian Foreign Minister's remarks (see above) calls for caution and must be confronted with reality. Nevertheless, Sergei Lavrov's return to centre stage - if confirmed - would be encouraging news, indicating that a diplomatic path is not completely closed. In the aftermath of the June putsch, Sergei Lavrov intervened to declare that the activities of the Wagner militia would continue in Africa. But at the same time, the Kremlin spokesman praised the efforts of Vatican diplomacy. Clearly, the shake-up of Russian power caused by Evgeny Prigozhin's Moscow escapade has created a new situation that could affect the conduct of the war in Ukraine. In any case, the discretion or visibility of Sergei Lavrov will remain an important indicator of the intentions of the Russian authorities in choosing between war and peace.

Cats on the roof

Not to mention the Brezhnev glaciation, the Moscow winter can be endless and snowfalls sometimes still occur in April or even at the beginning of May. However, temperatures gradually rise at the end of this period. They can still be clearly negative when, suddenly, unexpectedly, and while they had totally disappeared for many months, some cats make their appearance on the roofs of the capital still snowy and adorned with stalactites. The sign does not deceive who is heralding better days, not overnight, but in an inevitable way. It is difficult to tell from a distance what is happening in Kyiv, Washington or European capitals, where the discourse remains ambiguous, as it is also ambiguous in Moscow. But the alarmist calls that have been heard for weeks about the 'impeding' of an attack and the latest announcement by powerful intelligence services, about an invasion of Ukraine today, have been fortunately denied by the facts.

The crisis is far from behind us, but we witnessed 48 hours ago the surreal scene of a president questioning his Minister of Foreign Affairs on television live, in a pateline manner, on the possibility and relevance of a diplomatic solution. The 'always!' (*Всегда!*) expressed in response by Sergei Lavrov, rocked like a cry from the heart, while for his part the Ambassador of Ukraine in London was talking about the possibility for his country to renounce a request for accession to NATO. Yes it seems that the cats have begun to venture again on the rooftops of Moscow.

From one putsch to another

The putsch of June 2023 was not without similarities to that of August 1991 against Mikhail Gorbachev. In both cases, it was an operation organised by the most radical forces in the country: at the end of the Soviet Union, it involved some of the last defenders of the system, whether from the State apparatus or Communists, and nationalist currents; in 2023, it was a reaction by extremist forces whose objectives were not perfectly clear.

But there were three key differences between the two events: the 1991 putsch came from within the state apparatus, whereas Wagner was a militia, albeit one with certain links of consanguinity with the executive; the most conservative elements of the Ministry of Defence, the Ministry of the Interior and the KGB, which Gorbachev himself had brought into the government in the hope of neutralising them, turned against him. In 2023, the so-called democratic opposition - whether Mikhail Khodorkovsky from his exile in London or Navalny from prison - went astray, at the risk of discrediting themselves by immediately supporting Yevgeny Prigozhin. Finally, the people were absent from the debate in 2023, despite the fact that 1991 was one of the rare moments in the history of contemporary Russia when the popular masses played an important role: Boris Yeltsin was not alone on a float in front of the White House, but very much surrounded by the people; the street said no to a return to the past and defended, without necessarily being aware of it, the gains in freedom that Mikhail Gorbachev had brought it; it then proved ungrateful to Gorbachev.

Russian power vacuum

In these dramatic circumstances, it became clear that Vladimir Putin's undivided power of almost 25 years was not only being challenged, but was wavering in the eyes of Russia as a whole and the whole world. A civil war had even begun because, contrary to the rewriting of history by the main players, blood had been spilt between Russians along the road between Rostov-on-Don and Moscow.

It is premature to draw any conclusions from these considerable developments on the Russian domestic scene, which went far beyond the latter and affected both the war in Ukraine and the external perception of Russia. The first question that naturally arose was this: Was Putin now politically dead, as Gorbachev had been in the aftermath of the 1991 putsch, when he resigned a few months later on 25 December of the same year ? Faced with the mutineers, the Russian president had no choice but to make a very firm statement about '*treason*' and the '*stab in the back*'. But many pointed out that this martial tone had not been translated into action, in a kind of admission of powerlessness. Indeed, did V. Putin have the means to react, with the bulk of his regular troops deployed on the Ukrainian front, apart from blowing up a few fuel depots in the Voronezh region in an attempt to slow the advance of the insurgents? Since Prigozhin clearly has support within the state structures, could Vladimir Putin have taken the risk, if he had the capacity to do so, of using force at the risk of triggering a civil war in addition to an external conflict? This no doubt explains his reference, in his first speech at the start of the rebellion, to the events of 1917, on the understanding that he could not rule out the possible execution of Nicholas II and his family by the Reds in Yekaterinburg.

As for his opponent Prigozhin, he was somewhat hastily presented as the winner of the operation, having exposed the weakness of the government and even humiliated his former protector. But this interpretation was quickly corrected. The sudden about-face of his troops 200 km from Moscow was not understood. Did Wagner's leader have the means to reach Moscow without a blow? Could he control the capital? Did he have enough support? Doubts quickly set in and led to a pitiful retreat.

In the absence of a clear winner or an indisputable loser, what emerged from this dramatic episode was an abysmal power vacuum in a country that was previously thought to be characterised by a ruthless vertical distribution of power.

Yevgeny Prigozhin perpetrated a double deception: on the one hand, in relation to the war, Wagner's men may have been considered good fighters on the Russian side, and indeed it seems that they achieved results in Bakhmut, but even before the putsch, Prigozhin had denounced the war in terms that Kyiv would not have rejected, which created a great deal of confusion ; Faced with the Russian elites, the leader of Wagner embarked on a *march for justice*, developing an embryonic political programme based on the fight against *corruption, lies and bureaucracy*, even though he embodied the vices of an oligarchic system. In reality, his 'straight talk' was full of demagogy and lies.

As for the Russian President, he found himself in a double bind, faced with the war, the nationalists' one-upmanship, the media and all the forces he had mobilised for his project. The putsch brutally revealed to him that the war was corrupting his country and destroying the state. But committing to a way out of the conflict at that precise moment would only have confirmed his weakness. Strengthening the war, in the opposite direction, could only have fuelled the further disintegration of the country. The scenarios were therefore difficult to write.

In the context of a conflict that could not be controlled, it was the absence of a political project that could lead to a new wave of irrationality that was ultimately the most serious. In 1991, at the time of the putsch, the Soviet Union still formally existed and the putsch was carried out by the most conservative elements of the state apparatus (e.g. the Ministries of Defence, the Interior and the KGB), who were committed to preserving the system. Faced with them, Boris Yeltsin posed as the defender of the nascent freedom (NB: finally, thanks to Gorbachev), supported by the people who had taken to the streets of Moscow.

So what was the plan now? The stability that Putin had embodied for so many years? Or had we entered a 'period of unrest', as Russia had experienced throughout its history? Was the steady rise in living standards that Putin had been credited with, thanks to high energy commodity prices, still possible now that sanctions were taking their toll? Was there still a future for 'Bonapartist' figures like Prigozhin? Finally, the democratic opposition seemed extremely weak, with Khodorkovsky on the outside and Navalny on the inside who had fallen into the trap of supporting the business of Wagner's boss.

The transformation of Russian power thus seemed to have completed a complete evolution, i.e. to have returned to the starting point, namely the disappearance of the Soviet Union. *'Everything has changed so that nothing changes'*, to quote a famous phrase. But the essential difference was the absence of a project.

Vladimir Putin is fond of historical references, because he conforms to an imperial project. In his martial speech at the start of the putsch, he spoke of the risk of a repeat of the events of 1917, without mentioning Nicholas II. For him, the alternative was perhaps the model of Ivan IV the Terrible. Threatened by foreign invasions at the end of the 16th century, he chose to strengthen the absolutism of the State; he even had the Metropolitan executed, despite having been a childhood friend, believing *'that as a man he was a sinner, but as Tsar he was just'*. Another way forward would be to return to a great reformist project in the spirit of Peter the Great, namely enlightened despotism, i.e. change from above. Such a policy had for a time given him a certain legitimacy, but it would take time to restore his credibility, beyond the war in Ukraine.

7

Russia's economic changeover

The break-up of the Soviet Union, the rise to power of V. Putin, chosen by B. Yeltsin in 1999, the global economic and financial crisis from 2008 onwards, wars in the Caucasus and Ukraine - these are just some of the high points in contemporary Russian history. Beyond appearances, what was Russia's 'tipping point' during these years? What were the underlying forces behind these developments? What are the prospects today?

V. Putin became Prime Minister of Russia on 10 May 2008 at the end of two presidential terms; he has not left the presidency since 2012 and in 2024 has begun a third term of 6 years in a row, which is now permitted by the Constitution of the Russian Federation.

In retrospect, 2008 appears to be a pivotal date in Russia's most contemporary history, coinciding as it did with an international economic and financial crisis that affected the country, albeit a few months later than the world economic situation. Ignoring this pivotal moment does not help us to understand more recent developments. 2024 and beyond could also prove to be years of great danger for the Russian regime and the country as a whole; the Russian president re-established his authority after the Wagner revolt in June 2023, but the progress of the war in Ukraine and the conditions for ending it remain a major challenge.

Stability and change from 2008 onwards

An orderly political transition

Unable to stand for a third successive presidential term from 2012, V. Putin organised a transition by choosing D. Medvedev. He had carefully prepared in advance for his temporary withdrawal as head of government in a perfectly legal manner, setting the limits of the inheritance and usufruct of the government and even informing in advance certain foreign personalities in whom he had confidence. France had not been taken into confidence.

The key words of the new Prime Minister's general policy statement were modernisation of the economy, social well-being of the population and integration of Russia into the world economy. Only the Communists, behind their leader G. Zyuganov, voiced their opposition in the Duma. In an unusual reversal, these government policies were also imposed on the new Head of State.

V. Putin insisted on the need to strengthen the competitiveness of the economy and introduce structural changes; indeed, although Russia's GDP exceeded $2,000 billion at the time, placing it 7th in the world and enabling it to envisage overtaking the United Kingdom in near future, it also had to face up to tough international competition. The Prime Minister spoke of the achievements (e.g. cereal exports on a par with Canada) and the weaknesses of the Russian economy (e.g. lagging behind in products with high added value). Putin made macroeconomic stability a condition for opening up to the world economy, committing himself, for example, to reducing inflation to a single figure; he announced a tax reform project, particularly in the oil sector where taxes on extraction and other taxes accounted for 75-80% of profits; this was damaging to the maintenance of low-yield fields and the exploration and development of new sites.

This rather liberal economic discourse also focused on the defence of large groups (NB: 'corporations') and the government intended to rely on the sectors deemed essential: transport, high technology and ship and aircraft building. The Prime Minister gave assurances that Russian investment abroad - which he claimed had been hindered to the tune of $50 billion over the past year under the misleading slogan *beware, the Reds are coming* - would be pursued on the basis of reciprocity (NB: foreign investment in Russia was 10 times higher).

Another key player in the perfectly choreographed transition, the new president D. Medvedev, inexperienced on the international stage, took his first steps. His foreign policy novice's character was, however, corrected by his experience in 'energy diplomacy', acquired in particular as Chairman of Gazprom's Board of Directors. One of his first notable interventions was with the President of Ukraine to encourage that country, in the midst of a gas crisis, to fulfil its contractual obligations.

He quickly asserted the continuity of foreign policy (see *'the course followed for eight years will be continued'*), the fundamental directions of which the President was supposed to set under the Constitution. As with his predecessor, the CIS was quickly established as a 'first circle'; D. Medvedev even ventured into the regal domain par excellence of defence issues; he defended and illustrated *'Russia's national interests, which must be defended on all fronts and by all means, in compliance with international law'*; Europe was given a prominent place, without neglecting Asia in line with new strategic imperatives.

Continued modernisation of society

This trend was first reflected in the composition of the government. Among the ministers of the 'economic bloc', the following remained: A. Kudrin, a 'Petersburg liberal', as Finance Minister, and E. Nabiullina, Minister for Economic Development, now head of the Central Bank. Greater control by representatives of the 'power structures' (*Siloviki*) was perceptible with the relative disappearance of the Stechine-Ustinov-Patrouchev axis (NB: it should be noted that these personalities are still at the heart of power in the Kremlin). Although he did not have any major networks, D. Medvedev tried to make his mark by placing a number of people close to him in positions of power and by asserting his determination to fight against 'legal nihilism' (NB: he was a trained lawyer) and corruption.

D. Medvedev's economic views were perfectly in line with those of his mentor V. Putin. They took the form of 'pragmatic state capitalism' (NB: joint-stock companies, controlled by the state but 49% open to private capital; replacement of civil servants on boards of directors by 'professionals'; keeping the energy sector and defence industry in the state fold; attention to social problems). The St Petersburg Economic Forum was undoubtedly the highlight of the year (see D. Medvedev's opening speech on '*Russia's long-term development*'), with 9,000 participants, 65 countries, 200 managers and $13.5 billion in contracts signed.

Challenges, weaknesses and uncertainties

Demographics remained a major challenge (NB: with the four major national programmes: education, health, housing and agriculture) in a country that had lost 600,000 to 700,000 people a year in previous years, despite an upturn in 2007 and a resumption of the birth rate. From then on, the demographic policy was integrated into the major national programmes and was not dissociated from the regional development policy (see the obsession with an empty Russian Far East in the face of China).

State capitalism revealed both its needs and its limits. D. Medvedev, although he denied it, had a vision of capitalism based on state corporations; but the intention was also to open up capital (see above) in order to inject new money and import foreign technologies and skills; it was understood that strategic sectors would remain controlled for an indefinite period.

Macroeconomic contradictions remained visible: how to control inflation (NB: then in double figures) by increasing pensions and salaries, when supply was insufficient? How could supply growth be ensured without removing barriers to competition? How can we guarantee the emergence of SMEs in the absence of bank financing? How can we allow innovative SMEs to flourish in the shadow of state corporations? These were just some of the questions that arose.

The international environment began to look more uncertain for Russia, against a backdrop of crisis in the Caucasus (notably Georgia). But Russia also had major concerns in its '*soft underbelly*' (NB: Iran, Central Asia, Afghanistan). It struggled to position itself between East and West, aware that Europe was necessary for its modernisation but also waving a 'Chinese card'. The crisis in the Caucasus (NB: Georgia) ultimately boosted the popularity of V. Putin, who was in fact at the helm behind the curtain; it also aroused strong anti-Western feeling in Russian opinion, with Saakashvili's Georgia seen as an instrument of NATO, i.e. the United States. At the same time, Russia was concerned about the long-term consequences of this affair (e.g. the recognition of entities such as Abkhazia and South Ossetia, distancing it from close partners such as China, which were committed to territorial integrity).

The ordeal and the way out of the crisis

Impact of the crisis on the Russian economy

The Georgian crisis was the first intervention by a regular Russian army outside the country's borders since Afghanistan in 1979, and in the end it did not lead to any upheaval in relations between Russia and the European Union. The French Presidency of the EU played a calming role that was appreciated by all parties. The debate on economic sanctions against Russia came to a halt; indeed, the French Presidency had ruled out such a prospect beforehand.

But 2008/2009 was a year of change, and of danger, because of the delayed effects of the global financial crisis. Initially, the effects of the crisis were not as visible as in other economies. The banking system, for example, was not affected to the same extent. This was not the case, however, for the stock market, which fell more sharply than those of other emerging countries, to the point where it even had to be closed in October 2008.

The price of a barrel of oil, essential to the Russian economy, plummeted from \$147 in July 2008 to \$30 in September of the same year. Given this sharp deterioration in the terms of trade, the rouble should have been devalued. But the government, still traumatised by the syndrome of the 1998 financial crisis under President Yeltsin, refused to do so. The Central Bank confined itself to trying to limit the fall in the currency by intervening to the tune of \$200 billion between November 2008 and January/February 2009; this did not prevent a de facto devaluation of around 30%, when the considerable resources mobilised by the Central Bank could have been put to better use, for example in investments designed to strengthen the country's economy and enable it to emerge stronger from the crisis. A poor understanding of the modern mechanisms of the international economy and a continued attachment to the command economy were undoubtedly responsible for these mistakes.

Managing the crisis

Substantial public loans totalling $135 billion, or 10% of GDP, were mobilised to counteract the crisis; a special system for refinancing the foreign debt of large companies was also set up, via the Central Bank and the Foreign Trade Bank (*VneshEkonomBank*) for an amount of $50 billion. Despite these considerable resources, a lack of liquidity was felt, leading to a profound transformation of the banking landscape - which had already been predicted before the crisis - based on the fragmentation of the sector (NB: there were more than 1,000 banks in Russia at the time).

The increased involvement of the State in the economy, thanks to the crisis, was one of the most striking effects of the period; it was a question of tackling traditional weaknesses in a context that was more delicate than ever (see dependence on raw materials; dilapidated infrastructures; insufficient supply and double-digit inflation; regional imbalances).

Prospects at the end of the tunnel

The crisis undoubtedly eroded Russia's economic prospects over the next few years, bringing to an end a 10-year cycle of strong growth. After two successive shocks (cf. banking sector and terms of trade for oil and other raw materials), it became clear that Russia would continue to depend on the level of global growth (NB: 80% of resources come from raw materials); it would therefore not be in control of the scenarios, with a barrel price of at least $70 being required to balance the budget. The central bank would continue to defend the rouble with a costly policy of 'small steps', sometimes described as *wrong steps in the right direction*.

The political authorities, for their part, kept asserting as a leitmotiv that investment in strategic sectors would be maintained; major projects were nevertheless affected (e.g. Moscow City and the metallurgy industry). In January 2009, Russia and Ukraine settled their dispute over gas (NB: 20% discount for Kyiv compared with European prices), allowing deliveries to Europe to resume, but Prime Minister Putin stressed the need for new supply routes to the north and south. Against this backdrop, and to prepare for the recovery, Russia expressed its attachment to cooperation with the outside world. D. Medvedev, for his part, relaunched the project for an 'Innovation City' at Skolkovo, near Moscow, which is sometimes referred to as *Russian Silicon Valley*.

Russia in search of a new stability

A look back at 2009/2012

2009/2012 will have been a key moment for the most contemporary Russia, beyond the choice of men (see supreme leaders, renewal of governors), notably with regard to the choice of economic and social model. The crisis reminded the State of its ardent obligations, but destiny hesitated, because at the same time the already dominant theme of reform had taken hold and was developed extensively by D. Medvedev himself (see diversification of the economy, research and innovation); its corollary was new privatisations, after the so-called 'savage' ones of the 90s, and the opening up of the capital of public companies ('state corporations' to foreign investment).

The influx of petrodollars in the previous decade had not sufficiently encouraged investment. In the end, the crisis had some virtues. It reminded us of the structural weaknesses of the economy, in particular its heavy dependence on raw materials, and it led to a new voluntarism: an appeal to foreign investors for modernisation; a re-examination of the role of the State in the economy; and the use of the budget to manage the macro-economy, with priority given to infrastructure. In this new configuration, external capital needed the rules of the game to be defined and respected.

What is the point of recovery?

The system in force since 2000 has been one of stability guaranteed by an authoritarian mode of governance. A different path then emerged, one that was also possible in terms of fostering the investment climate: that of promoting the rule of law, which D. Medvedev championed during his presidency. This debate between Russia as it is in depth and Russia as it should be summed up, at the risk of caricaturing, the major challenge of the period ahead.

The Putin/Medvedev tandem, which was not a cohabitation (*'we are of the same blood'*, the former used to say) but rather a political and institutional formula, worked from the presidential election of 2008 onwards; internal consensus was sought outside political pluralism and this has always been the specificity of the Russian "recipe'. Prime Minister Putin always remained the strong man, controlling the power structures and managing the major economic issues. But President Medvedev tenaciously pursued a policy of change (NB: in the army, the forces of law and order and the bureaucracy), without necessarily opposing his mentor, which for a time seemed to give him credit with the population but ultimately cost him the loss of influential supporters. Strictly speaking, there were no real tensions within the dyarchy, but rather a sharing of roles that also had the advantage of giving the impression of a debate that did not really exist in society.

Externally, Russia was reassured to some extent on its western flank by the election of President Yanukovich in Ukraine (2010-2014) - a nagging problem since the end of the USSR; it controlled the political and military situation around Georgia; but it retained - albeit carefully disguised by apparent good relations - an obsessive fear of China that was revived by China's inroads into Central Asia. On this last point, we have to look at the long term and - at the risk of being surprising - we cannot totally rule out the possibility that the problem of the East will end up replacing that of the West, provided that the question of the European security architecture is put back on the drawing board and comes up with a formula acceptable to all.

A new era of unrest?

Since the end of the first decade of the 2000s, Russia has unquestionably been on a 'tipping point', if we are to look at the most recent phase in its history. The global crisis of 2008 and its lasting after-effects have contributed to this, as have international crises such as Ukraine, with which the conflict actually began as early as the post-Soviet partition of 91/92. The annexation of Crimea in 2014 has rendered some of the players unrecognisable. As has already been described, Sergei Lavrov, his country's legalist spokesman in international forums, has embodied this transformation by becoming virtually inaudible; D. Medvedev has become the herald of the most extreme ideas; the media, like *Russia Today*, a channel created with an air of modernism and directed by Margarita Simonian, have lined up entirely behind the banner of power.

The *Time of Troubles*, which preceded the Romanov dynasty, was a period of extreme violence in Russian history. History, without being seen as a repetition, is nevertheless a reference point. The Wagner revolt led by Progozhin in June 2023 could have led to civil war. Indeed, in the mad dash to Moscow from the town of Rostov, militiamen killed soldiers of the regular Russian army. Power, which had been shaken for a time, could not fail to re-establish itself, whatever the means, at the risk of sinking.

V. Putin's policies over the last few years, and in particular his 'imperial' project in Ukraine, have undoubtedly corresponded to a quest for identity in the face of a West that is likely to contaminate people's minds and that is perceived from then on as a threat to the Russian mode of governance. Putin's 'scheme' can be compared to the triptych of Nicholas I: Authority-Nationalism-Orthodoxy. Having re-established his authority, which had been violently challenged from within, a new necessity could arise for Russia's supreme leader, one that can be summed up in a new triptych in the spirit of Peter the Great: Authority-Reform-Openness. Indeed, the Tsar needed a great mobilising project, without which there could be no enlightened despotism.

One of the main conclusions drawn by Russia's leaders from the 2008-2012 crisis - which in reality never ended - was that the way out lay in continuing to open up to the West, in full accordance with Russian history, geography, demography and culture. Indeed, until the war of 2022, 70% of investment continued to come from the West - and not from Asia - against all the odds. Given Moscow's absolute need to re-establish the European market for its gas - an intolerable loss of income in the long term - the return could be comparable in 2024/2025 and the following years. The remedy for such a strategy will obviously involve putting an end to the war in Ukraine. For its part, Europe should encourage Russia in its own way by waving a 'light at the end of the tunnel' in front of it. The collective West, as it is now called in the global South, should ponder for its own part - and above all make its own - this famous thought of Lord Palmerston, who was at one time in favour of a warmongering policy towards Russia: *England has no eternal allies and no eternal enemies, only eternal interests*.

8

Russian gas, a global issue

In the crisis in Ukraine, Russian gas is as much an issue as a player in a conflict with global ramifications.

Since the start of the war in Ukraine in 2022, Europe has decided to drastically reduce its supplies of Russian gas imported via pipelines (NB: however, gas continued to transit through Ukraine - until the end of 2024 - in reduced quantities, particularly to Central Europe: the Czech Republic, Slovakia, Hungary and Austria). But purchases of liquefied natural gas (LNG) from Russia, to mention only European countries including France, have partially offset this sudden change. According to the President of the European Commission, the EU plans to stop all imports of fossil fuels from Russia by 2027.

Russia has responded to the Western sanctions by reducing its exports. It is trying to make up for its shortfall with Europe, both by developing its LNG capacity (NB: at its Yamal 2 site, for example) and by trying to move towards Asia. However, such an adaptation is coming up against both political and, above all, technical constraints, due to the lack of suitable gas pipelines for quantities that are many times greater than current gas pipeline exports to the Far East.

The sabotage of Nord Stream 2 in the Baltic Sea hit the headlines and illustrated - in a way that was visible to the public - the importance of what is at stake. The fact that the investigation is increasingly pointing towards non-Russian responsibility - which we cannot imagine was not authorised, supported or even seconded by one or more powers outside the region in question - could in itself confirm that Russian gas is an issue that goes beyond the European continent alone.

Nostalgia is not what it used to be

Against the backdrop of extreme tensions with Moscow, it is difficult to remember that the Soviet Union, and then Russia, were always perfectly reliable suppliers. Even at the height of the Cold War, the energy weapon was never used; on the contrary, long-term agreements were renewed, as was the case for Gaz de France (GDF). It should be noted that, in this type of agreement, a *Take or Pay* clause obliges the buyer to pay for a minimum quantity of gas, whether or not it is consumed, while the supplier undertakes to deliver a certain quantity of gas. Long-term contracts have thus contributed to the stability of gas prices.

The Russian group Gazprom has long preferred long-term contracts for its customers in Europe. These contracts were generally for 25 to 30 years. The United States, for its part, did everything it could during the Cold War to ensure that cooperation in the gas sector between Moscow and European countries did not develop. However, Soviet gas proved necessary for Europe's economic growth.

Russian gas made its appearance in Europe immediately after the Second World War (e.g. Poland in 1946); during the 1950s, other allies of Moscow within the socialist camp were also beneficiaries. During the 1960s, the development of very large gas fields, particularly in Siberia, led to the extension of the gas pipeline network westwards, although not beyond the borders of the Warsaw Pact countries.

It was not until the end of the 1960s that the first agreements with Soyuzneftexport were signed for limited quantities with Austria, then France and Italy. But it was the FRG that became the USSR's main gas partner, due to the development needs of its industry. In exchange for the gas, German companies supplied high-quality, large-diameter steel pipes, which only they and Japan could produce. Despite opposition from Washington - which declared an embargo, extended to Europe and Japan in the event of American components, on deliveries of equipment for the oil and gas industry to the USSR - deliveries of Soviet natural gas to Europe increased tenfold over 20 years, until the end of the Soviet Union. In 1981, there was a tug-of-war with Chancellor Helmut Schmidt over the construction - with

European funding - of a gas pipeline for quantities of up to 60 billion m3 per year, which was eventually reduced to just over 30%. In any case, towards the end of the 1980s, almost 15% of all gas in France was of Soviet origin (NB: this percentage was comparable before the war in Ukraine). In Germany, this figure rose to just over 50% before 2022.

The trigger for sanctions

By the end of 2021, the EU was importing just over 40% of its gas from Russia (NB: 30% of its oil). The situation has changed radically with the drastic reduction in imports by Europe and the Western sanctions. As a result of these sanctions (NB: the first sanctions, which do not directly concern gas, were not decided in Brussels until December 2023) - which, it should be remembered, are unilateral, as they were not decided by the UN Security Council - Russia reacted. But its attitude did not go so far as to envisage a long-term boycott of the European market.

The results of the voluntary reduction in imports of Russian gas by EU countries, compared with the first quarter of 2022, were as follows in 2023: the percentage of Russian gas fell from 39% to 17%; that of Norway - which dethroned Russia as the leading supplier - rose from 38% to 46%; the other main suppliers were the United Kingdom (13% instead of 9%), Algeria (13% instead of 6%) and Azerbaijan (7% instead of 6%). The major groups in the energy sector have diversified their supplies: TotalEnergies has signed a gas agreement with Iraq in 2023; the group has also announced the start-up of production from a field in Azerbaijan and strengthened its partnership with the Algerian company Sonatrach.

At the same time, the LNG market has changed dimension over the period under review, with US LNG in particular rising by 143%. European LNG imports increased by 60% in 2022 compared with the previous year. LNG has established itself as an alternative to traditional gas in the absence of pipeline transfer constraints. The gas is transformed into a liquid by cooling, which then enables it to be transported by sea. But LNG technology - which has an impact on the environment - is still required, as are suitable LNG carriers and refurbished loading and receiving ports. Germany has embarked on a development programme in this area (NB: Russian LNG is currently received in the Netherlands, Spain and France) and Russia has not been left behind, both in terms of maintaining deliveries to Europe and developing an Arctic route with nuclear LNG carriers (NB: including the *Christophe de Margerie)* bound for China. France has become the leading European recipient of Russian LNG by 2022. With Spain and Belgium, its imports of Russian LNG have increased by 55% compared with 2021 (NB: +12% over one year for the EU as a whole). However, the EU's main supplier of LNG remains the United States, which supplies 40.2% of Europe's total LNG imports from shale gas. The breakdown of sources of liquefied natural gas in 2023 compared with 2022 was as follows: United States (49% instead of 40%), Russia (up from 13% to 18%), Qatar (11% instead of 13%), Nigeria (6% instead of 4%), Algeria (4% instead of 7%), others including Norway with just over 6% (12% instead of 22%).

Dependence, new constraints and global uncertainties

LNG has helped the EU to adapt its energy policy to the war in Ukraine, but there is a risk of a new dependency - on the United States after Russia - and the environmental dimension should not be overlooked. Finally, LNG is 30% to 40% more expensive than gas delivered by pipeline, and Europeans now pay 3 times more for their gas than Americans, which has obvious consequences in terms of industrial and commercial competitiveness. The bottom line is that the major breakdown in energy relations with Russia - despite the preservation of now more marginal supplies - is damaging for us and ultimately for everyone.

For Russia, whose economy is dependent on hydrocarbon exports (NB: 25% of GDP, 40% of government revenue before the war), the stakes are even higher. In response to Western sanctions, Russia has also cut its gas supplies. In doing so, it lost $170 billion. As the world's 8th largest economy, Russia has tried to compensate for these losses by increasing its trade with China, the world's 2nd largest economy (NB: this reached a record \$240 billion, an increase of 26% on the previous year). However, Russia is not a major global supplier to China (NB: only 5% of total Chinese imports) and China exports as much to the Netherlands as to Russia, and less than to Vietnam (NB: \$111 billion). Moscow has tried to compensate for this shortfall by increasing its oil sales (NB: India imported 35% of its oil from Russia in 2023, compared with 2% before 2022).

After the 'Chinese card' that Russia is said to have played in recent years, there has been talk of a real 'alliance' between the two countries. But we need to be much more cautious. Despite the exponential growth of its trade with China, culminating in the record figure of 2023, Russia has remained dependent on EU investment, as it was at the end of the first decade of the 21st century (NB: 50% of its trade then was with the EU and 70% of foreign investment; the share of European investment even reached 75% before the war). In other words, technology was still coming from the West. It will be difficult for Russia to replace its energy relations with EU countries with a preferred buyer for gas, which would be China.

There are both political and technical obstacles in the way: Does Beijing want to forge closer political ties with Moscow? And in some way physically, in a sustainable way, through gas pipelines? A single gas pipeline currently links the two countries over a distance of 3,000 km between Siberia and the Amur river: *Power of Siberia*, which was inaugurated in 2019 after an estimated investment of \$15 billion, was commissioned in 2014. The pipeline is expected to transport 38 billion m3 of gas by 2025, or just 10% of China's needs. *Power of Siberia 2* is intended to replace *Nord Stream 2*, with a final capacity of 50 billion m3; the quantities delivered would then total 100 billion m3 and the equivalent in LNG (NB: 2.7 billion LNG in 2023). The objective is all the more ambitious given that work on the *Power of Siberia 2* (NB: 5 years of work, 2,600 km, 10 to 15 billion in investments) has not yet begun and a formal agreement on the project has still not been signed, despite the pressing demands of V. Putin. The Russian President's visit to China in May 2024 does not appear to have brought any progress. It should be noted that in

September of the same year, V. Putin visited Mongolia, a country which is also on the planned route and which also has a say in the implementation of the project.

On the other hand, Russian-Chinese cooperation on LNG seems to be making progress. An LNG 2 project, close to the Yamal site in the Arctic zone - and led by the Russian company Novatek in conjunction with the Chinese companies Zhejiang Energy Gas Group and Shenergy Group of China (NB: Total confirmed at the beginning of the year that it did not want to take part in the project) - should give rise to the first ship deliveries in the next few weeks.

Europe's ability to react and adapt to the new Russian gas situation has sometimes been seen as a *geopolitical disaster* for Russia. But isn't the same true for Europe? Not to mention the economic consequences for Europe. Only the United States, with its considerable energy wealth, and China, which can diversify its partners because of its new-found power, currently seem to have more control over the situation and their future choices. What will the European countries, excluding Norway and the United Kingdom, which have gas, ultimately decide? The question mainly concerns Germany, the main economic victim in Europe of the war in Ukraine. There has been talk of high-level German-Russian contacts during 2024 (NB: notably in Azerbaijan in October), as part of the so-called 'Petersburg dialogue' between the civil societies of the two countries, which had been dormant since February 2022.

The trap of economic sanctions

The ambassadors of the twenty-seven countries of the European Union adopted a 14th set of economic sanctions against Russia (NB: as Ursula von der Leyen welcomed the decision). The Heads of State and Government were no doubt expected to confirm these decisions taken ad referendum. The new measures target the energy sector in particular - by penalising the logistics of Russian liquefied natural gas (LNG) exports from the Arctic - as well as the system enabling financial transactions following Russia's exclusion from SWIFT.

These latest developments come at a time when the Russian economy's apparent resistance to Western sanctions is being confirmed; this is a far cry from the statements made in March 2022 by the French Finance Minister, who said that '*sanctions are frighteningly effective ; we are going to cause the collapse of the Russian economy*'; international institutions have repeatedly reported that the Russian economy is holding up well, and the World Bank has ranked Russia 4th among the world's economies. Statistics can always be challenged, and a somewhat forced soothing discourse on the theme of 'sanctions will strike in the long run' can be repeated in an incantatory manner, but we cannot avoid reflecting on the mechanisms of international sanctions, their legality if not their legitimacy, and above all on their effects in a globalised economy.

Is there anything better than international sanctions?

Sanctions policies have become a kind of Pavlovian reflex in international life. Sanctions can be aimed at weakening an adversary in the event of marked tension or a long-lasting dispute; they also often conceal economic issues behind the assertion of high principles; and they seek to punish for what is considered a breach of international order, in the absence of consensus on more radical measures.

In practice, these measures are increasingly deployed outside the multilateral framework - due to the fragmentation of the international order - even though the multilateral framework has made them the agreed instruments of its possible action (see article 41: coercitive measures not implying use of armed forces), but they require a certain consensus of the UN Security Council and cannot be adopted if only one of the permanent members of the Council opposes them (NB: this is improperly referred to as the use of a '*right of veto*', which is in fact simply a negative vote by a permanent member).
Major players in the international system - who could not be challenged head-on by other means - are targeted, such as Russia,

China and Iran. However, because of the divisions in the international community, sanctions are increasingly being adopted on a regional basis (e.g. EU sanctions against Belarus and Russia), further proof of the weakening of a global security architecture and a growing trend towards a more multipolar world.

Effectiveness and perverse effects of sanctions

Regardless of the method used - whether or not sanctions are imposed within the framework of international legality - they can have perverse effects, and have sometimes been criticised for their global impact on the target societies, i.e. their injustice if not their ineffectiveness. There are many examples of punishments inflicted on entire populations which, paradoxically, end up strengthening the authoritarian powers in place. Historically, it was not punishments that undermined, let alone ended, the apartheid regime in South Africa; arms embargoes led Pretoria to develop a powerful and flourishing national arms industry. Nor, from the 1991 Gulf War onwards, were they instrumental in overthrowing Saddam Hussein; on the contrary, they enabled the dictator to consolidate his power - through the distribution of humanitarian aid designed to correct the appalling effects of sanctions on the most vulnerable elements - and to hold on for a further ten years until the military intervention in 2003.

Today, although we cannot speak of the harmlessness of such measures, the question is whether they have any chance of making Russia or China, or even Belarus, give in. On this last issue, the need to sanction Lukashenko's regime became clear to Brussels, but Europe had difficulty defining 'targeted' sanctions, a term that has now replaced the somewhat shocking expression *smart sanctions*.

The Nord Stream 2 case, even before it was sabotaged, revealed the complexity of the sanctions mechanisms and their multiple dimensions, whether in terms of energy policy (NB: do we need additional quantities of Russian gas ?), environmental protection (see the reservations of certain States, such as Denmark, about the pipeline route), the economy (cf. German-Russian trade) and geostrategy (NB: would additional Russian gas increase dependence on Moscow or, on the contrary, would it assert the independence of Europe, whose major companies have regularly been hit in recent history by the application of US laws with extra-territorial scope ?)

A substitute for unspoken ambitions?

It is probably this complexity and combination of costs and benefits that led Washington to suspend (NB: by virtue of a waiver from the executive) certain measures taken against companies involved in the *Nord Stream* project, in addition to the opportunity to facilitate President Biden's first tour of Europe to the EU and NATO. In the final analysis, it is not a question of simply being in favour of or strongly opposed to sanctions, which have in any case become a fact of international life. But the sheer scale of the issue calls for clarification, the prerequisite being a clear understanding of the existing mechanisms and arrangements. Many questions arise: what is the legitimacy of national or regional sanctions under international law? What are the types of sanctions? What are their effects, including for industrial groups belonging to countries that use them frequently in the context of increasingly fierce competition between states that sometimes belong to the same political and military alliances?

Is the sprinkler being sprinkled?

In European circles in Brussels, many were delighted at the speed with which the EU had adapted, during the first year of the war in Ukraine, to the drastic reduction in Russian gas imports via pipelines (NB: these have not been completely interrupted and continue to transit - albeit in very reduced quantities - via Ukraine, through which three major pipelines pass). The ability of several European countries to adapt cannot be disputed (e.g. Germany has speeded up the construction of LNG delivery terminals).

But the cost of this considerable transformation is all too often overlooked. While the United Kingdom and Norway, both gas producers, have benefited from the new situation, it is above all the United States that has been the main beneficiary of sales of its shale gas. The cost of these changes in supply has been considerable for European economies, where gas is now three to four times more expensive than in the United States. We can therefore draw the necessary conclusions in terms of the profoundly affected competitiveness of European economies. Brussels does not seem to be moved by this, and has not abandoned its objective of imposing total sanctions on Russian hydrocarbons by 2027.

Over and above these considerations, it should be noted that as the European economic sanctions against Russia are not 'international', in the sense of measures that would have been decided by the UN Security Council, Europe is thereby promoting the principle of the 'extraterritoriality' of legislation on a continental scale: remember the $9 billion penalties imposed on BNP for dollar transactions with Iran) have been seriously affected. What's more, even if the United Nations Security Council is now paralysed on many issues, bypassing it can only contribute to the further disintegration of an international system that will have to be rebuilt.

A poorly conducted trial

As Europe's biggest importer of Russian LNG, France is sometimes stigmatised. But Ukraine itself allowed Russian gas to pass through in the middle of a war until the end of 2024, and received royalties for this transit. Until the end of the first decade of the new millennium, Ukraine paid less than $50 per 1,000m3 for the Russian gas it imported for itself, when the price of the same gas, for the same quantities, was $250 on the world market. Who knows? Who says so?

As for Total-Yamal, these are long-standing commitments that are not subject to sanctions, which are unilateral and in no way global, as they would be if decided by the UN Security Council. In addition, Total refrained from participating in the Yamal 2 project with Chinese companies for the exploitation and processing of LNG, even though it was not obliged to do so.

Europeans obviously prefer to buy shale gas from the United States - admittedly, they don't have much choice. As a result, they are now paying three times more for their gas than the Americans.

To take France to court, where over the years it has been one of the countries least dependent on Russian gas (NB: around 15% of its needs compared with over 40% for Germany, if I'm not mistaken), thanks in particular to nuclear power, is to miss the mark.

As for Germany (NB: but we could also talk about Italy or Poland, which used to be totally dependent), it pursued a logical supply policy, for economic reasons and given its geographical proximity to Russia.

Russia - and the Soviet Union before it at the height of the Cold War - had always been a perfectly reliable supplier, until the war in Ukraine and the sanctions to which it responded with its own weapons.

Russian gas, war and peace

The mention of a possible return of Russian gas transported by pipeline to Europe, and the role that Matthias Warnig, former East German Stasi agent and Managing Director of Nord Stream AG, could play in promoting this strategy, does not necessarily correspond to a perspective in the near future, but it deserves consideration and scrutiny.

Russia is an energy giant: gas accounts for 50% of Russia's energy resources; before the war in Ukraine, hydrocarbons (oil and gas) contributed 30% of Russia's GDP and 50% of the federal state budget. The lack of 'diversification' of an economy dependent on fossil fuels - which D. Medvedev's presidency sought to correct, but without success - and the impossibility of substituting the Asian destination for the traditional European market (see 200 billion m3 of gas per year) are sources of vulnerability for Moscow, given the lack of sufficient pipelines (NB: Russian gas covers only 10% of China's gas requirements).

Russian gas - which, incidentally, is not affected by the sanctions - covered 40% of Europe's gas needs (NB: 50% for Germany) until 2022. LNG, mainly American since that date, is 30 to 40% more expensive, while Russia also supplies liquefied gas to Europe, via France, Spain and Belgium, mainly for reasons relating to port facilities. The EU's interest therefore lies in a sort of 'back to business as usual'; Ukraine itself, through which most of the gas to Europe passed, with the exception of Nord Stream 1 (2005-2022), received substantial royalties from Gazprom, and this regime continued - albeit in reduced quantities - until 31 December last year.

Could there therefore be a certain convergence on gas; would this consensus, born of an inescapable economic realism, be a more important guarantee than possible 'troops on the ground', even if only as observers of a possible ceasefire? In the same vein, might there not be a 'virtuous' effect induced by the gradual lifting of unilateral sanctions by the United States and Europe, including those that are ineffective or even counter-productive against individuals, such as Matthias Warnig (see above) under US and UK sanctions, Leonid Mikhelson, the Russian-Israeli oligarch and CEO of Novatek (NB: LNG) or Alisher Usmanov, the Russian-Uzbek former owner of Arsenal football club, and so many other economic players ? Whatever the outcome, Russian gas will be at the heart of war or peace on the European continent.

9

The nuclear complex

The incidents over many months surrounding the Ukrainian nuclear power plant at Zaporijjia - Europe's largest in terms of capacity - in an area currently controlled by Russia but where the International Atomic Energy Agency (IAEA) nevertheless provides some supervision, and closer to home the uncertainties raised by military developments in the Kursk region on Russian territory, have drawn attention to civil nuclear power in times of war.

In less troubled times, civil nuclear power also represents a considerable challenge: This was the case in Ukraine, where the proportion of nuclear-generated electricity fluctuated between 25 and 30% until the mid-90s, before rising to over 50% before the conflict with Russia. Russia, for its part, is reputed to exploit fossil fuels first and foremost, which are a source of real income, but its 'nuclear complex', in the sense of all the structures and companies involved in the production of nuclear-generated electricity and also in the export of the corresponding technologies, is also noteworthy. Russia's nuclear sector is the only one of the former USSR countries that has been able to maintain and even increase its scientific potential since the *perestroika* period.

Nuclear renaissance

Russian technology is now mainly based on pressurised water WWER-type reactors of Soviet, then Russian, design. This is a different technology from that used at Chernobyl, although the latter is still used at the Kursk plant. An effort to standardise was made with a single type of pressurised water reactor rated at 1,200 megawatts.

There was a great upsurge in nuclear power, but for a while there was a clear downturn. This was followed by a revival that could contribute to the planet's 'energy equation', as well as its ecological equation. The aim was to promote technologies that did not emitCO2, such as nuclear, hydroelectric, wind and solar power. The process also had to aim for energy efficiency. Carbon dioxide had to be captured and stored.

The nuclear 'renaissance' can be dated back to 2008-2009 (NB: 56 reactors under construction at $8 billion each; China: 21 reactors, Russia: 11, South Korea: 6 and India: 5). Paradoxically, the global economic and financial crisis contributed to this. At the time, Russia was involved in the construction of 8 reactors, more than any other country, as well as on the world market in China, India, Iran and Bulgaria.

This renaissance has taken place in the context of the 'diversification' of the Russian economy, which was the leitmotiv of the presidency of D. Medvedev (2008-2012) and of the policies pursued by Prime Minister V. Putin. This diversification was reflected in the modernisation of Russia's nuclear fleet.

Russia has sought to secure *a stable position among the world's leading manufacturers of nuclear power plants* (S. Shmatko, Russian Energy Minister). This orientation mainly determined the rapprochement with Siemens, which was sometimes perceived - at the time and no doubt exaggeratedly - by Russia's other partners in the sector as a sort of 'nuclear Rapallo'.

As Russia embarked on the modernisation process, it also sought to improve its energy efficiency. Saving money meant acquiring know-how. At the time, Russia consumed 400 billion m3 of the 650 billion m3 of natural gas it produced annually. The aim was to achieve savings of 100 billion within ten years. Russia was also interested in the experiences of Japan and Italy in the field of energy efficiency.

2009 also saw the culmination of a gas crisis between Russia and Ukraine, which in turn gave a boost to nuclear power. Since the end of the Soviet Union, gas had been sold in Kyiv for less than $50 per 1,000m3, while the world market price was $250. Moscow therefore insisted that Ukraine - which had been de facto subsidised - should pay an appropriate price for Russian natural gas and guarantee its responsibility for the safe transit of gas to the West, as provided for in the European Energy Charter. In Moscow's view, the EU had to send a clear signal to Ukraine that it had breached the Charter.

Russia felt that it had developed a relationship of trust with Europe; indeed, it had regularly supplied Europe for 40 years, including during the most tense moments of the Cold War. It was also this general observation that motivated the construction of the Nord Stream and South Stream pipelines, with the obvious aim of bypassing Ukraine (NB: at the time, Russia estimated Europe's needs at 620 billion m3 in 2020, i.e. 100 to 120 billion more than in 2010).

Franco-Russian strategic cooperation/the case of the Arabelle turbines

The key to the success of major French companies was seen to be a long-term commitment, investing in Russian industries and infrastructures and participating in their development. This was the approach taken by Total with the project to exploit the *Shtockman* gas field in the Arctic Sea (NB: the project was ultimately shelved due to technical difficulties and costs), by Vinci and Bouygues in road infrastructure construction projects, and by Renault, which acquired a stake in Avtovaz.

The most important thing was undoubtedly to act solely through partnerships and not to target a market primarily for the sale of its own products, but for their adapted production in partnership with local companies. Under these conditions, the majority of employees were local and the percentage of expatriates was less than 10%.

Ten years ago, France was Russia's 6th largest investor and 9th largest trading partner, including its 4th largest EU partner (NB: after the Netherlands, Germany and Italy). In the gas sector, cooperation was

35 years old at the time, mainly because of the long-term agreements with GDF. GDF Suez made a commitment to Gazprom to acquire a 9% stake in the Nord Stream 1 project (€7.4 billion), while EDF agreed to acquire a 10% stake in *South Stream.*

For Alstom, the future of Russian and European high-speed trains could be decided in Russia. In the non-nuclear energy sector, for example, Alstom has successfully completed a project - launched in 2006 - to supply a turnkey thermal power plant to *Mosenergo,* an electricity producer majority-owned by the giant Gazprom.

In the nuclear sector, an ambitious joint venture project with *Atomenergomash* (51%), a subsidiary of Rosatom, took shape in 2007 with the famous *Arabelle* turbines, which would have been assembled locally on the basis of Russian orders. Strictly speaking, this was not a transfer of technology, but rather a transfer of equipment. An initial agreement was signed in 2008 to carry out the engineering for the turbine-generator set and the equipment for the machine room at the Seversk nuclear power plant in the Tomsk region of Siberia. This project was part of Russia's programme to build new power stations, with 26 reactors due to come on stream by 2025, producing 30% of Russia's electricity by 2030 (NB: instead of 16%).

These *Arabelle* turbines were never nuclear. They were part of the conventional part (NB: conventional island) of certain nuclear power plants. Although Alstom was involved in nuclear power by supplying turbo-generators, it did not supply reactors. Reactors are the heart of nuclear power plants, converting the heat produced by the nuclear reaction into electricity. In a power plant, to put it simply, public works accounted for around 40%, turbines for 30% and pure nuclear power for 30%.

It should be noted that one in three power plants in the world at the time used Alstom technology (NB: including 58 nuclear reactors in France) of remarkable, if not unequalled, efficiency, characterised by very high resistance to corrosion, impressive longevity (NB: up to 60 years), optimal maintenance and operation and minimised costs and downtime.

The advantage of an approach based on participating in the development of a strategic Russian sector - which, by definition, contributes to the country's long-term economic development - was that it could also result in less exposure to the crisis, which was soon to hit the energy sector in particular (see below).

The global slowdown of 2008-2011

Demand for electricity worldwide fell in 2009 for the first time since 1945; indeed, 2008/2009 brought disruptions to the international market, with traditional customers inclined to postpone their most significant projects. Alstom, for its part, has seen its order intake severely affected by the economic crisis (NB: a 39% drop between 2009 and 2010 compared with an admittedly particularly high level). In a period of weaker demand, the price factor takes on greater importance. Market recovery has been relatively slow (NB: this was the case at Alstom, where we had to wait until the last quarter of 2011), even though infrastructure has been less affected than other sectors.

This should not be confused with unmet domestic demand for electricity, which is due to specific and sometimes mistaken policies. If we look only at the delayed effects of the 2008 crisis, the example of Russia is worth considering. The crisis was also able to have effects that were not only negative by limiting inflation, putting an end to excessive external borrowing and reducing excessive staff turnover and recruitment costs. If the 'modernisation' and 'diversification' of the economy had been the key words of the presidency of D. Medvedev and Prime Minister Putin, they were not realised according to their stated ambitions. The opportunity was not taken to embark on development that was not based solely on the export of raw materials.

However, against a backdrop of global economic crisis, the Russian nuclear industry has continued to send out positive signals. The state-owned corporation Rosatom remained at the centre of a new strategic geometry, with an increasing number of tie-ups and one-off projects, with Siemens in 2009 - with a view to a partnership described as 'strategic' (see cooperation on power plants in Bulgaria and Slovakia) - and between Toshiba and *Atomenergoprom* the previous year; collaboration with Areva continued for the supply of fuel.

The Arabelle turbines were subsequently sold to General Electric (GE) as part of the sale of the Alstom Group's Energy (Power) division. Alstom is a private group. The sale to GE was approved by shareholders' meetings. The sale took place in 2014. The purpose of the sale was to preserve the rest of the group. Acquisitions, on the other hand, are a more positive process, because they are unconstrained: they aim to strengthen activities; they must be integrated in the best possible way; and the price paid must be acceptable. The latter process was undertaken by a private company; it was spread over several years and under a variety of governments; it was mainly driven, albeit regrettably, by economic and financial considerations, linked mainly to the development and decline in the market for major energy projects, particularly since the economic and financial crisis of 2008. Such was the cruel reality of a very complex issue.

The Russian nuclear complex

At the heart of industrial policy

V. Putin took an early interest in industrial policy, particularly in the energy sector, when he left St Petersburg to serve Mayor A. Sobchak in industrial policy, particularly in the energy sector. His objective was quickly to restore to the State the levers needed to drive policy in this area, which had been lost during the privatisations of the 1990s. Irrespective of industrial property, the government took the view that both the State and companies had to contribute to Russia's economic transformation. There was no recourse to nationalisation, but on occasion, pressure was brought to bear to appeal to private capital for solidarity.

It was in 2007 that the Russian nuclear industry accelerated its structural reform with a view to a massive renaissance (see above), with the dual aim of accelerating the development of nuclear production in Russia and becoming a world leader. It was President Putin who signed the law on the restructuring of the nuclear sector.

An X-ray of the Russian energy 'complex' reveals that it has been driven by figures such as S. Kirienko, Director General of Rosatom and former Prime Minister of Russia, and I. Sechin, who came from the heart of the Kremlin. But the list should be extended to include a larger number of personalities, such as S. Sobyanine, head of the Presidential Administration, who became Chairman of Rosatom's Supervisory Board and is now Mayor of Moscow, or S. Narychkin, once head of the Presidential Administration and now head of the Foreign Intelligence Service (SVR), and S. Prikhodko, who was President Medvedev's diplomatic adviser. This list, which is not exhaustive, illustrates the interpenetration of political circles, senior administration and the management of the economy. This is an essential feature of post-Soviet Russia.

At the end of the first decade of the new millennium, the aim was to develop 26 units by 2025, with a target of 30% nuclear power (NB: compared with 16%). It should be noted that the state corporation Rosatom, with its 300,000 employees, was the 'equivalent' of the CEA, including its military branch, Areva, EDF and Alstom combined.

Strategic cooperation with Russia is diverse and long-standing. French and Russian scientists have been working together since 1967 (see Agreement between the Soviet State Committee for Nuclear Energy GKAE and the CEA) in the field of the use of nuclear energy (e.g. ITER project at Cadarache for controlled nuclear fusion). France and Russia also shared a common vision for the development of nuclear energy. The continued use of nuclear energy involved recycling plutonium in fast neutron reactors, in strict compliance with a safety and non-proliferation regime.

Admittedly, industrial cooperation proved to be more complex than scientific and technical cooperation, with French and Russian industrialists competing on third-party markets. There were examples of cooperation, such as the purchase of uranium enrichment services from Russia by EDF and AREVA, and situations of head-on confrontation, for example in Finland and China; French industrialists wanted the Russian market to be opened up to French nuclear technologies, while the Russian industry demanded total liberalisation of trade in nuclear materials and enrichment services, while penetration of the EU nuclear materials market was regulated.

The tie-up with Siemens was wrongly seen as a surprise. The Russian power plant supplier had already integrated the digital control technology of its 'new' German partner into a reactor supplied to China. Ten years earlier, a WWER reactor model had been developed with Siemens. Peter Löscher, the company's CEO at the time, recalled that the company's first presence in Russia - which was then just a fledgling enterprise - dated back to 1853.

Russian soft power?

Russia has successfully completed the programme it set itself in the early 2000s. On the world market, it has continued to expand in the civil nuclear sector and has become a leading exporter. More than a third of the new reactors built around the world are Russian, in China, India, Iran and Egypt. Western countries have reacted by limiting Russia's access to the fuel market, and President Biden has signed a bipartisan law banning imports of enriched uranium into the United States (NB: 25% of American needs).

In Bangladesh, for example, Rosatom is continuing construction of a $12 billion power station whose 2,400 MW of capacity will supply electricity to 10% of a population of 170 million. While Russia's aim is to compensate in the energy sector for the losses it has incurred as a result of the war in Ukraine (see diversion from Europe, sabotage of Nord Stream), the objective is clearly not purely economic and commercial. And we could also mention Turkey.

Projects such as these create lasting links, since it takes around 10 years to build a power station whose reactors will have a lifespan of 60 years. The length of such a process was demonstrated by the Busher power plant project in Iran. Rosatom is able to provide the personnel to operate the plant and the role of the host country can be reduced to the purchase of electricity. Rosatom - whose external revenues have increased significantly since 2022 (NB: $16.2 billion in 2023 compared with $11.2 billion in 2022; 50% of its revenues come from external sources) - has thus been a powerful vehicle for Russia's influence in the global South by signing more and more memorandums of understanding (MoUs) in Africa and Latin America. Rosatom's total revenues are expected to double by 2030.

***

Speaking at the end of 2009 to the staff of the industrial group I represented in Moscow, which at the time covered Russia, Ukraine and Belarus, I said:

'…2009 is shaping up to be a year of international economic and financial crisis. As a result of globalisation, Russia has not been spared. The seriousness of this situation should not be underestimated, but it should not lead us to pessimism or, above all, defeatism. Russia has the means to overcome the difficulties and, in this context, Alstom has no intention of turning its back on it - quite the contrary. The Energy and Transport sectors, which are key components of Alstom's business, are also at the heart of Russia's ongoing modernisation process. In this respect, Alstom has made the strategic choice to be a partner of Russia and its companies. We are here for the long term, for joint actions in this country. We will succeed together.

All the talents brought together within Alstom in Russia will have the opportunity to express themselves and to be recognised. This is my dearest wish. As far as I am concerned, I will do everything I can to ensure that everyone feels at ease within Alstom, free and responsible at the same time. The challenges we face are an opportunity; they give us a mission that goes beyond our individual cases. Our future successes must be those of the wider communities to which we belong, and they must also be the foundation of wider cooperation between Europe and Russia, which is closely linked to it...'.

Reading these lines, one cannot help but notice that time has passed and even that we have moved on to a different era. The company's local staff, by far the most numerous compared to the number of expatriates, which is less than 10%, have always been respected; the commitments made to our partner have not been betrayed; but the constraints of international economic life and even more so the effects of government policy have imposed themselves, to the detriment of a great adventure. But the constraints of international economic life, and even more so the effects of national politics, have taken their toll, to the detriment of a great adventure. To take comfort from this, we should quote the optimism of General de Gaulle: '*Et tout recommencera*!' (And it will all start again).

10

Russia-China: partnership and competition

In the context of the war in Ukraine, China and Russia are sometimes presented as allies. This is not necessarily the case: while Beijing has not formally condemned the invasion, China did not vote with Russia at the United Nations on this issue, but abstained. Furthermore, Chinese leaders appear to have repeatedly expressed their concerns to Russian officials about the possible use of tactical nuclear weapons on the battlefield. This was the case with Indian Prime Minister Modi at the Shanghai Cooperation Organisation summit in Samarkand in September 2022, and at the Sino-Russian Xi-Putin summit in Moscow in March 2023.

The two former rival communist powers, which were on the brink of confrontation in 1969, now have converging geostrategic interests and have come much closer economically, with trade, for example set to reach record levels in 2022 and 2023. However, competition and ulterior motives are not absent between China and Russia, due to the marked imbalances between the respective powers. A ratio of 1 to 10 can be observed: the Russian population only represents 1/10 of the Chinese population; Sino-Russian trade only reaches 1/10 of China's trade with the West (NB: USA and EU); China's gas supply, due to the lack of sufficient gas pipelines, only covers around 1/10 of Chinese needs.

However, talk of Russia's vassal status in relation to China is exaggerated, or at any rate premature. In reality, the current Sino-Chinese relationship should rather be described as a partnership with a view to strengthening it. This partnership does not exclude a certain amount of competition, for example in Central Asia, at the heart of a new Great Game.

The international 'Great Game' has thus become difficult to master at times, but this complexity offers opportunities. The Washington-Moscow-Beijing triangle of the Cold War, perfectly exploited at the time by the American administration, has been replaced by the United States-China-Europe triangle. In a way, Russia is still partly linked to Europe. We need to bear this in mind as we rebuild the international system.

The new Great Game

Attention is focused on the Ukrainian conflict, even though perceptions of the war can vary significantly from one part of the world to another. In this respect, Central Asia, a former part of the Soviet Union where Russian soft power remains important and which often finds itself in an unbalanced face-off with China, particularly in economic terms, is a strategic zone of prime importance. There are at least two major issues at stake in Central Asia : the importance of its energy resources, which are a source of envy, and its location between East and East (see the eastern part of Russia on the one hand, and the power of China on the other), bordered to the south by Iran, Afghanistan and the Caspian Sea, the gateway to the Caucasus and Europe.

Paradoxically, without being neglected, the region remains a kind of 'hidden face of the world', despite the fact that in the 19th century it was the scene of what was known as the Great Game between the Russian and British empires, for almost a hundred years. Russia remained in the region, while the United Kingdom maintained its interest and a number of relays of influence. The Great Game is likely to take on new forms. Will Central Asia be able to free itself from its powerful neighbours, commensurate with its immense potential and its location at the heart of the new Silk Roads? Or will it have to resign itself to being no more than a hinge between several worlds, or confine itself to playing the role of cordon sanitaire between a new East and the powers of Europe and the West?

In Russia's shadow

The independence gained by the five Soviet republics of Central Asia at the end of the USSR did not mean a total withdrawal from Moscow, but a significant transformation in relations between the former centre and its periphery. Russia has maintained its positions in the region in a number of ways, whether through modes of governance often inherited from Soviet practices, economic networks (eg. Kazakh oil can only be exported via the Russian port of Novorossiysk on the Black Sea), the dependence of the states concerned on remittances from migrant workers (NB: 8 million people in Russia and up to 30% of the national wealth of certain republics), cultural soft power through the language and expatriate Russian communities (NB: over 40% ethnic Russians in Kazakhstan at the time of independence, officially 20% today) or dual nationals (NB: several thousand in Turkmenistan, where the question of a single nationality has still not been implemented) or border security and a military presence (see the border guards in Tajikistan and an air base in Kyrgyzstan near the capital Bishkek).

But Russia has not contented itself with this legacy of the past; it has tried to organise multiple links between the components of the former Union of Fifteen Soviet Republics. With the exception of the Baltic States and Ukraine, they have all come together within the Commonwealth of Independent States (CIS) created by the Minsk and Alma Ata agreements in 1991. All the Central Asian states, with the exception of Turkmenistan which registered its permanent neutrality with the United Nations in 1995, are members of the Eurasian Economic Community (EurAsEc) created in 2000 by the Treaty of Astana, the Collective Security Treaty Organisation (CSTO) of 2002 and the Shanghai Cooperation Organisation (SCO) launched in 1996, then renamed in 2001 - which includes Russia and China in the same multilateral system - aimed at three major security objectives: terrorism, extremism and separatism. The Eurasian Economic Union, made up of Russia, Belarus and Kazakhstan, joined by Armenia in the absence of the hoped-for Ukraine, was created in 2014 in response to the Eastern Partnership launched by the European Union in 2009. Russia's economic presence has diminished but not disappeared, and

Kazakhstan in particular remains a major partner for Moscow and its major industrial groups such as Lukoil, Rosneft and Rosatom.

At the heart of China's ambitions

Kazakhstan, which is more than five times the size of France, is the world's 11th largest oil producer, and since 2009 has been the world's leading producer and exporter of uranium, ahead of Canada and Australia (NB: 36% of the world's supply, 2nd largest reserve in the world, with more than 20% of known reserves), and is also rich in coal (ranked 8th in the world). Kazakhstan is therefore a major trading partner in Central Asia. Trade with China and Russia is now comparable in terms of volume, but China's role in the country continues to grow. For example, Chinese companies have accounted for over 20% of Kazakhstan's oil production for more than 10 years. Turkmenistan has the world's 4th largest gas reserves and is - it's not stressed enough - the world's leading supplier of gas to China. The Chinese company CNPC is the figurehead of the Chinese presence in the country. The opening of the Turkmenistan-Uzbekistan-Kazakhstan-China gas pipeline in 2009 marked a turning point in Turkmen gas flows, which turned away from Russia. In recent years, Russia has even stopped buying Turkmen gas it no longer needs. For a time, in order to maintain a symbolic activity in the energy sector, Russia offered limited purchases (1 billion m3), but at knock-down prices, which Ashgabat was unable to accept, at the risk of exposing itself to a counterclaim by China.

Russia has never had a problem with Turkmen gas exports to the East. On the other hand, it has always sought to slow the emergence of competition from Turkmen gas in Europe, a fact sometimes acknowledged by its diplomatic representatives in the region. As President Medvedev had done in his time, it has on several occasions put forward environmental considerations to delay the construction of a gas pipeline across the Caspian Sea. In the end, this policy turned out to be short-sighted, given the quantities involved (NB: the pipeline in question could not have absorbed more than 30 billion m3 per year, whereas Russian deliveries to Europe were well in excess of 200 billion). It wasn't vital for Russia, but it was for the Turkmen, whom it had alienated. Azerbaijan did not help its Central Asian neighbour in this area either, fearing competition in the energy sector. China, the region's almost sole gas customer, also buys quantities from Uzbekistan and is involved in gold mining in Kyrgyzstan (see Kumtor gold mine).

The new Silk Roads

The perception of the Chinese in Central Asia is not always very good, starting paradoxically with its Turkmen gas supplier, who sometimes resents its economic dependence. President Berdymuhamedov, father of the current head of state, has on occasion voiced his concerns on this point to trusted interlocutors, and Chinese nationals are rarely seen in the capital Ashgabat. Kazakh and Kyrgyz feelings have not always been more favourable.

It was in autumn 2013 that the newly elected President Xi Jinping announced this Promethean project, known as the *One Road One Belt or Belt Road Initiative* (BRI). The ambition was to increase China's trade with a large part of Central Asia and Europe by land, and with South Asia and Africa by sea. This would involve a third of the world's GNP by 2049, which would coincide with the 100th anniversary of the People's Republic of China. The project is not just economic, it also has a historical and political dimension (see Xi'an, once the world's largest city, which was the point of departure or arrival of the ancient Silk Roads). In this respect, with reference to the 1955 Bandoeng conference, where China asserted itself, alongside the Third World, as a revolutionary against the colonialism and imperialism of the great powers, Beijing wants to set itself up as the protector of a world that is still the subject of international relations, at a time when China's ambition is to become the world's leading economic power. Hence a phraseology that uses concepts such as *'building a community of destiny for all mankind'*. More prosaically, it is clear that China's project is part of its energy dependency, economic slowdown, ageing population and global competition with the United States. But while the project involves risks and is likely to have perverse effects, its appeal should not be underestimated in countries that are sometimes relatively neglected, such as landlocked Central Asia. After the 'string of pearls' strategy (NB: Burma, Bangladesh, India, Sri Lanka, Maldives, Pakistan), the heart of Central Asia is now a major target. Indeed, it seems that around half of the BIS's activities will be concentrated in Asia.

A 'BRI' label has been created, covering a wide range of projects, particularly in the transport and energy sectors. This is not just wishful thinking, as an estimated $300 billion has already been invested between 2015 and 2018. The pandemic has slowed the process down considerably, and the war in Ukraine is also bound to have a major impact. But it's a safe bet that the Promethean enterprise will continue, in line with China's obligation to permanent growth. Since 2013, China's trade with BIS countries has amounted to trillions of dollars, or around 30% of its total trade.

A terrorist threat?

Radical Islam is generally contained, thanks in part to the traditions of moderate Islam inherited from the Soviet Union, but extremist groups periodically erupt to exploit acute social tensions. There is recurrent unrest, for example, in the Caspian Sea region of Kazakhstan. The risk is not nil in Uzbekistan, the hotbed of Islam in Central Asia, where externally-funded Koranic schools sprang up after independence, but were dominated with an iron fist by the late President Islam Karimov.

Radical movements have exploited a breeding ground of ethnic rivalries and regional imbalances, against a backdrop of war in Afghanistan and latent opposition from the major powers. The risk of a 'clash of cultures' is always present: from 2001, the Manas airport in Kyrgyzstan (Air Transit Center) welcomed American soldiers and war material for Afghanistan under a rental contract. Uzbekistan, meanwhile, abruptly suspended its air services in 2005. Military cooperation with Kazakhstan is limited under NATO's Partnership for Peace (PfP) programme.

A wide range of opportunities, including for Western countries

Significant trade relations have developed with Kazakhstan, Turkmenistan and Uzbekistan, the three largest economies in the region, although Europe, and even the United States, sometimes lag behind in certain countries such as Turkmenistan. However, American companies have a strong presence in Kazakhstan, particularly in the energy sector (NB: the Tengiz oil field, the first in the country, was prospected by Americans; Chevron controls 50% of production and ExxonMobil 25%).

Washington's attitude towards Turkmenistan is often one of indifference, even though the country has played an important bridging role, particularly during the American presence in Afghanistan (logistics, military leave, etc.). Turkmenistan, in the name of its neutrality and good relations with all Afghan parties, has not agreed to be used for military purposes. For the same reasons, the complex withdrawal of foreign military equipment from Afghanistan, including French equipment, could not be carried out via a Turkmen route, which would have been much easier.

In 2014, the United States built a new embassy in Ashgabat at a cost of more than $250 million (NB: Sergei Lavrov, for his part, inaugurated the impressive new Russian embassy). We can imagine that this is not without reason, given the stakes and the proximity of the Iranian border, just 25 km from the Turkmen capital.

Europe remains a relatively marginal political player, despite the intense efforts made a few years ago by its special representative, Ambassador Pierre Morel, which led to the formulation of the EU's 2007-2013 strategy for the region. Specific cooperation projects, for example in the field of training, are appreciated. The emphasis on democracy and human rights, however legitimate, does not necessarily facilitate the promotion of European interests. However, partnership and cooperation agreements have been signed with several Central Asian countries, including Kazakhstan and Turkmenistan.

The British sometimes pretend not to be overly interested in the region, even though, as experts in the Great Game, they are constantly thinking about it. British interests are particularly well represented in Kazakhstan's energy sector (Shell and British Gas); cooperation is organised with the best British universities, notably in Kazakhstan and Uzbekistan; annual military exercises are organised with Kazakhstan.

Germany is Kazakhstan's leading European partner and is also active on the cultural front, working with diasporas and cultural associations. Alongside the UK, Germany and France, Italy is particularly active in Central Asia. Matteo Renzi, Italy's prime minister, visited Turkmenistan on his way back from a G20 meeting, the only head of a Western government to have done so.

France is eagerly awaited, including politically, and a strategic partnership has existed with Kazakhstan since 2008. More than 100 French companies are present in Kazakhstan, including Total, Alstom (see electric locomotive factory in Astana), GDF Suez, Areva and Airbus. Turkmenistan is France's3rd most important economic partner in Central Asia: it was once the leading international market for Bouygues Construction; Accor, Cifal, Schneider Electric, Thales (see satellites), Total and Vinci are also present. President Mitterrand's visit in 1994 to accompany the young state on its baptismal font had lasting economic repercussions for French companies, over and above the French president's passion for the ancient city of Nysa. In this respect, it is regrettable that a new presidential trip could not take place as envisaged in 2016. Confirming France's interest in the region, the ministers are continuing their visits to the region (NB: Kazakhstan and Uzbekistan in particular).

The dawn of Eurasia

In 2018, Bruno Maçães, the Portuguese Minister for Europe from 2013 to 2015 and then a consultant to the City of London, wrote *Dawn of Eurasia* following a sabbatical of several months in this immense space stretching from Europe to China. It is simplistic to conclude that Europeans generally think in terms of norms and rules that they want to extend, whereas in this case we should be thinking in terms of power (*'If you think Russia and China have an expansionist approach, you can't respond with a rule'*). The question is not to build a neutral framework of rules, but to know which one will prevail. Another idea, seemingly paradoxical in the light of the foregoing, is that the challenge to the global economic order does not ultimately come from the periphery, but from the centre, in other words from ourselves. Are we still attached to a 'liberal' order? Does the Brexit vote, for example, reflect this? These huge questions bring us back to our identity and our ambition. Is it still our destiny to export our ideas to Asia, or to welcome theirs from now on? The new Grand Jeu asks these fundamental questions.

Big manoeuvres in Central Asia: business as usual

Vladimir Putin's trip to Tajikistan and Turkmenistan in June 2022 came as a surprise. At a time when the war in Ukraine was raging, when questions were being asked about the Russian President's state of health and when there was talk of possible cracks in Moscow's ruling circles, this could not have been a routine trip, but a trip of the utmost importance that we must try to decipher.

Russia, which left Central Asia at the end of the Soviet era, has never turned its back on the region. As it happens, Tajikistan is a reliable partner for Moscow, representing a major security issue on the border with China and Afghanistan, and at the crossroads of the unrest fuelled by various extremist groups that are far from being limited to the Taliban, who focus above all on the problems of South Asia. This is why Russia has a large military base in Afghanistan, and also controls its borders with specialised units.

On the other hand, Turkmenistan, a republic that was little regarded during the Soviet era and whose resources were never exploited, distanced itself from Russia when it became independent more than 30 years ago. The country is not, therefore, one of the most reliable allies that some of the media are talking about today on the occasion of Vladimir Putin's visit. But the country, aware of its relative weakness, has had the intelligence to spare its relations with all its neighbours and former partners. This was the philosophy behind its official neutral status at the UN in 1995. Of all the multilateral bodies created or run by Russia since the end of the USSR, Turkmenistan is only a member of the CIS. Despite this, the country receives at least one high-level visit from Moscow every year.

The first message from Vladimir Putin's presence in Central Asia is undoubtedly that *'everything has changed so that nothing changes'*. With a language and means that are naturally very different, it is not a question of denying the existence of a nation in the post-Soviet space, as in Ukraine, but of suggesting that it remains a tangible reality where Russia is at ease, if not at home. Ashgabat's participation in a summit of the Caspian states is a further means of broadening the perspective and giving an appearance of unity, at a time when relations between the members (see Russia, Kazakhstan, Azerbaijan, Iran and Turkmenistan) are sometimes difficult. In Turkmenistan, Russian soft power has continued to assert itself, notably through culture and language. President Berdymuhamedov, who handed over the reins of power to his son Serdar, was a Moscow-trained stomatologist, and the young Turkmen president also speaks perfect Russian with President Putin.

Russia's openness

It is paradoxical that the Russian President should have visited Turkmenistan, a landlocked country surrounded, even encircled, to the south and east by the Iranian and Afghan mountain ranges, and separated from the Caucasus and more distant European prospects by the Caspian Sea, which remains a climatic, geographical and economic frontier. The question of the status of the Caspian remains a subject of complex debate, and both Russia and Azerbaijan have never done anything to facilitate the construction of a trans-Caspian gas pipeline enabling Turkmenistan to export part of its gigantic gas reserves to the West (NB: the 4th largest in the world).

Today, it is Russia which, despite its vastness and lack of options, is turning in on itself, not least because of the sanctions. Talk of a 'Chinese card' that Russia could quickly play is not very coherent. If we are talking about a 180° reorientation of energy exports, particularly gas, it will prove extremely costly, technically complex in a Russian Far East devoid of infrastructure, and will take years to implement. Just as Merkel relied too much on Russia, Russia may now feel that it has given too much priority to its European customers, and is also in a bind.

Moscow can explore and find a solution in the South. In this respect, Turkmenistan is of considerable strategic importance, as there is already a network of gas pipelines linking Russia to this country. It was Moscow which, in recent years, decided it no longer needed Turkmen gas, reducing its imports to token quantities before ceasing to buy it. Moreover, Turkmenistan is linked to Iran, to which it has supplied gas, particularly for its northern regions far from Iran's major gas fields. In any case, a route exists that could provide access to vast markets.

Finally, the famous TAPI gas pipeline project (NB: Turkmenistan-Afghanistan-Pakistan-India) was never abandoned. Unable to export to the West (see above), it was considered vital by Turkmenistan, which wanted to increase its export quantities and avoid a face-off with China, its exclusive customer. Given the regional context (war in Afghanistan, recurring tensions between India and Pakistan, huge investments), the project has still not seen the light of day. The Turkmen government would have liked the Total group to be the figurehead of an international consortium. In retrospect, it would have been in Russia's interest to make a decisive contribution to the realisation of this major undertaking, for the greater benefit of its new major energy trading customers, such as India. A kind of new Silk Road, reversed and parallel, would not displease either India or Moscow, which is doomed to subjection to Beijing because of its turning away from the West.

A message for China

Vladimir Putin's rapid trip was also a strong message to China, which essentially said: Yes, we are turning away from the West, but our relative economic weakness compared to a co-leader of the world economy must not lead us to vassalage; Russia retains strategic assets that are not limited to its nuclear forces, but stem from its history and geography; Moscow still has its place at the heart of the *Heartland*, control of which will be an important key for the powers of tomorrow; it is not turning its back on it, but will be able to confront it.

The Russian and Chinese presidents met in Moscow on 20 March 2023 (see below) for the first time in four years, apart from meetings in third countries, such as in Samarkand in September 2022 for a summit of the Shanghai Cooperation Organisation (SCO).

It is fashionable to talk of a Sino-Russian rapprochement fostered by the war in Ukraine. The convergences between Moscow and Beijing have in fact been apparent during the period under consideration, since the famous handshake between Vladimir Putin and Xi Jinping on the sidelines of the Beijing Winter Olympics in February 2022, a few days before the start of hostilities against Kiev. It was on this occasion that there was talk of an *'eternal friendship'* between the two countries.

In reality, this is not a new concept. It emerged in the 1950s between Mao's New China and the Soviet Union, which had emerged victorious from the Second World War, but it has not prevented the bilateral relationship from undergoing numerous ups and downs, against a backdrop of ideological competition and national interests. These developments even led to armed clashes within the 'peace camp', which degenerated at the end of the 1960s on the rivers Ussuri and Amur.

In reality, this concept is not new. It emerged in the 1950s between Mao's new China and the Soviet Union, which had emerged victorious from the Second World War, but it has not prevented the bilateral relationship from undergoing numerous ups and downs, against a backdrop of ideological competition and national interests. These developments even led to armed clashes within the 'peace camp', which degenerated at the end of the 1960s on the Oussouri and Amour rivers.

So what are the realities and facts of relations between Moscow and Beijing today? What are the prospects, beyond the novel of eternal friendship? President Xi Jinping's visit to Kazakhstan on 14 September 2022, his first foreign trip since the Covid pandemic, and the Shanghai Cooperation Organisation summit in Samarkand, Uzbekistan, on 15 and 16 September, are evidence of major manoeuvres in Central Asia, far beyond Sino-Russian relations alone. For his part, President Putin surprised everyone with a bilateral visit to Tajikistan on 28 and 29 June, in the midst of the war in Ukraine, followed by a meeting in Turkmenistan of the states bordering the Caspian Sea.

Xi-Putin: the summit of fantasies

With a three-day state visit to Moscow in March 2023, President Xi Jinping made his first trip abroad since his reappointment as head of China. It was also the first time in four years that he had seen his Russian counterpart, with the exception of a meeting with a third country in Samarkand in September 2022 on the occasion of a summit of the Shanghai Cooperation Organisation (SCO).

Against a backdrop of heightened tensions with the United States and above all the war in Ukraine, this Sino-Russian summit gave rise to radical interpretations even before it took place: shortly after Beijing published a 12-point 'peace plan', some anticipated a Chinese move towards a rapid settlement of the conflict; others feared that the meeting of the two heads of state would lead to the de facto formation of a quasi-alliance, accompanied in particular by the supply of military equipment to Russia; in both cases, many observers agreed that China had great power status, and even a unique ability to establish a new world order.

It is fashionable to talk of a Sino-Russian rapprochement fostered by the war in Ukraine. So what are the facts and realities of relations between Moscow and Beijing today? What are the prospects, beyond the novel of eternal friendship? Isn't the first perception of the summit a fantasy?

Even before it was possible to draw up an assessment, the Russian-Chinese summit in Moscow was seen as a striking confirmation of the recomposition of international society to the detriment of an order that was no longer dominated by the West. But it is the timing that must also be taken into account. On the one hand, a powerful China, but also somewhat weakened by years of isolation due to a pandemic, new internal economic and social difficulties and growing American pressure, wanted to demonstrate its preferences and ambitions to play a global role on the international diplomatic stage; on the other hand, the timing could not have been more opportune to break the risk of ostracism made acute by the launch of an international arrest warrant for the country's supreme leader (NB : in this respect, the meeting immediately followed Vladimir Putin's trip to Sevastopol and Mariupol).

But what is the real state of bilateral relations between Beijing and Moscow? For at least fifteen years, we have been hearing that Russia is playing the 'China card'. The conceptualisation of Russia's turn towards Asia goes back even further, and can be attributed to Evgeny Primakov, former Minister of Foreign Affairs and short-lived Prime Minister of the Federation in 1998.

At the end of the first decade of the 2000s, half of Russia's trade was with the countries of the European Union and 70% of foreign investment came from European countries. While it's true that China has since become Russia's biggest trading partner - and that bilateral trade has reached a record $190 billion by 2022 and $240 billion by 2023 - the share of European investment has risen to 75%. In plain English, this means that technology was still coming from the West before the outbreak of war in Ukraine.

Since then, purchases of Russian energy products, particularly oil, have risen sharply, while China has been supplying high-tech components that Russia desperately needs, including for its weapons production, such as microprocessors. But the gas issue will be more difficult to resolve, as Europe has ended its dependence on Russia due to the lack of suitable gas pipelines that will take years to build and require investment running into tens of billions of dollars (NB: on the sidelines of the Beijing Olympics in February 2022, the construction of a new gas pipeline and the signing of a 30-year contract for the supply of Russian gas were announced). Contrary to popular belief, however, Russia is still not China's main supplier of gas, which continues to come mainly from Central Asia. At the Moscow summit, President Putin promised his Chinese counterpart 98 billion m3 of gas deliveries by 2023. But this target seems totally unrealistic, since it is conditional on the construction, via Mongolia, of the Siberia 2 gas pipeline. President Xi Jinping seems to have remained cautious on this issue.

On the diplomatic front, China and Russia also seem to have grown much closer in recent years, both bilaterally and multilaterally, for example within the framework of the Shanghai Cooperation Organisation (SCO), which is both economic and political in nature. The latter structure, which in 2001 was limited to the two countries and those of Central Asia, with the exception of Turkmenistan, opened up fifteen years later to India and Pakistan, then to Iran in 2021. Ironically, one of the Organisation's missions is to deal with 'separatism'.

But this marriage of reason does not exclude competition, even in strategic areas. The competition between the powers in Central Asia is a case in point. President Xi's visit to Kazakhstan in September 2022 - his first trip abroad after the pandemic - before the SCO summit in Uzbekistan a few days later, and President Putin's visit to Central Asia in June of the same year, in the midst of the war in Ukraine, are evidence of major manoeuvres in the region. This new Great Game is not limited to China and Russia, but should also include Turkey (NB: four of the five Central Asian republics are Turkish-speaking), India and even Iran, where the West is not sufficiently present, except perhaps in Kazakhstan - the world's leading producer and exporter of uranium - through the intermediary of very large energy and mining companies.

It is no coincidence that Xi Jinping invited Vladimir Putin to Moscow for an investment forum as part of his *One Road One Belt or*

Belt and Road Initiative (BRI) (NB: 300 billion dollars invested between 2015 and 2018).

While the Primakov doctrine was based on the idea of a triangular relationship with Asia and Europe, aimed at breaking with the Washington-Beijing-Moscow triangle of the Cold War, the war in Ukraine marks a break with both Washington and Europe, and now places Moscow in an almost exclusive tête-à-tête with Beijing, which is likely to be more restrictive. The new Sino-Russian relationship is likely to prove demanding, even stifling, for Moscow. In the energy sector, in addition to the above considerations, China will be able to influence prices and already benefits - like India - from substantial tariff reductions. Nor will it see Russia as a major export market, for example in the new and rapidly expanding automotive sector, capable of ensuring a significant flow of finished products from the 'workshop of the world'.

Keeping up with its rank

China is considered a founding member of the UN, but the seat of the Republic of China was not awarded to Beijing until October 1971 by a vote of the General Assembly. Since then, the People's Republic has played a relatively discreet role. Beijing is now keen to present itself as a responsible state, as befits a power worthy of the name. Today, this attitude seems at odds with the behaviour of a permanent member of the Security Council that does not respect the fundamental principles of the United Nations Charter.

The Sino-Russian Treaty of Good Neighbourliness, Friendship and Cooperation of 2001 established a strategic partnership between the two countries that had existed since 1996. As far as Taiwan is concerned, Moscow has since aligned itself in a classic manner with the thesis of the uniqueness of China, and the emphasis has also been placed on defending the national unity and territorial integrity of states.

In this respect, it should be noted that China did not support the declaration of independence of the two Russian-speaking entities in the Donbas region, nor the subsequent annexation. At the *Wehrkunde* in Munich, shortly before the outbreak of war in Ukraine, the Chinese Foreign Minister defended and illustrated the principle of territorial integrity. The justification for intervention in Ukraine (see genocide, denazification), however crudely expressed, will not necessarily be any more convincing in Beijing than it is in Washington and the capitals of Europe. At most, at the UN Security Council, which was meeting at the same time as the Russian President's statement, China said it understood Moscow's security concerns.

The Moscow summit gave rise to in-depth discussions on the war in Ukraine, and Xi Jinping and Vladimir Putin reportedly had a 4-hour tête-à-tête at the start of the talks. The tone of the exchanges does not appear to have been the same as at the SCO summit in Samarkand, where the Chinese President reportedly clearly warned his counterpart about the possible use of unconventional weapons. It should be noted that the final Moscow communiqué takes up this theme, while ruling out the prospect of a nuclear war.

The relative understanding that Beijing continues to show publicly towards its Russian partner is not incompatible with a certain distancing that translates into a desire to exercise a form of mediation in the conflict. A few months ago, the Ukrainian Foreign Minister, Dmytro Kuleba, reported that his Chinese counterpart had told him that '*China was interested in ending the war*'. President Zelensky himself has never closed the door on a diplomatic role for China, and there is talk of President Xi having a telephone conversation with his Ukrainian counterpart after Moscow.

A hyper-calculating power

Some analysts have been quick to point to China as the big winner in the war in Ukraine. But it is still far too early to make such a claim. It is true that China was initially satisfied with the fact that the crisis diverted somewhat, for a time at least, the pressure that was weighing more and more heavily on it, particularly with regard to Taiwan, and which had materialised, for example, in the formation of the Western alliance AUKUS in the Indo-Pacific.

From a global geostrategic point of view, western China lies not only to the east of the Pacific, but also at the extreme west of the Eurasian continent. The fact that Ukraine, far from its borders, is becoming a stumbling block, and that Russia is being used to push back a group inclined to regard China as a 'systemic rival', may a priori present advantages for Beijing.

But there is no doubt that China would have preferred the war to have been limited to a minor incident, to use the language used in Washington by President Biden even before the Russian aggression. A large-scale, long-lasting crisis is likely to undermine China's vital need for growth - forecasts for 2023 put it at 5%, the lowest figure for 30 years - which is the source of its internal balance and power, as well as the sacrosanct principle of the territorial integrity of states, a cornerstone of the international system for China.

A scrupulous analysis of the global economic situation and the consequences of war for its own interests determines the Chinese position. Beijing must balance its strategic partnership with Moscow against its relations with the rest of the world.

The two great powers, China and Russia, which have revised the international system - in geopolitical terms and not in the traditional sense of rewriting the United Nations Charter - have an interest in maintaining their unity, even if this is more apparent than real in all respects. Both countries need 'strategic depth' in the face of the West. This approach is also a component of the tensions with the United States over Taiwan, whose 'lock' Beijing intends to loosen. Surprisingly, China is relatively landlocked, as the South China Sea - covering 3.5 million km2 - is semi-enclosed and controlled by six straits. The Taiwan Strait is the most direct route for its nuclear submarines, which sail from the island of Hainan towards the vast Philippine Trench. Aside from this military dimension, it should be noted that 90% of China's foreign trade and almost 50% of world trade passes through this area. Coming back to the West, cooperation with Russia, given its size and the influence it retains in Central Asia, is essential in the perspective of the new Silk Roads.

Chinese growth is likely to be severely disrupted by the prolongation of the war in Ukraine (see above), even if the forecast rates would be the stuff of dreams for many economies - in China's case, they represent its weakest performance for thirty years. Yet maintaining growth is essential to satisfy its middle class, guarantee social peace and even the stability of its political order.

While China's trade with Russia has grown very strongly since 2020, reaching a record level in 2022, this impressive result needs to be put into perspective, as it should be compared with China's trade with the countries of the European Union and the United States, of which it represents only around one tenth.

Ukraine itself is an important trading partner for China, particularly in the agricultural sector. China is the world's largest importer of agricultural products, and over 80% of its grain imports come from Ukraine.

As far as the huge energy projects between China and Russia are concerned, it should be noted that the construction of the latest gas pipeline announced at the Beijing Olympic Games will require considerable investment. These will no doubt be largely financed by China itself, as has already been the case with certain Central Asian countries. This will involve Chinese state-owned banks, which are likely to be subject to international sanctions.

In the light of all this data, which is of course not exhaustive, it is hard to imagine the hyper-calculating power selling out its national interests and jeopardising the economic growth that is vital to it. Beijing has solid arguments for steering the war in Ukraine towards a diplomatic solution. It is also in our interest to encourage it.

The handshake between Xi Jinping and Vladimir Putin on the sidelines of the Winter Olympics in Beijing, which made such an impression and perhaps gave rise to over-interpretation, probably deserves to be put into perspective. Given its economic interdependence with the West, which is ten times greater in quantitative terms than its trade with Russia, and even greater in qualitative terms, if China were forced to do so - which it is currently trying to avoid - it would choose the United States and Europe. In addition to these constraints, the Chinese economy is running out of steam and the population is ageing. But we have not yet reached this Cornelian choice and, ultimately, the real nature of the Sino-Russian relationship is also a barometer of Sino-American tensions and is determined by the West. In the future, China will also be what we make of it.

Russia, China's vassal state?

While the G7 was meeting in Hiroshima, President Xi Jinping was hosting a summit in Xi'an with the five Central Asian countries (C5), the third of its kind. Xi'an was once a capital and the largest city in the world, and its ramparts still bear witness to this. Xi'an was the starting point of the Silk Roads, and the summit will coincide with the tenth anniversary of the Chinese President's launch of the Belt & Road Initiative (BRI) in Kazakhstan.

Central Asia represents multiple challenges for China: security, with the issue of Xinjiang - and it is no coincidence that China has deployed border guards in Tajikistan; the economy, with energy supplies, particularly gas, and mining resources; trade (70 billion dollars with Central Asian countries by 2022), with rail transit to Europe (80% of this loan is operated through the region in question).

Central Asia has also become a zone of influence, even domination, between China and Russia. Russia has retreated since the end of the Soviet Union, but retains important links there, beyond binational communities and the lingering influence of the Russian language. In some cases, remittances from Central Asian migrant workers to Russia account for a significant proportion of the GNP of certain Central Asian states. The latter, which aspire to emancipation, are also reluctant to confront a China that sometimes worries them. Moving from one 'big brother' to another is not a particularly attractive prospect for them.

Central Asia is undoubtedly destined to become the scene of a new Great Game. And this will not be limited to China and Russia, close allies if not allies today, but competitors in the name of power interests.

There is an imbalance in Sino-Russian relations that can be summed up by a ratio of 1 to 10: Russia's population is 1/10 that of China; Sino-Russian trade represents, with some fluctuations, 1/10 of trade with the United States and the countries of the European Union; Russia does not yet supply even 1/10 of China's consumption needs. But 'vassal status' would imply a tension that does not currently exist between Beijing and Moscow, at a time when *unlimited friendship* is being declared. While Russia accounted for around 50% of its trade with the EU just a few years ago, Sino-Russian trade has grown rapidly, reaching a record $190 billion in 2022 and $240 bn in 2023.

The relationship is therefore more complex than it seems, for both technical and political reasons. It is in China's interest to obtain energy products from Russia at the best possible price; Russia must imperatively replace the traditional gas market with that of Europe, because of the sanctions. But the gas pipelines needed for massive exports have insufficient capacity. The Siberian Force 2 project, whose stated final objective is to supply 50 billion cubic metres a year, will not be launched before 2024; five years of work will be needed to build 2,600 km of pipes, for an investment probably of between 10 and 15 billion dollars. Faced with this mutual dependence until 2030, what will the two countries do?

11

The South, collective and specific

The 'global' West is sometimes contrasted with a 'collective' South, but since the emergence of the Third World on the international scene at the Bandoeng Conference in 1955, the South has above all been the expression of a claimed non-alignment with the blocs of the Cold War, which constituted its most common denominator. Is the South now more homogeneous than it was with non-alignment within the framework of the United Nations, notably within the Group of 77? The difference with that period is the emergence of powerful entities aspiring to the forefront, such as China and India; these entities, beyond geopolitical convergences (China-Russia, India-Russia or Brazil-Russia) are developing 'à la carte' relationships, as New Delhi perfectly illustrates. These powerful entities are not strictly speaking 'allies', but juxtaposed, they constitute a vast group capable of challenging the international system and offering an alternative to the way it has operated in the past.

Secrets and treasures of Africa

Hasn't Africa drifted away, even from our mental universe? Haven't we forgotten about it at the same time as it has been distancing itself from the old tutelary powers? Doesn't it deserve a more positive presentation? The expression 'international community', however overused, nevertheless generally expresses an ideal that rises above differences and reflects an aspiration for good and a certain sense of justice. It contains the idea of reunion rather than division. It is opposed to the solitude of national egoism. It is not necessarily an abstract reality, a construct of the mind; it is also tangible, made up of lived experiences and encounters, based on dreams that are our software and enable us to move forward.

Africa is a natural part of this picture, and we don't talk about it enough, except to highlight problems that are often our own. This extraordinary continent harbours many secrets and, above all, treasures, discovered during diplomatic missions some forty years ago, which have brought it into our intimacy for ever, despite considerable changes and upheavals.

The UN and Africa

The field of agriculture and food was then covered - as it still is today - by one main specialised UN agency, the FAO (Food and Agricultural Organisation), and several other organisations linked to it, such as the WFP (World Food Programme), which was particularly dedicated to emergency food aid. All these bodies and organisations were based in Rome, a capital that was by definition open to the South and all the more legitimate for dealing with development issues.

The FAO had to be taken to heart. It was a forum where the 'countries of the North', particularly those with large cereal surpluses in some cases, and the countries of the South that were poor or afflicted by scourges, first and foremost war, could work together on agricultural development issues. The problem was complex, and did not stop at setting up transfers, for example in the form of endowments in kind, which could have perverse effects leading to the destruction of local production. The organisation provided much-appreciated expertise to countries that lacked it, and the 'FAO label' was authoritative.

State representatives were responsible for guiding the work of the multilateral institution, conceptualising it, managing its resources and deciding how to allocate them. The delegations therefore called on mixed teams of generalists and specialists. As far as France was concerned, the Quai d'Orsay endeavoured to ensure coordination and also arbitration between the Ministry of Agriculture, which was as close as possible to the interests of our rural world, and the Ministry of Cooperation and Development, whose primary aims could differ considerably.

To top it all off, and this was a considerable help, Michel Rocard was Minister for Agriculture at the time, and his passion for development and his open-mindedness in general were to make things a lot easier and, more than that, to be a powerful driving force. What's more, in the years immediately following François Mitterrand's election as President of the Republic, the Ministry of Cooperation no longer confined itself to Africa - in the sense of France's 'pré carré' - and was given a new lease of life. For me, at least, it was a privileged moment when diplomacy was no longer a matter of what was sometimes called *'Kriegsspiel'*, but seemed to respond to really concrete questions concerning vast groups of people.

At the end of a dry, white season

These Roman international organisations took us into the field. The regional conference devoted to Africa, the FAO's main field of action, took place in Zimbabwe, a country in the throes of transition. On the way to Harare, the stopover in Johannesburg, when the apartheid system was still in place in South Africa in the mid-1980s, proved depressing. The very modern city centre, bristling with skyscrapers, had the appearance of the cities of the Anglo-Saxon world, but the whole was strange and oppressive even for visitors.

While the regime of international sanctions had forced the country to turn in on itself, confinement also produced a reaction in the form of great and benevolent curiosity towards visitors. Kindness towards foreigners was equal in the two communities, black and white, which were still completely separate, and the very fact of being a foreigner helped to break down many barriers. A bourgeoisie seemed to be emerging within the black community, but the overwhelming majority of the latter left the city centre in the evening to return to the townships by bus. Johannesburg emptied out, as if Manhattan became deserted at the end of the day. It was time to cut short this desolate experience, as described by the South African writer André Brink in *A Dry White Season*, and get to the former Rhodesia as quickly as possible.

The southern winter was not the season for bougainvilleas and blooming jacarandas, but these high plateaux brought a gentler climate that was not just climatic. The country had already moved towards a form of government in which the minority no longer dominated unchallenged. Harare was immediately appealing. In all places, the high plateaux, whatever their elevation, in Kenya, Ethiopia or Vietnam, can provide comparable sensations; they seemed to provide distance from the hustle and bustle and contributed to a certain inner calm.

In stark contrast to the deep tensions felt in South Africa, the city of Harare, with its wide, somewhat deserted and then oversized avenues, sparsely urbanised and close to nature, seemed provincial and peaceful in the very pure light of the southern winter. Scattered Mozambican refugees, having fled the violence nearby, were looking for work; they were a reminder, however, that we were in the eye of a cyclone heralding the ultimate end of colonial empires and the transition from one world to another. The time of Frederic de Klerk, sometimes described as the 'Gorbachev of Southern Africa', would soon come. But Zimbabwe had a head start, perhaps because the separation of communities had not been institutionalised there, and no doubt also because the geostrategic stakes were lower than in South Africa, the continent's colossus.

Eden, savannah and ice

The East and Southern Africa we travelled through during these years was grandiose, with breathtaking beauty. From the huge herds of elephants in *Hwange National Park*, as big as Switzerland, where you landed on a runway cut through the forest, to the Zambezi or Victoria Falls, nearly two kilometres wide and twice as high as Niagara Falls, whose roar shook the ground that Livingstone had walked on, to the Ethiopian plateau and the gorges of the Blue Nile, right up to the still-preserved Kilimanjaro icecap, emerging in the early hours of the morning from an intense mist over the savannah, everything was awe-inspiring. We must preserve these images and sensations provoked by a super-powerful nature, rich in species and populated by a fascinating humanity, a kind of Eden to be rediscovered or re-established, which had its coherence and was a world in itself.

Another Middle Kingdom, a thousand years old and timeless

Experiences like these let Africa get under your skin. But should we be talking about Africa or Africas ? The question was obvious, if only because of the discovery on the continent of a particular country that was a world in itself, a kind of Middle Kingdom: Ethiopia, which had still been an empire just a few years earlier.

The country hosted the headquarters of the Organisation of African Unity (OAU) in Addis Ababa. At the time, the OAU was an organisation that carried weight in the international system, as the colonial presence and that of foreign troops - including 50,000 Cubans - for whom the African continent was a battleground, drew to a close. The immense Ethiopia, a sumptuous ex-empire in some respects and now governed by Colonel Menguistu, was then in the grip of drought and famine.

So what a surprise it was when the effect of altitude - Addis is 2,500 m above sea level - and, above all, heavy rain suddenly interrupted sleep. The images of starving people, displaced with their meagre herds in search of water to survive, that the media carried at the time corresponded well to the reality of the terrible famine that hit the country in the early 80s. But in fact, there were considerable regional disparities and a wide variety of climatic conditions across the country.

The province of Shoa, at the centre of which was the capital Addis Ababa, with a surface area of around 80,000 km2 and set on high plateaux, was relatively well-watered. It is in this region that the Blue Nile cuts through the high plateaux to form dizzying gorges before joining the White Nile in Sudan. On the way to the gorges, you would meet horsemen riding their colourful mounts, their shoulders covered with a shimmering stole, giving them a hieratic despite the movement, almost religious attitude.

These images were out of time, or at least out of our time, and even beyond our imagination. But the Province of Shoa also had its hardships. The demographic pressure on the capital was one example. As elsewhere in Africa, access to increasingly scarce firewood was vital for the population. In Addis, the expansion of the city's surface area, which coincided with the growth of the population, meant that the inhabitants had to make daily journeys on foot, which were increasingly long and arduous, in order to obtain supplies. To reach the heights of the city, they had to cross a pass over 3,000 m high and enter deep into the high plateau.

Menelik's eucalyptus and Haile Selassie's lion

The French embassy was located in the heart of this city of hills and terraces. In the 19th century, Emperor Menelik II offered France a vast 42-hectare plot of land for its diplomatic presence. The eucalyptus trees grew to a considerable height of several dozen metres. It was highly inadvisable to venture out onto the perimeter of the compound on foot at night, as hyenas prowled the area. The embassy itself emerged from the highest part of the grounds. The enclosure, made of a high wall, had been weakened by the years and in some places revealed gaping holes. This gave access, which was authorised once a week, to the inhabitants of a neighbouring village who came to gather firewood. Such was the spectacle that could be seen from the offices and meeting rooms. It was like a resurgence of our Ancien Régime on African seigneurial lands. This tolerance was quite natural and helped to limit deforestation around Addis - a matter of concern to the relevant international organisations. It was also a fair return for land granted to France.

From the Diplomatic Chancellery, where these scenes straight out of the Middle Ages could be seen, the lion of the emperor could no longer be heard roaring as it once had. The emperor had been overthrown in 1974, a decade earlier, but his memory remained close, and the new practices of power, inherited from the Soviet Union, had borrowed from the imperial tradition. As in Ryszard Kapuscinski's book *The Emperor*, in which this former correspondent for a Polish press agency recounts his search, after the revolution, for the emperor's missing relatives, I left for Addis with only a letter addressed to the former news presenter of the only television channel at the time that had had links with the embassy. Had she survived all this upheaval? If so, where was she and what was she doing now?

The revolution after the empire

It was not a question of investigating the end of a reign, which had been the end of a world, but simply of helping to reconnect the threads of a personal history. Even if it was a case of looking for a twig in a haystack, the search eventually came to fruition after many twists and turns. One meeting was finally fixed with an elegant Eritrean woman. Her apparent serenity and the visible absence of fear in her attitude and words were striking. She was no longer working in television and had clearly been 'crossing a desert' for a long time. Her new position had enabled her to make a few trips to 'sister countries' over the previous few years. Married to a lawyer, a member of the imperial family, but herself from a much more modest background, she had been able to help her husband - and perhaps even save him - during the 'events'.

In reality, even if she herself did not explain it clearly, Haile Selassie's last years had been complex, even confused. Faced with the ultra-conservatives, the large landowners who were present in the Palace but who wanted to maintain their powers in the provinces, the emperor had appealed to an educated youth from modest backgrounds. Their representatives were hated by the dignitaries. Over the last few years, before the final degradation and the seizure of power by a military committee - the Dergue - several antagonistic currents had coexisted right up to the pinnacle of power, encouraged in turn by an emperor who refused to make a decision unless he became incapable of doing so due to his age. The hardliners were led by the emperor's daughter, while the reformers, seeing disaster on the horizon, urgently called for radical change.

This interlocutor, heir to both the Empire and the Revolution - in that order which is the opposite of French history - had witnessed a country crushed under the authoritarianism of the powerful, repeatedly prey to the worst famines, which ended up giving free rein to outbursts of extreme violence. These brutal upheavals had even reached the capital, but it was impossible to imagine a cosmogony in which the King of Kings was not the centre. As a result, the revolution had infiltrated the Palace, initially masked in the name of the monarch, who sometimes even supported it if it could do the country some good. But more and more arrests were made at Court, in increasingly massive numbers, sparing only the emperor and a few rare, insignificant followers. After his deposition, the Negus remained in the Palace, still adorned with some of the trappings of his former power. The star was dead, but still shone brightly. Perhaps Haile Selassie still thought he was ruling, at least within the limits of the theatrical exercise of power that had been the hallmark of the final phase of his imperium.

In this context of extreme complexity and opacity, where did this interlocutor fit in? Had she been promoted with the talented youth of the rising social classes intended to contain the feudalists? Had her husband been one of these liberal reformers, as the imperial family, a vast tribe, had included a few? Had her Eritrean origins spared her from the ferocious confrontation confined mainly to the Amhara people who had dominated since the 13th century? The rise to power of the Tigrayans, from 1974 onwards, would appear to be a revolution within a revolution. There were only partial answers to this wide-ranging question, but was there really a global explanation? Only a door had been half-opened that was to close hermetically on so many mysteries.

Africa at the heart

Fifty years after the deposition of the emperor, this Middle Kingdom remains little known and little understood. The conflict in Eritrea, followed by that in Tigray, sometimes hits the headlines in bits and pieces, resembling a Hundred Years' War that escapes our contemporary time reference points. But we have to live with these secrets, which are also inexhaustible treasures. We think we've turned the page, but Africa remains in our hearts.

India, a centre of multipolarity

The contract signed in 2023 to supply Air India - which is now been owned by the Tata Group - with 430 aircraft produced by Airbus and Boeing, including 40 long-haul A350s, has confirmed the place that India now occupies in international politics, even beyond the economy.

The 'world's largest democracy' in terms of size is poised to overtake China in terms of population; it is also asserting itself as a major economic power, including in the field of cutting-edge technologies. In regional terms, it is no longer simply the colossus of the subcontinent, but has the potential to shine as a global power, rooted in non-alignment since its origins at the end of partition in 1947.

Does this mean that the state of the world cannot be reduced to all-out competition between China and the United States? Would international relations be limited to a simplistic East-West opposition, as described in the narrative of Putin's Russia? This new order in the making - characterised by a multiplication of poles of power evolving towards a truly multipolar system - would therefore not simply reproduce the confrontation between blocs, like that of the Cold War. In this new context, where do the interests of France and Europe lie?

The mega aircraft contract

Let's take a moment to look at the aircraft contract. It is one of the largest ever signed in civil aviation. It was announced during a videoconference between Prime Minister Modi, the President of the French Republic, the CEO of Airbus and a representative of the Tata family, which owns Air India.

The Airbus CEO said that *'the time was right for India to become an international hub'*. Partners within Airbus will naturally also benefit from the contract. It is in the United Kingdom that the Airbus wings are designed and produced; Rolls-Royce powers the A350s. The first 6 A350s will be delivered in the first year of the contract. Within the decade, India will become the 3rd largest air transport market, behind the United States and China. This prospect confirms the place that India now occupies in the field of high technology, as well as its role as the 'workshop' of the world, which is no longer the exclusive preserve of China. Apple, for example, is in the process of relocating iPhone production from China to India. But the process is proving complex.

Tradition of non-alignment and emerging power

For decades, India has been a regional power playing a significant role in multilateral forums. Because of the quality of its nationals, their language skills and the involvement of the Indian armed forces in UN peacekeeping operations, India has long been over-represented in the international civil service in relation to its budgetary contributions. This is exactly the opposite of the situation in Japan, for example.

Reflections on UN reform have always included an Indian 'factor', for the reasons set out above. For more than twenty years, consideration has been given to enlarging the UN Security Council to make it more representative of the state of the world. While this complex process has come up against major political obstacles, France has on several occasions publicly declared itself in favour of India, Germany, Japan and a major African country joining the Council. India and France have had a strategic partnership since 1998. But if we consider the case of India alone, whose candidacy was indisputable on the basis of several criteria (demographic and economic weight, participation in UN activities), it was clear at the time, when the issue seemed to have reached maturity at the end of the 90s, that such a candidacy would inevitably give rise to a counter-request from Pakistan. Pakistan was also a considerable country, but it also had the disadvantage of having carried out nuclear tests in 1998, as did India. In addition to the respective relations of the countries concerned with the major powers, this was not possible at a time when nuclear proliferation had become a major concern and could not be 'rewarded' in any way. What is the situation today, when India is on the verge of acquiring the status of a world power? And was India ever simply a regional power?

The characteristics of the current period, highlighted in particular by the war in Ukraine, are the breakdown of the international system and the temptation to reconstitute power blocs. While these trends are a priori unfavourable to India, which is traditionally non-aligned and inclined towards multilateral cooperation, New Delhi can paradoxically benefit from the new situation. India is being courted from all sides: Prime Minister Modi was entitled to a state visit to the United States during the Biden presidency; he also received a *red carpet treatment* at the BRICS summit in Kazan in October 2024.

For a Mediterranean Republic

After the fall of the Berlin Wall in 1989 and the reunification of Germany in 1990, the Member States of Europe expressed different priorities: Germany and its neighbours, linked to it most strongly in economic terms, focused on *Mitteleuropa*, i.e. on Central Europe and beyond on the East in general, while France, less polarised and not yielding to the same tropism, continued to give priority to its neighbours to the south of the Mediterranean. The end of the war in Ukraine - currently a kind of obsessive 'blue line of the Vosges' - could well reshuffle the cards and the Mediterranean neighbours, whether we like it or not, remain unavoidable for French policy.

Memory rent and common interests

Coinciding with recurring controversies over immigration issues, the Algerian President's state visit to France, initially scheduled for May 2023, has been postponed several times. But the Franco-Algerian bilateral relationship cannot be reduced to economic disputes and recurring crises over visas, as in October 2021 when they were reduced by 50% in retaliation for Algiers' alleged refusal to accept illegal immigrants who had been expelled from the country. Nor can the eternal quarrel over memory prevent the relationship from flourishing, and it is only by moving forward that so many wounds can be healed. The 'official' histories will not be abandoned, but citizens will experience theirs in a different way.

In January 2023, a former French ambassador to Algeria (see 2008-2012 and 2017-2020) published a resounding tribune. The former diplomat explained that 'the new Algeria', to use the expression in vogue in Algiers, *'is in the process of collapsing before our very eyes and that it is dragging France down with it, no doubt more strongly and suddenly than the Algerian tragedy brought down the Fourth Republic in 1958'*.

A few days later, the President of the French Republic also spoke to the press about Algeria, a subject about which he has had changing views over the years. During his first presidential election campaign, he described colonisation as a *'crime against humanity'* (NB: a concept defined by the Nuremberg Tribunal). More recently, on the other hand, he has denounced the *'memory rent'* that Algeria has endlessly exploited against France since 1962.

Since then he has done it again, in a way, contradicting his initial comments in Algiers by declaring that he would not ask Algeria for *'forgiveness'*, even though he made a major trip to Algiers in August 2022 and his Prime Minister and many members of his government also travelled there to seal a 'new Franco-Algerian reconciliation'. *'The work of remembrance and history is not about settling scores. On the contrary, it is about supporting the fact that there is something unspeakable, perhaps unspeakable, unforgivable'*, declared the French President. For its part, Algeria had criticised the report commissioned by the Élysée Palace from French historian Benjamin Stora, which recommended gestures of reconciliation while ruling out *'repentance'* and *'apologies'*.

By relying too much on the virtuosity of the language and on the intrinsically contradictory nature of thoughts, the risk is eventually to fall into the trap of declaratory politics. Official communication is coded, because if we can't move forward, we mustn't go backwards. The discourse is therefore stereotyped, repetitive, wearying and ultimately depressing in terms of expectations and needs: that 'everything changes so that nothing changes' still corresponds to too many interests. In the end, what counts are the actions that no commission of historians or cunning politician can produce. Algeria and France, and perhaps some of their Mediterranean neighbours too, need a grand project.

Our mutual interests remain considerable and link us together, but the substance of our expression is minimalist. We need to avoid anything that could be perceived as provocative on either side of the Atlantic, and to avoid any polemics. A form of silence is still needed for an indefinite time. Does this right to remain silent even become a duty? But passion holds us and in this state will be even stronger.

Algeria, Germany and France: intersecting destinies

All things considered, Algeria is the most important country for France to the south, as is Germany to the north. In both cases, wars have marred our relations with these neighbours. With what was then 'Rhenish' Germany, a spectacular reconciliation was initiated in 1958 by de Gaulle and Adenauer. Despite the *'peace of the brave'* proclaimed by the General and a few too timid attempts to 'turn the page', such as during the 'Cross Cultural Years' between the two countries (NB: 2002 and 2003), such a reunion did not occur with Algiers. Paradoxically, this has rekindled differences, for example on the highly sensitive issue of remembrance, which have continued unabated despite the Commission of Historians co-chaired by B. Stora.

But, before coming together, do the opinions embrace the whole problem? If Franco-German animosity belongs to the past, do the French really know Germany, beyond the mechanical and convenient expression of the Franco-German 'couple'? Do they know its history, culture and language, including French diplomats? Do they follow developments in the Federal Republic's policy with the attention required by Germany's power at the heart of Europe? Do they even go to Germany on holiday? With Algeria, in a relationship made up of passions, the intimacy is ultimately greater:

the million repatriates was also one of the vectors, after a common history dating back to 1848; but also in a negative way, the scoriae of the war and the excesses of either the FLN or movements such as the OAS have irrigated part of French politics, including after independence.

For a long time, Germany was perceived - with more than a touch of envy for its economic success - as too powerful, before being perceived as too weak, because of its energy dependence or its insufficient contribution to the security of the continent, which was deemed insufficient. With Algeria, the crises are recurrent, whether it's the thorny issue of visas and immigration or the aforementioned question of memory. There has been a constant oscillation between warm reminders of what unites us and paroxysmal bitterness. This is illustrated today by the debate on the 1968 migration agreement, at a time when the derogatory advantages in relation to ordinary law - which were very real before family reunification was accepted from the mid-1970s onwards - have been largely eroded. This text is not the be-all and end-all for settling the Franco-Algerian dispute.

The strategy of tension is doomed to failure. We should prefer the breath of fresh air that the vision of Algiers the White gives us, or the dazzlement that seizes us in the Roman ruins of Tipasa on the Mediterranean coast. It was this vision that inspired Albert Camus, a great lover of Algeria, to write that '*outside the sun, the kisses and the wild perfumes, everything seems futile*'. It was on the right bank of the Rhine, also by the water in his house in Rhöndorf, that Konrad Adenauer liked to tend his rosebushes. It was here that he found rest and serenity; he even made it a kind of base camp for his political action, in a process that is the reverse of that described by the Latin adage: '*Arx tarpeia Capitoli proxima*' (it's not far from the Capitol to the Tarpeian Rock). Indeed, close to this retreat on the right bank of the Rhine was the famous Drachenfels (Dragon's Rock) in the Sibengebirge, where, according to the legend of the Niebelungen, Siegfrid fought the dragon; a little further south, the Lorelei Rock recalled another tragedy, that of a prudish young girl who threw herself into the Rhine to escape dishonour and was transformed into a fearsome nymph.

The arrest of the writer Boualem Sansal in 2025, who was awarded the Grand Prix du roman by the *Académie française* many years ago and naturalised as a French citizen in 2024, is nothing less than a hostage-taking operation, with a violent message addressed directly to France. Boualem Sansal is the expiatory victim of the deterioration in Franco-Algerian relations, yet his only natural place is in the world of freedom that he has always embodied. But what does the arrest of a free thinker reveal about the no-face power that governs Algeria? Is the fragility of this power such that an essayist should be accused of jeopardising the security of the Algerian state? Is it possible, more than 60 years after independence, to imagine a relationship that finally emerges from the infernal cycle of unsolvable mutual accusations? Boualem Sansal, now a dual national after having embodied two cultures, undoubtedly expresses all this, including perhaps even the unquenchable bitterness of the power that imprisons him. Boualem Sansal is also our hostage, and we must set him free.

The word "apaisement" does not have a good press and is generally used in its English translation "appeasement" to express the culpable weaknesses of a policy in relation to the threats that ultimately led to the Second World War. Yet this is the direction that is taking shape, in an obviously totally different context, towards Algeria at the end - it is to be hoped - of a new crisis in the bilateral relationship with France. A policy aimed at resuming a dialogue that cannot be ignored seems to be taking shape at the top of the French government and is being echoed on the other side of the Mediterranean, as illustrated by the visit to Algiers by the French Minister of Foreign Affairs.

Not all the issues have been resolved and probably never will be, but that should not prevent us from moving forward. The Boualem Sansal affair - Algerian in Algeria and French in France - for which we hope for a rapid solution, has been both the tree that hides the forest and a decoy. Focusing exclusively on it, in a public way, has not so far contributed to its resolution, as is generally the case in this type of affair, where more discreet diplomacy almost always proves more effective. The error of approach has mainly been made on the French side, relegating for a time to the background the substantive issues that needed to be dealt with; the advantage will have been mainly on the Algerian side if it has finally reminded France that forgetting Algeria's considerable importance for it is contrary to history, geography and its permanent interests.

General de Gaulle declared that '*Algeria is France*'. Although he did not necessarily renounce this thought in his heart, it was he who was the main architect of the '*peace of the brave*' and Algerian independence. But independence in no way meant breaking off such a passionate relationship.

The great project of France and Algeria is not the completion of separation, which is clearly impossible. General de Gaulle, born in the nineteenth century, was a man of the twentieth, and who can say, with all due respect, that his thinking is in any way relevant to the major issues of the twenty-first century? Has France's withdrawal from Algeria worked? Can migratory flows be controlled simply by raising portcullises of drawbridges in an age of migration fuelled by conflict and climate change? If France is likely to be dragged into an abyss by a decomposing Algeria, what is the former ambassador proposing? Pursue sterile historical quarrels ? Is he not basing his peremptory and definitive judgement on an analysis of the internal Algerian situation, which is a form of interference? If there is any basis for his thinking, he should not express it, because it only leads to deadlock. A diplomat should not play the Cassandra; his job is to be positive and always try to find solutions. As for the politicians who substitute themselves for historians, when history is so complex and they don't necessarily master it, or even for psycho-sociologists, they would do better to devote themselves by definition to politics. This means moving in a clear direction with a firm resolve to build, which is quite enough.

'*Egypt, a French passion*', wrote Robert Solé. Sixty years after independence, France-Algeria is also - but differently - a French passion, incandescent but at the same time stagnant. The language of the relationship is veiled, made up of euphemisms, and generally fails to name the facts and realities. This mental block doesn't even entirely escape generational change, because distance, whether temporal or geographical, doesn't prevent radical discourse and sometimes even action.

From the Maghreb to the Eastern Mediterranean

The Mediterranean Republic should be an unprecedented impetus on both sides of the Mediterranean. Sometimes this would mean more Republics, but it would also mean more Mediterranean, i.e. more orientation towards the South. Barriers must be abolished because they cannot be erected effectively. This vast project should not be limited to France, but should also be extended to southern European states such as Spain and Italy, which could be associated with it.

The southern shore of the Mediterranean cannot exclude the eastern part of that sea, and we are naturally thinking of Syria in the Levant, which is so dear to us. It was France that put the Alawites still in power on the flagstaff, until then driven back into the mountains above Latakia, and who have since pledged eternal gratitude to France, albeit tempered by the vicissitudes of recent years.

Every 11 November, a ceremony was held near Damascus, at the French military cemetery in Dmeir on the road to Palmyra, in the presence of the French community and the civil, military and religious authorities of both countries. The aim was to honour the victims of the war in Cilicia in 1920-1921, the operations in Jebel Druze and in Damascus itself in 1924-1925, and the fighting in the Second World War, in a place containing 4,000 graves, some of them in a Muslim 'plot'. We can still see that France without Syria, a factor of regional stability, are not at all the same thing.
The Mediterranean Republic should be an unprecedented impetus on both sides of the Mediterranean. Sometimes this would mean more of the Republic, but it would also mean more of the

Mediterranean, i.e. more orientation towards the South. Barriers must be abolished because they cannot be erected effectively.

The dizziness and dazzlement that the Mediterranean world can arouse should not lead us to ignore the meaning of words: the Mediterranean Republic - whatever it is called - should be a great project for the future. And efforts have already been made in this direction. The Mediterranean, which has long been analysed, notably by the great historian Fernand Braudel in his famous thesis The Mediterranean and *the Mediterranean World at the Time of Philip II* (see study of the environment, collective destiny, events and the politics of men) implies a community of positive or negative destinies; but the sine qua non condition is the progression of republican ideas and practices, without which any rapprochement is illusory.

Afghanistan, an adjustment variable

Unfortunately, the months of August are not free of disasters, and summer lethargy is no obstacle. We are reminded of Hiroshima and Nagasaki on 6 and 9 August, the construction of the Berlin Wall on 13 August, the invasion of Czechoslovakia on 21 August 1968, not forgetting the Kursk submarine disaster almost twenty-five years ago and many other tragedies. Today, all eyes are on the Near and Middle East.

The Taliban regained power in Kabul in 2021, on 15 August; they had already occupied it in 1996. We went to Afghanistan, we left, we abandoned the country in a way. At the time, a French minister told a UN committee, with reference to women and young girls, among the most vulnerable sections of the country's population, that there were '*those who left and those who stayed*' and that '*in both cases, we would help them*'. But in both cases, it was a tragedy. If Afghanistan has sometimes been called *The Graveyard of Empires*, has it not also become the '*Graveyard of the Innocent*'?
International relations are not about feelings, but about raw interests. Should we not evoke a humanitarian and even moral duty, given our past involvement? The worst thing would be silence, or even

oblivion: in any case, we must not give in to the humiliation caused by the conditions of abandonment, or to the fear or rancour that are leading us today to paralysis and to look the other way; humanitarian issues, refugees and displaced persons, should be the concern of the international community.

The eye of the storm

This region, at the heart of major strategic issues, is bound to catch up with us in the end. Afghanistan has been conquered many times, but never completely subdued. Ethnic and even tribal divisions have given rise to endless disputes and conflicts, which have also been exploited by outside powers. The country has been the strategic focus of a merciless struggle in the subcontinent between Pakistan and India since the latter's partition in 1947.

Afghanistan is thus the revelation and crucible of threats both old and more recent. The latter were visible to the whole world, such as the terrorism that struck New York, which was conceived and coordinated from the Al-Qaeda hideout in the almost inaccessible mountains.

Afghanistan is in the eye of a nuclear storm. In addition to India and Pakistan, which carried out their first experiments in 1998, Russia and China, respectively the old and perhaps the new guardian power, are not far from this theatre. Iran, with its large Shiite Hazara community, its rejection of a competing religious model, the large migratory flows it has experienced as a result of the war and its status as a nuclear 'threshold' country, cannot be insensitive to what is happening in and around its neighbour.

Can Europe and even the United States, which withdrew at the end of a twenty-year war, lose interest in the medium and long term in this area, which is destined to be at the heart of major economic projects such as the new Silk Roads? Will we remain passive on this new front line, as in the 'Tartar Desert', where waiting undermines the defenders and does not prepare them to meet the challenges? Will we simply say to ourselves, thinking of all the civilian and military victims on all sides over the past decades: was it all for this?

The situation in Afghanistan is like starting all over again. The history of the 'students of religion' (Taleban) movement, officially set up in the Pashtun areas, goes back a long way and is in fact linked to the 'mujahedin' struggle - organised with Western support - against the Soviet Union's ten-year occupation of the country (1979-1989).

From the late 1970s onwards, a dream could have been entertained. It would have consisted of supporting a power that was religious and capable of transcending the tribes, appealing to the figure of a King - whose return from exile in Italy had sometimes been mentioned - and developing a vast economic project. The idea was to turn Afghanistan into a transit zone for hydrocarbons, from the production zones to the markets and ports of South Asia. Basically, the plan was reminiscent of a Saudi 'model', with essentially strategic aims. The TAPI gas pipeline project, still not completed but not abandoned (NB: Turkmenistan-Afghanistan-Pakistan-India) corresponded to a similar scheme, all things considered.

For the international community, the primary concern after the withdrawal will remain trying to ensure that the de facto extension of Pakistan's tribal areas does not become an uncontrolled hotbed of the most extremist activities. The spectre of terrorism on a vast scale, which has not dissipated since the World Trade Center in 2001 - which provoked the last war in the country - will continue to haunt the world for a long time to come.

The second objective, whoever is in power, will be to work towards stabilising the country and the region. This is a matter of both our humanitarian duty and our security interests. Although rural areas have largely escaped progress, the past twenty years will have enabled the transformation and modernisation, in terms of infrastructure and lifestyle, of a country whose population has doubled over the period to 40 million. Honesty dictates that the considerable resources spent by the United States and its allies were not all wasted. In any case, it was impossible to achieve *nation building* with armies alone. The question now is what can be preserved. This latter approach may be one justification, albeit not the only one, for the decision of certain powers to remain in the region and maintain their embassies there.

An eternal Kriegsspiel?

Afghanistan has always provoked immediate rejection, but also lasting addiction. The shock comes, for example, when newcomers are confronted with the barrier of the Hindu Kush, a 5,000 metre high wall at the bottom of the Central Asian desert, marking a clear boundary and signifying the landlocked and impenetrable nature of the country.

The Taliban problem is not confined to Afghanistan. The Soviets' ten-year war was followed by the Americans' twenty-year war. Some people talked about China's moment, but it is a safe bet that China will take previous experiences into account. The 'new old' Afghanistan could pose problems for China, particularly by complicating its relations with other states in the region, especially Islamabad and New Delhi.

What is certain is that the 'Great Game' in the region, as it has been called since the 19th century when the Russian and British empires were pitted against each other, will continue in another form. Whatever the case, we must not forget the Afghan people - the adjustment variable in so many tragedies - who have been actors in the *Kriegsspiel* for some of their components, notably the warlords, but also an expiatory victim of opposing powers. Conflict and desolation should not be seen as an inevitability for populations that are supposed to be developing. Starting with Europe, we need to define a new form of 'engagement', a term that is undoubtedly preferable to 'intervention', which now has a worse reputation, even if it is defined as humanitarian.

12

The old West and the new East

Cracks in the West, renewed anti-Americanism

Like the reflex of the same name, 'Pavlovian' anti-Americanism is still with us. Against the backdrop of the war in Ukraine, where the future of the European continent is at stake, some prefer to turn their sting towards the 'US takeover of Europe' as the ultimate culmination of an 'old dream of domination'.

Anti-Americanism is nothing new in France. It stems in part from the amnesia of our oldest ally with regard to a shared history rooted in the independence of the American colonies and magnified by the liberation of 1945. It may have been fuelled, though not for its own sake, by a certain extremely sensitive Gaullist discourse on independence. The French, who at the same time were dreaming of the American civilisation popularised in particular by the cinema, ended up really liking a country that they had really discovered relatively recently thanks to increasingly accessible travel.

French disappointments

This has not prevented powerful relapses of an affliction that has never completely disappeared. And it cannot be otherwise, given that the powerful 'protector' within and on NATO is an empire whose interests can only be selfish. The Bretton Woods institutions and even the Marshall Plan also corresponded in part to this attitude. Closer to home, in the summer of 2021, the withdrawal from Afghanistan, without consultation, confirmed this recurring behaviour of going it alone.

France, for its part, has had its share of disappointments. Australia's cancellation of the so-called 'submarine of the century' contract - for 12 conventionally-powered *Barracuda* submarines to be built by the French company *Naval Group* - was seen as an affront by the

European power with the strongest military presence in the Indo-Pacific region, not to mention the 1,600,000 French citizens who live there. The formation of the AUKUS alliance under the impetus of the United States, between the latter country, Australia and the United Kingdom, immediately reduced to ashes the strategic partnership between France and Australia marked by the visit of the President of French the Republic in May 2018 and numerous agreements in the security and economic fields.

The transatlantic relationship remains intangible

On the international stage in general, a 'Suez syndrome' has perhaps never been fully overcome, and some analysts believe that it is the residue of such a trauma that still fuels orientations such as the objective of European 'strategic autonomy'. But we should also talk about an economic competition in which the term 'allies' no longer has any meaning. We all remember the extra-territorial application of American laws, as in the case of BNP, which was ordered to pay $9 billion in penalties for dollar transactions in Iran, which were perfectly legal under European regulations. Equally shocking, in another area, was the revelation in 2016 that the US Security Agency (NSA) had been eavesdropping over a long period on French leaders, part of the political class and diplomats and other officials, with the help of the intelligence services of a European country reputed to be a close friend of France.

But the transatlantic relationship remains intangible despite so many accumulated grievances and recriminations. The differences in culture between Europe and France are great, and the French often even delude themselves about the closeness of their French-speaking 'cousins' in Canada, who in reality are first and foremost North Americans. But the concept of the Euro-Atlantic 'community' is not an empty word, and the emergence of great autocratic powers helps to remind us of this closeness. It is in this context that the disturbances experienced by American democracy are felt in Europe, as are the risks of legal regression facilitated, if need be, by a Supreme Court that has become more conservative as a result of the appointments made under the Trump presidency, and the tragedies caused by the liberalisation of the arms trade, not to mention the death penalty still in force in certain states of the Federation.

See further

General de Gaulle, who was extremely concerned about France's independence - and probably never overcame the difficult relationship he had with President Roosevelt throughout the Second World War - was often characterised by his anti-Americanism. In reality, it is well known that he was always the first to side with the United States in major crises, such as those in Berlin and Cuba. He had great respect for President Eisenhower, was fascinated like everyone else by the Kennedy couple and appreciated Richard Nixon, whom he tried to advise on the Vietnam affair.

The context is no longer the same, and it is not certain that the war in Ukraine will give rise in the long term to a 'resurrection' of NATO and a lasting 'return' of the United States to Europe, whose priority, to the point of obsession, remains China. It is therefore desirable that the crisis be resolved as quickly as possible so that a new 'iron curtain' is not erected on the European continent. Clearly, between American egoism and the risk of hegemony from a powerful dictatorship, the choice will always be in the same direction. But we need to look further ahead in the long-term interests of a European geostrategic entity whose eastern limits could one day turn out to be Asian.

At the crossroads of forgotten Europe

The old West and the new East need to shed light on a part of Europe that is all too often neglected or passed over in silence: the Romanian lands in Danube Europe. The trips made by the President of the French Republic to Romania and Moldova at the end of his European Presidency, and to Ukraine in the company of the German Chancellor, the Italian Prime Minister and the Romanian President for the latter destination, cannot be dissociated, but the different stages also had their own specificity. If the Romanian lands had indeed become the western flank of a major conflict, it was also time for them to be developed for their own sake.

If not too late, why?

The President of the French Republic, who spoke directly to his Russian counterpart for dozens of hours before the start of the Ukrainian crisis and was in contact with all the players in the current war, has information that we do not have and, in fulfilling a responsibility that he does not share with regard to the prerogatives of his office, we must respect his approach. Nevertheless, the mission to Kyiv, the capital where he had stopped over on his way back from Moscow before the conflict to meet President Zelensky, seems to have been put off for too long. We can't say 'too late', but we can certainly say 'at last'. Fortunately, the Head of State was preceded by the visit of his Minister of Foreign Affairs, who also travelled to Bucha before a presidential audience in the Ukrainian capital.

The European team, which brings together a northern European country, two southern European countries and an eastern European state, is unusual and rather unusual from a diplomatic point of view, but it clearly sends out a message of seeking a diplomatic path that goes beyond war. It should be noted that it was the Minister of Foreign Affairs who accompanied the President of the Republic and not the Minister of Defence. France, which has rarely shied away from dialogue with Russia, is not, however, in the same position as Germany and Italy, which are doing everything they can to break the deadlock they find themselves in because of their dependence on energy supplies from the East.

It was time for the European Presidency to go to Kyiv, and the fact that France was accompanied does not reduce the significance of the Member States' assertion of European leadership. This is a return to an old debate on the respective prerogatives of the Member States and the Commission, and it should be noted that Ursula von der Leyen had already visited Ukraine twice during the conflict. The late appearance on Ukrainian soil by the Troika, extended to include Romania, had the disadvantage of clearly marking a split in Europe's approach to the current crisis. Warsaw and the capitals of the Baltic States will no doubt consider that 'finesse' is not the right approach when faced with a Russia that has long dominated them and from which they no longer expect anything.

The French 'en même temps' is in danger of becoming the sole focus of criticism following misunderstood and sometimes even misappropriated statements. If the French intellectual tradition is that of the 'juste milieu', as it was understood in the 17th century, it should in fact mean the search for a synthesis on which we try to elaborate and build, and not a permanent pendular movement.

The only way to overcome these difficulties was to make a trip to Kyiv that was not symbolic but a vehicle for concrete commitments, in the absence of a genuine plan to end the crisis, even if its implementation was delayed. What's more, the Romanian and Moldovan preliminary stages, by showing clear support for countries worried about Russia, will have had the merit of providing a more balanced colouring to the diplomatic manoeuvre.

This last condition was finally fulfilled with the Four's commitment to Ukraine's immediate status as a candidate for membership of the European Union, on which the Commission and the Member States were subsequently to vote. On the French side, the deliveries of additional *Caesar* mobile guns (NB: 6 in addition to 12), taken from national stocks which are not considerable (72) given France's external military commitments, will have constituted a strong gesture.

Apart from his unfortunate reference to Russia's 'humiliation', which was particularly offensive to Ukrainians faced with such appalling aggression, the French President affirmed a consistent line: to stand by Ukraine for as long as necessary; to encourage a negotiation process if Kyiv so decides; to work in the immediate future, if not to lift the blockade on Ukraine out of its reach, at least to circumvent it, and it is here that the role of Romania and the presence of its President Klaus Iohannis in Kyiv took on its full meaning.

Latin lands and fierce resistance

The presence of the French Head of State in the capitals of so-called Danube and Balkan Europe should not be reduced to the war in Ukraine. His presence in Romania and Moldavia was valuable in its own right, because the history of the Romanian world is a lesson for the very contemporary period.

It is often forgotten that Romania has been a member of the European Union since 2007, and of NATO since 2004. It is in this context that France has just provided military support by positioning some of its soldiers at the Mihail Kogălniceanu forward base, named after a great Romanian statesman. Moldova, whose remarkable President Maia Sandu has been received in Paris on several occasions, is also destined to become part of Europe, in parallel with the accession process, as envisaged by the President of the French Republic and outlined in his speech in Strasbourg.

Romanian lands are first and foremost Latin lands. Romania was born into history as a frontier march, as the Dacia of the emperor Trajan, whose story appears on the colonnade near the Forum in Rome and its replica on Place Vendôme in Paris. It therefore originally embodied the human rampart of Latinity against the assaults of the peoples of the steppe. The Slavic invasions of the 6th and 9th centuries had the strength of numbers but lacked the political organisation that Rome had established. After a century under the Pax Romana, Romania was submerged for ten centuries by the hordes from Asia, and for five centuries was occupied, shared or re-shared between the powers and Great Empires (Magyars, sometimes served by monastic orders such as the Knights of the Teutonic Order; Ottomans between the 15th and 17th centuries; Austro-Hungarians after the siege of Vienna was lifted in 1683) whose interests clashed on the Danube. Romania straddles the arc of the Carpathian Mountains and is bounded to the south by the Danube, which flows into a majestic delta, now beyond the strategically important port of Galati.

Historians have argued that it was thanks to the *'immolation of the Balkans and Eastern Slavs'* that Western civilisation was able to continue in Western Europe. The country's most emblematic figure was *Stefan cel Mare* (Stephen the Great) in the 15th century, who turned submission to the Hungarians and Poles into an exceptional cultural renaissance in Moldavia, as witnessed by the monasteries with their exterior painted facades.

The nation's development was also forged thanks to France's respect for its Christian tradition (NB: part of its so-called 'Uniate' Church, in a country dominated by Orthodoxy, even attached itself to Rome), its language and the development of its culture. The message of 'Greater Romania', the largest territorial extension of the country after the First World War, was that of Western civilisation, on the shores of the Black Sea, *At the crossroads of dead empires*, to use the title of a book by Lucien Romier written almost a century ago.

Like Trajan's Dacia, it was caught up in the clash of the two irreconcilable ideologies of the Cold War, but once again it was able to resist - under Eastern influence, being administered under the Ottomans by the Greeks of Constantinople and in the West by the Magyars and Germans of Transylvania - and to be a troublemaker in the European socialist camp under the leadership of Nicolae Ceausescu, whose audacity should not be forgotten. From the end of the 1960s onwards, it even relied on China, playing on the strong Sino-Soviet tensions. Romania knows what is meant by unity and independence, fully asserted today in a European Union that is not a hindrance but a framework and a necessary support for its development and progress.

A message from the Danube region

The message from the Romanian lands brings us back to our own identity, that of the Latinity inherited from Rome and that of a Europe that remains that of the Enlightenment. A similar message is coming from the neighbouring Slavic world, in the Ukraine, where Kyiv is, if not a new Rome, at least a Constantinople fighting foot to foot against the invasions and striving to postpone a fatal outcome for the benefit of a greater whole.

If it was high time to recognise and honour this part of Europe, it was also time to send a message of recognition and solidarity directly to these lands of civilisation. But Kyiv, Bucharest and Chisinau are asking us some fundamental questions: is the message of the Romanian lands really ours? Is Kiev's message compatible with that of Romania and Moldova?

Europe's relationship with the Russian world is a centuries-old process. But so too was resistance in the Danube region, and beyond from the Dnieper to the Dniester. The real message or DNA that has never been lost in these Romanian lands, which we have neglected for too long, is that of a great Roman country, which was a contemporary of the Emperor Hadrian, Trajan's successor in the first century. Marguerite Yourcenar has given us the *Memoirs of Hadrien, a scholar and philosopher*, determined to put an end to an expansionist policy, to pacify and to build, even within borders that remain porous.

East/West: neglected convergences

Caucasus and Central Asia are in many ways a black hole in our knowledge: large-scale Islamist terrorism erupted in Moscow in a concert hall in March 2024, with the attack claimed by the Islamic State of Khorasan; this may have led Russia to fear - despite initial denials and the insinuation of a Ukrainian lead - the creation of a second front on its own territory.

Attacks on Orthodox churches and a synagogue, which were also claimed by the Islamic State, took place a month later in Dagestan - an entity of the Russian Federation - in June 2024; around twenty people were killed and dozens injured, and several official and historic buildings were set on fire.

The *modus operandi* of the first event, the location and the number of victims, brought back memories of the Bataclan and the Paris attacks in November 2015, prompting expressions of compassion and even a willingness to cooperate in the fight against terrorism. The second incident received relatively little media coverage and a deafening silence on our part.

While the Russian authorities were quick to suggest a Ukrainian connection, some commentators in the West did not rule out manipulation by the authorities to justify an even stronger commitment to the war in Ukraine and increased repression of the opposition at home; these analyses did not question the need for the President of the Federation - who had just been re-elected - to assert his authority and his position as guarantor of the country's security. Both of these arguments proved to be misguided.

In reality, Islamist terrorism was not and is not a new phenomenon for a country stretching from Europe to the Far East, and whose international commitments are bound to expose it to the complexity of contemporary conflicts. But the threat of terrorism from the Caucasus and Central Asia is of a different nature today. A real threat, it is also more diffuse and may have internal ramifications. Central Asia, often forgotten in the West, is in fact the scene of a New Great Game after the one between the Russian and British empires in the 19th century.

In addition to its soft power, Russia has maintained its positions in Central Asia, despite a decline since the end of the Soviet Union (NB: 40% Russians in Kazakhstan then, only around 20% ethnic Russians today). This area of influence has been encroached upon by China and its economic ambitions (cf. the New Silk Roads; Turkmenistan is its leading gas supplier). Western countries have a variable economic presence in the region, with the colossus that is Kazakhstan (NB: 5 times the size of France) taking precedence over the other Central Asian republics.

The latter are part of the Commonwealth of Independent States (CIS) and, with the exception of Turkmenistan, a neutral state, of a network of regional organisations; the Shanghai Cooperation Organisation (SCO) has set itself security objectives, including the fight against terrorism, extremism and separatism.

The question today is: New Great Game or cordon sanitaire? Faced with the terrorist threat (cf. recurring unrest in Kazakhstan's Caspian region, Koranic schools financed for a time from outside in Uzbekistan, ethnic rivalries and regional imbalances), a vast field of opportunities is also opening up, including for Europe as a still relatively marginal player (NB: France and Kazakhstan have had a strategic partnership since 2008). As a counterpoint to these economic rivalries, there is also scope for developing convergences in security, so as to avoid a 'second front' for all concerned.

The challenge of the Moscow attacks

It should be noted that the Soviet power - with the exception of Stalin, who deported minorities, including the Crimean Tatars - and then Russia, managed the Muslim question on their territory quite well, guaranteeing a moderate Islam (NB: the Great Mosque of Moscow, rebuilt in 2015). The wars in Chechnya and the sporadic violence in the Caucasus should not make us forget that Muslims are part of Russia's history, at the heart of it. Kazan, the capital of Tatarstan, is 800 km to the east of Moscow, founded after it, and the Tatars, with a population of 6 million, are the second largest people in Russia. Muslims are estimated to number between 25 and 30 million, or 17-20% of the total Russian population. It is true that recent economic immigration from Central Asia (NB: an estimated 1 million Tajiks) poses new challenges.
The fact that President Putin did not immediately refer to Daesh, but instead directed the accusations towards Ukrainian accomplices, was clearly in the service of his war against Kyiv. But it may also have been a question of preserving relations with the Muslim world, particularly the Arab world, and beyond that with the 'global South'.

The Moscow bombing represented a major challenge for the Russian authorities, in much the same way as the Prigozhin uprising in June 2023. The security apparatus showed its vulnerabilities and V. Putin will have to prove once again that he is capable of guaranteeing domestic stability, the source of his legitimacy. This will not be enough for him without a major project to reform and modernise the country. With this in mind, Russia will not be able to put up with the war in Ukraine for long. It will have to remember that it is also part of the northern hemisphere and that it faces the same challenges, be they climate, migration or nuclear proliferation. A kind of normalisation with the West is a necessity.

The bitterness felt in Moscow after 11 September

It is too often forgotten that Vladimir Putin was the first leader to express his solidarity with the United States and its President George Bush Jr after the attacks on the World Trade Center in New York and the Pentagon in Washington. This was not just rhetoric limited to feelings of compassion for the victims and a vague solidarity whose contours were never precisely defined. Russia immediately took action and offered the United States facilities to transfer troops and military equipment to Afghanistan, which had been the US administration's preferred target for its response to 11 September. Nor should we forget the role that Moscow played with certain Central Asian states, such as Tajikistan, where Russian border guards were stationed on the border with Afghanistan.

In a way, Russia behaved as if it had been a member of the Atlantic Alliance and had made use of Article 5 of its Charter (NB: for the first and only time in the history of the Alliance, the US allies complied with this commitment of solidarity defined by Article 5). This very special moment of rapprochement with the West did not last and Russia felt that it had not been 'rewarded' in return, for example in 2004 with the first wave of enlargement of NATO to include six countries that had formerly belonged to the USSR (NB: after Poland, Hungary and the Czech Republic in 1999), at the Alliance Summit in Bucharest in 2008 - where the question arose for Ukraine and Georgia - and under President Obama (2009-2017) with the Maidan 'revolution' in Kiev. After the Orange Revolution of 2004, *Euromaidan* or *Euro-revolution* were the names given to the demonstrations that followed the Ukrainian government's decision in 2013-2014 not to sign the association agreement with the European Union.

A look back at the Cold War: tensions and search for stability

While it is not a question of justifying anything, it is at least important to put events into perspective in order to understand the psychology and logic of the players. The current period is sometimes improperly described as a new Cold War, even though the system has lost the stability that, paradoxically, nuclear weapons - apart from the Cuban missile crisis - had guaranteed. The period when the blocs faced each other but did not clash directly actually allowed for cooperation.

In May 1981, between the two rounds of the presidential election in France, a leading French figure - who was no longer a member of the government at the time - came to East Berlin to work in the industrial sector and met the highest East German leaders. The Euromissiles crisis (i.e. the threat of deployment of American cruise missiles and Pershing II rockets in response to Soviet SS-20 medium-range missiles aimed at Europe) was then in full swing. Nevertheless, the message was one of cooperation and restoring balance to the international system. In a vision that could have been premonitory - and will perhaps one day be seen to be so - the personality in question developed the prospect of eventual convergence between the powers of the northern hemisphere, which were then opposed to each other in the face of the problems specific to the countries of the south, which they would have to deal with in a preponderant manner.

At the same time, the French ambassador received his Soviet counterpart Pyotr Abrassimov in the same GDR 'capital'. Pyotr Abrassimov, who had been stationed in Paris and had known General de Gaulle and President Pompidou, was a leading figure in Soviet diplomacy; in fact, he was the USSR's negotiator for the 1971 Quadripartite Agreement on Berlin. He had just returned from Moscow, where he had taken part in the last Congress of the CPSU and had held talks with Leonid Brezhnev; he spoke to the French ambassador about the forthcoming French presidential election and distanced himself clearly from a possible victory for the Left in France, including the PCF, in the name of the stability that Moscow said it was seeking above all else.

Objective convergences, if not elective affinities

These historical references illustrate what is known as state-to-state relations, which at the time could take precedence over any ideological considerations. Later, in the early 90s, the KGB, now the FSB, under the leadership of Evgeny Primakov, helped France to free French airmen taken prisoner by the Serbs during the fighting in the former Yugoslavia.

Russia has shown itself to be particularly prudent and responsible with regard to the development of Iran's nuclear programme. The efforts of the so-called P5+1 (i.e. the five permanent members of the UN Security Council plus Germany) culminated in the agreement of 14 July 2015, which was ultimately broken by Trump's United States, in a way that did great damage to the *in situ* controls of the International Atomic Energy Agency (IAEA).

Today, V. Putin's Russia is showing a rapprochement with North Korea, because of its need for equipment and munitions for its war in Ukraine and also for geopolitical reasons. It is not certain that Moscow has any real intention of transferring sensitive and, a fortiori, proliferating technologies to Pyongyang in return. Shouldn't the message to Washington be: we could do it, but please stop us agreeing to it, and let's resume a dialogue on the major issues on which world peace depends. Between the risks of Islamic terrorism and those of nuclear proliferation, the scope for cooperation, if not solidarity, is vast; these prospects require, in particular, an end to the high-intensity war on the European continent and the adaptation, if not the reconstruction, of an international system that takes account of the new power relationships in the world.

Is China in NATO's sights?

The 75th Anniversary Summit of the Atlantic Alliance was held in Washington from 9 to 11 July 2024. Paradoxically, despite this longevity and at a time when the Organisation has just enlarged to include two new members, Finland and Sweden, the commemoration is sometimes perceived as taking place at a time of uncertainty (see the prospect of the American elections in November; conditions for ending the war in Ukraine; relations with the 'global' South). International crises, including Ukraine and the Middle East, were naturally at the centre of attention, as the replacement of the Organisation's Secretary General, the Norwegian Jens Stoltenberg, by Mark Rutte, the former Prime Minister of the Netherlands, became official. But the Asian dimension of current geostrategic challenges must not be overlooked either, so it is worth pausing for a moment to consider how the Alliance and its members perceive this part of the world, i.e. the rise of China and the way in which we are adapting to it or, for some, attempting to oppose it.

Genesis of the Atlantic Alliance

The genesis of the Atlantic Alliance is well known, but a reminder sheds us of its identity at a time of possible transformation. It was the break with the USSR from 1947 onwards that led the West to look for a new alliance system, and the 1948 Berlin blockade, which lasted almost a year, can be seen as the beginning of the Cold War. The idea of a defensive pact, in the form of automatic assistance in the event of aggression - on unspecified terms - then emerged; it was translated into the famous Article 5 of the Charter. The then Secretary-General of the United Nations initially expressed some reservations about regional alliances, which could have developed to the detriment of collective security (NB: even though Article 52 of the UN Charter recognises the existence of regional agreements or organisations, Article 53 specifies that no *coercive action* shall be taken at the regional level without the authorisation of the Security Council).

On 4 April 1949, an Atlantic Pact limited by definition to a specific area was signed in Washington at the State Department (N.B.: the first departure from the 'Atlantic' nature of the Alliance - and the issue was debated at the time - came with the admission of Greece and Turkey in 1952). General Eisenhower was the first Supreme Commander in Europe. SHAPE (Superior Headquarter of Allied Powers in Europe) was established at Roquencourt, near Versailles.

In September of the same year, the first atomic explosion in the USSR was detected. But 1948 had already seen the extension of the Soviet zone of influence in Eastern Europe, while in the Far East the positions of the Chinese nationalists led by Chiang Kai-shek had deteriorated. The USSR immediately recognised the People's Republic of China as soon as it was proclaimed in September-October 1949; it was followed in early 1950 by India and Pakistan, and also by Great Britain - which is sometimes forgotten - which no doubt wished to preserve important commercial interests in China.

An extension of the geographical scope?

NATO member states, including France, intervened in Afghanistan, in support of the United States, after the attacks on the World Trade Center; this was the only time in the Alliance's history that Article 5 of its Charter was applied. This important development did not, however, imply a formal extension of the geographical scope of the Organisation's intervention.

Talking about NATO and China today also means talking about Japan. Japan should, however, be wary of the role that the United States might see for it, as part of its campaign - not to say crusade - against Beijing, which is going from strength to strength. The Atlantic Alliance summit in Washington was therefore worth watching in this respect, as it could confirm a worrying development in this direction, following the opening of a NATO office in Tokyo.

Irrespective of China's fairly recent rise to power, especially over the last thirty-five years or so in economic terms under the impetus of Deng Xiao-ping and after 1995 in military terms, we must never forget America's identity as a country bordering the Pacific. It was the attack on Pearl Harbor on 7 December 1941 that determined the United States' entry into the Second World War. The Vietnam War, following on from the Indochina War, was part of a vast project to set up an anti-Beijing system; the Vietnamese communists, led by Hô Chi Minh, whose relations with Moscow and Beijing were complex and underpinned by ardent nationalism, paid the price. Closer to home, the formation of the AUKUS alliance between Australia, the United Kingdom and the United States coincided with the loss of a very important contract to supply Canberra with French submarines, and appeared to be the emergence of a new bloc in the Indo-Pacific area to confront China.

Values and legitimacy

Unlike Germany, Japan has never really looked back at its contemporary history. Hiroshima may have made it possible to disguise, if not forget, the country's history by portraying it as a victim.

Rana Mitter, in *China's War with Japan, 1937-1945*, reminds us that in the spring of 1939, while Europe was still at peace despite many concerns, the Second World War was already raging several thousand kilometres to the east. We should also mention the conditions of the Japanese occupation throughout South-East Asia right up to the battle for Australia (see the famous Battle of the Coral Sea in May 1942). French Indochina was not spared either. Just remember the Japanese 'coup de force' of 9 March 1945.

Although Japan has become a peaceful and sometimes even pacifist country, it was also an imperialist power in Asia (cf. Edwin O. Reischauer, *Japan, Past and Present*) and this fact has sometimes remained a vivid reputation. It was at the Yalta and Potsdam conferences in 1945 that it was decided that Korea would be freed from the domination exercised by Japan since 1910. In the aftermath of the Second World War, from 1947 onwards, the United States distanced itself from the Chinese nationalists and focused its attention on establishing good relations with Japan. Japan's international status was forged at the San Francisco conference in 1951, immediately followed by the conclusion of a security treaty between Washington and Tokyo. It was envisaged that Japan would not have its own means of defence (NB: 'self-defence' forces instead of a real army), which would mean temporarily maintaining American bases, such as in Okinawa; Japan would gradually acquire a defence capability while avoiding any offensive weaponry (see art. 9 of its constitution, which was imposed on it by the United States: '*Japan forever renounces war as a sovereign right of the nation*').

The Japanese Self-Defence Forces (JSDF) are no longer limited to a simple domestic policing capacity. In fact, the country has increased its military budget as a percentage of GDP (NB: from 1% to 2%). With an annual budget of 50 billion dollars and around 200,000 men, Japan has significant conventional capacities, but they cannot be compared with those of China. However, it is important to bear in mind the very high technological level of its equipment. It should be noted that Japanese armed forces have been taking part in United Nations peacekeeping contingents for some thirty years (e.g. Cambodia in 1992, UNDOF in the Golan Heights from 1996 onwards; withdrawal from Southern Sudan in 2017). The tragically deceased Prime Minister Shinzō Abe helped to move the Japanese defence forces towards greater autonomy.

Can Thucydides' trap be avoided?

Graham Allison, author of the seminal book on the Cuban rocket crisis (*Essence of Decision*), described in a more recent book (*Destined for War*) the scenario that would lead to the current superpowers eventually colliding (NB: '*on a collision course for war*'), unless certain delicate and painful arrangements were made. It was this perspective that led him to define his 'Thucydides trap', now widely popularised, whose initial conception was based on an analysis of the Peloponnesian wars in ancient Greece: the emergence of Athens would have led Sparta to react with a conflict that had become inevitable in order to preserve its power. G. Allison lists a series of conflicts throughout history which were the result of a pre-emptive reaction to an emerging power despite an imbalance of power.

Seen from Washington, the Sino-American relationship has been approached with great continuity over the last few presidencies: B. Obama was the first to define the 'pivot' to Asia, thus favouring

China, both positively and negatively, above all other considerations; at a summit with President Xi Jinping in 2015, he nevertheless expressed the assurance that the two countries should be able to *'manage their differences'*, while his counterpart did not rule out *'the risk of miscalculations'*. D. Trump, for his part, used more antagonistic language, although this did not affect trade, and major American groups continued to expand their presence in China (e.g. Tesla, Apple). President Biden has endeavoured to maintain a firm stance towards China, which remains a priority; William Burns, former ambassador and current director of the CIA, confirmed this publicly at the very heart of the war in Ukraine. However, Sino-American contacts at the highest level have never broken down (e.g. visits to China by Secretary of State A. Blinken and Treasury Secretary Janet Yellen).

Collateral victims and boomerang effect

Does Japan, whose trade with China in particular is profitable, have an interest in pandering to the United States' obsessive preoccupation with Beijing? But will it have a free choice, given that Washington has never ceased to 'twist the arm' of the vanquished of the Second World War, be it Japan, Germany or Italy? Italy, for example, has a public opinion that is clearly pro-Russian by tradition and by interest, in particular because of its energy dependence, but it is clear that Mrs Giorgia Meloni does not deviate from a rather Atlanticist line, for example with regard to Kyiv. In fact, she reconciles all these demands with skill. Japan seems to be on its own and has no prospect of 'strategic autonomy' which, even for Europe, will not consist of a rose-lined path.

The warning also applies to Europe. Is it not already 'under influence', as Brussels' agreeable language on China attests (see *'a partner, a competitor and a systemic rival'*)? Contrary to what is regularly announced in the run-up to the American presidential elections in November, the United States has no a priori interest in withdrawing from NATO. Before the war in Ukraine, the French President rightly observed that NATO was *'brain dead'*. Moreover, the Alliance is not engaged as such in this latest conflict. After the Cold War, NATO was converted into a privileged instrument in the service of

American policy in Europe. Why then should D. Trump or any other presidential candidate do without it?

More reassuringly, the economic interdependence of the world's economies could play a stabilising role. This can be seen in the war in Ukraine, where China, which is clearly leaning towards Russia for geopolitical reasons, cannot afford to jeopardise its trade with the West (NB: United States, European Union), which is ten times greater than its trade with Russia, the latter having reached record figures in 2023 (NB: 240 billion dollars).

Despite trade controls on certain high-tech products (e.g. microprocessors) and the gradual withdrawal of certain US companies from the Chinese market (e.g. Apple relocating to India or Vietnam), the figures are still staggering, and only a partial list is available: China holds at least $860 billion of US public debt (i.e. 12%); the volume of Sino-American trade reached around $700 billion in 2022; the United States remains China's main destination for foreign investment. Japan and Australia, whose trade with China has just reached unprecedented levels, would also have a lot to lose from a clash of blocs in the Indo-Pacific.

For Graham Allison, Thucydides' trap is not fatalism, and need not lead to pessimism. China is clearly in the firing line, but it is to be hoped that it is also in the firing line for the right reasons.

A whiff of the Cold War

The new world sometimes still smacks of the Cold War. In August 2024, for example, the United States and Russia exchanged prisoners, generally referred to as 'spies' by both sides - even if they do not, of course, refer to their own nationals in this way. The best-known American prisoner was Evan Gershkovitch, a *Wall Street Journal* journalist who was convicted of espionage by a Russian court after a trial behind closed doors; on the Russian side, Vadim Krasikov, a former FSB officer convicted of murdering a Chechen in Germany, was the case in which V. Putin seemed to be most directly interested.

Putin. The scale of the exchange, involving the release of 24 people, was unprecedented in the post-Cold War period. It should be noted that this settlement followed that of December 2022, which enabled Brittney Griner, an American basketball star, to be exchanged for Viktor Bout, a Russian businessman with close ties to political power, specialising in the arms trade.

The memory of Glienicke's Bridge of Spies

This development could not have been expected, as this type of affair is generally handled with the utmost discretion, sometimes despite pressure from public opinion in the West. Negotiations had been going on for many months and seem to have accelerated towards the end of June, when a meeting took place in an unspecified capital in the Middle East between the services of the two countries. The outcome was a spectacular contrast to the 1962 exchange on the Glienicke bridge, near Potsdam in the Berlin region, between U2 pilot Gary Powers and Rudolf Abel, the Soviet agent imprisoned in the United States. Although S. Spielberg's films have since immortalised the scene, it was not publicised in the media and footage of the exchange was not broadcast in real time. What's more, the context is not comparable: in 1962, the people exchanged were valuable in their own right; Gary Powers had carried out an operation using a spy plane that the Soviets might have feared had transmitted highly sensitive information using technology that they themselves did not possess; Russia might also have feared, almost paranoid, that agent Abel, who had infiltrated the United States, might end up delivering valuable data on the political system in Moscow.

The negotiations therefore focused mainly on the individuals involved and aspects linked to the strict sphere of intelligence. This does not seem to be the case today, as Washington does not accept that the journalist, as was the case with the basketball champion, has any connection with the world where the shadow war is being waged on an ongoing basis.

Domestic and foreign policy dimensions

The affair therefore went beyond the ultimately happy fate of the people who were freed. Paradoxically - but this was necessary by definition if there was to be a denouement - the Russian and American presidents can be said to have found a comparable interest in it on their domestic stage, and the denouement received a great deal of media coverage on both sides. J. Biden went in person in the middle of the night, accompanied by K. Harris, to a military base to welcome the guests. V. Putin did the same in Moscow, with Vnukovo 1 airport reserved for officials. But that's not all. The most important aspect was undoubtedly the international dimension of the event, partly reflected in the fact that, on the Russian side, eight nationals were imprisoned in NATO countries and that several states were involved in the negotiations, namely - in addition to the two main protagonists, of course - Belarus, Poland, Norway, Germany, Slovenia and Turkey.

The return of the former American prisoners was a success for President Biden. After withdrawing his candidacy for a new presidential term, he had indicated that he would devote his final months in the White House mainly to international affairs. This result was likely to enable him to present a more positive final assessment of a foreign policy tarnished, from the first months of his presidency in August 2021, by the chaotic withdrawal from Afghanistan. However, the war in Ukraine and, above all, the situation in the Near and Middle East remain factors of uncertainty that are still likely to tip the balance in favour or not of the outgoing Democratic administration.

President Putin also ensured that the return of his nationals was widely publicised in the media. He welcomed them himself on the airport tarmac, where a red carpet was rolled out and a guard of honour deployed. Although the general opinion in the West is that there is no public opinion in Russia, this is not entirely true, even if the channels of popular expression are strictly controlled. After the revolt of E. Prigozhin's revolt, during which the power of the Kremlin trembled, if not wavered, it was felt at the time that the Russian president could only ensure his political longevity on three conditions: re-establish the authority of the state, in particular by bringing the militias to heel; regain his role as arbiter between factions and different powers - contrary to the exclusive vision of the verticality of power; once again take on the role of reformer with a programme of modernisation - in the tradition of Peter the Great - and social progress. The return to Russian soil of those whom V. Putin considered to be *'patriots who have fulfilled their military duty and faithfully served their country'* enabled the Head of State - in addition to his renewed consideration for "structures of strength' - to emphasise his attention to individuals within a society marked, more than is often thought, by the war in Ukraine.

Longer-term strategic choices

But the key issue in this prisoner exchange was strategic. What were the respective motivations of the two main powers involved? Unlike domestic motivations, which may show some convergence (e.g. the successful completion of J. Biden's term of office; the rebuilding of V. Putin's popularity), the strategic prism offers a more fractured vision.

From Moscow's point of view, the Russian government was able to give the impression that it was betting on, if not choosing, a Democratic victory in November; it would have been a question of 'investing' in Kamala Harris' candidacy before 'prices' soared, and the timing was quite right. If Russia had then considered that Trump had a serious chance of winning, the possible prisoner exchange could have been postponed until the autumn at the earliest, or even January (NB: it should be remembered that the Iranians did not free the hostages from the US embassy in Tehran until the day after Reagan's election, which had a negative impact on the end of Carter's campaign). Since then, however, things have evolved in line with the uncertainties of the November presidential elections in the United States.

In any case, there will be a price to pay in Washington, and we can think in particular of the conditions for ending the war in Ukraine. D. Trump indulged in ranting and raving, pledging that he would settle the war in Ukraine in 24 hours. Although Russia is no longer the superpower that the Soviet Union once was, Moscow and Washington continue to work together on issues that carry great weight, starting with nuclear arms control. And there is no doubt a realisation in Washington that Russia could play a useful role in the Middle East, which has become a highly volatile area, and even in dealing with proliferation in North Korea. From this point of view, since the Soviet era, Moscow has always been wary of democrats (see the diplomacy of values and the defence of human rights and democracy in general); but Kamala Harris can also be seen as rational and predictable, while the Republican Party now appears to be just as ideological - even messianic - as it is committed to *Realpolitik.*

The Biden administration's Ukrainian policy has remained ambiguous from start to finish. The watchword in the months leading up to the election was the status quo. The debate on the supply and authorisation of long-range Western missiles for use on Russian territory fizzled out despite some spectacular announcements, including in Kiev on the occasion of a joint visit by A. Blinken and his British counterpart. In the Near and Middle East, the United States, especially since 7 October 2023, does not give the impression that it is in control of the situation, or even of its ally Israel. This general line between past interventionism, for example that of the neo-conservatives, and an isolationism that the state of the world probably does not allow, will have to be clarified.

13

An American in Paris

Kamala Harris' moment?

The last televised debate between Biden and Trump - improperly described as 'presidential', since neither of the two protagonists had then been officially endorsed by their respective party conventions - turned into a nightmare for the incumbent President, even though he had asked for it. In fact, the question of choosing the champion to fight the war did indeed arise, particularly in the Democratic camp, after the calamitous performance of the incumbent President in front of more than 70 million American television viewers and around thirty million more on the Internet in the United States alone.

The names of new Democratic presidential candidates were then circulated on a short list drawn up by the media, including those of the Vice-President and several governors, including those of California and Michigan. Even before the disastrous debate, a rumour had been circulating that the Democratic Convention might have to make a drastic decision, with a view to the November referendum, by finally choosing a candidate other than J. Biden.

The Democratic candidacy for the presidency of the United States came down to the wire over a weekend in the Delaware state residence where J. Biden was recluse to treat a Covid. Initially, there were conflicting signals: under growing pressure from Democratic figures such as Mrs Pelosi and B. Obama, the impression had been gathered that the incumbent President might abandon his candidacy; then, a J. Biden, on the contrary, despite the withdrawal of major donors, stated his intention to resume the campaign (NB: until then, the campaign had been run almost single-handedly and very loyally by K. Harris). President Biden, whom many Democrats felt was no longer fit to govern, finally announced on 21 July 2024 that he was withdrawing his candidacy.

This immediately raised many questions in the Democratic camp: could Kamala Harris now be the real alternative? Despite the relatively low level of popularity that she was criticised for in her own camp, and even a firmness that was seen as harsh, she quickly emerged as the most natural option, particularly given the short time available to make a radical decision. D. Trump's campaign team immediately set to work on this hypothesis after the Republican Convention in Milwaukee.

The Kamala revelation

A bet was made on K. Harris, but it was undoubtedly the last chance for the Democrats to win in November. In this hypothesis, another crucial question had arisen: by giving up the candidacy, would President Biden at the same time resign as Chief Executive? In any event, this would not necessarily have affected the choice of delegates who were to vote at the Democratic Convention scheduled to take place in Chicago from 19 to 22 August. President Biden ultimately 'recommended' Kamala Harris, a course of action that was not legally binding on them but which an overwhelming majority of them, having rallied behind the Vice-President in record time, would logically follow. Even without J. Biden's resignation, K. Harris did not need the whole of the time, which was in any case very limited until November, to show that she was presidential material. An excellent number two does not necessarily become a good number one, but the costume of the vice-presidency - by definition self-effacing - is often a handicap that the candidate obviously quickly overcame.

In the end, the scenario proved ideal for the Democrats, giving K. Harris - who closed the gap between J. Biden and D. Trump in the polls in record time - a chance of leading a real contest if not winning. One of Kamala Harris's assets is that she embodies the United States of today and tomorrow (multi-ethnic and Pacific-oriented). It is worth remembering that in the 1988 election, G. Bush Sr, the outgoing Vice-President under R. Reagan, was 17 points behind his rival Dukakis in July, and he eventually won.

A tale of reason, love and dreams

Kamala Harris is nothing like the wealthy heiress in Vincente Minnelli's 1951 film *An American in Paris*, set to music by Gershwin and starring the unforgettable Gene Kelly and Leslie Caron. In the end, the heiress is not the central character in the happy ending between these two stars.

In the end, it's good for her that she can't be equated with someone who embodies impossible love. The question for her from then on was her personal relationship with America and its people. A presidential election is in fact a double story, her own and that of those whose votes she was likely to seek. These two journeys come together in a project, which can also be a dream and is not just a matter of rationality. For this reason, J. Kennedy, R. Reagan and even B. Obama will have left their mark on contemporary history and the collective memory of the United States, even more so than H. Truman, despite the atomic bomb, L. Johnson, despite the height of his commitment to Vietnam, and G. Bush Jr. Bush Jr, despite 9/11, Afghanistan and Iraq.

Skills and working methods

Kamala Harris has devoted herself to the human sciences, but her working method is inherited from her mother, who was a top-level scientist. Her obsession was the search for innovation that can benefit the public and political spheres. With this in mind, the right approach, in her view, is first to formulate hypotheses, to carry out more in-depth research and, above all, to carry out tests to verify, through experimentation, pre-established theoretical schemes. The result must be a plan of action - always oriented towards the world of reality - because in politics there is no question of limiting oneself to rhetoric and not proposing solutions. That's why her favourite slogan was always '*Go to the scene*'. This is what she has done throughout her career, including in the judiciary, witnessing the ravages of pollution in her home state of California, working alongside the contingent in Iraq and visiting Syrian refugee camps in Jordan. Lastly, according to the Vice-President, 'public capital' cannot be designed on the basis of the interest it might earn, but must be spent entirely for the benefit of the people.

The popularity test

Did this general approach to problems enable her to overcome the 'protocol fatality' that generally afflicts the Vice-Presidents of the United States, however dynamic they may be, making them by definition self-effacing personalities ? Thomas Jefferson, the third President of the United States in the early years of the nineteenth century, after assuming the Vice-Presidency, was an exception; he had already been the principal author of the famous *Declaration of Independence* in 1776.

But there is a long list of vice-presidents who have been forgotten by history, or whose mark came after or outside the office in question: who remembers Spiro Agnew, elected with Nixon in 1968, if not the conditions of his departure for tax evasion and corruption? Who remembers Walter Mondale - who embodied the industrial, progressive and industrialised north of the Great Lakes with the southerner J. Carter - even though he was the first 'modern' vice-president, participating in the development of foreign policy and more than symbolically obtaining an office in the White House, but who failed badly in the presidential race against R. Reagan in 1984 with, for the first time, a co-lisor at his side ? Even George Bush Sr, whose career never ceases to impress us (ambassador to the UN in 1971, head of the US representation in People's China from 1974 to 1975, director of the CIA in 1976), despite being Reagan's vice-president for eight years, has only left us with vivid memories of his presidency, in particular the Gulf War in 1991 after the invasion of Kuwait. Closer to home, Mike Pence only really came to prominence because of the circumstances of the assault on the Capitol on 6 January 2021, when he dissociated himself from D. Trump.

Moreover, the American public's perception of K. Harris' actions is ambiguous. Her past as California's District Attorney gave her a reputation for toughness, particularly when it came to cracking down on crime; indeed, she ended up becoming the target of the *Black Lives Matter* movement. But she was also part of the classic Democratic tradition of American progressivism. She wanted more gun control, a taboo subject if ever there was one; she was committed to raising awareness of climate change; she opposed the ban on same-sex marriage and defended the right to abortion during the debate at national level, which was finally settled by the Supreme Court, which referred legislation back to the federal states. Paradoxically, the visibility afforded by all these positions - which lifted her out of the relative anonymity of the Vice-Presidency - did not necessarily work in her favour in terms of popularity.

The responsibilities of America and the world

In a cyclical process throughout its history, Washington has oscillated between isolationism and involvement in the world. In recent years, D. Trump has embodied the nostalgia for a white, prosperous, dominant America that is rather focused - if not inward-looking - on its own interests, China excepted. President Biden is also part of an evolution that B. Obama embodied with his concept of the 'pivot to Asia', but this orientation was tinged, if not corrected, by a traditional internationalist ideology among the Democrats.

K. Harris can be compared, in certain respects, to B. Obama (born in Hawaii and having lived in Indonesia). Both can be described as 'alchemists of the new world'. In her early youth, Kamala accompanied her mother to her research laboratory, where she handled and cleaned cruets.

The story of Kamala Harris is a beautiful American story. Does it still conform to one of those success stories, such as we like them, that the United States likes to stage? The rest of the world would like to think so, in these troubled times, when the two main protagonists of the country's political debate seemed outdated and questionable in so many ways. Whether or not we like the dominant power in the Western world, it is still indispensable in dealing with world affairs, including our own interests. But our needs have their limits and our judgement can be distorted by our own prism.

Throughout her career, Kamala Harris has projected an image of energy, optimism and commitment to the values we love. Kamala Harris naturally came to Paris, notably for the 4th edition of the Paris Peace Forum, but she lived in Montreal with her mother, where she attended French primary school.

Because of her Californian origins and long career, she is seen as by definition Asia-Pacific-oriented. In this respect, she embodies the United States as it has become, at the cutting edge of modernity, but also because of her upbringing in the fine traditions that have fuelled America's appeal. *'Paris is like love, art and faith'*, says an actor in the film *An American in Paris*. It would be so welcome if Kamala Harris could remind us of this, in addition to her ambition for excellence. She collected first prizes: after being the first woman Attorney General of California (elected in 2010 and re-elected in 2014), US Senator (NB: she was sworn in by Vice-President J. Biden at the time), she became the first woman Vice-President, and by the same token the first African-American and Afro-Asian.

Hadn't the path to the presidency been mapped out for her a long time ago? B. Obama was in a sense 'caught in a vice grip' between G. Bush Jr and D. Trump; K. Harris, all things considered, finds herself in a comparable situation, under the combined pressure of a legacy of traditional American politics - embodied by a J. Biden, who for decades spent most of his career in the confines of Congress - and the demands, impulses and appeal of a vast new world.

The man/woman of his/her time

The age of the captain is not the only criterion for judging the fit between a personality and its time. The main issue is the embodiment of aspirations, responses and decisions in return, major projects developed in response to profound changes and developments that are not always perceptible without hindsight. Joe Biden was, in his own way, a young president. He even gave the impression that, in his new role as supreme head of the Executive, he had completed the 'Hundred Days', a period that is something of a yardstick in political history. The *'flight of the eagle'* had come to a halt at Waterloo, while Joe Biden completed the first phase of his journey at a breakneck pace after a rather hesitant start.

The new President of the United States was thus, in the first months of 2021, a beginner taking his first steps; you never know whether a loyal and even 'brilliant second-in-command' will ever become a real number one. This path and this status correspond, in all proportion, to the situation in which Kamala Harris finds herself; the questions about her are even greater because the situation is unprecedented since the resignation of President Lyndon Johnson in 1968, due to the developments and impasses encountered in the conduct of the Vietnam War.

Joe Biden gets off to a flying start

It was therefore time for an initial assessment of Joe Biden's presidency, to which Vice-President K. Harris immediately paid tribute with a vibrant defence and illustration. A presidency that is now clearly out of breath should not erase Joe Biden's brilliant start, particularly in the wake of the Covid pandemic and its effects on the American economy even before the end of D. Trump's term of office. On the domestic front, particularly as regards the economy, Joe Biden quickly appeared bold with a massive programme of Keynesian-style demand-led stimulus, in other words a break with all the theories and practices since the Reagan era, which even led to him being described as revolutionary.

This was reflected in its early orientations: In addition to the $1.9 trillion *American Rescue Act*, which was specifically aimed at small businesses and individuals who had suffered from the Covid disaster - comparable in terms of the sums involved to the space programme of the 1960s in response to the launch of Sputnik in 1957 or, at least in spirit, to the New Deal of the 1930s - there was the *American Jobs Plan* ($2.3 trillion) for infrastructure renewal and the *American Families Plan* ($1.8 trillion) aimed at reducing social inequalities and the racial divide; Among other things, it involved modernising schools and introducing maternity leave at federal level.

This last measure, which seemed self-evident in the light of current social policies in Europe, marked a radical change and constituted a veritable revolution. However, it was not enough for Joe Biden to have set out such ambitions; he also had to reckon with Republican opposition, initially in the form of *filibustering* in Congress. In addition to a brief but intense vaccination campaign against Covid - which produced results - there was an undeniable recovery, illustrated by annualised GDP growth in the first quarter of 2021 of 6.4% and 1.6% compared to the same period the previous year.

A mixed international record

Following in President Obama's footsteps, it is not hard to imagine that J. Biden would not have wanted to comply with the *'Washington handbook'* either, a sort of unwritten doctrine requiring every American president to resort to military means. In 2013, his predecessor decided not to sanction the use of chemical weapons in Syria, thereby ruling out the risk of a new military adventure, even though he had been elected to put an end to the interventions in Iraq and Afghanistan.

The final withdrawal from Afghanistan was supposed to be an illustration of this policy. After twenty years of presence and 2,300 American casualties in the conflict, it had been negotiated by the Trump administration for 1 May 2021 and set for 11 September of the same year to signify by this date that a loop had been closed and also to leave open the possibility of a more orderly withdrawal including the allies according to the principle: *'In together, Out together'*. Unfortunately, things did not turn out as planned and the departure from Kabul, which was accompanied by the Taliban's seizure of power on 15 August, was totally chaotic and resembled a parody of the Capitol. This debacle, which was not unlike the fall of Saigon in April 1975, was bound to have an impact on the management of the war in Ukraine, a country which could not conceivably win against Russia but could not lose either.

But, generally speaking, Joe Biden's early foreign policy attitudes were classic in the Democratic tradition. He was helped in his task by a highly experienced foreign policy Dream Team , the like of which perhaps no administration had ever known, with John Kerry, Antony Blinken, William Burns, not forgetting Robert Malley for the Near and Middle East - already present at Bill Clinton's side - and of course Vice President Kamala Harris, whose position included important tasks, however discreet, of foreign representation.

This classicism, which had been undermined long before Donald Trump by the Reagan administration, led to a return to multilateral diplomacy. An executive order immediately put an end to the procedure for leaving the WHO, and the decision was taken to rejoin the Paris climate agreement. The new President and his team showed a talent for forming 'thematic coalitions' of variable geometry.

Classicism could not mean a return to the balmy days of 'duopoly' dating from the Soviet era, but it could mean preserving, as a first step, a substantial and constructive dialogue between the United States and Russia on politico-military matters, which was in fact in Washington's interest. Joe Biden therefore decided to extend for five years the *New Start* Treaty, which remains the only one on strategic weapons between the two countries. The war in Ukraine has clearly profoundly disrupted this process.

The downside of classicism has also been the difficulty in innovating, in the face of China, for example, after Obama's pivot towards Asia and Trump's tough trade policy. This is perhaps why J. Biden sometimes delegated to his Secretary of State Antony Blinken and to the Director of the CIA, the diplomat William Burns. He has also relied, especially in his first steps, on his Democratic DNA, which incorporates 'values diplomacy', clearly dissociating himself from his Republican predecessor. The Near and Middle East, especially after 7 October 2023 and the reaction against Gaza, posed an unprecedented difficulty in terms of both intangible solidarity with Israel and the radical left of the Democratic Party, which had clearly evolved on the

Palestinian question. This Cornelian situation may explain a certain American restraint with regard to Iran, the regional organiser.

The main thrust of the presidential campaign

It is difficult to pinpoint the contours of D. Trump's foreign policy programme. Is he in a better position than anyone else to put an end to the war in Ukraine, as he claims? Does he really want to distance himself from NATO, the essential instrument of America's presence in Europe, if not its control and domination? What are his real intentions with regard to China, with which American *big business* intends to maintain substantial trade? Is the question of isolationism or interventionism not an artificial debate in today's world? The Republican candidate's lack of clear guidelines is in fact largely due to an approach to international relations that is totally devoid of ideology. This is undoubtedly Trump's true compass. Threatening Taiwan, as he did recently, with a reduction in security assurances if the island did not contribute more to the defence effort, is merely an echo of the warning addressed during his presidency to the member states of NATO, guilty in his eyes of insufficient budgetary commitments for their protection and that of the Alliance.

But, as has traditionally been the case in the United States - even at the height of the Vietnam War - it will inevitably be domestic issues that take centre stage in the current presidential election campaign. Questions of purchasing power, inflation, security and immigration are not just for European voters.

Faced with Trump's unbridled economic liberalism, will Kamala Harris preserve the new line of a Democratic Party - moving away from the market-friendly management of the Clinton and Obama years - insisting, under the pressure of contemporary constraints, on a greater role for the State? Will the post-liberal orientation of US economic policy be confirmed at the ballot box? Will there be a *Bidenomics* without Biden?

Faced with the paradox of a billionaire who knows how to make himself heard by blue-collar workers, will Kamala Harris have succeeded in establishing a link with the world of industrial and agricultural workers? Even if the Democratic administration's responsibility for the return of inflation is also due to external factors, will the candidate have acquired sufficient credibility on this subject, as well as to deal with the issues of housing costs, healthcare and education? Whatever the case, she will absolutely have to correct the image she has sometimes been saddled with - whether well-founded or not - of a *'brilliant Californian adored by Wall Street'*.

Back to the past and new horizons

Does Trump's MAGA (NB: *Make America Great Again*) slogan really sum up a vision for the future, or is it a dream inspired by declassed sections of the population nostalgic for a bygone era? Kamala Harris was quick to launch her first attacks on her rival's backward-looking vision.

Can evangelical America be central in a post-modern world? Is the *Swing State* of Ohio, whose Governor has just been nominated by Trump to be on the Republican *ticket,* the engine of innovation and growth in the United States, or is it rather the West Coast, where Kamala Harris is the embodiment of an 'elite' that is in the process of replacing the WASPs of the East Coast? The candidate will inevitably be strongly attacked on immigration issues, but her origins are only an apparent weakness, because America has become multicultural through a process that is ultimately as old as its origins. More than 30 years ago, the United States was already welcoming 500,000 illegal immigrants a year, most of them Hispanic. Was Trump's wall a panacea? Is there any particular Democratic culpability? America is undoubtedly changing profoundly: is the answer refusal, violence or regulation and better integration of external contributions, America's salt?

The historian Jon Meacham, who is said to have been an influential speechwriter for Joe Biden, especially at the beginning of his term in office, questioned the meaning of the presidential office by quoting President Lyndon Johnson in the aftermath of the assassination of John F. Kennedy. The question *'what the hell is the presidency for?'* was in fact an expression of determination to achieve great things, in this case - a new conversion for him - to complete the *Civil Rights Act* that Kennedy had initiated. This sudden change, under the shock of tragedy, had been matched in American history by Lincoln's conversion in a single year between 1861 and 1862 to a determination to abolish slavery.

Joe Biden was once presented in the guise of Roosevelt and his policy of major works. When it came to a policy of massive investment, the discreet and pragmatic Senator from Delaware - who had already learned a lot from the 2007-2008 crisis when he was in charge of Obama's Recovery Plan - had the audacity of his Hundred Days. Will they remain a benchmark for a new century? '*To be a man of one's country, one must be a man of one's time*', said Chateaubriand. This inescapable principle will apply to the contenders for the supreme office and will define the conditions of their failure or success, even beyond 6 November.

The verdict of the people and the world

The virtual election

The great show of the American election, which swallowed up billions of dollars while breaking records, ended up giving people hangovers before the electoral consultation had even been truly completed.

Faced with a reality TV artist who played his role as former and future president (see '*Kamala you are fired, get out*'), a reputed swindler who has been convicted by the courts and whose greatest claim to fame is having supported a 'putsch' against the very state he was supposed to be defending, we saw and heard a candidate without much charisma, having difficulty killing the father - or rather the grandfather, the outgoing President - and therefore barely sketching out the contours of a future policy beyond a few slogans that inflamed the crowd of supporters (see '*We will not go back...,when we fight, we'll win*').

These excesses and at the same time this staggering emptiness were inflicted on the world, condemned to contemplate a spectacle supposed to be that of the new Athenian democracy. There was little or no mention of the world: the Republican candidate, who prides himself on resolving conflicts in 24 hours, was no less ambiguous than the foreign policy of a Democratic administration that began with the abandonment of Afghanistan and ended with impotence in the Near and Middle East and neglect of Ukraine. But what would the vigorous septuagenarian do tomorrow in the face of China, which only yesterday he was condemning to the flames, when he has now included among his supporters the richest man in the world, who is doing a profitable business there?

As for the media, they happily participated in the excesses of the show. Hordes of correspondents followed Barnum circus from one place to another without giving us the slightest information about local realities; in fact, they had no idea because they had not worked on their subject and their aim was above all to appear on the screen by providing a stereotyped image. We are in the age of virtual information, just as we are in the age of virtual democracy. Autocracies have a bright future ahead of them.

D. Trump's total victory (see large lead in votes nationwide and in the number of grand electors; conquest of all the 'swing states'; majority in the Senate and the House of Representatives; largest number of votes ever obtained by a Republican candidate in the history of the United States) and the Ukrainian impasse, programmed in reality from the outset, are two concomitant events but not directly linked. The human and material destruction of Ukraine, its lack of prospects, are more the result of the hypocritical, ambiguous and ultimately irresponsible messianism of the Biden administration and the West in general.

On television, the Trump tsunami has caused utter disarray on most channels. CNN, a quasi-democratic party mouthpiece and back office, deserves our deepest sympathy; it had a gloomy election night, with star presenters whose voices were strangled by emotion if not humiliation. It was a veritable wake when the people had spoken.

The bleak outlook for Ukraine could have been avoided a long time ago. It is not Trump who is responsible for it; he is no doubt thinking today of a 'freeze frame' for the war: freeze the positions, stop the destruction and the ruin - which in the end, apart from Kiev, concerns Europe (NB: isn't that Chancellor Scholz ?) rather than the United States - in the absence of an improbable negotiation, which Moscow has no need of, as it has already shown in Georgia and Transnistria.

However, not all illusions have yet been dispelled. On television, we still hear talk of Ukraine having been a nuclear power (NB: although Moscow has always controlled this armament) and even that it could become one again. If the aim is to make Western supporters feel guilty, is this also the 'plan for victory' over a nuclear superpower? Not to mention the insane, and still persistent, dream of NATO membership.

In the age of 'Trumpian' realism, Kiev will have to come to terms with its history and geography, which make it - if the word hurts - a 'buffer' zone between East and West. Such a situation, well exploited, is not without its advantages, particularly in economic terms. For a long time, Ukraine benefited from Russian gas at five times the world price.

In France, the commemoration of 11 November has become that of all wars, which are not necessarily victories. Naturally, we must remember the victims of all conflicts. But we must also ask ourselves about our present responsibilities. It will be time for a Requiem if we are to avoid yet another cruel Oration.

A funeral oration in the media, a requiem for Kyiv

D. Trump's total victory (see large lead in votes nationwide and in the number of electors; conquest of all the swing states; majority in the Senate and the House of Representatives; largest number of votes ever obtained by a Republican candidate in the history of the United States) and the Ukrainian impasse, which was in fact planned from the outset, are two concomitant events that are not directly linked. The human and material destruction of Ukraine, its lack of prospects, are more the result of the hypocritical, ambiguous and ultimately irresponsible messianism of the Biden administration and the West in general.

On television, the Trump tsunami has caused utter disarray on most channels. CNN, a quasi-democratic party mouthpiece, deserves our deepest sympathy; it had a gloomy election night, with star presenters whose voices were choked with emotion if not humiliation. It was a veritable wake when the people had spoken.

The sad state of affairs in Ukraine could have been avoided a long time ago. It is not Trump who is responsible for it; he probably has in mind today a 'freeze frame' of the war: we freeze the positions, we stop the destruction and the ruin - which ultimately concerns, apart from Kyiv, Europe (NB: isn't that Chancellor Scholz?) rather than the United States -, in the absence of an improbable negotiation which Moscow has no need of, as it has already shown in Georgia or Transnistria.

However, not all illusions have yet been dispelled. On television, we still hear talk of Ukraine having been a nuclear power (NB: although Moscow has always controlled this armament) and even that it could become one again. If the aim is to make Western supporters feel guilty, is this also the 'plan for victory' over a nuclear superpower? Not to mention the insane dream, which still persists, of joining NATO.

In the age of Trumpian realism, Kyiv will have to come to terms with its history and geography, which make it - even if the word hurts - a 'buffer' zone between East and West. Such a situation, when properly exploited, is not without its advantages, particularly in economic terms. For a long time, Ukraine benefited from Russian gas at five times the world price.
In France, the commemoration of 11 November has become the commemoration of all wars, which are not necessarily victories. Naturally, we must remember the victims of all conflicts. But we

must also ask ourselves about our present responsibilities. It will be time for a Requiem if we are to avoid an even crueller Oration.

Populism and the people

It is not a question of drawing definitive conclusions from D. Trump's victory, and it would be risky to do so in the heat of the moment. Could it be the victory of populism?

Kamala Harris, a late coming, has not managed to detach herself from the Biden presidency, and she has undoubtedly run out of steam herself, as her last rally in Philadelphia showed. It is a serious mistake to be absent from the outcome and to abandon the bluster of the party in the middle of the campaign, reflecting at the very least a lack of consideration for the people, reminiscent of the *'deplorables'* described by H. Clinton or more recently the *'rubbish'* stigmatised by J. Biden.

During the latter part of his term in office, Biden inflicted the spectacle of his own degradation, which deserved only commiseration from a human point of view but was unacceptable coming from a President. His term of office began in 2021 with the cowardly and chaotic abandonment of Afghanistan - reviving the syndrome of the fall of Saigon - and the barbarity of its people; it finally ended in his absence on the deserted campus of Howard University, which resembled a wasteland swept by an ill wind.

The delegation accompanying the President of the French Republic to meet Mr Trump when he was President was sometimes surprised by his lack of attention and comments that were considered to be disjointed. But did this lack of interest not also serve to show his interlocutor his rightful place in the concert of nations? The status of 'cayman of the swamp' is now reserved - and this is likely to increase without a reaction from Europe - only for non-European powers, in particular China.
If there has been a victory for populism, wouldn't it be better to talk about populism in its various forms - non-interventionism, protectionism, sovereignism, even nationalism - from one region of

the world to another? From the American Middle West to Prime Minister Modi's Hindu India, from Russia's return to an imperial project based on Orthodoxy to parts of Europe contesting its federalist drift, beyond the control of nations and peoples? In the end, the common denominator of these upheavals seems to be the quest for or preservation of an identity. And that identity is the people; it comes from them and their history, and is in turn vital to them. This could be the message from an American in Paris.

When analysing populism, we often talk about mimicry or sudden influence. For example, the sovereigntist Nigel Farage and Boris Johnson in the United Kingdom are said to have had links with Donald Trump; the Brexit is said to be a kind of matrix for a possible Frexit; populism is said to have been exported to the Americas, as far afield as Brazil and Argentina; the victory of Giorgia Meloni and Fratelli d'Italia across the Alps may have foreshadowed electoral successes of Marine Le Pen and the Rassemblement National in France - even though the two parties have so far kept their distance from each other; Victor Orban is said to be close to Russia because of its national approach to problems.

In reality, we need both to respect national specificities, which populists pride themselves on (see the 'Make America Great Again' or MAGA of the Republican current in favour of Trump), and to look for root causes that may be common to different large groups or converge.

The New International Order, celebrated by President George Bush Sr in the early 1990s, was in reality a unipolar world - in the process of coming to an end - dominated by the United States; it gave political expression to the globalisation already underway, under the banner of a liberalism conceived as humanity's unsurpassable horizon (see Fukuyama, The End of History). The idea that the market would regulate the world and replace inter-state relations has in fact led to the deregulation of the international system and a process of levelling out societies, particularly under the influence of GAFA. The phenomenon of massive and uncontrolled migration has greatly contributed to the disorientation of the latter and has accentuated the turmoil.

Could populism in its various forms - non-interventionism, protectionism, sovereignism, even nationalism - be the chaotic result of these major phenomena, from one region of the world to another? From the American Middle West to Prime Minister Modi's Hindu India? From Russia's return to an imperial project based on Orthodoxy to parts of Europe contesting its federalist drift, beyond the control of nations and peoples? Isn't eventually the common denominator of these upheavals the quest for or preservation of identity?

Hubris, politics and law

'Hubris' in politics is an age-old phenomenon, as the Greek word suggests. This is not about ancient history, but the very contemporary period. The 'Trumpian' surge is the latest illustration of this. Even before the end of the Cold War, what has more recently been called American 'hyper-power' was expressed; the Reagan years were notably characterised by attacks on the multilateral system, with, for example, the withdrawal of the United States from certain international organisations, such as UNESCO; Washington subsequently backtracked. Gerorge Bush Sr, on the other hand, had the intelligence to maintain a balance between the New International Order dominated by his country, after the break-up of the Soviet Union and the Gulf War, and multilateral cooperation, particularly within the framework of the UN Security Council.

The complex and sometimes antagonistic relationship between politics and law has been multiple and recurrent in international politics. The accusations cannot be reserved for the American Republicans alone. At a certain point in the conflict in Ukraine, President Biden decided to supply Kiev with cluster munitions, now banned by 111 states that have ratified the 2008 Oslo Convention and which the United States - which made massive use of them in Vietnam - has not used itself since 2010 in accordance with domestic law. When it comes to extrajudicial executions, a former president of the French Republic once boasted of having resorted to them. A Ukrainian intelligence official claimed during the conflict that his country would continue to 'kill Russians everywhere and in all places'.

The recent sanctions taken by D. Trump against the International Criminal Court (ICC) - whose statutes the United States has not ratified - are an unacceptable attack on an international justice system that is still embryonic and defenceless against the powerful. However, it can be argued that the most recent initiatives of its Prosecutor aimed at issuing arrest warrants against state leaders have not necessarily respected the principle of 'complementarity' to which the Court is bound, i.e. that it can only intervene when states have been unwilling to judge crimes within their jurisdiction.

Today's political hubris, which is most visible in the United States, reveals a double paradox: it is occurring in a state renowned for its system of checks and balances, where the 'government by judges' has sometimes been feared; the unlimited assertion of a single power runs counter to a general evolution of the world characterised by the emergence of new and considerable poles of power.

Signs from Heaven

The Romans tried to decipher the signs of heaven and read animal viscera. It's hard not to think about this in these troubled times of wars, climatic disasters and martial discourses. Are these manifestations indicative and harbingers of a general disruption that could lead to even greater threats?

D. Trump was elected last November by a majority of Americans. His presence since then on the American and international stage seems to have been in anticipation of his forthcoming enthronement. The ascendancy he has already gained over the other players has made him, with E. Musk at his side, the world's new master and supreme reference to whom we must inevitably give in and pledge allegiance.

And yet, the signs from heaven could indicate otherwise. The well-deserved, moving and highly successful tribute to Jimmy Carter in Washington's National Cathedral was, in the end, a grand mass for

Democratic values, attended by the President-in-Office and K. Harris, as apparent winners, as well as by the President-elect. The President-elect's ambitions for Greenland, Canada and the Panama Canal gave early legitimacy to the generalised primacy of force over law that we are seeing in Ukraine and elsewhere, and the resurgence of a world in the state of nature. The interference of the space genie and the electric car in Europe's domestic policy has caused offence. The uncontrolled conflagration of Los Angeles, surrounded by flames, may not be the destruction of Gomorrah, but the rain of fire is at least the punishment for unpredictability and neglect of the community and public services. The fact that the dominant Democrats in California may be held responsible for this also has a serious impact on the message about the greatness of an America based solely on the deployment of unbridled energy and the apology of natural selection to the detriment of necessary solidarity.

In the 1980s, a literary bestseller about the 'golden boys' of Wall Street - then already masters of the world - was called *The Bonfire of the Vanities*. Whether or not you believe in signs from heaven, flags will be flying at half-mast in Washington on 20 January.

14

Facing permanent revolution in China

President Xi Jinping made a State visit to France in 2024, this time to mark the 60th anniversary of the establishment of diplomatic relations between France and China. He continued his stay on the European continent, in Hungary and Serbia.

Behind the image of the Red Emperor, we can also look beyond the evolution of political power since the founding of the People's Republic of China (PRC) to the great personalities who have shaped this immense country, which has become the world's second largest power. This is not to minimise the role of the 'masses of the people', who have been a major agent of change under Mao Tse-tung, but it is also important not to overlook the influence of individuals, their social environment and education, which have enabled leaders who have become 'revolutionaries' to contribute to the far-reaching changes in a nation and a civilisation that go back thousands of years.

In his Three Messages to France, immediately prior to his visit, President Xi Jinping himself recalled that *'France was one of the first countries to welcome Chinese government scholarship holders on its soil, a century ago, young Chinese students, some of whom were eminent and made a remarkable contribution to the foundation and development of the new China'*.

Xi, Sun, Chou, Deng and the others

Xi Jinping was born in Beijing, the son of a former high-ranking official in the Chinese Communist Party who was demoted during the Cultural Revolution. As such, and because he was brought up in a privileged environment, he was and still is sometimes referred to as a *'Red Prince'*. Like many of his predecessors who had held eminent positions at the head of the State, he travelled abroad to

207

further his education; in 1985, for example, he went to the United States to study fashionable agricultural techniques and stayed with an American family.

The father of the Republic

But we could also mention Sun Yat-sen, the first President of the Republic of China proclaimed in Nanjing in 1912, one of the founders and then President of the Kuomintang Party, Chou En-laï, with his patrician appearance, and Deng Xiao-ping.

Sun Yat-sen is regarded today in China as the father of modernity in that country and even of the contemporary Chinese nation. His initial programme was to expel foreigners, found a republic and redistribute land. He tried to form an alliance with the Chinese Communist Party from Canton and is now revered by both the latter and the Kuomintang. This unanimity alone should lead us to think more deeply and cautiously about Taiwan.

Sun came from a peasant family but, having quickly acquired his fortune, he went on to become part of the intellectual and political elite of the late imperial China of the Manchu Qing dynasty, whose last representative was the young Pu Yi. His lifestyle in Shanghai bears witness to this. You only have to look at his residence in the French Concession in Shanghai to see that it was just a few hundred metres from Chou En-laï's, but the latter, occupied for a relatively short time until the break with the Kuomintang in 1948 after an alliance against the Japanese, bore only external similarities, even though it was organised in a Spartan manner, with a view to the Communists taking power, like the future Chinese Ministry of Foreign Affairs.

The Red Patriot Patrician

Chou En-laï was one of the greatest figures of the PRC, serving as Prime Minister from 1949 until his death in 1976, a few months before Mao's death. He was born in Jiangsu, the capital of Nanjing, one of China's richest coastal regions. His mother was the wife of a high-ranking civil servant, and all his life he gave the image of a patrician. From an early age, he had read the great classical Chinese novels of the 18th century, such as *Dream in the Red Pavilion* and *Jin Ping Mei* (Flower in a Golden Vial). He himself declared: '*I am an intellectual from a feudal family... my revolutionary career began abroad*'. Belonging to the elite and training abroad - which was a guarantee of social advancement on returning home, whether in the United States or Japan - were indeed the dominant characteristics of the future cadres of the revolution on the march.

But Chou was a rebellious pupil and student from a very early age. This later enabled him to understand, and even contain, the Red Guards of a devastating Cultural Revolution and thus ultimately to save the structures of the Communist Party and the State. It was in France that he organised the first group of the Chinese Communist elite before Mao took over the leadership of the movement. In China, he attracted to his cause the best cadets from the Military School founded by Chiang Kai-sheck and converted many of the upper echelons of the Republican army to Communism. And yet, in a paradox of his thought and action, Chou, from his youth, never believed in revolution from above, but rather in the transformation of the masses, particularly through education.

Deng, reform in double digits

Deng Xiao-ping came from a family of wealthy landowners in Sichuan and took part in the 12,000 km Long March in 1930. Encouraged by his father - who had studied law and political science - and given the mission of learning in the West to save China, he embarked for France (NB: Shanghai-Marseilles) in 1920; as a student, he even worked there, notably in the Renault factories in Billancourt; he lived for a time in Place d'Italie, where he even shared a room with Chou En-lai. He did not return to China until 1926 after a stay in the Soviet Union.

He was subjected to Mao's purges during the Cultural Revolution and it was he who launched economic reform in 1978. He was in charge of the country during the Tiananmen Square uprising. He put in place a system, under which China still lives but which may have reached its limits, based on the leadership of the Communist Party but within the framework of an open and sometimes even hyper-capitalist economy; his adage, dating back to 1960, that '*It doesn't matter whether a cat is black or white, as long as it catches a mouse*' has become famous.

Deng is associated with the lightning economic development of a China that, in 30 years, has risen from poverty to achieve double-digit growth rates. Does the system, characterised by both authority and extreme economic liberalism, still work? The country's new demographic problems, the State's takeover of the economic sector and ideology, and a certain muted and in some cases more visible protest, such as during the Covid pandemic - the paradoxical effect of rising living standards and young people's access to information - all lead us to ask this question. This is the major challenge facing Xi Jin Ping, as the masses have themselves become an elite.

General Bâ, Kuomintang Maoist

We could also talk about General Bâ, who is less well known, but whose career illustrates Chinese political syncretism. Here again, we need to look to southern China, in this case the city of Guilin (see André Malraux's *Les Conquérants*, published in 1928, begins with: '*General strike declared in Canton*'; It was in this city that President Xi received the President of the French Republic). The general, a Kuomintang figure, collaborated with the Communists and with Mao himself in the fight against the Japanese invaders.

Even today, the memory of the general (NB: a Kuomintang general glorified in Communist China) is honoured. His residence has become a sort of museum, with many photographs of this heroic period on display.

This rapid kaleidoscope should not obscure the major stages of a troubled history, to which eminent personalities had to adapt and who were often completely subjected to it: The reform of the Hundred Days in 1898 in a vain attempt to save an Empire stuck in a mortifying state of immobility; the Boxer Rebellion in 1900; the

Republican Revolution of 1911, which coexisted for a time with imperial rule in Beijing; the Communist Revolution that saw the triumph of Mao Tse-tung in 1949. Throughout these events, history should not forget that more modern institutions were springing up - encouraged by foreign religious missions - most often based on English and American models. Foreign travel (NB: Chou himself travelled abroad in 1917, before his stay in France and his discovery of several European countries) had also had its effect.

From the Soong sisters to Xi Jinping

President Xi Jinping is a contemporary leader, but also the embodiment of China's permanence, if only through his 'imperial' style of governance.

Despite this consistency over time, China cannot help but continually seek ways of governing a bloated population that has now reached 1.4 billion. The Chinese often say that *there are never any small problems in China* and that the balance is always unstable, given the challenges.

Today's challenges are particularly demographic, economic and environmental. Outside the country, the leader often described as an 'autocrat' and the regime in which the Communist Party (CCP) retains control of the country may inspire fear. But there is no doubt that things need to be seen in a different light: what is to be feared is the force of inertia of a kind of Chinese 'machine' of gigantic and incomparable dimensions; in order to ensure high levels of growth guaranteeing social peace and political stability, China absolutely must constantly conquer new market shares, and this 'necessary' gigantism can only weigh heavily on society and the environment, as well as on relations with the outside world. More than Xi or any other Chinese leader who might replace him, the real danger lies in the force of inertia of gigantism.

In this context, is the model put in place by Deng Xiao-ping - based on economic openness while maintaining the power of the CCP -

still appropriate? Xi seems to have taken the gamble of confirming this in part by re-emphasising an ideological dimension in his governance, while reintroducing the state into the management of the economy, which in part distinguishes him from Deng. Will the gamble pay off? Isn't a new Chinese revolution inevitably underway, which the leaders themselves will have to bring about under pressure from the population? Who will be the players in the changes that are bound to occur throughout China's history? With this in mind, a few references to the past may be useful. China remains a Middle Kingdom, centred on its own history, and it is the sole object of its policy, whatever the currents that may sometimes tear it apart. The story of the Soong sisters is a case in point. The Soong sisters made a major contribution to major changes in China, and it could even be said that their father Charles Soong had 'programmed' them to do so.

The Soong sisters

We must focus on the extraordinary destiny of the three Soong sisters - Ai-ling, Ching-ling and Mei-ling - which is also a way of talking about the role of women in contemporary Chinese politics. In the end, the Soong sisters represented the entire Chinese political spectrum, from the Kuomintang to Communism. In their own way, they embodied the Three Principles of the People (Nationalism, Democracy, Socialism) proclaimed by Dr Sun Yat-sen as early as 1898. Mao is said to have said *'The first loved money, the second China and the third power'*. This apocryphal statement is simplistic but flattering for Ching-ling.

They overcame the differences in their respective backgrounds, making education and the modernisation of China their common cause. The fight against the Japanese invaders also brought all the Chinese together. In 1931, the Japanese intervened in Manchuria, where the following year they created the artificial state of Manchukuo, entrusted to the last deposed emperor Pu-Yi. They occupied Beijing in 1937, at the end of the Second Sino-Japanese War, and the photographs taken by their military leaders at the

Temple of Heaven are reminiscent of Hitler posing at the Trocadero in 1940.

The Soongs were not wealthy, because the head of the family, Charles Soong, one of the first Chinese students in the United States - at a time when the Protestant churches were looking for missionaries to evangelise the Middle Kingdom - who had returned to China in 1881, was a Methodist minister; their mother, a descendant of an illustrious mathematician from the Ming period, had been converted to Christianity by the Jesuits. Generally, only boys were sent abroad to study, but Charles Soong - who also had a friendly relationship with Dr Sun Yat-sen - had a project that was nothing less than to contribute to the liberation of China, and this began with the transformation of minds. So he enlisted the help of the *Southern Methodist Church* to send his daughters to study in the United States. Ailing, aged 15, was the first to go. In 1908, Ching-ling and Mei-ling joined their elder sister in Georgia. They returned to China (Shanghai) just before the revolution of 1911.

Ching-ling was the most academically inclined. She was already the most idealistic and the most interested in Chinese affairs. At a very young age, she began to write thoughts on how China could be changed by students returning from abroad. They found the country (NB: like Ai-ling, who returned after 6 years in the United States) a conservative and rigid society. There had been the alarm of 1898 and 1910/1911 was approaching. But the young reformers bringing back American ideas were often perceived as an outsider. In 1910, China could be considered the most conservative of the great nations; the imperial power in Peking was mired in isolation, outdated traditions and immobility.

The September Revolution of 1911 was first fomented in Shanghai where Dr Sun had returned, having fled China in 1895 and returned in 1900 (NB: Ching-ling was then starting school; Chiang Kai-check was only 14 and Mei-ling, his future wife, was 1) after stays in Europe and Japan. The Dowager Empress Tseu-hi had already died and the Tsing dynasty, while realising the need for change, was unable to implement it. Chiang (NB: Kuomintang means 'People's

Party') and Mao were, in their own way, two revolutionaries working towards the same goal of profound change in China (NB: in this respect, it is worth noting that Sun and Chiang met in Japan).

Sun Yat-sen, who became the first president of the Republic of China in 1912, was Cantonese and remained in the south of the country, initially coexisting with the last emperor. He was Ching-ling's secret hero, and she returned to Shanghai in 1913 to live on Avenue Joffre in the French Concession. She married him the following year. Ching-ling first lived with her husband in Shanghai, on rue Molière in the same concession, then in Canton in 1920. After Sun's death in 1925 at the age of 58, Ching-ling continued to be involved in public affairs; like Sun, she showed an interest in the Russian revolution and visited Moscow, but came to the same conclusion as Sun that *the Soviet revolution could not be introduced into China*. Although she was Sun's widow, this did not prevent her from endorsing the People's Republic of China after its proclamation on 1 October 1949. She was even co-president of the People's Republic and held several other high offices at the head of the State, including that of Honorary President, a few weeks before her death in 1981.

Chiang was also effectively advised by the Russians (NB: Joffe and Borodin) to reorganise the Kuomintang; he even spent a year in Moscow studying military issues. But he broke with the Communists after the Canton Commune of 1927. The failure of the workers' revolution led Mao to turn towards the rural world and to distance the Communists from the Kuomintang.

There was thus a sort of 'consanguinity' of contemporary power in China. It was in Dr Sun's house that Chiang met Mei-ling for the first time. Mei-ling had returned to China in 1917, after 10 years in the United States, and she even boasted that she knew every state; she even had to relearn her native language. On her return, she devoted herself to educational issues and social and charitable activities. When she married Chiang, she became part of the plan to unify China, which was then in the grip of the warlords. Chiang Kai-shek realised his plan in 1928 and became Head of State. She was First Lady of the Republic of China, before becoming First Lady of

Taiwan. A fluent English speaker, she became a celebrity in the United States in particular. She retired there after Chiang's death in 1975 and permanently in 1991, and lived in New York until 2003, at the age of 105.

The Makioka sisters

The Japanese Makiokaka sisters are no less endearing and interesting than the Soong sisters. But they are fictional beings - more real than life - described in the great novel *Sasameyuki* (Snow Drizzle), published between 1943 and 1948, by the Japanese writer Tanizaki. Tanazaki, with bombs raining down on Japan, thought that his country was going to disappear, but he had also noticed that Japanese society had changed considerably over the previous years. The story of *the Makioka Sisters* covers the period from 1936 to autumn 1941, ending a few months before the attack on Pearl Harbor. But it is clear from the date of publication that the spectre of the Second World War and the possible occupation of Japan haunted the writer's mind. The meticulous description of a gigantic tsunami ravaging the province of Kansai sums up the anguish of collapse.

The Four Japanese sisters from Osaka - Tsuruko, the eldest, Sachiko, Yukiko and Takeo - had to face up to a Japanese society in the throes of transformation, even before the Second World War, as a result of economic and social changes and the shift of wealth away from the traditional large families. The two most distant characters were Tsuruko and Yukiko. Tsuruko is the guardian of these values, which in the end are still alive in Japan despite the apparent modernism; Yukiko (*Yuki* means snow), in her free-spirited thirtysomething youth, foreshadows a different future.

The big difference between the Soong sisters and the Makioka sisters is that the former succeeded in becoming players in history and in major changes in China that were not just political. The Malika sisters were subjected to history, but *volens nolens* were both the receptacles and the relays of a new Japan.

The revolutions of liberty, equality and fraternity

Mao Tse-tung practised permanent revolution in China, using it to govern the country, albeit chaotically, and also to maintain his power. Just look at the *Hundred Flowers* in 1956, the *Great Leap Forward* in 1958 and the youth insurrection (NB: Red Guards) that he sparked off from 1966 to 1968 with the violent *Cultural Revolution* that Chou En-laï finally tried to curb. Deng Xiao-ping was in power in 1989 at the time of the Tiananmen uprising, which was bloodily suppressed, but in 1992 the major economic reforms were launched, resulting in double-digit growth rates.

But the singularity of the Chinese revolution may ultimately lead us to attempt to establish a typology of revolutions around the world, however artificial. Schematically, and at the risk of caricaturing, we could speak of the revolutions of liberty, equality and fraternity, based on the republican triptych.

'Liberalism is one of the great achievements of the 19th century', says historian René Rémond. It is a global, political and individual philosophy of history (NB: history is made by individuals) and knowledge. In this respect, the Chinese revolution was never liberal. The religion of freedom is also opposed to religions and traditions, and this was not the case in China as a matter of priority, despite the denunciation of the immobility of imperial power from the beginning of the twentieth century onwards.

Liberalism transformed Europe, as it appeared in 1815 with, in France, the *Sun of July 1830* and the *People's Spring of 1848*; Russia experienced the decabrist movement in 1825 and liberalism triumphed there, albeit fleetingly, during the revolution of 1905; the Congress Party in India was inspired by liberalism; the Meiji (Enlightenment) revolution in Japan, from 1868 onwards, was undertaken from the top down by the imperial powers and was therefore an elitist movement: It was a process of modernisation without a break with the past.

Wealth and education are the two pillars of the liberal order, and there was a time in China under Deng Xiao-ping when this orientation was reminiscent of Guizot's famous '*Enrich yourself*'; it led to double-digit growth for many years and enabled China to become one of the world's two leading economic powers.

The equality revolutions were part of the '*era of democracy*'. The democratic movement did not have to attack the Ancien Régime, which the liberal order had already done. The revolutions of equality are above all the socialist revolutions; they are most often about democracy combining authority and a popular foundation. Democratic revolutions are often anti-parliamentary, anti-liberal and plebiscitary; today they may be embodied in populist movements.

Historically, socialist revolutions have taken place under the influence of Marxism. There was an interest in them and the Kuomintang itself (NB: People's Party) was not insensitive to them; but the Chinese model was specific and based on the rural masses (see Mao's strategic choice) and not on workers' insurrection (see Chou En-lai's hopes); Stalin therefore never believed in the Chinese revolution and hence the schism between the two communist powers which culminated in serious military confrontations in 1969 along the Amur and Ussuri rivers.

To put it simply, the revolutions of fraternity are those of the Third World. Miserable revolutionary China was one of them, and even became its torchbearer after the Bandoeng Conference of non-aligned nations in 1955. Now rich and powerful, the PRC is striving to be one of the leading figures of the 'global South'.

Nationalism, the dominant feature of the 19th century, was not incompatible with all these revolutions; it changed from liberal to democratic, and the Castro revolution was described as 'Cuban', another name for a 'tropical' revolution; Ho Chi Minh in Vietnam combined nationalism with communism. Similarly, there will be a 'Chinese revolution' that will not be proselytised; although socialism will have contributed to the evolution of nationalism, the Chinese revolution will remain nationalist to this day. The European Union defines China as '*a partner, a competitor and a systemic rival*', but this language is inappropriate. Are we really in a systems confrontation with Beijing? Do we want to convert China? China has no such plans, because it wants to ensure its continued development through trade with the West (NB: the United States and the European Union).

Georges Pompidou's testament

In his posthumous book *Le Nœud gordien* (The Gordian Knot), Georges Pompidou wrote that '*revolutions are often the work of dissatisfied privileged people*', referring in particular to the events of May 68 in France. But what was the final outcome in Asia?

On a global scale - and here we can also include a reflection on the West - the following question could be asked: will increasingly educated societies be exclusively a factor of progress? Or will they be a source of destructive, nihilistic upheaval? Part of the answer to this question is another question about the nature and results of education systems. The Chinese revolutionaries were, in a way, mandarins. But the dissatisfied privileged, identified and so aptly described by Georges Pompidou, have now been joined by countless and increasingly indocilent multitudes, as shown by the more than turbulent reactions to the Chinese government's management of Covid. The revolution in China is likely to continue.

15

Russia's Eurasian temptation

In 2024, the Russian President and his Chinese counterpart held their third bilateral summit in two years in Beijing (see V. Putin's visit to China in October 2022 and President Xi's visit to Moscow in March 2023). This attests to the density of the Sino-Russian bilateral relationship (NB: 43 meetings in total between the two leaders) between two major states with converging geopolitical analyses, if not formally true 'allies'. This latest meeting came at a key moment in the war in Ukraine, but also in the longer term.

Enemies with unlimited friendship

Russia and China, once fraternal enemies under Communism, have undeniably grown closer in recent years, as evidenced by the exponential growth in trade between them since 2021/2022. They have not, however, become formal allied powers, but rather close partners. The convergence of geopolitical interests that led to the rapprochement, at a time when the ideological dimension of these poles of communism had disappeared or at least had weakened under the influence of reality and necessity, does not rule out the persistence of a state of competition, particularly in the economic sphere. As Russia recalls its Asian dimension - as illustrated by the Putin-Kim Jong-un summit - competition for the *Heartland*, be it the Russian Far East or Central Asia, must be taken into account.

While there has been talk in recent years of the United States' Asian 'pivot' - formulated above all since the Obama presidency - there is also an increasingly visible and assertive Eurasian dimension to Russian policy. This is rooted in the evolution of the Slavophile movement, which has evolved into a more nationalistic conception of Russia, distancing it from its historical and cultural links with Europe. From the mid-1990s onwards, Evgeny Primakov pragmatically sought to promote a new triangle between Europe, Russia and Asia, replacing the conflictual relationship between Washington, Moscow and Beijing.

The question today is to know whether Russia's clear orientation towards Asia is dictated by circumstances or whether it is a process which, if not definitive, is more profound and lasting, commensurate with the considerable, multi-year investments, for example in the energy sector with the construction of new gas pipelines (see '*Power of Siberia* 2', theoretically from 2024) serving China. The duration of the war in Ukraine will be an important factor in this respect: it is clear that the continuation of the conflict on the European continent would consecrate the rupture of a long-standing proximity with Europe in many areas. Both Europe and Russia will have to make major strategic choices in this area, which will commit them in historic terms.

Sources and meaning of Russian communism

The Eurasian temptation is in fact a question of identity, which is not unique to Russia, but is generally due to accelerated modernisation, the effects of globalisation and uncontrolled migration around the world as a result of climate change, war and global inequality. Russia is a bicontinental, multi-ethnic, multi-religious and multi-cultural empire, and its Eurasism appears more as a protest against the West than an attachment to Asia (NB: this marks a difference with the Russian Slavophiles of the 19th and early 20th centuries). It should be remembered, in a country where history is part of the permanent collective memory, that the Mongol invasions of 1214 to 1552 - the most dangerous in the history of the Russian nation - came from the East and that the history of Russia, once its territorial expansion was complete, was always turned towards the West.

Russia's Eurasian orientation is not unrelated to the ancient debate between Westerners and Slavophiles. The philosopher Nicolas

Berdiaev was one of the theorists of this difference in his research into the deep roots of communism. According to him, Russian thought was forged in a territory that was too vast and had imprecise contours. As a result, Moscow has long imagined itself as a 'third Rome', a sort of lost Byzantium.

Paradoxically, communism contributed to a certain westernisation of Russia, but Vladimir Putin - who differs from this - is clearly a proponent of Eurasia, in a contemporary version of the Slavophile with an unquenchable hatred of the West. This is also why he relies on the hierarchy of the Orthodox Church. In this way, he reproduces in his own way the triptych of Nicholas II: Autocracy-Orthodoxy-Nationalism.

Marxism-Leninism was subtly influenced by Eurasian ideas. Even more than Slavophiles, Eurasians condemn Europe and its civilisation. The Eurasian debate reappeared in the early 1990s; the communist Zyuganov supported an alliance with China; the nationalist politician Zhirinovsky drew on the geopolitics of Haushofer and McKinder, emphasising the *Heartland*, and feared China as much as the United States; The philosopher Dugin was firmly in the anti-Chinese camp; Eurasians in general emphasised the specificity of Russian civilisation, but other thinkers stressed that post-Soviet Russia was and should be oriented towards Europe.

Evgeny Primakov's legacy

For Evgeny Primakov, former Director of the Institute of Oriental Studies at the Russian Academy of Sciences, who was Head of External Intelligence (SVR), Minister of Foreign Affairs and Prime Minister under Boris Yeltsin in 1998, it is more a question of an ad hoc interest in Eurasia, driven by necessity, than a belief.

Primakov's analysis was that the Soviet Union had lost the Cold War, but that it had not been annihilated as Germany and Japan had been in 1945. A single superpower had emerged and, while the mental patterns of the Cold War had persisted, a transition to a multipolar world was under way. It was therefore important for Russia to take advantage of this development within the framework of necessary and profitable cooperation (*'enemies are not permanent, but interests are'*).

Primakov undoubtedly understood better than Putin that post-Soviet Russia - sometimes described as a *'poor power'* - no longer had the means to pursue a project in the imperial tradition. He therefore advocated cooperation, which could sometimes be conflictual, but resolutely ruled out the use of force; For him, it was a question of absolutely avoiding a break with the West, which would be contrary to Russia's DNA and its history of looking towards both the European continent and Asia.

Primakov first conceived of a Moscow-New Delhi-Beijing triangle, which was naturally integrated into his strategic thinking. This project, which was conceptualised in what came to be known as the 'Primakov Doctrine' in 1998, prefigured the BRICS. But this triangle could also be described as a 'trio of asymmetries'. China's *Belt and Road Initiative* is likely to weaken Russian influence in the region. In their own way, these new realities confirm the Russian President's view that the demise of the Soviet Union was *'the greatest catastrophe of the twentieth century'*.

It is hard to imagine more different personalities than Putin, who appeared distant, cold and almost autistic, and Primakov, an outgoing bon vivant from the South. But Putin took on board the foreign policy 'software' of his predecessor at the head of the government, whom he revered for having been an undisputed master of intelligence. As well as the need for a strong state, the dialectics of the unipolar/multipolar world and the question of not enlarging NATO have brought the current Russian President closer to his mentor.

It is hard to imagine more different personalities than Putin, who appeared distant, cold and almost autistic, and Primakov, a bon vivant extrovert from the South. But Putin took on board the foreign policy 'software' of his predecessor at the head of the government, whom he revered for having been an undisputed master of intelligence. In addition to the need for a strong state, the dialectics of the unipolar/multipolar world and the question of not enlarging NATO have brought the current Russian President closer to his mentor.

Friction points with the East, Dialogue with Moscow

A 'definitive' break with Russia would not be to our long-term advantage either, particularly in the face of China, and we will have to rebuild a relationship with Moscow. But we could also talk about the proliferating countries of Iran and North Korea, where dialogue with Moscow is absolutely essential. The world's major balances are at stake. As far as China and Russia are concerned, they are not allies and it will be difficult for them to become so because too many interests separate them. For example, Central Asia, the heart of tomorrow's power, is already a place of competition from which we are far too absent. We will therefore have to manage, if not try to exploit, such differences in all directions in a world characterised by the multiplication of poles of power and a weakened international system that needs to be rebuilt.

In addition to Central Asia, North Korea - under a certain degree of Chinese tutelage - could be a stumbling block between Beijing and Moscow. The main significance of North Korean leader Kim Jong-un's visit to Russia in September 2023 was probably not what it seemed.

V. Putin was probably trying to send a message to the West, i.e. Washington. Other interpretations have also been put forward: the immediate need to obtain munitions for the war in Ukraine, thanks to the compatibility of the two countries' equipment of Soviet origin; the search for North Korean workers for Russian factories, particularly arms factories, to compensate for the sending of Russian fighters to the front; the provision in return of food aid to Pyongyang, or even more broadly economic aid; the start of a dialogue on possible transfers of sensitive technologies, for example in the space field if not nuclear. We did not get the precise conclusions of this visit by the North Korean Head of State, so we will have to make our own assumptions. But the communication developed by the parties, starting with the welcome extended to Kim Jong-un on his arrival at the Vostotchny cosmodrome in the Russian Far East, is likely to guide our analyses.

The issue of sensitive technologies, in the context of an already nuclear North Korea, is central. The interests of North Korea and Russia do not entirely overlap, and there are differences: Pyongyang, a power turned in on itself and ostracised to the extreme, very likely sought in this spectacular visit a means of asserting itself on the international stage; on the Russian side, the objective was not to overtake China, and a Moscow-Beijing-Pyongyang triangle is already taking shape.

Vladimir Putin's Russia has rarely sought to seduce, and is instead part of a historical and cultural tradition dominated by the cult of strength and power. Since the start of the war in Ukraine, Russia's rhetoric and actions have been consistent with a strategy of terror, as evidenced by the recurrent references to the possible use of nuclear weapons.

In the case of North Korea, over and above Kim Jong-un's visit, the aim was to show that an Asian 'front' can also exist and be strengthened, and that Russia, judged until now by the UN Security Council to be a rational and responsible power when it comes to nuclear proliferation, whether against Iran or North Korea, could abandon this attitude.

The *'hold me back or I'll do something bad'* message was clearly a reminder to the United States of its ability to cause harm, and was not without links to the European theatre, where Washington has been hesitating over what policy to adopt towards Ukraine and where the campaign for the American presidential elections is already well underway. Doesn't Pyongyang's 'message' ultimately correspond in every respect to the profound meaning of Russia's Eurasian 'temptation'?

16

Western responsibility? Neutralising Ukraine?

To understand the war in Ukraine, it is necessary to take stock of the last thirty years, both as regards Russia and its relations with the West. The argument that the West is responsible - not to say guilty - for the failures of the transition from the Soviet system and, above all, for the policies pursued by President Putin in recent years has been put forward several times by Moscow. The subject, on which historians will continue their research, is extremely complex, but it is important to re-establish certain facts that qualify assertions that are often more political, or even ideological, than actually documented.

The nagging question of NATO's westward expansion

The most frequent criticism, mainly from the Russian side, relates to the enlargement of NATO, to which Moscow is said to have responded in order to re-establish a protective glacis on its borders. The expansion of NATO is said to have run counter to the 'promises' made at the end of the Cold War. It is true that NATO expanded in phases from 1999 onwards - notably with the accession of the Baltic States in 2004 - and that Russia has repeatedly referred to the 'commitments' that were allegedly made to Mikhail Gorbachev, notably by Secretary of State James Baker, at the time of German reunification. As a result, the former Russian President remains reviled in his own country for his supposed weakness - and in this case for not having formally negotiated the withdrawal of Soviet forces from East Germany in exchange for non-expansion of NATO - while he still enjoys an unrivalled aura outside for having peacefully transformed the Cold War world. But in reality, the West made no formal commitment, apart from the soothing words of James Baker.

In any case, the process of enlargement to include Ukraine - as well as Georgia - was frozen in 2008 at the Atlantic Alliance summit in Bucharest. The French President and the German Chancellor opposed such a prospect at the time, and at most an 'open door' was left in the summit's final document, at the insistence of US President George Bush Jr, to allow for the future. During the course of the war in Ukraine, under the pressure of events and in the interests of conciliation, President Zelensky himself realised that it was impossible to envisage this option.

It is therefore paradoxical that the expiatory victim of a Russia that is in reality confronting the West by proxy should be a country that is still not a member of the Atlantic Alliance and does not appear to be close to joining it. Since the annexation of Crimea and above all the armed and murderous tensions in the Donbas, it has become impossible to integrate a country at war into NATO. Article 5 of the Alliance's Charter, which provides for solidarity between members in the event of aggression - but leaves them free to decide how to react - should be applied ab initio. Ukraine's accession would therefore be a form of declaration of war on Russia that the West cannot or should not contemplate.

Russian obsidional complex

The Russian obsidional complex, which is long-standing and rooted in a long history of invasions, clearly prevents Moscow from being equally concerned about the threat it poses to European countries. It is clear that the war in Ukraine has accelerated the rapprochement of countries such as Sweden and Finland to NATO and has led them to become members of the Alliance. The Kaliningrad exclave, formerly East Prussia between Poland and Lithuania, now belongs to Russia. It is highly militarised and we need to make sure that hypersonic missiles are not installed there. This would certainly resurrect a debate of the kind that Europe experienced with the Euromissile crisis in the 1980s. At that time, the Soviet Union launched a vast campaign against the deployment of American cruise missiles and Pershing II rockets - which were never deployed in Europe, incidentally - even though these weapons were a response to the deployment of SS 20 missiles aimed at Europe by the USSR. If there is mistrust, it is also conceivable that it is mutual.

The West, winner of the Cold War?

There has recently been a resurgence of the thesis, set out as a postulate, that *'for the West, the only thing that mattered was that the USSR should be brought down'*. A former foreign minister of a major EU country has even expressed himself in these terms , referring in particular to Ronald Reagan's 'star wars' programme in the final years of the Cold War. In this respect, it should be noted that the American President himself, who had described the Soviet Union as an 'evil empire' as early as 1983, seemed to have converted to total nuclear disarmament at the Reykjavik Summit in 1986, which, moreover, made his own administrations, clearly taken by surprise, dizzy. During the last phase of the Soviet Union and the period immediately afterwards, President George Bush Sr. showed himself anxious to spare Mikhail Gorbachev and then the new Russia. His support for the last Soviet leader was motivated in particular by the fear that nuclear weapons aroused in a country in the throes of decomposition, especially as the arsenals were stored not only in Russia, but also in Ukraine, Belarus and Kazakhstan. The nightmare of a 'Yugoslavia with nukes' even haunted people's minds at the time. Sensing that the country was teetering on the brink, George Bush Sr endeavoured to bring forward the Moscow Summit as soon as possible, which was finally held in July 1991, during which the START 1 treaty on nuclear arms reduction was signed.

For these major reasons, it has now been established - on the basis, for example, of documents from the *George Bush Library* consulted by the American historian of Ukrainian origin Serhii Plokhy - that the American President could live with the survival of the Soviet Union and the existence of a Communist Party that was, in any case, greatly weakened. Boris Yeltsin's 'blows' against his rival Mikhail Gorbachev did not arouse the initial enthusiasm of the West, including François

Mitterrand in France. A number of Western chancelleries subsequently had to make efforts to establish and develop a more peaceful relationship with the new Russian leader, at the risk of not judging the 'Battle of Parliament' in October 1993 - when Yeltsin had his opponents shot at - or the first war in Chechnya as they should have.

Western sirens in the economy

In economic terms, the picture needs to be qualified. While the new Russia, lacking both the reference points and the skills to implement a form of management that radically departed from the command economy, was overly sensitive to the siren calls of a liberalism that was inapplicable at the time, it cannot be denied that the Western experts who were sometimes present in Russian ministries at the time were not always the best advisers. Mikhail Gorbachev, who had already been shaken internally and whose popularity had waned, also had cause to complain about the indifference felt towards his country's needs. Invited to the G7 summit in London in July 1991 - the forerunner of the G8 - he returned empty-handed, without the financial aid he had been hoping for, despite the support he received from Mrs Thatcher and President Mitterrand. In retrospect, he took offence at the fact that, a few months earlier, President Bush had found it easier to finance his Gulf War than to agree to the financial aid (NB: $20 billion) that Russia sorely needed at the time.

While the '500-day programme' devised by economists around Gorbachev - including Iavlinsky - for the years 1990-1992 was never implemented because it was considered too radical a transition, the 'shock therapy' of the Russian government led by Egor Gaidar and inspired by the Chicago School is generally presented as the illustration of a policy that was ill-adapted to Russian realities. Privatisation and price liberalisation were policies that were ultimately maintained throughout the 1990s, including by Prime Minister Victor Chernomyrdin, Gaidar's successor, whose entire career up to that point had been spent working for the state-owned Gazprom Group. Russia was encouraged to embrace free trade, which also marked a break with the Soviet era. The country was not prepared for this, and many of its products - such as lorries and cars, as the privatisation of the ZIL factories showed - were not competitive on the world market, resulting in the dislocation of the Russian industrial fabric.

Shared responsibility

We can therefore dare to speak of shared responsibility, insofar as Western aid, via the IMF or the World Bank, was not insignificant. The 'savage' privatisations of the first years of the transition under Boris Yeltsin, which allowed what is known as an 'oligarchy' to emerge, are a phenomenon specific to the country's society and economy during the period in question. The 'consanguinity' of the oligarchs and state power is undoubtedly the main phenomenon that has prevented the country from achieving more harmonious and less unequal development.

The question of responsibility brings us back to Mikhail Gorbachev and Ukraine. Mikhail Gorbachev fought with all his might to prevent the break-up of the Soviet Union, and his plan for a new Union Treaty in the summer of 1991 was one of the factors that triggered the putsch in August. His rival, Yeltsin, on the other hand, sought to promote an independent Russia based on nationalist rhetoric. It was Yeltsin who, on 8 December of the same year, concluded an agreement with his Ukrainian and Belarusian counterparts to create the Commonwealth of Independent States (CIS). However, the current Russian President is not the heir to Mikhail Gorbachev, but was brought to power by Boris Yeltsin, who enjoyed the understanding and support of the West. Although Yeltsin and Ukrainian President Kravchuk agreed to break up the Soviet Union - and consequently deprive Gorbachev of his power - strong dissensions began at that point with the thorny issue of sharing the Black Sea fleet and the naval base at Sevastopol, and escalated to the conflict we know today.

Buffer zone, ceasefire and neutralisation?

In the current stalemate, it may seem out of the question to think about a way out of the crisis in Ukraine, or at least an easing of tensions. And yet, on the French side, have the efforts of conventional deterrence (NB: the hypothesis of 'ground troops' in a conception of greater strategic ambiguity) been credible in an isolated approach? Is a traditional deterrent (NB: the France-Ukraine security agreement refers to an 'active deterrent') not an adventurous approach?

In view of the current military impasse in Ukraine (see shortcomings or uncertainties in US policy; inadequate armaments; recruitment problems), we cannot rule out the possibility that Russia is also likely to seek a way out by 'updating' the initial special operation.

V. Putin's reference at one point to a 'buffer zone' was not necessarily a simple reference to a de facto ceasefire (see frozen conflict) or a formalised ceasefire (see Panmunjom in Korea). It is more likely that, in the minds of Russian officials, the buffer zone would be equivalent to a form of 'neutralisation' across the whole of Ukraine. At this stage, this objective would not inevitably require wide-ranging negotiations on European security.

Russia may find it advantageous to limit itself to a de facto ceasefire. In the absence of a formal settlement, the demarcation line between Russia and Ukraine would remain blurred, as in the case of Georgia or Transnistria; the possibility of a resumption of the conflict would prevent Kiev from being included in an alliance such as NATO or even the EU. This is undoubtedly another reason for V. Putin not to negotiate a more global agreement. Does every conflict necessarily end at the negotiating table, contrary to what is repeated ad nauseam? Let's not forget that the Soviet Union, and then Russia, have never signed a peace treaty with Japan since 1945.

Kiev, for its part, could find advantages in this 'provisional' outcome - which could even last - apart from the fact that it would put an end to intolerable material and human destruction. In this way, Ukraine would not have to formally ratify the loss of territory, and it would be saving itself for better days.

Neutralisation and neutrality

Neutralisation is not synonymous with neutrality. Neutrality, which excludes participation in a military alliance, does not mean disarmament. It is important to correct preconceived ideas about neutrality by first distinguishing between states that have a policy of neutrality and those that opt for a status of permanent neutrality. The former express a desire to remain outside the blocs and alliances and determine their policy accordingly. This was the case for Sweden and Finland until they applied to join NATO. The latter opt for a special situation with international rights and obligations established by treaty.

Permanent neutrality is worth considering. It corresponds to a State's commitment not to use force except to defend its independence and territorial integrity. This commitment is recognised by the other States, which for their part undertake not to use force against it and sometimes undertake to guarantee its neutrality, i.e. to act by force against those who fail to comply with the status of neutrality.

This latter status of neutrality is historically ancient and generally reflects a desire to avoid armed conflict in particularly sensitive areas. The legal foundation of Swiss neutrality was laid by unilateral acts adopted in 1815. The Austrian State Treaty of 1955 put an end to the occupation of Austria and contained a commitment by the USSR, France, the United Kingdom and the United States to respect Austria's independence and territorial integrity. An Austrian constitutional law of the same year proclaimed Austria's perpetual neutrality. This position ruled out alliances and military bases on its territory.

Turkmenistan offers a very contemporary example of permanent neutrality. This Central Asian republic gained independence in 1992 following the dissolution of the Soviet Union. In a Declaration registered by the UN in 1995, the country opted for permanent neutrality. This status resulted from the exercise of a sovereign right and was confirmed, on its twentieth anniversary, by a resolution adopted by the United Nations General Assembly on the proposal of Turkmenistan, which France also co-authored.

Each example of permanent neutrality, a status that is not very widespread, is specific and the Central Asian model cannot be compared to Switzerland, Austria or even a former Soviet Republic that is now at war. A certain amount of thought was nevertheless given to Ukraine after the Crimea affair. Military scenarios are unfolding before our eyes from which it will not be easy to extricate ourselves, but the question of regional security, in ways yet to be determined, would inevitably be included in the event of an overall settlement.

We can imagine the very strong reservations that will inevitably arise from the prospect of external 'guarantees', with Russia's failure to comply with the 1994 Budapest Protocol - following the military denuclearisation of Ukraine - constituting in itself a trauma that is difficult to overcome. But permanent neutrality should be conceived differently and become a matter for the entire international community. There is nothing to prevent us from exploring all possible ways and means of putting an end to a destructive conflict, and neutrality can also have some virtues in this quest.

Is war an infinite spiral?

War, beyond the human losses and material destruction, is an infinite spiral, even when it is no longer visible, because it corrodes minds, sustains the desire for revenge or at least gives rise to negative and paralysing mental representations.

The economic dimension is likely to weigh just as heavily on both the direct belligerents and their supporters. If the sanctions affect Russia, can the resulting disruption to the world economy and the direct consequences of the war itself - such as the role played by Ukraine before the conflict as the world's 'granary', particularly for China - be sustained over the long term by all the economies already weakened by the consequences of the pandemic?

And then there are the mental consequences of a war experienced first-hand, of contemplating destruction on the scale of Berlin in 1945, and of witnessing massive and repeated war crimes. Armaments, alliances, violations of the laws of war and international jurisdictions, military budgets, new hypersonic weapons and the trivialisation of the language of deterrence have become obsessive themes in these times of anachronisms and a conflict that we would have imagined in another age.

What does not seem negotiable on the Ukrainian side at this stage is the recovery of sovereignty over the entire territory. The question then arises of how this territory is to be delimited. Even if the annexation of Crimea by Russia in 2014 has not been recognised by the international community, the peninsula's 'belonging' to Russia - which invokes history and where it has strategic interests including the presence of nuclear submarines - will almost certainly also be considered non-negotiable by Moscow. But will Ukraine be able to forget its history and extricate itself from the geography that shapes its destiny?

For Russia, the gradual lifting of sanctions, according to a timetable determined by the implementation of other agreements reached, will be decisive. It is also conceivable that a European 'perspective' could be offered to Moscow for the longer term, according to specifics to be determined, and even that the horizon could be set for a new security architecture on the continent involving Russia. NATO, despite its revival due to the Russian invasion and its enlargement, is not an immutable structure and will depend in particular on the commitment of the United States according to its priorities on a global scale.

After the war, time for diplomacy?

The facts of the war in Ukraine have not fundamentally changed in almost a year. It is important to recall them now that the war in Ukraine is only occasionally at the forefront of our radar screens.
At the time, it was asserted that military scenarios would determine the way out of the crisis. The war, whatever its motives, had naturally led to a reaction from Kiev; the UN Charter had been

violated and the international system had been disrupted; a high-intensity war on the European continent could not fail to handicap Europe's prosperity and development.

But the context had already changed, more than a year after the start of the conflict: if the Ukrainians had been unable to reach the end of the negotiations, 'with a gun to their heads' (see Istanbul talks, March 2023), a counter-offensive on their part did not augur well; the powerful Russian artillery and Russia's control of the skies had to be taken into account; public opinion was becoming weary (war fatigue) in the United States and Europe; the cost of the war, as well as the foreseeable cost of reconstruction, were beginning to appear as unbearable burdens for Kyiv's supporters.

Diplomatic initiatives were emerging here and there (e.g. China, Africa) which, taken together, raised hopes of achieving a result. The G7 debates in Hiroshima had confirmed that the United States had set itself limits that could not be exceeded; on the Russian side, the question of Crimea was an implicit red line, revealed by more than subliminal statements on the possible use of tactical nuclear weapons. France, which had endeavoured to maintain channels of communication with Moscow in the run-up to the crisis, had perhaps prematurely envisaged negotiations and no longer really got involved when it should have in order to avoid the situation getting bogged down or, worse still, escalating. Will there be a return to diplomacy now that a first international conference has been held in Switzerland and a second conference, in which Russia will not be taking part this time, has not been confirmed?

The war in Ukraine has profoundly affected Europe's prosperity and disrupted its mechanisms, even beyond the Treaties that govern it. This is untenable. The 'NATOisation' of Europe - after the contrary diagnosis of *'brain dead'* - with the accession of Finland and Sweden in particular, can only ruin plans for a 'European strategic autonomy' in the long term, which would not be limited to military issues, but would also encompass high technology. The revision of the international system, if not its overhaul, will also have to take account of the new poles of power: they see the conflict in Ukraine as just another war and have their own interests. The American elections in November will clearly be decisive. The Republican team's Settlement Plan, mooted during the campaign, would basically consist of freezing the current situation on the ground.

Neutralisation of Ukraine

It's a truism that Ukraine lies between East and West. It should not forget its history and geography, which destined it, at the end of the Soviet Union, to be a 'buffer zone' or a 'bridge', a more positive term. It benefited from this situation, for example by being virtually subsidised by Russia until 2009/2010, with gas priced at less than $50 per 1,000 m3 at a time when the world price was reaching $250. Tensions in the energy sector clearly preceded the annexation of Crimea, let alone the current war. At the same time, Kyiv could have benefited from its proximity to EU countries, particularly in terms of trade. Geopolitical factors, combined with the negligence of many of its leaders and the divisions within society, have prevented Ukraine from opting for skilful external orientations.

Today's challenge is twofold: the end of hostilities between Russia and Ukraine; the reconstruction of the latter and the normalisation of a relationship with Moscow that is essential for Europe. It is hard to see how the cessation of hostilities - which could even be de facto (frozen conflict), without being formalised (Panmunjom formula), and a fortiori accompanied by a settlement on the status of Ukraine - would be anything other than a 'freeze on image' of sorts, depending on the situation on the ground. As for Russia, the threat of new sanctions, if things did not go smoothly, would not necessarily be effective, as the country has adapted to such a situation; moreover Moscow - in the tradition of an empire with blurred borders (see Transnistria, Georgia) - is not absolutely eager to obtain a formal agreement, unless it ratifies that Ukraine has no vocation to be in NATO or the EU; a Ukraine with uncertain borders would be an insurmountable handicap for it in the perspective of membership of larger entities. The concept of a buffer zone is undoubtedly, in the mind of the Kremlin, a neutralisation on the scale of the whole of Ukraine, the main aim of the war for Russia; it should be noted that neutralisation would not exclude bilateral security guarantees for Kiev from its main supporters.

As for the reconstruction of Ukraine, it is to be feared that Europe, already economically punished by the war, will be made to feel guilty for not having been able to help Kiev more. Have we ever seen the United States take on such a responsibility, even if it was overwhelming? Just remember Vietnam, Kuwait/Iraq and Afghanistan.

The cacti of Vladimir Putin

V.Putin's 'yes, but' on the truce agreed between the USA and Ukraine in Jeddah is more than the famous 'cactus' of a former President of the French Republic.

Not all the Russian President's obvious reservations are based on valid arguments. For example, the fear that the 30 days of cessation of hostilities will be used by the Ukrainian army to reconstitute its forces may also be felt a fortiori by Kyiv.

The Kremlin's lack of 'eagerness' can obviously be explained first and foremost by its fierce determination to settle the issue of the Kursk area; it is out of the question that Russian territory, even a very marginal portion in relation to the vastness of the country, should still be occupied before negotiations begin.

Beyond this apparent procrastination, it is the question of 'guarantees' that is at issue. On the Ukrainian side, there is no longer any hope of NATO membership or the presence of American troops on the ground. The 'rare lands' affair remains unclear to this day; is it not ultimately an illusion both in economic terms (NB: Trump could boast to his public that he has taken pledges, but does he really believe in the viability of the project except in the very long term) and in security terms (NB: will the presence of American companies and their employees be enough to ensure a degree of sanctuary ?) There remains the veiled threat waved by Trump - it could be new sanctions - likely to penalise a Russia eager to quickly lift existing penalties.

On the Russian side, these are sometimes the same demands but in reverse (see NATO, American and even European troops), plus recognition of the annexations and demilitarisation of the country, or even a regime change.

D. Trump and V. Putin have the most cards in their hands: the American president wants to move quickly to meet his commitments to the public and because he wants to 'turn the page on Ukraine'; the Russian president could wait and even do without a peace agreement, contenting himself with 'blurred' borders compatible with his imperial-inspired project of 'frozen conflicts'. For him, the limit that must not be crossed remains the preservation of a normalisation with the United States, which was unhoped for until recently.

Warmongers of all countries, unite!

Friedrich Merz is not yet officially Chancellor of Germany, but he won the recent parliamentary elections (NB: by just a few points over the far-right *Alternative für Deutschland* - AfD). He took advantage of his relative legitimacy to call an emergency meeting of the Bundestag from the previous term (NB: the new parliament resulting from the elections will not take office until after 25 March) in order to proceed with a major constitutional reform that can only be adopted by a two-thirds majority.

The stratagem succeeded and a qualified majority was largely obtained. But the compatibility of the approach, which is certainly in line with the letter of the law but not with the spirit of democracy, is questionable. Indeed a two-thirds majority on the proposed reform would undoubtedly not have been achieved in the new parliamentary configuration.
By virtue of the vote that has just taken place, the federal state and the sixteen Länder will no longer be limited in their capacity to incur debts. F. Merz is planning an investment programme of €1,000 billion, divided more or less equally between military equipment and infrastructure (schools, hospitals, roads, etc.).

According to the future Chancellor, whose coalition has still not been formed, this will be '*a first step towards a European Defence Community*'. This needs to be clarified: initial statements by F. Merz's initial statements indicate that he could be satisfied with both the American nuclear umbrella and the extension of the French deterrent; during the war in Ukraine, the outgoing Chancellor O. Scholz had a €100 billion defence plan adopted, which was immediately used to buy American F-35 fighter jets, which are responsible for 'nuclear service' within NATO, i.e. carrying nuclear weapons.

Germany's massive rearmament project will not necessarily reassure all its neighbours and those who are supposed to be its partners. From a German national point of view - but it is up to the FRG itself to decide on this point - is a great Germany possible without an *Ostpolitik* ? After the limits reached by Konrad Adenauer, often referred to as the '*Kanzler der Alliierten*' (Chancellor of the Allies), great chancellors such as Willy Brandt, Helmut Schmidt, Helmut Kohl and Gerhard Schröder have proved the opposite. Nor is the European out of time - when a ceasefire in Ukraine is within reach - rearmament frenzy any comfort.

17

The eternal question of politics and law

Law and international relations

The recent US Supreme Court ruling on presidential immunity is an illustration of the close relationship between law and politics. While the Court's ruling did not affect the presidential campaign to any great extent, it could, if necessary, influence the outcome of the election by giving former President Trump the theoretical possibility of pardoning himself if elected. A decision to the contrary by the Court could have had very different consequences. Although force is currently taking precedence over law in international relations, with the UN Security Council paralysed - due to one of its permanent members breaking away from the basic rules contained in the Organisation's Charter - the law nevertheless remains a reference point for dealing with many international problems. Here are just a few examples.

The ICC at a disadvantage

The announcement by the Prosecutor of the International Criminal Court (ICC) that he would file applications to issue arrest warrants for the Israeli Prime Minister, his Defence Minister and three Hamas leaders has given rise to heated controversy. The point here is not to enter into the debate on the apparent equality between those responsible for the gigantic terrorist pogrom of 7 October and those responsible for the war in Gaza, but to confine ourselves to a consideration of international criminal justice.

First of all, it should be emphasised that the institution of the ICC, which is not a UN body, is not universal. Major states, including the United States, China and Russia, have not signed or ratified the

Rome Statute, which was adopted in 1998 and came into force in 2002. In this case, Israel is not a party to the Statute and Hamas does not represent a state. Furthermore, the ICC should have respected the principle of complementarity, meaning that it can only intervene when States have been unable or unwilling to judge the crimes falling within their jurisdiction.

Secondly, international criminal justice can only be an illusion in the absence of political authority; this applies both to the international system and to national jurisdictions. In reality, Prosecutor Karim Khan's announcement appears to be political because of the above considerations, and it has come at an inappropriate time. One cannot imagine the possibility of a judicial power intervening in the middle of a conflict. William II was not prosecuted until 1919, by decision of the negotiators of the Treaty of Versailles and in the total absence of international criminal law; he then had to take refuge in the Netherlands, a neutral state. The Nuremberg and Tokyo Tribunals convened after the end of the Second World War and tried the representatives of defeated and crushed states. This was perhaps the only time in history when international criminal justice was truly applied.

Since its inception, the ICC has only tried people from weak states, or states that it considered to be weak. The same is true today, with all due respect, and neither China nor the United States - for the Second Gulf War, for example - have ever been implicated by the Court; the exception is the international arrest warrant for V. Putin. In so doing, it has moved away from impartial justice.

In reality, by abandoning this noble ambition and seeking to play a political role at the wrong time - and this also applies to the astonishing press release from the Quai d'Orsay, published in the middle of the night and in a hurry - the ICC has paradoxically only strengthened Prime Minister Netanyahu, behind whom the whole of Israel's population and political class have rallied.

At a time when the Israeli-Palestinian conflict has reached a paroxysmal level, many voices have once again called for a 'two-state solution'. Ireland, Norway and Spain have decided to formally recognise the Palestinian state.

Such an outcome has already suffered setbacks, including those attributed to the Palestinians themselves, at the end of the discussions in 2000 between Yasser Arafat, the leader of the PLO, and Prime Minister Ehud Barak, under the aegis of President Clinton at the Camp David II Summit; it would not be without posing immense political problems: can the Palestinians be 'rewarded' after the extreme violence of 7 October last? What would become of the security of Israel, whose fragility has just been exposed? What about Jerusalem, whose status was a major stumbling block at Camp David II? Not to mention the nagging question of refugees.

In concrete terms, there is the question of the borders of the new state, the population that would make it up and the political power that would govern it: the Palestinian Authority in the West Bank or Hamas in Gaza? These are eminently political questions, but they are also matters of international law.

There are traditionally four constituent elements of a state: population, territory, political organisation and sovereignty. Sovereignty cannot be absolute and must be compatible with the UN Charter.

The legitimacy and legality of the State of Israel are based on the Partition Plan adopted by the United Nations in 1947, but also on the famous Security Council Resolution 242 of 1967, passed after the Six-Day War, which applies to 'every State in the region' and therefore to Israel, whose existence cannot be called into question. Resolutions 242 of 1967 and 338 of 1973 remain the basis for an international settlement.

But in the absence of such a settlement, and given the uncertainties surrounding the constituent elements of a Palestinian state, can such a state be formally recognised? Wouldn't this mean reversing the order of priorities? Doesn't the solution still lie, today as in the past, above all in the will of the parties? Under these conditions, aren't the recent recognitions 'virtual'? Are Madrid, Oslo and Dublin prepared to exchange embassies with Hamas? For its part, the Quai d'Orsay has just declared that *the conditions have not yet been met for this decision (of recognition) to have a real impact*.

Cluster munitions: the Vietnam syndrome

At a point in the conflict when Ukraine appeared to be running out of ammunition - failing to supply F-16 aircraft and/or long-range missiles directly - President Biden decided to supply cluster munitions, which are now banned by 111 States that have ratified the 2008 Oslo Convention and which the United States itself has no longer used since 2010 in application of a domestic law.

This decision reflects a hesitation on the part of the United States about its political line in Ukraine and confirms a general American tendency to consider that there is always a technical solution to a problem. On the eve of the NATO summit in Vilnius, the Biden administration's choice can only have created fissures within NATO's partners, including the Europeans who signed up to the Oslo Convention.

Cluster munitions, invented by the Soviet Union, were used during the Second World War by Nazi Germany and the USSR. They were also used on a massive scale by the United States during the Vietnam War. They are considered particularly inhumane by public opinion because of their delayed effects on populations, years or even decades later.

Contrary to what some experts claim, Western cluster munitions are not necessarily more discriminating (cf. higher initial explosion rate) than those from Soviet stockpiles, which were also used by the Ukrainians but which no longer have them. In Laos, 50 years on, it is estimated that 30% of cluster bombs have still not exploded. In Vietnam, the United States did not hesitate to use methods against civilians and the environment that offended its own public opinion. They did so on the territory of their ally, South Vietnam: the famous *Napalm Girl* photograph was taken in 1972 just a few kilometres from Saigon. In Ukraine, Washington will allow the country it supports to carry out irreversible destruction on its own occupied territory.

Resistance and extra-judicial executions

France commemorated the memory of a hero on 8 May in Lyon. Jean Moulin was the organiser and unifier of the Resistance within the CNR (National Resistance Council). He paid for it with torture and his life. He entered the Panthéon on 19 December 1964, as André Malraux's unforgettable cavernous voice resounded under the gaze of General de Gaulle. He will forever embody the legitimate struggle for the survival and independence of a nation.

Another resistance is developing today in a Ukraine whose very existence and sovereignty are under threat. The virulence of the comments made by its head of military intelligence is understandable in such a context. But his statements that *'we have killed Russians and will continue to kill Russians all over the world'* raise questions. If they are aimed at those involved in the war, they may also suggest that extra-judicial executions of Russians are also being advocated, wherever they occur and without discrimination.

State-to-state relations

Traditionally, France does not recognise regimes or governments, but states.

We still have diplomatic relations with Russia, with which we are not at war. During the Soviet era, we distinguished between state-to-state relations and the role of the Communist Party of the USSR, which was involved in an international organisation. France's position in this case is therefore perfectly consistent. The question is whether it is also consistent with other recent positions.

There are countless examples of the consistency of French diplomacy in this area. When the Taliban took power in 1996, France expressed no formal recognition, by virtue of the same unwritten doctrine. But it maintained its embassy in Kabul.

In another case, contrary to what public opinion often thinks, France did not break off diplomatic relations with Bashar al-Assad's Syria. It recalled its ambassador, who was no longer ambassador to Syria but ambassador for Syria (NB: in practice, ambassador for the Syrian opposition) and closed its embassy, which it still owns. The Résidence de France, formerly the summer residence of the Ottoman Governor of Damascus, is a historic residence that welcomed the short-lived King of Iraq, perhaps Lawrence of Arabia and General de Gaulle during the Second World War. The defence of its interests there (for example, the protection of dual nationals) is ensured by another European State, a member of the EU.

Beyond the knee-jerk reactions that the presence of the French ambassador to Russia in the Kremlin for the inauguration ceremony of the Russian president may provoke, it is important to take account of the rules of diplomacy, to put events - which may surprise or even offend a priori - into historical perspective and to realise, as the French government has just stated, that it is necessary to 'preserve channels of communication', all the more so in an increasingly dangerous world.

Law and society: the memory of Simone Veil and Ruth Ginsburg

Let us also look at the domestic order to examine the relationship that can be established between law and politics. The recent decision of the Supreme Court of the United States, immediately presented as the abrogation of the constitutional right to abortion and a victory for American religious conservatism, sent shock waves. The tremor, which undoubtedly affected the image of the United States after other developments raising concerns about the country's democratic life, quickly spread to Europe.

In France, the idea of enshrining the right to abortion in the Constitution was taken up again with a view to drafting a bill along these lines, and the process was brought to a conclusion. The debate has taken an ideological turn by transposing the American climate, whereas the issue could also be approached in a more pragmatic way from the angle of equal rights and justice. The legacy of Simone Veil and the work of the late US Supreme Court Justice Ruth Ginsburg could help us in this approach.

Federal law and state powers

The Court's decision must be seen in the political context of the United States and its federal structure. The process has been completed. There is no doubt that the current composition of the Supreme Court, to which President Trump appointed three judges during his term in office, helped to shape the Court's ruling. The judges, who are considered to be conservative, adhere to an 'originalist' doctrine, i.e. an original reading of the Constitution, interpreting it according to the context in which it was drafted.

But it must also be admitted that American society has always been very divided on the issue of abortion, and the 'pro-life' movements are also very powerful, particularly within the Republican movement. Although the 1973 *Roe v. Wade* ruling recognised women's constitutional right to control their own bodies, this was due to a Supreme Court that was reputedly very progressive fifty years ago. A boomerang effect has therefore just occurred in a society where one legitimacy is opposed to another, even though there seems to be an overall majority of opinion (NB: 60%) in favour of upholding *Roe v. Wade*. This overall figure is itself misleading and conceals a great diversity of opinion. Abortion is more widely accepted by Republican voters than might be thought, and the debate is more about the methods of regulation, in particular the length of time abortion is permitted.

In upholding a Mississippi law prohibiting abortion after 15 weeks, even though voluntary termination of pregnancy (abortion) is practised up to 24 or even 28 weeks in some US states - legislation that could be considered extremely permissive from a European perspective - the Court ruled that the Constitution did not confer a right to abortion.

Contrary to what was sometimes claimed when the decision was announced, abortion is not prohibited in the United States, but the Court referred responsibility for regulating and, where appropriate, prohibiting it back to the federal states (*'The Constitution does not prohibit the citizens of each State from regulating or prohibiting abortion'*). It is estimated that in around twenty States, abortion has become illegal or subject to strict restrictions. However, it is not possible to prejudge entirely the measures that will be adopted in each State, and what are known as 'restrictions' are generally more flexible than French law even as far as time limits are concerned (cf. 15 weeks in the Mississippi law that the Court has just upheld; 10 weeks, then 12 weeks, in the French law of 1975 amended in 2001). If, as the saying goes, *'what can live by the Court can die by the Court'*, how can the Court be criticised for allowing a democratic debate to be re-established, when we are inclined to denounce the power of judges?

An ideology-free approach

In a society that remains divided on the issue, as is the case in the United States, despite a majority opinion in favour of abortion, the question cannot be decided in an absolute way at federal level and we can also consider - at the risk of appearing to be going against the tide - that there is a form of wisdom in the recent Supreme Court decision.

Recalling the memory and actions of Simone Weil and Justice Ginsburg, who shared a pragmatic approach, may prove invaluable in this context. Ruth Ginsburg was sometimes accused of being a radical ideologue (cf. *'a radical, doctrinaire feminist'*), as she was during the Senate hearings on her nomination as a Supreme Court Justice. This judgement came from representatives of 'pro-life' groups.

But the opinion she expressed on the case of Struck v. Secretary of Defense, which was heard by the Supreme Court in 1972 - when Ruth Ginsburg was not yet on the bench - provides an illustration of her attachment above all to equal rights. A captain in the US Air Force in Vietnam, who would have been able to have an abortion in the army but refused to do so, had been dismissed by the institution. Justice Ginsburg supported the mother's case, ruling that fathers did not face such difficulties at the time. In this case, a few months before the famous Roe v. Wade ruling, it was not a question of defending the right to abortion per se independently of any other consideration, but of working in favour of equal rights.

Even more audaciously, Ruth Ginsburg later considered that Roe v. Wade had prevented a necessary debate among legislators, while at the same time a trend towards the liberalisation of abortion throughout the country was underway. This trend towards legislative change was, for example, underway on the issue of divorce, which won nationwide support in the mid-1980s. Justice Ginsburg's approach remains relevant today.

Facing up to distress

To put it bluntly, the decision by the main party of the French presidential majority to take up the issue of abortion, echoing the upheavals on the other side of the Atlantic, seemed to reflect a certain ignorance, if not of the realities then at least of American societal developments over a long period.

It was even a misguided tropism, since the issue of abortion, settled by the debate of the 1970s and the 1975 Veil law, was not a topical subject in France. If this was not a misunderstanding, it was clearly a crude political diversionary tactic in the face of the deadlock revealed by the recent legislative elections. Having failed to resolve the problems of purchasing power, taxation or even retirement, the government preferred to invoke so-called 'societal' debates. Didn't the 'marriage for all' of a previous five-year term also have such a purpose, at least in part? Instead of bringing people together for a common cause, the risk is to divide the country even further and, in this case, to ultimately damage women's rights by calling into question what has already been achieved.

The reference to Simone Veil is also relevant in this context. The Health Minister of the time succeeded in bringing about a considerable reform when Jean Lecanuet, the Justice Minister who should have brought it before Parliament, had failed to do so, citing reasons of personal ethics. The law of 17 January 1975 on voluntary termination of pregnancy decriminalising abortion was finally adopted despite opposition from a significant section of the government majority. The law was extended indefinitely in 1979.

Simone Veil's strong words in the National Assembly have stayed with us. The minister's conviction, stated many times, was that abortion should remain 'the exception'. In this spirit, a separate law was passed to make contraceptives available free of charge and anonymously to minors on medical prescription. The 'tragedy' referred to by Simone Veil was echoed by the 'distress' defined by the law and transposed into the Public Health Code (cf. '*A pregnant woman whose condition places her in a position of distress...*'). Article 1 of the law is the keystone, and it is essential to reread it: '*The law guarantees respect for every human being from the beginning of life. This principle may not be infringed except in cases of necessity and in accordance with the conditions defined by this law*'.

Roe v. Wade and the spectre of division

Jane Roe, who brought an action in 1970 against the Texas law (NB: prosecuted by Henry Wade) banning abortion, was the emblematic figure of pro-abortion activists before joining the pro-life movement. She herself never had an abortion. Her life, which ended in 2007, illustrated the social and psychological misery that can lead to voluntary termination of pregnancy; it also reflected the division of America not only into two camps but also in individual consciences. This is also a European phenomenon, and while we must be careful in France, where a consensus was reached on the basis of the Veil law, not to revive the spectre of division in a society that is already quite fractured, women must always have a say in the matter.

The Fourth Republic lost its way in the Algerian War, which sank it. After the 'Toussaint plot' of 1 November 1954, the first tragic mistake was made by Guy Mollet, who in 1956 replaced Governor General Jacques Soustelle, a supporter of the integration of Muslims into the French community, and then increased the number of troops to 400,000; not to mention the hijacking of Ben Bella's plane and the systematic use of the guillotine by Interior Minister F. Mitterrand. After so many victims, to whose memory some of the headstones in our villages in mainland France bear witness, the ceasefire of 1962 brought about the 'peace of the brave' sought by General de Gaulle.

The absence of vision and the impotence of a political system with no real head, the almost hysterical frenzy of a war party, the partiality of the justice system and the many denials of democracy are now threatening France with collapse, against a backdrop of social injustice and contempt for those outside the microcosm.

The judicial night of the long knives' that has just taken place under the sunlights of the cameras was aimed at nothing less than decapitating, outside the ballot box, the head of a political movement. In the political sphere, the 'provisional execution' of judicial decisions is a fate from which the current head of the French government has escaped, a new illustration of double standards. After Romania and even Georgia, what if J.D. Vance had not been completely wrong in his famous speech at the Munich *Wehrkunde*?

Marc Bloch's *L'étrange défaite* (The Strange Defeat) described the surprise provoked by the fall of a great continental power in 1940, even though it had been rearmed as a matter of urgency. On the other hand, a weakened country, which continues its international rantings in total incoherence, is now programmed for further collapse. In the absence of popular support, will the Fifth Republic even avoid collapse?

A former minister and member of the Constitutional Council, made a remarkable speech on television considering that *'the court decision - concerning provisional execution - is not founded in law'* (see the use of references to recidivism or the risk of disturbing public order).

'In the system of liberal democracy, the presumption of innocence must be guaranteed' (NB: provisional execution, which was not automatic but depended on the decision of the judge alone, was therefore not mandatory; appeal should in principle preserve the presumption of innocence).

'The prosecutor mentioned his political opinions' (see the idea that Marine Le Pen must be prevented from standing as a candidate and being elected).

'The court's decision is also a slap in the face to the Constitutional Council' (NB: the latter laid down the principle of the 'proportionality' of the decision, preserving the 'freedom of the voter').

Ms Lenoir recalled that F. Mitterrand was quoted as saying at his last Cabinet meeting: *'Judges have killed the monarchy, they are going to kill the republic'*.

If we really wanted to be controversial, without any partisan activism, we could talk about 'judicial mush and political adventurism'.

The judge - while acknowledging that this text was not relevant in this case - applied the provisions of the Sapin 2 law relating to automatic ineligibility and provisional execution, even though this law was enacted after the events in question.

The political scandal lies in the fact that a trial judge probably eliminated - and this was the intention stated, including by the Public Prosecutor - the person who, at that stage, was the favourite in the next presidential election scheduled in 2027.

It is a sad for France sinking in all areas. Has France become a country, like some others that are not paragons of democracy, where *'it is better to know the judges than the law'*?

18

Democracy in France

In full compliance with its constitutional procedures, in 2022 France elected its President of the Republic, appointed a government and renewed the mandates of its deputies in the National Assembly. The line that won the largest number of votes in the election of the Head of State was quite clearly liberal, social, reformist and European. However, dissatisfaction with the policy that was to be implemented was expressed in advance. These found an outlet in 2024 in the elections for the European Parliament and, a few weeks later, in the legislative elections that followed after the dissolution of the National Assembly.

As a result, the legitimacy of those in power is sometimes subject to constant challenge, with some political parties talking of a 'third round' of parliamentary elections, or even a fourth round in the streets if they fail to get their way. The media complacently echo what is supposed to be the *vox populi*, and even help to amplify it.

Yet representative democracy is a privilege in the face of the rise of authoritarian regimes that sometimes claim to set themselves up as models, and it should show something other than such feverishness. But what is it really? How does it define itself? Is it identified with a particular type of regime? Is it strictly conditioned by institutions alone? Does it not also depend on a historical legacy, a state of mind and a culture ? Does it not also rely on practices outside the strictly political sphere, for example in the social sphere or today in the all-important field of information and communication?

A reflection in the mind of Alexis de Tocqueville

'I confess that in America I saw more than America; I sought there an image of democracy itself, of its inclinations, of its character, of its prejudices, of its passions ' (Alexis de Tocqueville).

Alexis de Tocqueville and Gustave de Beaumont were sent on a mission by the French government in 1831 to investigate the American prison system. It was at the end of this specific ten-month study throughout the United States that Tocqueville wrote *De la démocratie en Amérique* (Democracy in America) , the first book of which was published in 1835. The work focused on a descriptive analysis of this republican representative democracy and reflected on its particular forms. The result was often premonitory visions of the abolition of slavery, the fate of the Indians, the emergence of the United States and Russia as a power, the growing role of the administration in favour of equality over liberty, political violence and the judgement of the wise by the ignorant...

A contemporary reflection on democracy, however modest and embryonic it may be, cannot be limited to the political system and institutions alone, and all aspects of life in society must be taken into consideration. Education must be a priority, but so must the media system and the poorly regulated world of the Internet, which has become a de facto space for direct democracy. In this respect, we should remember the 'Drama on Capitol Hill' in Washington on 6 January 2021, from which a number of lessons can be learned.

If the main question then was naturally: how is it possible in a democracy for free elections, observed, scrutinised, judged and certified, to be open to question? Another question, just as important after certain social networks banned messages from the President of the United States, was: how can private entities be allowed to regulate the operation of new channels of freedom of expression without any possibility of appeal or recourse? The German Chancellor and the French Minister for the Economy denounced the risk of a 'digital oligarchy', and the latter pointed out that *regulation is a matter for the sovereign people, governments and the courts*.

The field of democracy is therefore immense; it has even widened, and that is fortunate. It would be good if, in a historical reversal, we could say: From democracy in France to democracy in America. *Democracy and the political system*

Democracy is a mode of relationship between the governors and the governed that cannot be reduced to a single type of political regime. No one would dispute, for example, the democratic nature of the British monarchy and its parliamentary system, at the centre of which is the House of Commons. This parliamentary system is generally considered to be a model.

At the end of August 2013, the House refused the Conservative government led by David Cameron authorisation to undertake a military operation in Syria in response to the alleged use of chemical weapons by the government in Damascus against its own population. This vote had been preceded by a genuine, but not public, rebellion by Conservative MPs against Foreign Secretary William Hague. The underlying reason was that the British people were still suffering from the 'syndrome' of the 2003 Iraq war, into which Tony Blair, the Labour Prime Minister at the time, had dragged his country in the name of supposed Iraqi weapons of mass destruction. The hundreds of thousands of people who took to the streets to protest against the war alongside George Bush Jr's United States were not heard. In 2013, however, they were heard by their representatives in their constituencies.

President Obama was impressed by this strong act of democracy and it was one of the reasons why he decided not to take military action in Syria, given that the US Executive was not guaranteed a majority in Congress. By the same token, France abandoned the idea of military strikes, for which preparations had already been made. But the French Parliament had not had to make a decision.

On the other hand, there are countries with little democracy whose official name is the Republic. There have also been patrician republics, such as that of Venice, which in retrospect can be likened to oligarchies. But there has never officially been an oligarchic regime. As with the 'formal' and 'real' freedoms that Marxist-Leninists liked to distinguish, we could speak of formal republics and those where the sharing of the common good is a reality. The criterion of authenticity is ultimately the degree of this sharing. If this is not assured, we cannot speak of a Republic. Without it, where relative social harmony is assured, there is no true democracy.

Democracy and political institutions

The debate in France on how to improve the way democracy works recurs time and time again around the reorganisation of institutions. It is a French peculiarity to 'number' republics, as if there were several possible ones. The last three were born of profound historical upheavals: the delayed effects of the Franco-Prussian War of 1870 for the Third Republic (see Proclamation of the Republic in 1870 and the Constitutional Laws of 1875), the aftermath of the Second World War for the Fourth Republic and the Algerian War for the Fifth Republic. Some people are talking about a Sixth Republic, but are they really talking about a Republic, or is the term just a smokescreen for other ambitions to bring about a profound break with the past?
Whatever the case, in the light of institutional practice over the last twenty years and electoral processes over the same period, the debate has come to focus on a few points such as the length of the presidential term, the role of Parliament and electoral law.

The reduction of the presidential term of office from seven to five years by the constitutional referendum of September 2000 (NB: supplemented by the July 2008 revision limiting the number of terms to two) was motivated more by the personal convenience of the then incumbent president than by any substantive reasons. The 'modernity' of such a reform is in fact questionable, and it is fair to say that the seven-year term is appropriate to the role of referee, which is supposed to be above partisan battles, in the spirit of the founders of the Fifth Republic. In turbulent times, it is good that the Head of State has a long-term vision. It should be noted that during the last presidential election, a number of candidates came out in favour of a seven-year term.

Shortening the term of office has also altered not only the spirit but also the practice of the institutions of the Fifth Republic. The current coincidence of presidential and parliamentary terms deprives the country of a democratic 'breathing space' during the term of office of the Head of State. Until now, cohabitation has only occurred in the context of seven-year terms (1986-1988, 1993-1995 and 1997-2002). Cohabitation has perverse effects but has the merit of reflecting the political state of the country and forcing a society that is not naturally inclined to compromise to do so.

While a consensus is not out of reach on the question of the length of the presidential term of office, we are still a long way from it as far as the election of deputies according to the rule of proportional representation is concerned. It is not unfounded to wish that the National Assembly should reflect the state of political forces as closely as possible, but the risk of instability that such an electoral law would bring must be seriously considered in a country that is already fragmented. The UK has a first-past-the-post system, while proportional representation is limited in Germany to a 'second vote' for Bundestag elections. President Mitterrand had wanted to 'instil' proportional representation and we could, if necessary, use this term again in a proportion to be determined. The fact remains that the two-round majority system was designed to eliminate extremes and guarantee majorities.

One way of controlling proportional representation would be to introduce a strict separation of executive and legislative powers. This transition to a presidential system would also have other virtues. As soon as the Head of State returns to a longer term of office, the power of Parliament should be enhanced. It is time for Parliament, with its powerful committees, to play its full role in a system that guarantees the stability of the Executive. Representative democracy will always be preferable to direct democracy, and so-called 'popular initiative' referendums cannot be a substitute or an effective solution.

Clearly, any institutional 'project' is always a large-scale affair that must be approached with caution and after careful consideration. Tinkering with elements of an institutional balance is likely to affect the whole system. Presidential term of office, separation of powers, electoral law - the list is not exhaustive, and we should also mention the 'third pillar' of the constitutional order, namely the judiciary. The development of the prerogatives of the Constitutional Council - marked in particular by the introduction of the preliminary question on constitutionality (QPC), which came into force in 2010 - towards the establishment of a genuine 'Supreme Court', should indeed be pursued.

France, which is supposed to be the land of Cartesian reason, also suffers recurrent bouts of sudden, irrational, nihilistic and destructive fever. The myth of revolution and of a 'brighter tomorrow', the admiration for great orators, even if they turn out to be demagogues in the end, repeatedly inflame a community that is reputed to be astonishingly prone to depressive tendencies. The dormant revolutionary eruptions were in fact moments of rupture in an ensemble that was also underpinned by monarchical traditions and aspirations.

Aren't we talking about the republican monarch of the Fifth Republic? Aren't we seeing microcosm phenomena throughout society that have nothing to do with the Capetians but are rather reminiscent of the Court of Versailles? We want a king, but we don't want any heads to stick out, and that leads to tragic 21 January tragedies. Evil would systematically be at the top and good at the bottom, knowledge and science would be haughty provocations, ambition and the aspiration to progress unhealthy passions, work and competence outmoded values. Republican merit would have had its day.

On meritocracy

The *Entretiens de Royaumont* (Dialog of Royaumont) were devoted specifically to the theme of meritocracy. The concept is broad, complex and needs to be understood in many different ways. Beyond a general understanding of the term, we need to distinguish the notion from that of equality or even freedom. Isn't meritocracy an inherently unequal system that allows individual talent to flourish? If it is the opposite of levelling out, it immediately raises the question of freedom, which can be formulated as follows: does society allow the development and affirmation of personal freedoms? To the major questions raised in this way, should we not add another specific to the

French education system: is elitism legitimate, not in the sense of inequality, but by virtue of the fact that a tiny proportion of an age group - in any case well below 1% - is admitted to what are known as the 'Grandes Écoles' ?

The meritocracy system at the service of all: The answer to all these questions should take into account both respect for innate talent, willpower and hard work, for the greater benefit of individuals, and the needs of a society eager for dynamism, excellence and progress. In very concrete terms, this means that public schools and universities need to be constantly adapted to meet the needs of the community, with fair selection, scholarships, tutoring, mobility for second and third chances, and lifelong learning. The meritocracy system must serve everyone, at every stage of their personal and professional lives.

Meritocracy is therefore a system that should not be confused with the notion of merit, which is more personal, even if it is sometimes recognised externally (see the Ordre du Mérite). The subjectivity of merit is essential if everyone is to progress, but it also has its limits. As one eminent participant in the *Entretiens de Royaumont* put it, '*there are those who never get over their failures, just as there are those who never get over their successes*'.

The latter must always be kept under control, especially in a society where jealousy is a national pathology. Lastly, merit must be given as limited a time frame as possible, to prevent it from being transformed into a form of income, which may even be transferable. At a time of fragmented societies and fierce international competition, merit must remain a central, common, shared concept that is inseparable from justice.

Towards the end of the republican monarch?

The dissolution of the National Assembly, decided by the President of the Republic on the evening of the European Parliament elections on 9 June 2024, was a shock. And this may have been one of its aims:

to chase one disturbance after another. Taking an unvarnished look at the current political and institutional realities in France, and drawing on the science and wisdom of the great public law jurists, may help us to reflect on this unprecedented scenario in the Fifth Republic.

Appeal to the people

In the spirit of the institutions of the Fifth Republic, 'Appeal to the people' seems entirely appropriate when it comes to breaking a political or institutional deadlock; in this respect, however, the President of the Republic could have chosen another moment, for example by means of a referendum - under Articles 11 and 89 of the Constitution - during the debate on pensions or later on immigration legislation; on the evening of 9 June, when the presidential camp had just suffered a crushing defeat, the President could even have proceeded with a 'semi-dissolution', acknowledging the failure of his troops but announcing that the dissolution would only take place in a few months' time if the government failed to achieve a particular result; this would have given him time to organise his supporters and also the hope of benefiting electorally from successful Olympic and Paralympic Games and a possible improvement in the economic situation.

Political uncertainty

A different choice has been made, which is not without its dangers and uncertainties, with the risk of increased instability. Given the current balance of power between the political groupings, two main scenarios could be envisaged:

The *Rassemblement National* (RN) and its allies obtain an absolute majority of seats in the National Assembly. In this scenario, the President of the RN would agree to form the government and a new cohabitation would begin. It would be in the interests of the new dominant party to ensure that this cohabitation took place as smoothly as possible, in order to demonstrate a genuine republican spirit, which has sometimes been called into question, and a sense of responsibility and of the country's higher interests, particularly against the backdrop of the 2027 presidential elections.

The other hypothesis was that the legislative elections of 30 June and 7 July 2024 would fail to produce an absolute majority in the National Assembly. Such an outcome would prove more complicated than the situation ex ante, where the government had had to resort on numerous occasions to Article 49.3, which was deemed likely - a fortiori if used repeatedly - to prevent any 'democratic breathing space' for the country through elected representatives. What's more, according to forecasts, the new configuration of the Assembly will be characterised by a decline in the number of parties supporting the President's line, and will give pride of place to parties with more radical leanings.

In both scenarios, one question could not be avoided: would the President of the Republic - whatever his 'assurances' - be able to stay in office and complete his term of office? Everything would depend on the score achieved by the former presidential 'majority' on the evening of 7 July. If the Ensemble movement and its supporters were to be reduced to a bare minimum, or even virtually disappear, the President's position would have proved extremely weak. This was not the case, but the political crisis has not been overcome. Moreover, in the event of scenario 2 (see absence of an absolute majority in the Assembly), the question of the President's resignation could be the only institutional solution - over and above the political problem - as a dissolution is no longer possible for another year, under the Constitution.

The shift to parliamentarianism

In his book on the constitutional history of France (see Between despotism and democracy), Professor Zorgbibe explains clearly that the 1958 Constitution allows for several interpretations and applications.

Its 'presidentialist' version (NB: a president elected by universal suffrage and a parliament reduced to the strict work of parliament) was weakened by the reduction of the presidential term of office to 5 years (cf. Constitutional revision carried out by President Chirac in 2000). Since then, the President of the Republic has ceased to be a referee, and as his term of office coincides with that of the National Assembly, he has increasingly become a 'super Prime Minister' managing day-to-day affairs. This trend has intensified with the current holder of the Élysée Palace. This situation, until the dissolution of 9 June, had not been corrected beforehand, either by a majority contract in due form with formations joining the presidential party, which would have given meaning to a government reshuffle, or by a referendum, including the so-called 'popular initiative'. Under these conditions, the Executive's direct link with the people has become much weaker.

The 'parliamentary' constitution was revealed during the cohabitations of 1986 (Mitterrand-Chirac), 1993 (Mitterrand-Balladur) and 1997 (Chirac-Jospin), the latter ending with an 'earthquake' caused by the presence of the Front National candidate in the second round of the 2002 presidential election. A fourth cohabitation, from July 2024, could be of a new type and prevent the President from being the 'leader of the opposition' in the face of an absolute or relative majority at the ballot box. This unprecedented scenario would be the result of presidential unpopularity unprecedented in the Fifth Republic, dissension in the presidential camp - whose leading figures have been very critical of the hasty decision to dissolve the government since before the legislative elections - and a possible extreme weakness in the contingent of elected representatives in favour of the President in the National Assembly (see scenarios above).

The virtues of referendums

In view of the above considerations on institutional development and the new political configuration, is the Fifth Republic not de facto called into question? The President of the Republic has finally respected the spirit and the letter of the institutions, allowing supreme arbitration to be reserved for the people, through referendum or dissolution.

But a final question now arises. Will the Assembly be sovereign or will it comply with popular sovereignty, which is not exactly the same thing? Elected representatives are the expression of the national will and do not have an imperative mandate; they are elected in a constituency, but express themselves and legislate in the name of the nation. Here we return to an old debate, dating back to the revolutionary era, between parliamentarianism and the 'representative' principle, in which the question of democracy is central. Article 3 of the 1958 Constitution defines a semi-direct democracy (*'national sovereignty belongs to the people, who exercise it through their representatives and by referendum'*). The referendum may ultimately prove to be a last resort designed to 'democratise' the French parliamentary system. It would then become a kind of safeguard, whether or not the National Assembly has a clear majority; it would ultimately be a matter of supervising the 'republican monarch', whose *diminutio capitis,* if not forfeiture, it could thus ratify.

A return to the roots or a Sixth Republic without the name?

Thanks to Pr Zorgbibe, let's take a look back at Michel Debré's constitutional project, within the Conseil National de la Résistance (CNR) in 1944, which was parliamentary in essence. It was envisaged that the 'republican monarch' would not govern himself; he would be above the daily political ups and downs, guiding the government's action in broad terms; he could, if necessary, support the government by dissolving it; he would only intervene directly in the event of a crisis.

Michel Debré's nostalgia for a 'classic' parliamentary system was opposed by a 'democratic anti-parliamentarianism', the aim being to reduce the effects of an abusive transfer of the people's sovereignty to the 'representatives' sitting in Parliament. This was the conception of René Capitant, an early Gaullist and disciple of Carré de Malberg.

The Constitutional Act of 10 July 1940, which conferred full powers on Marshal Pétain, was the culmination of the 1875 regime and undoubtedly fuelled the fears that gave rise to this latest approach.

The Ordinance of 17 August 1945 therefore instituted a consultation of the French people by means of a referendum. But the promises of 1945 were not kept with the Constitution of 27 October 1946 establishing the Fourth Republic. The representative system then made a comeback, but it should be noted that it was the Parliament of the Fourth Republic that delegated constituent power to General de Gaulle in 1958.

The 1958 Constitution was originally more liberal than democratic. The constitutional reform of 1962 - concerning the election of the President of the Republic by universal suffrage - fundamentally corrected this initial orientation. Be that as it may, the solution lies in the division or distribution of sovereignty between the 'monarch', the Assembly and the people. The return in force of the Assembly to the centre of the institutional and political game, in the current situation, even in the event of a relative majority, while the Executive is weakened, leaves no other solution than the most regular possible consultation of the people in order to decide on the main arbitrations. A constitutional adaptation that would not bear the name would then have been introduced. The age of the republican monarch, according to a Constitution carved out for General de Gaulle and to which Georges Pompidou aspired, would then have come to an end. The famous words of the Duc de La Rochefoucauld addressed to the King on the evening of 14 July 1789 (*'But this is a revolt ? No, Sire, a revolution!'*) are bound to come to mind. But if a revolution is an accomplished revolt, it is also the completion of a complete turn and therefore a return to the starting point.

Fifty shades of cohabitation

With the possibility of political cohabitation looming - which would be the fourth under the Fifth Republic - and the 'reserved domain' of the President of the Republic sometimes evoked in public debate, it is important to examine these concepts, not only theoretically but also in the light of French institutional practice.

Cohabitation and the reserved domain

The cohabitation of the Head of State with a majority of Parliament hostile to him is a major problem posed by the Constitution of the Fifth Republic. It should be pointed out that such a situation can also arise even when the President and his Prime Minister are from the same political current.

For example, Prime Minister Jacques Chaban-Delmas gave a speech to the National Assembly on the '*New Society*' that made history, provoked the ire of President Pompidou and led the latter to part company with his head of government in 1972, replacing him with the loyal Pierre Messmer. The incompatibilities between President Mitterrand and Michel Rocard were also very real and lasted three long years, from the end of the first cohabitation. But in such situations, where there are differences of opinion and even open conflict, the solution remains for the Prime Minister to be replaced by the President, in accordance with the latter's constitutional right.

In the event of cohabitation - in the strict sense of the term - resulting from the emergence of a majority different from that of the parties supporting the President of the Republic - the 'parliamentary' reading of the Constitution prevails.

Does the transfer of majority power from the President to the Prime Minister make the latter the true head of the Executive? The answer to this question needs to be qualified, if we examine both the institutional aspects and the balance of political power. Political scientists and constitutional experts have been able to distinguish between 'cohabitation-compromise', 'cohabitation-submission' - which President Mitterrand in particular refused to accept - and 'cohabitation-conflict', which presupposes that two clearly established legitimacies can clash.

The myth of the reserved domain

Let us say straight away that the concept of a '*reserved*' domain does not appear in the Constitution of the Fifth Republic, original or amended. The expression was used by Jacques Chaban-Delmas in 1959 at a political meeting.

Nevertheless, the extent of the specific and joint powers of the two heads of the Executive and the question of their reciprocal powers of veto must be carefully examined.

The area in which the President has his or her own powers consists of the acts that he or she may commit without ministerial countersignature. The list is limitative but covers theoretically important powers: the President may thus have recourse to a referendum (art. 11), dissolve the government (art. 12), take exceptional measures (art. 16), address the Assemblies by message (art. 18), refer to the Constitutional Council concerning an international commitment (54) or laws (art. 61). The fact remains that the President - a ritual formula inherited from the Third Republic? - is *'the head of the armed forces. He presides over the higher national defence councils and committees'* (cf. art. 15). In addition, we must not forget the question of a possible non-shared decision on the use of nuclear weapons.

The Prime Minister, for his part, is not powerless. Under Article 20: *'The Government shall determine and conduct the policy of the nation. It has the administration and the armed forces at its disposal'*. In the latter area, Article 21 states that the Prime Minister *'shall be responsible for National Defence'*. The fact that *'The Government shall inform Parliament of its decision to have the armed forces intervene abroad, no later than three days after the start of the intervention...'*. (art. 35) reinforces the powers of the Head of Government in the event of the armed forces being deployed.

Kriegspiel and reality

Cohabitation must be analysed from a legal point of view, but the way in which it unfolds is also, and above all, the result of the reality of the political balance of power; we cannot confine ourselves to purely theoretical schemes. The popularity of the main players, the numerical strength of the parliamentarians who support them, and the resources at their disposal (e.g. the media system) are all important factors. A dissolution having just taken place, the 'hand weapon' defined in art. 12 at the disposal of the President cannot be used for one year; the application of art. 16, except in the case of a national tragedy, cannot be envisaged and is strictly regulated; a referendum was not resorted to in the case of pensions or the law on immigration, so why should it be any different today ?

In 1981, President Mitterrand ruled out the idea of cohabitation and dissolved the National Assembly as soon as he was appointed. Today, by declaring in advance that his mandate was not under threat and that he would complete his term of office in 2027, the President of the Republic has preserved the prospect of cohabitation. However, in the event of a major political deadlock, the only way out - democratic in nature - would undoubtedly be an early presidential election. For a time, during the first cohabitation, Jacques Chirac was considered to be the most powerful Prime Minister in the history of the Republic; this did not save him from failure in the 1988 presidential election. But wouldn't this governmental ascendancy be even more marked, given the current configuration, in the event of an absolute majority in the National Assembly, hostile to the President of the Republic? Should we not add a category, that of 'unbalanced cohabitation' to the typology of cohabitations outlined above?

Raymond Aron once said of the international situation: *'Impossible peace, improbable war'*. Could we now say - using his expression - 'impossible cohabitation', i.e. ineluctable but inevitably conflictual, and 'improbable reserved domain', i.e. limited in practice and conditioned by circumstances? In this general context, is it out of place to talk about the *'honorary'* function of the head of the armed forces, in the event of cohabitation, and the blocking power of the head of government - whose only reason, incidentally, is not that he *'holds the purse strings'* - for the deployment of troops in a foreign country? If it is not a question of encouraging extreme positions on both sides, is it not time for the restoration of politics - expressed by a clear will and a clear direction - whereas a 'peaceful' cohabitation, i.e. the dream of some, would once again be tantamount to an absence of determined government in France?

The sovereign Republic

Looking back to 2022

The second round of French parliamentary elections in 2022, following the last presidential elections, had already been described as a tsunami, which was no doubt an exaggeration at the time and had to be put into perspective. The situation certainly seemed deadlocked in the absence of an absolute majority in the National Assembly and any serious prospect of forming a grand coalition 'in the German style'. Nevertheless, the centre of gravity of the political debate had shifted to the Chamber, and this could be judged rather positively in terms of the parliamentary reading of the 1958 Constitution.

Democracy through the voice of the people's representatives was better than the direct democracy of the street or even social networks. Better effective parliamentary democracy than a recording chamber dominated by one or more *godillot* (clodhopper) parties, i.e. parties that were as submissive as they were lethargic. The essential question was therefore one of effectiveness for the country: how could we get out of this? What needed to be done?

Two legitimate powers were then facing each other: an Executive which was no longer able to implement its programme by legislative means, or at least with the greatest difficulty by resorting to the famous '49.3'; an Assembly where no political party or group of parties had an absolute majority; opposing extremes sometimes appealing to socially close but irreconcilable electorates; pivotal parties open to dialogue, but running the risk of a total loss of identity and even eventual disappearance.

Consultation of the parties was therefore unlikely to produce any significant results or bring about any real clarification. René Coty and the Fourth Republic were in fact from another era, and the separation of powers should also protect us from such encroachments - which could ultimately be reserved for a head of government accountable to Parliament - when the country had already spoken. Couve de Murville, General de Gaulle's minister, used to say that '*France does not speak twice*'.

Breaking waves and cohabitation before time

The Republic ran the risk of being tossed about, plagued by confusion, threatened if not close to being submerged by breaking waves. It had to be '*brought into port*', as the great historian François Furet wrote of the advent of the Third Republic. This period of our history, which René Rémond, another great historian, described as a 'sovereign Republic', was born of the imperial defeat at Sedan and lasted through three wars until the fatal collapse of 1940. In its early years, it was characterised by the opposition of the monarchist right and the republicans in a sort of 'cohabitation' before its time.

Despite these considerable difficulties, and despite the fact that no constitutional experiment had lasted more than twenty years since 1789, it was the ascendancy of the Republic that ensured its longevity, which was only surpassed in the end by the Fifth Republic. The year 1879 marked the end of hopes for a monarchical restoration with the death in battle of the Prince Imperial, the death without heir of the Count of Chambord, the unexpected control by the Republicans of the High Assembly and finally the resignation of Marshal Mac Mahon. But democratic 'breathing space', at a time when ministerial cabinets were alternating wildly, also played an essential role thanks to elections and universal suffrage. Yes, the sovereign Republic was a supreme guarantor.

Contemporary France has long retained a nostalgia for the monarchy, and there has been talk of a 'republican monarch'. Paradoxically, this atavism, which has lasted through the constitutional ages, has often developed in a permanent pre-revolutionary climate likely to provoke a swing in favour of the extremes. It was perhaps this analysis, in the wake of the traumatic Algerian war and its outgrowths in metropolitan France, that led the fathers of the Fifth Republic to devise a constitution that was half-presidential and half-parliamentary. The system - tailored primarily to the needs of General de Gaulle and which President Mitterrand even managed to take advantage of during two periods of cohabitation - effectively required a kind of monarch insofar as it was not protected by a strict separation of powers.

Resolving a latent constitutional crisis?

The current context, which could if necessary take on the appearance of an institutional crisis, does not allow us to imagine a profound reform with a view to a strict separation of powers, i.e. an increase in the powers of Parliament, accompanied if necessary by a modification of the electoral law which would incorporate a dose of proportional representation. But the time is not right, or not yet, because the changes would appear to be expedient and of a nature to protect a besieged citadel, even if in spirit the aim would be to limit the 'solitary exercise' of power so often criticised under the Fifth Republic.

One solution, at least a temporary one, to prevent the country from falling into disastrous stagnation, would be to seek inspiration in the message of the sovereign Republic: the whole Republic, nothing but the Republic. Recourse to the people, through dissolution, when the country had already expressed itself four times in the space of a few weeks in 2022, potentially presented the risk of aggravating the crisis and strengthening more radical, even extreme movements; but this, in the absence of referendums that could have been held earlier, for example at the time of the debate on pensions or the law on immigration, was made necessary by the message of the European elections and the need for democratic clarification. The resignation of the President of the Republic? The disadvantage described above - unless parliamentary confusion made this the only possible institutional outcome - could have been multiplied, given that the President of the Republic, even weakened, is supposed to remain a major guarantor of the institutions.

Photograph of the National Assembly

Much ultimately depends on the picture of the National Assembly, after a rather blurred video of the last presidential election. In 2022, despite its decline compared to the previous legislature, the presidential party had retained a certain momentum that gave it room for manoeuvre, such as a possible governing coalition. This is no longer the case in 2024. The choice of the leader of the largest parliamentary group as Prime Minister should a priori have been a necessity, with the Head of State drawing the consequences of the country's political state for a second time in a row. But the absence of a majority from any party has complicated the process. It is nonetheless imperative that the new government, even if it is not necessarily a single-coloured one, should be able to tackle the most essential issues, both internal and external, as a matter of urgency.

A major risk would be that the fourth cohabitation would be approached with Machiavellianism, as has already been the case in the past. It will be in the interest of the new dominant party - clearly aspiring to confirm its respectability - to lend itself to a cohabitation that is not perceived as purely confrontational, if only to hope for electoral benefits later on. The choice of dissolution may have been criticised, especially for its timing, but it could later be re-evaluated in a more positive light if it had helped to avert a political and social explosion.

A laboratory for political regimes

France's constitutional history shows that the country has had no fewer than eleven written constitutions and that it was the greatest laboratory for political regimes. Should there be a monarch or a president? One assembly or two? Censal or universal suffrage? A single vote or several rounds? A dose of proportional representation in the electoral mechanism? Referendums and supreme judges? The Fifth Republic was equipped with instruments - including dissolution - to overcome this contradiction. But there is no doubt that this is not the time for new experiments, even if they may be dictated by circumstances. Apart from the fact that the absolute priority is to get the country back to work over the long term, the compass must above all remain the reference to the sovereign Republic.

Betting on instability?

On the evening and the day after the first round of the legislative elections, the New Popular Front (NFP) cannot envisage an absolute majority, and a fortiori the 'Ensemble' movement, the figurehead of an ex-'majority', whether alone or with others. In the absence of a clear majority, the latter movement would then find itself in the National Assembly in a new configuration of relative majority, but in a clearly diminished position and subject to the left, including the most extreme.

Consequently, to declare that the main objective is to prevent the Rassemblement National from obtaining an absolute majority of seats at all costs (NB: is this also the position of Horizons or the Parti *Les Républicains*?) is, in practice, to bet on the instability of the country.

The objective of blocking the *Rassemblement National* at all costs - failing a cohabitation with the latter, however conflictual - could end up forcing the President of the Republic to resign and call an early presidential election. This is what Marine Le Pen had indicated in recent days, while making it clear that she was not formally calling for this, but that it could prove to be the only political outcome. In the immediate term, her party may find it advantageous, in the run-up to the second round of legislative elections and beyond, to develop the argument of the risk of instability with voters.

Leaving aside a priori the possibility of resignation, would the only realistic ultimate objective of a clearly diminished President of the Republic be only a negative one (unless we imagine that the Left could still be beneficial to the country and truly believe in the concept of the 'Republican Front')? Would volatility and instability be preferable to cohabitation? Would destruction be creative, as some economists believe? Or is it more a question, in the end, of doing harm above all else in the belief of saving face?

Dissolution has given the people back their say and cannot therefore be contested a priori. In fact, 'appeal to the people' is a fundamental principle of the institutions of the Fifth Republic.

In so doing, the President of the Republic asked the people to clarify their aspirations, or even to make a decision, and he had to remain above the political fray by adopting the position of referee. This is apparently not what is happening. Many have criticised the Chief Executive for his decision on 9 June, including and perhaps even especially in his own camp.

But to try to 'muddy the waters' even further, and to use unnatural arrangements to curb or even pervert the expression of the sovereign people, can only deepen the political crisis and send the country into uncontrolled turbulence.

If anything, it would be worse than what has already been done. A coincidental rapprochement with LFI - a movement that is undoubtedly more anti-Republican than other supposed extremists who have been pilloried - would also be a moral failing with regard to a manipulated and deceived public.

The advocates of the Sixth Republic do not just act on impulse and there is no doubt that they have a strategy. We have to give them credit for this talent. Those who think they can live with it, or even take advantage of it, when they are in a position of great weakness, are deluding themselves. It is astonishing to note that one of the pillars of the semi-presidential system of the Fifth Republic is working - out of blindness, spite or misplaced pride? - to its own collapse, in a manner reminiscent of the Fourth Republic. In reality, the result of these strategies, developed behind the backs of the French people, could lead us to great disorder in the streets, the ultimate goal of Trotskyite-style tactics.

A narrow path of ridges

As a result of institutional and political juggling, for which he himself was in no way responsible, the neo-Gaullist Michel Barnier became Prime Minister of France. Given the parliamentary situation and the challenges to be faced, the path ahead of him - and the expression may seem appropriate for a mountain man - was a narrow path of ridges and ultimately a journey along vertiginous and abysmal precipices.

Even if the Gaullists are pachyderms, firmly rooted in the clay, but still obsessed with movement - and they have, moreover, modernised France - their immense memory and incomparable physical weight, which can trample over more than one if necessary, was not enough. Lacking boldness and clear commitments on the budget, the Barnier government was censured by the National Assembly, something that had not happened since Georges Pompidou in 1962.

'President' Bayrou

He was succeeded by the centrist François Bayrou, heir to the Christian Democracy movement and also a supporter of Europe. In the current political context, his choice of Prime Minister seems coherent. However, his past positions in favour of left-wing personalities have not spared him from enmity within the so-called democratic left, to the outcry from its more extreme fringes; his republican respect for the Rassemblement National and its voters may be paid in return by a form of non-aggression pact a priori from the right, which considers itself patriotic. A certain longevity at the head of the government could thus be assured, but under certain conditions.

The final composition of his government team, made up of the heavyweights of French politics, could strengthen his hand, but much will depend on the programme he intends to implement. The question of adopting the State budget for 2025 will be the first major obstacle: mimicking his predecessor - whose only readable budget line was to raise taxes - would be fatal. And even more so a reverential attitude towards the President of the Republic. Let's be quite clear: F. Bayrou is not taking the helm of the government to save a weakened President without a solution, but for higher ambitions, starting with his own.

Having finally realised part of his lifelong political dream, anything is now possible. To put himself in a favourable position for the next presidential election, he will have to dissociate himself to the breaking point from the other branch of the executive. Uniquely in the annals of the Fifth Republic, he could well take the ascendancy within the dyarchy at the top. Certain appearances may be preserved because, as with Henri IV, whose biography the new Prime Minister wrote, Paris will be worth a mass.

But apart from the immense responsibility in this context, the function of head of government as defined by the Fifth Republic can be considerable. It should be remembered that since 1958, there has been no 'reserved area' defined by legislation.

On the road to Bordères

François Bayrou is firmly rooted in a family, a history, a terroir, a landscape. When his national obligations allow, he lives in Bordères in the Pyrénées-Atlantiques about twenty kilometres from Pau, where he intends to remain mayor. This rural village community has well under 1,000 inhabitants. His home is his parents' house, which he has never left. The village is light and airy, dotted with large, solid farms and dwellings in the traditional Béarn style; horse-breeding and small-scale industries linked to agriculture are the dominant activities facing the grandiose Pyrenees mountain range. The village is dominated by two churches, which is hardly reminiscent of Colombey, let alone a guardian of the two holy mosques. The village gives an impression of quiet strength, and if the slogan didn't exist we'd have to reinvent it. This solidity is enhanced by the charm of a lively school where the children are delighted to be picked up by a cheerful cart pulled by two draught horses. The bells and heavy footsteps of the animals echo through the narrow streets, providing a natural concert of simplicity. Henri IV, about whom the new Prime Minister wrote a biography a long time ago, is a permanent reference for him. Bordères lies on the famous Henri IV trail from Pau to Lourdes, which the king used to travel on horseback and which is still popular with horse riders, cyclists and hikers.

On the road to Bordères, on the road to Lourdes... happy surprises may also await the citizens of France, Navarre and beyond, despite the turbulent and gloomy climate, despite the tragedy due to a hurricane in the island of Mayotte and the terrorist act in Magdeburg.

The nobility of politics

The thunderous arrival of the new Prime Minister shook up what was still left of the Fifth Republic. For the first time in the history of the Fifth Republic, the Prime Minister was imposed by forceps; can we imagine that G. Pompidou or M. Couve de Murville could have done the same with General de Gaulle? For the first time, the Prime Minister was able to put together his own government team quite independently. Finally, for the first time, the head of government could take the ascendancy over the head of state in a new type of cohabitation; the condition, however, would be to avoid any new controversy that the public would not understand.

A few years ago, the new Prime Minister painted an ideal picture that was far removed from the majority system that is the essence of the Fifth Republic, which the French no longer seem to want. The definition of the political 'centre' is that of a sort of receptacle for pluralism. It also seems more linked to parliamentarianism than to a semi-presidential system that no longer works. His reference to W. Churchill - a model for the Prime Minister - is in fact a tribute to British parliamentarism, but we could also mention German institutions and political life, which allow coalitions to be formed. If F. Bayrou is a history buff and can speak knowledgeably about it, his remarks of a few years ago - which reflect a certain idealism - seem highly topical and also correspond to a necessity on a narrow path of ridges.

19

Spirituality without the Churches?

It has sometimes been predicted that the century will be a religious one. It is still too early to say, and the violence and clashes under religious banners do not necessarily confirm this. Rather, the prediction refers to a possible spiritual revival, and the question arises first and foremost for the two largest religions in terms of the number of believers, Catholicism and Islam (NB: 2.2 billion Christians and 1.8 billion Muslims, mainly in Indonesia and India).

The spirit and the time of the Reformation

The Catholic Church today undoubtedly finds itself at a time that is similar to that of the Protestant Reformation. Some similarities can even be identified with sixteenth-century Germany, although, as always, comparison is not reason. At that time, it was a question of dealing with the dysfunctions of the Roman Church (see the debauched 'curetons'; the Popes behaved like sovereigns, such as Leo X, a sumptuous patron of the arts, son of Lorenzo the Magnificent) in a climate of profound economic and social disorder (see the *Peasants' War* of 1525). We should mention Thomas Münzer - one of the religious leaders of the Peasants' War and one of the great protagonists of the Reformation - as much as Martin Luther, who in the end sided with the powerful (*'Dear lords, stab, slaughter, slit throats'*) and put an end to revolutionary Protestantism. The essential inspiration of the Reformation movement was the need to return to the origins of Christianity, i.e. in practice to the Scriptures. (See '*The true treasure of the Church is the Holy Gospel*', Wittemberg Theses). For Luther, the author of these theses posted on the eve of All Saints' Day in 1517, '*a Christian is the master of all things and the subject of no one*', which is an affirmation of free interpretation (*sola fide*), if not of free will.
Mozart and Francis

Benedict XVI's funeral Mass was a somewhat truncated event. There is no need to go back over France's absence at the appropriate level. We need to read or reread Benedict XVI's testament, written in 2006 and now revealed, to appreciate the light - the word comes up several times - that emanated from Joseph Ratzinger's personality and the hope that animated him right up to his last day. The sobriety and simplicity of the funeral, in accordance with the wishes of the Pope Emeritus, did not exclude grandeur and emotion.

Joseph Ratzinger expressed himself, particularly in his native language, in such a clear and crystalline manner that one had the impression of hearing Mozart, whom he loved so much and whom he played on the piano every day. But instead of dull reciters and a homily strangely focused on suffering, we did not hear the music in which Italy abounds with incomparable talent. We missed, for example, the Andante from Concerto No. 23, filled with the zephyrs of the Elysian fields, or the touching *Soave sia il vento* from Cosi fan Tutte, particularly well-suited to the circumstances. Or Biber's glorious baroque *Missa Salisburgensis*, created and performed near his beloved Bavarian Alps.

We would then have been at the heart of European civilisation, where Benedict XVI has always placed his reason and his faith, and from which he has developed his Pontificate towards the whole world. But the greatness was that of the recumbent, for Wolfgang 'Amadeus' will always remain with him. 'May the breeze be light to him...' (*Soave sia il vento*).

France, the reprobate daughter of the Church and of Europe

The funeral of Benedict XVI took place in Rome under the gaze of the whole world and in the presence of many heads of state and government. France was represented by its Minister of the Interior and Religious Affairs. Despite the respect due to the Minister, this underlined the distance France has taken with the Vatican.
France, which was long considered the Eldest Daughter of the Church, did not have the courage to include a reference to Europe's

'Christian roots' in European texts. Today, intellectually and morally adrift, it prefers to think about enshrining - uselessly because of the Loi Veil - the right to abortion in the Constitution and to seek to advance a freedom, which would then be misused, in the choice of the moment at the end of life. These erring ways perhaps explain the distance we have taken from Rome.

Cardinal Ratzinger was a lover of French culture, thought and language, in which he expressed himself as Mozart - whom he adored and played every day on the piano - did with his music. He was awarded the Légion d'Honneur at the Villa Bonaparte, the residence of the French ambassador to the Holy See. That day, he gave a memorable speech in French.

Since the 17th century, after the Kings of France, the Presidents of the Republic have been Honorary Canons of the Roman Church of St John Lateran. This archibasilica is also the Pope's episcopal church in Rome. By forgetting its roots, a France that has turned in on itself and often gives the impression that it is no longer governed is on the way to becoming the 'reprobate daughter of the Church and of Europe'.

A Europe rooted in great values

The insignia of Commander of the Legion of Honour were conferred on Cardinal Joseph Ratzinger by the French Ambassador to the Holy See, on behalf of the President of the French Republic, on 11 May 1998 at Villa Bonaparte in Rome. For a long time little was known about the speech given by the recipient, apart from those who attended the ceremony. In April 2005, just after the conclave that elected Benedict XVI, the French ambassador to the Vatican, Pierre Morel, sent this text with a diplomatic telegram to several French embassies and consulates around the world. This is the speech in its original and unabridged version (NB: delivered in French).

At this moment when words fail me, I can only say thank you from the bottom of my heart: thank you to the President of the French Republic, who made me a Commander of the Legion of Honour; thank you to you, Mr Ambassador, and to you, Madam, for your friendship and your commitment. I never imagined the honour and happiness of finding myself so truly and deeply connected to the great French cultural and spiritual tradition.

From a young age I was a zealous admirer of sweet France. In a Germany destroyed and humiliated by the war, the first drama I saw was Le Soulier de satin by Paul Claudel. It was an important turning point in my life. The symbolism of love and renunciation, of fertility and renunciation, of divine grace in human weakness, had become a very personal message for me, a fundamental indication of the path in life I would take.

We started to read the great contemporary French writers: Bernanos, Mauriac, Péguy, but also secular writers such as Anouilh and Sartre. At that time the German borders were still closed, but in 1948 we were introduced to the 'supernatural' book by Father Henri de Lubac: with his new anthropology, his deep sensitivity for modern man and his profound faithfulness to the true message of the Christian faith, he was a revelation for us. He opened up a new vision of the world and presented a new synthesis between modernity and tradition. A little later, I also discovered other French theologians such as Congar, Daniélou and Chenu: my way of thinking took shape through contact with these teachers, in whom I found an exemplary synthesis between spirituality and science, between intuition and methodological rigour.

For me, the great moment came when I had the opportunity, for the first time, at the Council of 1962, to greet the venerable Father de Lubac, and I was amazed at the humility and cordiality with which this great man welcomed the obscure young German theologian that I was. Father de Lubac had been one of the courageous inspirers of the resistance in France during the war. He had fought against an ideology of lies and violence, but not against a people. This resistance carried with it the true force of reconciliation: Christian humanism, based on universality and the unifying force of truth. Truth is also a sword - against falsehood, and Father de Lubac wasn't afraid to use this sword against falsehood inside and outside the Church, before and after the Council. But above all he was a man of peace and brotherhood in the love of Christ.
For me, the friendship with Father and Cardinal de Lubac, which developed during the Council and the period when we worked together in the International Theological Commission, is one of the greatest gifts I have received in my life.

This great Christian was for me the embodiment of authentic Christian humanism, capable of founding a Europe in fraternal communion with all the continents. Cardinal de Lubac stood out for me as the embodiment of noble France and a perfect model of evangelical savoir-vivre.

I congratulate France for these great personalities. I thank France for the gift of its humanistic culture. I hope that all of us can contribute to shaping a Europe steeped in the great values of its Christian tradition, to bar the way to ideological temptations of every kind. I thank you once again for the honour of belonging to the Legion of Honour. Long live the friendship between France and Germany, long live France!

The shadow of two Popes

The Vatican, the Pope and international politics are inextricably linked. As the Vatican is also a State and has a renowned diplomatic service, notably with its network of apostolic nuncios, it is not surprising that the Pope should express his views on the war in Ukraine. This is what he did on Swiss television, but with remarks that sometimes came as a surprise.

Referring to 14-18 and 39-45, the Pope first of all considered that we had entered a Third World War. This point of view is questionable, because the countries that support the parties to a conflict, which is certainly now global, are not co-belligerents in the legal sense of the term. What was most surprising - after previous highly controversial statements about '*NATO barking at Russia's door*' - was that he equated the aggressor with the victim, that he ignored war crimes and even genocide, and that he alluded to another form of imperialism in the war in Ukraine.

Unlike his predecessors, the Pope did not have the understanding of a European, for whom peace at any price can be tantamount to submission. John Paul II clearly understood what '*order reigns in Warsaw*' meant under the Soviet boot. It is not enough to say incantorily '*negotiations, negotiations!*' to put an end to destruction and injustice.

Since he likes to demonstrate by example, some people would have liked to see the Pope in Kyiv and even more so in Butcha. But isn't this deliberate retreat also a reminder that man is free, including to stray into the worst errors? And in such a conflict between two Christian nations, can the Vatican confine itself to an attitude other than that of neutrality and condemnation of all war? Its more recent comments to the effect that *'tomorrow could be worse'* or advocating *'the courage of the white flag'* were shocking in Kiev because they implied a form of surrender.

Decidedly, the dogma of papal infallibility - contested from the outset in 1870, notably for fear of an extension of the Church's temporal power - is a long way off. And we cannot fail to think of Pius XII, whose Christmas message in 1942 brought despair to so many believers, because it merely alluded to the Shoah. Will we ever speak of Francis in the same polemical terms?

John Paul II, Pope for the nuclear age

We still live in the shadow of John Paul II, who made a powerful contribution to shaking off totalitarianism and continues to be a guiding light for Roman Catholicism. From 1978 until 2005, Karol Wojtyla was the first non-Italian Pope since the 16th century. He guided the Catholic Church in the latter part of the century. This period was marked by a number of milestones the trip to his native Poland in 1979, which aroused national passions and vividly confirmed the country's desire to emancipate itself from the socialist camp; the attack on St Peter's Square in Rome on 13 May 1983; the first visit by a pope to the synagogue in Rome in 1986; and the establishment of diplomatic relations with Israel; the meeting in the Vatican with Mikhail Gorbachev on 1 December 1989, which led the following year to a law on freedom of conscience and religion in Russia; the rejection of the Gulf War in 1991, the opening up to Islam and at the same time the rejection of fundamentalism; the 'purification' of the Church's historical memory, in line with Paul VI. But more than the Pope, we should refer here to the thinker, philosopher and politician that he was perhaps above all. His thoughts on Europe, the nation and man, expressed for example in his speech to UNESCO in Paris in 1980, still resonate today with astonishing topicality:

'The whole of Europe - from the Atlantic to the Urals - bears witness to the link between culture and Christianity in the history of each nation and of the community as a whole'.

'My wish is that Europe, sovereignly giving itself free institutions, will one day be able to unfold the dimensions that geography and even more history have given it... the culture inspired by the Christian faith has profoundly marked the history of all the peoples of our unique Europe, Greek and Latin, Germanic and Slavic, despite all the vicissitudes and beyond the social systems and ideologies' (see speech to the UN, 1995).

'The nation is the great community of men. It exists through and for culture. It is always a stable element of the human experience and of the humanistic perspectives of human development'.

'Protect what is the apple of your eye, do not allow this fundamental sovereignty to fall prey to any political or economic interest, a victim of totalitarianism, imperialism or hegemony for which man counts only as an object of domination and not as the subject of his human existence'.

In this age of multiple nuclear threats, we should add this thought to the conclusion of a major speech:

'It is said that nuclear weapons have acted as a deterrent, preventing the outbreak of a major war, and this is probably true... but at the same time we can ask ourselves whether this will always be the case'.

'We must convince ourselves of the priority of ethics over technology, of the primacy of the person over things, of the superiority of spirit over matter'.

John Paul II loved France very much. It was during his homily at Notre-Dame de Paris on 30 May 1980 that he asked his famous, haunting and inescapable question: *'Do you love ? Do you love me?'*.

Woman, Life, Freedom, at the heart of Shiism

The Iranian Shiite revolution shook the world, starting with the revolution led by Ayatollah Khomeini forty-five years ago. Paradoxically, it is the very heart of Shi'ism that is now being shaken, if not cracked, both by strong internal dissent and by extreme regional tensions in the Near and Middle East.

Masha Amini, our sister, our daughter

Every 16 September, the civilised world - which includes first and foremost the young people of Iran in revolt - will remember Masha Amini, the 22-year-old Iranian woman of Kurdish origin who fell victim to the ferocious repression of the mullahs' regime in 2022. An expiatory victim, she will also have shaken one of the most criminal regimes on earth (NB: almost two thirds of the world's capital executions take place there) and perhaps contributed through her martyrdom to changing the future of her country forever.

The murder committed by the police sparked off a huge movement against the hijab, for the first time since the Shiite revolution in 1979. And this revolt in the heart of the cities, and in particular the university, has spread throughout the country against a backdrop of economic stagnation, with 30 to 40% of Iranians living below the poverty line and uncontrolled inflation (NB: estimated at between 40 and 80%).

In a country where the average population is under 40, most of the protesters were under 25. These young people, who had only known the Islamic regime and the Internet, met at Sharif University in Tehran and Ferdowsi University in Mashad in the north of the country; it involved many sections of the population, including small traders in the bazaar and part of the rural world, whether in Kurdish country or in Iranian Baluchistan in the south; it was composed equally of men and women; it was spontaneous in the sense that it had no leading figures.

While the initial slogan was *Woman, Life, Freedom*, the demonstrators also demanded a '*democratic, secular and non-discriminatory system*'. Theocratic rule was clearly called into question. But a revolt, however deep and long it may be (NB: this one lasted for many months) does not necessarily lead to a revolution, a fortiori in the face of a regime whose conservatism had been reinforced since the election of President Raissi in 2021. Iran experienced the 2009 protest against the results of the presidential election and the 'economic' revolts of 2017 and 2019. But the telluric tremor this time, in a country where there are 4.5 million students, the engines of change, will not be without lasting consequences, even if they are delayed.

Masha Amini, a prudish and innocent young woman from Kurdistan, has become, perhaps in spite of herself, the standard-bearer of a movement that will not disappear. We'll be thinking of her again during the '*Night of Yalda*', on the winter solstice, a very ancient tradition in Persian culture dating back to Cyrus the Great. Yalda also means 'rebirth', that of the sun, and therefore the triumph of light over darkness. You could even say over obscurantism and barbarism.

Nowruz in Iran

The sadness of the Iranian people is our sadness. It is due to the ferocity of the repression, to the cult of force, to the denial of so much intelligence, to the discrimination that amounts to virtual apartheid, to the destruction of beauty, finesse and sensitivity, which also means art. But Iranian pride remains immense and legitimate, and nothing will stop it from blossoming in the end. It will then be our Iran, the one that already exists and is being denied.

Nowruz, the first day of the year 1401, is celebrated every March throughout the Persian cultural and traditional area, from Iran naturally to Afghanistan and India, as well as Central Asia. This day corresponds to the spring equinox when, everywhere in the world, as the sun's rays strike the Earth at right angles and there is no inclination in their trajectory, the days and nights are of equal length.

Nowruz is preceded by the longest night of the year for the winter solstice, called 'Yalda Night' (*Shab-e Yalda*), which should have been celebrated in Tehran, in accordance with a very ancient tradition of Persian culture dating back to Cyrus the Great. For obvious reasons, however, it was not celebrated by a huge proportion of the Iranian population.

But Yalda also means 'rebirth', the rebirth of the sun, and therefore the triumph of light over darkness. We could even say over obscurantism. So Nowruz follows the night, and let's hope it will be so, especially for young people and Iranian women.

How can we celebrate Christmas in peace in other countries if it is not possible in Kiev or Aleppo? Restraint in our celebrations will express an awareness of what is at stake and what is also essential for us: peace, freedom and progress.

Christmas will also be a time to remember an Iranian woman, of Kurdish origin, who at the cost of her life undoubtedly changed the destiny of her country. She expressed her country's youth and beauty, and represented not just Iranian women, but all the women of the world.

The controversy and beauty of the veil

The issue of the veil, which carries with it many other issues such as Islam, immigration, Islamism and even terrorism in the greatest intellectual disorder, periodically and almost compulsively erupts in the political debate in France, particularly during elections.

For example, a controversy arose when an association in the city of Nantes put up a photo of a woman wearing a hijab on a billboard during Women's Month, possibly with the support of the city council. It is stated that the photograph is part of an exhibition entitled 'Visages de Nantaises' ('Faces of Nantes Women') on the lives of women living in the City of Nantes in 2021. While the controversy seemed to focus as much on the support given by the city of Nantes as on the photograph itself, it illustrated the hysteria of a section of the French political class, relayed without distance by the media.

Had the woman in question been involved in drug trafficking? Had she used a Kalashnikov in the northern districts of Marseille? No, she lives in Nantes. Was her only crime that she wore a headscarf rather than a traditional outfit from neighbouring Brittany? Her French region? The world. These fits of fever generally give rise to one-upmanship in the name of a secularism that is often misunderstood, narrow and itself sometimes fundamentalist. While the subject is not unique to France, it is likely that its polemical evocation is also the revelation and catharsis of an older, repressed trauma, associated both with the suffering endured and that inflicted on others during decolonisation.

The debate on the veil can consist of unproductive, confusing and frustrating exchanges, but it can also lead us to reflect further on sensitive, important and unavoidable issues. The aim here is not to assert expertise, but to encourage nuance and moderation.

Persian letters

The controversy surrounding the headscarf has provoked a number of reactions in the Muslim world, which it is only fair to report. The perception from within a Shiite Islamic society, based solely on the comments recorded, which do not constitute a survey of scientific value, points in two main directions.

The first is concern about what may appear to be excessive tolerance of the veil. It states: '*In my opinion and that of many Iranian women who are obliged to wear it, the Hijab is not a beautiful thing at all and only limits and hinders our progress. We are also human beings and we like to dress as we like and appear freely in society*'.

In order to clear up any misunderstanding, it must be made clear that this is in no way about encouraging people to wear the veil, but precisely about advocating freedom and defending it. Our interviewee agreed, echoing this concern by saying that '*there is no problem in choosing the hijab consciously and voluntarily*'.
The second feeling, aroused by campaigns and polemics on the issue, is that of the opprobrium we would bring upon a Muslim society

that is not as one-dimensional as we might think and where aspirations to freedom are extremely strong in depth.

The opinion on the veil, in this case the Hijab, whether positive or negative, would be a second punishment or at the very least a wound to each person's self-esteem for their own identity, which is always complex. It is asserted that the veil cannot always be equated with the application of religious law, but is very often a matter of cultural tradition.

Our interviewees did not equate the hijab entirely with Islam, but with a rigorous version of it (see '*Islam invites people to think wisely...Hijab or Veil became a frightening strong law for women...*').

We should leave the conclusion to these Persian Letters: '*Dress is dress, the real Hijab comes from insight and thoughts... insight needs to be improved in the whole world...*'. The message is clear: the Hijab can also protect free thought and the greatest dreams. Freedom is in fusion, like the volcano under the ice.

'*Truth below the Pyrenees, error beyond*', wrote a great philosopher. What is an instrument of oppression can also be an instrument of freedom. The dividing line also lies within the same soul.

Crossed spiritualities

The Night of Destiny, the light of day

The preaching of the Patriarch of All Russia, Kirill, reduces religion to another form of power. The incomparable sumptuousness of Orthodox rites in the cathedrals of the Kremlin, in the Novodevichy monastery where the Metropolitan of Moscow officiates, and in Sergiev Possad, the Mecca of Orthodoxy, are no substitute for the religiosity of large sections of the population.
Islamism obscures the beauties of Islamic civilisation since the Umayyads, from Damascus to Cordoba. So we need to forget about

religion as an institution or a power, in favour of the spirituality that will always exist. It is the antidote to all disturbances, the refuge of the greatest of freedoms, the privilege of the individual being, the guide to his thought and his existence.

Ramadan, the holy month that is one of the five pillars of Islam, ends with the breaking of the fast on Eid-el-Fitr. The 'Night of Destiny' precedes Eid. The Night of Destiny (*Laylat Al-Qadr* - لَيْلَةُ الْقَدْرِ) is the holiest night in the Muslim calendar, as it is during this night that the archangel Gabriel is said to have revealed the Qur'an to the Prophet ; It is therefore a reminder of the greatness of the event, but also of the moment when each person's destiny is determined; it encourages peace and serenity, before the return to the light.

The Islamic world has become vast and diverse, no longer confined to the geography of its origins. The Organisation of the Islamic Conference (OIC), created in 1969 as a political organisation for countries with large Muslim populations, brings together dozens of nations from Africa, Central Asia, the Indian subcontinent and South-East Asia. The largest Muslim country, in terms of the number of followers, is still by far Indonesia. China and Russia, two great secular empires, have large Muslim communities.

Even for a non-believer, the Night of Destiny in Ramadan can evoke powerful experiences, albeit from a more external perspective. It has the breadth of the metaphysical landscapes of the Arabian Peninsula in the Nejd region; it echoes the calls of the muezzins igniting the shores of the Red Sea in Jeddah at sunset and reverberating across the mountainous barrier near the Hedjaz ; It is illuminated at dawn by countless green falots from the mosques of Damascus and draws us into the dizzying whirl of Sufi dances in the courtyard of the Palais Azem; it envelops the solitude of the deserts of Central Asia as far as the wall of the Hindu Kush; it has the sumptuous brilliance of the Iranian Nowruz in the Shiite world.

The sense of the collective cannot drown out the individual, transcendental dimension of the famous Night of Destiny, whose name alone makes you dizzy. If it is indeed the revelation of the Word, then everyone, even non-believers, can make this great moment their own, and it can happen in any circumstances, to give it the meaning of a unique experience, that of perceiving a greater light - as through the marvellous screen of an Indian mosque - that of life. So the Night of Destiny brings the first glimmers of a great Day.

The Vow of Louis XIII

The feast of the Assumption of the Virgin Mary, i.e. her elevation to heaven, which is distinct from the commemoration of the Ascension of Christ, is, as this brief description reminds us, a Christian feast. In France, it is celebrated by Catholics on 15 August.

France, the 'eldest daughter of the Church', had Catholicism as its state religion. The Assumption cult originated as a plea to the Virgin by King Louis XIII and Anne of Austria, who were unable to have children until the birth of Louis XIV. Since then, processions on 15 August have multiplied in France - following the Vow of Louis XIII in 1638 (cf. *taking the most holy and glorious Virgin as special protector of our Kingdom*) - and their preferred location later became the grotto at Lourdes, from the second half of the 19th century onwards. The date of 15 August was even chosen to mark the bank holidays until the proclamation of the Republic in 1880 and its replacement by 14 July. The cult was later made official by Pope Pius XII in 1950.

The Assumption is not a celebration exclusive to France, and today it remains a tradition that is sometimes even more vibrant outside France, as in Central Europe. The cult of Mary is undoubtedly stronger than that of Christ in the popular imagery of the Christian world, in the Near East, as in Christian Syria. The same is true of the Orthodox world, as evidenced by the icons, including the sublime Our Lady of Kazan, which can be found in every home.

It is Mary who is the first to be seen by believers in places of worship, whereas Christ is reserved for the dome of Byzantine churches. She is also respected in the Muslim world. In a way, this level access to Mary provides a symbolism for everyone, even for non-believers. Mary is the mother, the sister, the woman, the incarnation of femininity. And the Assumption raises her above everyone and everything, like a permanent reality and dream at the same time.

Pope Francis' cry from the heart

The Pope's refusal, in the form of a sudden cry from the heart, to respond favourably to the official invitation extended to him to come and consecrate Notre-Dame de Paris for its reopening on 8 December 2024, has not failed to surprise, if not shock, the community of believers.

Does the Pope have a particular problem with France? Didn't he take care to emphasise when he came to Strasbourg, and then more recently to Marseille, that he was not visiting France but for events outside it?

But Francis is Pope and does not a priori have to express personal sensitivities. So does the Vatican have any issues with France? Is the eldest daughter of the Church now considered to have gone astray with its accelerated de-Christianisation, with the evolution of its legislation on so-called 'societal' issues, whether it be the inclusion of abortion in the constitutional principles of the Fifth Republic, marriage for all or the possible evolution of its legislation on the end of life? Not to mention the scandals in the Church of France in recent years?

Whatever the case, the reopening of Notre-Dame de Paris will be a global event. Notre-Dame is a shining symbol of Christianity and the nation as a whole, an expression of the 'genius' of Christianity, to use a term dear to Chateaubriand, and the embodiment of an immense institution.
Shouldn't Pope Francis naturally have honoured it and been associated with this major event? If the Pope despairs of the way the so-called developed world is evolving, can he be sure that Christian

thought is no longer deeply irrigating France? Couldn't this latent spirituality express itself again in a sudden resurgence and make France an unexpected centre of its renaissance? The great institutions are characterised by their permanence and their purpose. If spirituality can develop outside the Churches, the latter can also be its guardians, as in the case of Notre-Dame de Paris and Saint Peter's in Rome.

Francis and the power of life

The last breath: the strength of the weak

Pope Francis had left the Gemelli hospital in Rome where he was treated for five weeks for a serious lung condition. A convalescence period of *'at least two months'* - which is an eternity for the head of a state that maintains diplomatic relations with 184 nations and is above all the spiritual leader of a Catholic community estimated at 1.4 billion people worldwide.

This had raised the question of whether he would be able to carry out his pontifical duties to the end. The Pope himself had addressed the issue before his hospitalisation, ruling out a withdrawal that he felt should not become the norm; he was referring to his predecessor Benedict XVI and to the dozen or so Popes in history who have not completed their term of office.

The question became then even more acute. It should be noted, however, that despite his hospitalisation, the Pope had been able to continue his activities, both in terms of the governance of the Church and in taking important written positions - no longer from the balcony of St Peter's - on the major problems of the world, be they the war, the situation in Gaza or cross-cutting issues such as artificial intelligence.
In reality, the continuation of the pontifical office, whatever the difficulties and handicaps, can be interpreted as having a double meaning: the Pope cannot be an ordinary retiree and his mission is

for life. The dogma of papal infallibility concerning faith and morals was proclaimed in 1870 by the first Vatican Council; it has not been formally abandoned, but it has been, if not forgotten, at least relativised with the collegiality of the bishops with the Pope affirmed at the Second Vatican Council. By his proactive attitude in the face of adversity, Pope Francis is helping to remind us of the unique character of his magisterium.

The second important meaning is not unrelated to the debate in some Western societies on the end of life. In this respect, the Pope's message is very clear: the last breath is precious and an incomparable power that is also that of fragility.

Francis and the figure of life

In his 'Spiritual Testament 'written in 2022, Pope Francis expressed the wish to be buried in the Basilica of Santa Maria Maggiore, one of the four basilicas in Rome. The last pope to be buried in this fifth-century building was Clement IX in 1669; the Baroque architect, sculptor and painter Le Bernin, who designed the great colonnade of St Peter's, also found his final resting place there in 1680. The icon of the Virgin Mary above the altar is attributed to Saint Luke.

Pope Francis has systematically visited the site for many years, and on the occasion of his apostolic journeys; he came here again to venerate the Virgin (NB: called '*Vergine Salus Populi Romani*'), on 12 April this year, before the start of Holy Week. Whatever his motives, it is worth noting the importance of the Marian cult for recent popes; John Paul II, who was close to Our Lady of Czestokowa near Krakow, and Benedict XVI, visited Lourdes on several occasions.

The cult of Mary is inherited from a Byzantine tradition, but the Virgin is systematically represented with the infant Jesus in her arms (see The Virgin of Vladimir, Kazan or Lviv) or at the foot of the Cross. In the case of Lourdes or Fatima, these are apparitions to children, not representations of Mary's sacred role in history. But isn't the popular fervour for Mary due to her image of peace, serenity and life, whereas Christ, to whom her cult is inextricably linked, is the embodiment of suffering?

Pope Francis' wives, as he himself said in interviews with Dominique Wolton, were his grandmothers and his mother, as well as Esther Balestrino De Careaga, who taught him '*to think about politics*' and was a communist activist; one of the founders of the Mothers of the Plaza de Mayo, she was a victim of the dictatorship. Pope Francis was reunited with his three daughters, who came to meet him during his visit to Paraguay, their mother's country of origin ('*they kept telling me how much their mother loved me* 'François emphasised).

The funeral of a Pope and the spirit of the Jesuits

The triumphant Church

In October 1958, Pope Pius XII died in Castelgandolfo. His mortal remains, surrounded by a sumptuous protocol, were brought back to the Vatican via the Via Appia, alongside the Coliseum and crossed Rome in front of huge crowds. The body lay in state for three days in St Peter's Basilica, and the broadcast of the funeral, then in black and white, was one of Eurovision's first televised events. At the start of the Fifth Republic in France, led by General de Gaulle, the funeral of the archbishop of Avignon took place at the same time in a similar manner, albeit with different proportions.

Another city of Popes

In this other city of Popes - the last of the seven French pontiffs, Gregory XI, returned to Rome in 1377 - a number of confraternities developed, including the White Penitents, dedicated to the sick, whose 14th-century chapel still stands, and, from the 16th century onwards, the Black Penitents, dedicated to prisoners. But in a slightly more remote and popular area, *rue des Lices*, was the Jesuit congregation, which developed a College there.

Jesuit education

In those years, Jesuit teaching was classical, with classes called 'Rhétorique' or 'Humanités'. Michel Debré's 1959 law on education made it possible for the State to support public schools, including denominational ones under contract. This legislation made it easier for more modest families to access such education. The great names of some Jesuit teachers were not incompatible with their proximity and originality; Father Franchet d'Espèrey, a philosophy teacher - a descendant of the famous general in the 14-18 war who concluded the armistice with the Turks at Moudros - visited the town's prison every day, very early in the morning; Father de Montgolfier taught physics; Father Bernard was close to the gypsy community that made the annual pilgrimage to Saintes-Marie-de-la-Mer; another Jesuit was a former ski champion and another an evening jazz singer.

An unfulfilled dream

A destiny is never fully fulfilled. Benedict XVI could have visited Russia, something that was inconceivable for John Paul II. But the controversial interpretations of his 2006 speech in Regensburg — which focused primarily on the dialectic between faith and reason and was not specifically aimed at Islam — may have prevented him from doing so. Pope Francis, for his part, met Patriarch Kirill in Havana in 2016. This historic meeting — which also had a geopolitical dimension at a time of tension between Russia and the West — was the first between the heads of the Catholic and Russian Orthodox Churches since the schism of 1054 between Eastern and Western Christians.

It has been sometimes reported that Pope Francis had planned a visit to China that was ultimately consistent with logic and tradition. The logic is that of a magisterium without geographical boundaries and of taking into account the realities of the world. However, the Vatican was one of the few states that had established diplomatic relations with Taiwan (see the opening of an apostolic nunciature in Taipei in 1954). Francis has nevertheless constantly strived to improve relations with China; in 2018, the Holy See and China signed an agreement allowing for the joint appointment of bishops in China. The Vatican even respected Beijing's unilateral choice when appointing the bishop of Shanghai. As for tradition, it dates back to the first Jesuits at the end of the 16th century.

Matteo Ricci and Alexandre de Rhodes

Matteo Ricci, born in Macerata in the Marche region and trained at the Jesuit novitiate in Rome, was a missionary in Ming China. He entered China from Macao in 1583 and spent eighteen years in the Canton region, where he carried out important scientific and technical work (notably in clockmaking) and was received at the Imperial Court in Beijing in 1601. He is considered the founder of the Chinese Church and is buried in a cemetery near the Forbidden City.

Alexandre de Rhodes, a Jesuit from Avignon at the end of the 16th century, was born in that city into a Jewish family originally from Aragon. He attended the college of the Fathers, which was still in its infancy, before studying philosophy in Rome. Following in the footsteps of François-Xavier and Ricci, he was seized at an early age by a dream of the 'Indies 'and also arrived in Macao, but a century later than Ricci in 1683. Denied access to Japan, he turned his attention to Dai-Viêt, which became Vietnam. Was religious and commercial penetration in this country seen locally as a counterweight to China? Among his achievements, he took part in transcribing the Chinese written language into the Latin alphabet. Zhou Enlai once said that China had missed out on such a revolution, which would have facilitated the opening up of his country.

Unbroken tradition and modernity on the brink

The funeral of Pope Francis will not be conducted with the same pomp and ceremony as those of Pius XII or the Archbishop of Avignon. This was already the case for Benedict XVI, and Francis will have wanted it that way thanks to a reform that took place at the end of 2024. But, without prejudging the last Pope's assessment, which will require a certain amount of hindsight, we can already say that Francis will have remained faithful to the Jesuit tradition.

What is this Jesuit tradition ? The interpretation is naturally subjective. The spirit of reform originally opposed to the Inquisition, evangelisation in Asia in particular, the utopian dream of the Missions in Paraguay, the unwavering defence of the papacy, the education of the 'elites', the ability to adapt to the secular world ? But we should probably add the pursuit of freedom to the extreme, without straying from the path; when you're on the edge of the abyss, you don't fall.

Salus Populi Romani: richness of symbols, vertigo of centuries,
humility of a Pope

Pope Francis was buried near the most famous Marian icon, which tradition considers to be 'not painted by human hands 'and which is closely linked to the 'Salvation of the People of Rome '(Salus Populi Romani), of which the Pope is the bishop. This Byzantine representation of the Virgin Mary and the Child Jesus is attributed to Saint Luke, the most mysterious of the Evangelists; it is said to have been found in Jerusalem at the site of the Holy Sepulchre and brought to Rome in the 4th century by Saint Helena, the mother of Emperor Constantine. It has been venerated since the Council of Ephesus in 431, when Mary was proclaimed Mother of God. It is associated with several miracles and divine interventions in the history of Rome. It is venerated every year on the last Sunday in January, when the Feast of the Translation is celebrated (NB: solemn transfer in 1613 of the icon to the Pauline Chapel of the Basilica of Saint Mary Major, where it is located today).

It is in this 5th-century basilica, the smallest of the four papal basilicas, the only one dedicated to the Virgin Mary, the only one that has never been destroyed and the oldest dedicated to her in the Christian West, where relics of the cradle that held the Child Jesus at his birth are kept, located near Termini Station in a working-class neighbourhood, and finally where Ignatius of Loyola - the founder of the Society of Jesus to which the Pope belongs - celebrated his first Mass on Christmas Day 1538, that Francis chose his final resting place.

It was here that before his election, Monsignor Jorge Mario Bergoglio would go 'always, on Sunday mornings, when he was in Rome'. It is there that he made 126 visits during the twelve years of his pontificate; it is there that he went on 14 March 2013, the day after his election and on the eve of Holy Week in that year 2025. The icon 'Salus Populi Romani 'was at his side on 27 March 2020 when he stood alone in St. Peter's Square during the pandemic.

The Pope's tomb will be located between the Pauline Chapel of the Basilica, where the icon is usually kept, and the Sforza Chapel, near the altar of St. Francis. The tomb will be covered with stone from

Liguria, the homeland of the Pope's maternal ancestors, and engraved with the single inscription 'Franciscus 'and a reproduction of his pectoral cross. The Pope will be in a basilica where seven other sovereign pontiffs are buried, including the first Franciscan Pope, Nicholas IV, and the first Dominican Pope, Pius V; they will welcome the first Jesuit Pope in history.

Rome, 'Una giornata particolare'

Rome is renowned as the embodiment and illustration of power, and considerable events have taken place there. However, the Italian peninsula entered history relatively late compared to the East; the country was fragmented, with no major rivers to irrigate it except the Po; it was influenced by the Greeks, particularly in Sicily, described by Polybius as the 'Peloponnese of Italy', and by the Etruscans, especially in Tuscany (see Tarquin the Elder, the first Roman king of Etruscan origin in the 7th century BC; pre-republican Rome was therefore a great city).

At its peak in the 3rd century BC, Carthage was the largest city in the Western world, and mutual interest in trade and military expeditions led to conflict between the landowners of Rome and the sailors of Carthage. Cato the Elder contributed to the revival of the Roman Republic, which was more favourable to Hellenism – in keeping with Italian traditions – and to imperialism, the destruction of Carthage in 146 BC being a major milestone. In defending Italy in the West in the 3rd century BC, Italy became a Mediterranean power.

But when Rome turned its attention to the East, it did not face a divided Greece, but another great power that dominated it, that of a Seleucid (Antiochus III), descendant of the followers of Alexander the Great. The Eastern question then became a matter for the empire born with Augustus in 27 BC, paradoxically at the end of the rise of the plebeians over the patricians, which established a Pax Romana abroad.

This grandiose story – which can only be summarised at the risk of caricaturing it – should inspire modesty in those in power, such as those who gathered for Pope Francis' funeral. Nevertheless, it is good that they made the effort to attend, if only to show the world, despite themselves, their smallness and the limitations of their power in relation to a moral authority of global dimensions.

Their words were inaudible, their attitudes insignificant, and their presence, even if amplified by gigantic loudspeakers - as in a famous film - would have been nothing more than a faint, muffled echo. The real rumour, almost silent but immensely powerful, was that of a countless crowd, from the streets of Rome and from all over the world: *Vox Populi, vox Dei* (the voice of the people is the voice of God). Here we must quote the Latin scholar Pierre Grimal, who wrote in *Rome, les Siècles et les Jours* (Rome, the Centuries and the Days): '*...one of the secrets of Rome...its piety, its sense of the divine, and a kind of humility that makes it feel the greatness, the triumphs, the power, as well as the small successes of everyday life as gifts from the gods...*'

20

Historical perspective

From Antiquity to the present day

History is not necessarily new, and references to the past are not necessarily relevant. But we must endeavour to place events in the context of long-term historical perspectives. Our thinking should not be purely explanatory, but should lead us to favour valid orientations over time. Here are a few key moments in history by way of illustration.

Nero and Agrippina: the height of ubrism

The apparent stability of power is not necessarily incompatible with the existence of highly controversial figures. The Roman Empire of the first century AD, for example, was not overly affected by the derangement of figures such as Nero and his mother Agrippina, who were synonymous with excessive passions. But it is true that the emperor's death in 68 AD led to a two-year civil war, which was as brief in relative terms as it was intense.

Nero and Agrippina epitomised debauchery, the power of boundless ambition, corruption at court - where ancient Roman virtue had faded - and murder. The Stoic Seneca, Nero's tutor, failed to educate the young man. Agrippina took over, hoping to control the young emperor by paradoxically encouraging him to dictate to his passions, which coexisted with great indifference in the running of the state.

Instead of trying in vain to channel, the strategy was to accompany the erring ways. Nero's mentors were older men and women who acted in this way. Excess and madness were the real levers of influence over the emperor.

Agrippina, Caligula's sister and empress in her capacity as wife of his successor Claudius, who was also her uncle, had the latter assassinated. She herself was killed in 59 by her own son Nero, who had officially called her 'the best of mothers'. The same fate befell his wife, the virtuous Octavia, and his half-brother Britannicus, to mention only the closest family circle.

Agrippina's death paved the way for a chaotic period in power, even though nothing had shocked the Romans so much as the tyranny of the emperor Caligula, who had revived the Eastern absolutism inherited from his great-grandfather Antony. As for Nero, he chose to end his life by having a freedman kill him. A few years earlier, in July 64 AD, he had reached the climax of his power, his own megalomania and vanity, as he gazed with delight at the burning of Rome. The city was then at its height, with a population of between 800,000 and one million. Accident, criminal act or self-destruction?

Carthago delenda est: Europe faces its destiny

Europe's destiny is at stake not only in the resolution of the war in Ukraine, on which a first diplomatic conference has opened in Switzerland. Above all, it is a question of making the essential choice of identity and seeking strategic autonomy, which is not limited to the military sphere but also encompasses high technology. In the long term, this presupposes that the Member States regain a degree of sovereignty that has been lost and diluted by a 'federalist' drift. Europe will have to be rebuilt in one way or another if it wants to truly exist in the face of global challenges, between China and the United States.

Carthago delenda est (Carthage must be destroyed) was the watchword proclaimed in every speech to the Roman Senate by Cato *the Elder* or *the Censor* in the second century BC. This obsession encompassed the quest for total victory over an unarmed city whose misfortune was its insolent prosperity. Indeed, the Third Punic War ended with the destruction of the city.

After this '*Hiroshima of the ancient world*' - the annihilation of a nation and a culture - it is no longer just a question of knowing whether Ukraine will have to give up its arms on the current confrontation lines or whether the Russian regime, finally a victim of having been ostracised, undermined from within and having lost its legitimacy, will be profoundly transformed. The European challenge also exists in the face of other challenges.

The contemporary Carthaginian, faced with the new poles of power, is no longer simply a conqueror, but should have freedom and independence as his name. The Carthaginians are now us. From this perspective, ancient Rome is the embodiment of superpower domination.

Cato the Elder, in reality hysterical, closed to the cultures of the world like Hellenistic civilisation, sickly austere in his confinement, in fact brings together the figures of all the attackers. Overall, he represents the war party and at the same time embodies the Hannibal who destroyed the Roman army at Cannes in the bloodiest battle in history.

Hannibal never succeeded in taking Rome, which was within his grasp after the battle of Lake Trasimeno in 217 BC, mainly because he lacked 'siege machines' and also because his plan was falsely conceived (NB: '*I have not come to confront populations, but to fight in their name against Rome*') and out of reach (NB: to destroy Rome not just as a city, but as a political entity). Today we talk about defending 'values' and democracy.

In the desperate defence of the Roman Republic, the figure of Fabius *Cunctator* (the temporiser) came to the fore - as early as the lost battle of Trasimeno - who believed that head-on battles should be avoided. Was there a choice between Fabius and Flaminius, the latter of whom favoured the classic attack? This was the dilemma for a long time, until the strategy of evasion prevailed and the attacker's entrenchment until the 'delights of Capua' finally bore fruit.

This historical parallelism can be dizzying, and even the mercenary war in Carthage, imagined by Gustave Flaubert in *Salammbô*, is reminiscent of contemporary militias and clashes on the European continent. Be that as it may, we cannot allow Cato/Hannibal - whose battles were largely symmetrical and based on power politics, and who in reality had little concern for the people - to get away with it. Europe, in the throes of a war that in the end was only one revelation among many, now faces its destiny alone. It is important to know whether it really wants to have one.

Memory of Syria: near and eternal

Syria has become distant and difficult to understand; for too many years now, it has only made its presence felt in the news in the form of tragedy, and even in a sort of one-upmanship of tragedy. But it has always remained dear to our hearts, because it is itself an incomparable melting pot of Mediterranean civilisations and the Arab world, beyond the contemporary criteria of apparent wealth and power that apply to the region in question.

Syria has an impressive history: from its origins to the Hellenistic kingdoms, from the Roman era to Christianity, from Islam and Ottoman domination to the present day. It is a civilisation whose time span covers 'ten thousand years', it is often said, or even a million years since the Palaeolithic. The richness and complexity of this history form a universe that is both fabulous and dizzying, and so important for our understanding of the world, including today.

The evolution is the following: the appearance of the first agricultural villages at the beginning of the eighth millennium BC, i.e. in the Neolithic period; the sudden acceleration in the third millennium BC at Mari on the Euphrates, where Sumerian cuneiform characters were written and the 'Ur treasure', made up of ivory statuettes, was discovered. C. at Mari on the Euphrates, where Sumerian cuneiform characters were written and the 'treasure of Ur', made up of ivory statuettes, was discovered; the preserved independence of Ugarit on the Mediterranean coast from the Hittites a millennium later, and Ugaritic, considered to be the first alphabet in history; Syria under the Neo-Babylonian empire in the 7th century B.C., then Persia in the 7th century B.C.; and the emergence of the first agricultural villages at the beginning of the 8th millennium B.C., i.e. the Neolithic period. C., then to Achaemenid Persia; the great meeting of East and West under the Seleucids, heirs to Alexander the Great, as witnessed by the cities of Antioch, Latakia and Apamea, in memory respectively of the father, mother (Laodicea) and eastern wife (Afamia) of Seleucos I, as well as Dura Europos on the Euphrates.

Syria was Roman. In the 3rd century AD, Rome's emperor was Philip the Arab (NB: He re-established peace on the Danube and is sometimes considered the first Christian emperor) and, at the same time, the kingdom of Palmyra developed in the face of the Sassanids, who had succeeded the Parthians; the apogee of Palmyra was the reign of Zenobia - at once resistant, courageous and also excessively ambitious for having proclaimed herself empress - who eventually capitulated to Aurelian in 272, but the cultural and economic influence of the city never waned.

Christianity preceded Islam and Ottoman domination. There are many Christian churches dating from the 5th century on what is known as the 'limestone plateau' or 'dead cities' to the south of Aleppo. At the end of the fourth century, Christianity became established and Syria became part of Byzantium. From the outset, Islam flourished there, and the Umayyad mosque, completed in 715, became a model even in Muslim Spain (see '*Andalusia from Damascus to Cordoba*'); with the Abbasids, Baghdad became a new centre; from the 16th century, Syria came under Ottoman rule, leaving Damascus with the Sinan-Pasha mosque and the Azem Palace, which for a time housed the French Institute.

Apamea, on the edge of a plateau overlooking the Orontes valley, is a magical place. For several centuries, around the beginning of the first millennium, it was a military town which, at its peak in the 2nd century AD, was home to royal stud farms, cavalry horses and 500 elephants, a kind of deterrent force before its time. Conquered by Pompey in 64 BC, who made it a Roman province, it was home for a time to Antony and Cleopatra. The queen found herself pregnant. This encounter is reminiscent of the marriage of Alexander and his generals to Persian princesses in Susa, sealing the meeting of East and West. But if there is romance in history, which is sometimes no more than a myth, history as a whole is devoid of it. It is often tragic.

As we list these periods, which are superimposed like geological strata, we come to the contemporary period, and today we are just as stunned by the shock of the ongoing war in Syria. This nation seems to have fallen out of history, sucked into a spiral of destruction, far from the echoes of the world.

But to better understand the nature of the Syrian Arab Republic, we also need to look at the place occupied by religions, minorities and culture. In this land that has been Christian since the first centuries of our era, but which has become predominantly Muslim, eleven Christian religions have been officially recognised by the Damascus regime.

Other minorities included the Armenians, who have lived in Syria since Cilicia was part of the Kingdom of Tigran in the 2nd and 1st centuries BC. Some families have lived in Aleppo since the 15th century, where a large part of the community resides. The flow increased with the genocide of 1915, much of which took place in the Euphrates region around the town of Deir Ezzor. The Alawites, like the Druze, belong to Shiite Islam, but it is difficult to see clearly the religious dimension of this community. What's more, President Assad, although an Alawite, married a Sunni, a British woman of Syrian origin born in London. In the early years of his presidency, the country's relations with Saudi Wahhabism seemed to have calmed down, while Crown Prince Abdallah, the future king, had a Syrian wife from the nomadic Chammar tribe, scattered from the Nejd to Palmyra and other states in the region.

At the heart of the old city of Damascus was the Jewish quarter. Reduced to a synagogue and a few houses, the community dispersed, especially after the Six-Day War and the Yom Kippur War. But none of the houses were desecrated and the Syrians said they would always be preserved in anticipation of their return. At the National Museum in Damascus, the most beautiful pieces were figurative frescoes from the 2nd and 3rd centuries, still unique to this day, from one of the oldest known ancient synagogues. This immense edifice, buried deep underground - which had protected it for so many centuries - along the ramparts of Dura Europos on the Euphrates, the *'Pompeii of the East'*, was unearthed in 1930 and restored under the French mandate.

The Kurds, for their part, agitated on several occasions in what is known as the 'duck's beak', in the far north-east of the country. But the situation remained under control before the current conflict, as they enjoyed relative autonomy. The Palestinians formed a large community. They had status and could find work. We employed some of them at the French embassy. Finally, the Shiites were not clearly identifiable as such, with the exception of large groups of Iranians, who were mainly seen at the airport and who came on pilgrimage to the mausoleum of Saida Zeinab, on the outskirts of Damascus, dedicated to a granddaughter of the Prophet.

Feelings, nostalgia and compassion today, can never be dissociated from interests in state-to-state relations. In Damascus in 1984, when he was received by Hafez el-Assad as the first French head of state since the country's independence in 1943, President Mitterrand summed up our fundamental position when he declared that *'nothing* (could) *be achieved in the Middle East without Syria's help'*. President Chirac was the only Western head of state to attend Hafez el-Assad's funeral in June 2000. He was criticised for this outside Syria, but it strengthened his strong historical ties with the country. The Syrians looked to France without any partisan preference; for them, it was a country that embodied the search for balance in the service of peace and justice, which was particularly strongly felt by the Alawite community, which had long been discredited and which came to power thanks to France.

For reasons that belong not only to the past and to the apogee of our bilateral relationship a little over twenty years ago - when France had, as it were, baptized a young president under the age of 40 - but also to today's geostrategic imperatives, we must once again turn our attention to this land of high civilization, despite the incongruity of the term in view of the violence that continues to ravage it.

There was a 'Damascus Spring' that preceded by more than ten years an 'Arab Spring' that turned into a nightmare; it gave rise to hope and even euphoria and resulted in a ferment of debate within the intelligentsia and the promotion of reforms. These embryonic developments were thwarted by internal inertia and regional upheavals. But we must continue to believe, as General de Gaulle said of young people, that *everything will begin again* and that a long descent into hell will stop in the heart of Damascus, at the end of the Roman Via Recta, where Paul of Tarsus converted. Like all of us, Paul is the Jesuit Paolo Dall'Oglio, who disappeared during the conflict, probably in Raqqa, and who appealed to us to do our 'humanist and universal duty' (*sua humaniste ed universelle devozione*).

It was Beirut, it was Damascus

But in Damascus, time was not the same. The 10,000 years of history had learnt to bend to other rhythms, other demands and hierarchies of priorities. Just as in the shade of the high walls of the Damascene houses in the old town, cradled by the spray of water from the central basin of the inner courtyard, people talked at nightfall for all eternity. The essence was there, in this concrete exchange, seemingly innocuous, but ultimately serious. It was the language of friendship for ever.

The first approach from the Arabian Peninsula was preceded by a stopover in Beirut. The western quarters, the corniche, the lighthouse, the military baths, places known from history and current events, mythical places and also the scene of more recent tragedies, those of the civil war. All the Mediterranean was there in a nutshell: a place of opulent life that the elements alone offered, but a tragic destiny; the fatum of Greek tragedy: the outcome of the story was known in advance, but a morbid voyeurism was going to focus on observing how people reacted to the ineluctable chain of events. Beirut was a kind of Sisyphean rock of the good life, ambitions and pleasure, a miracle of permanent rebirth. The comfort of the corniche, the volumes, the rich and voluptuous decoration of the homes, brought to life a kind of waking Orientalism, reminding us of our dreams. The death of Sardanapalus stood next to the modest, old-fashioned but delicious restaurant of the 'Bride of the Sea'.

The road to Damascus, from this lost or threatened paradise, was an ascent, an initiatory journey. After the presidential palace district of Baabda on the heights of Beirut, from where you could dominate the sea surrounded by peaks sometimes snow-capped, everything finally came to a head, after crossing the Bekaa plain, at the Umayyad square, the true entrance to the land of the Sham. The districts of Malki and Raouda preceded the Ottoman mosques designed by the architect Sinan and their gardens; then, further on, the old town and its Christian quarter, its marvellous palaces often so discreet, so secret. On leaving the Hamidiyé souk, after passing the citadel and its ramparts, the incomparable Umayyad mosque stood out, as did the Roman via Recta and the eternal presence of Paul of Tarsus, a Jew from Cilicia, and his conversion. These historical, cultural and human riches shaped a strong Arab identity, incomparable, inevitably and eternally militant; they also determined eternal wars, giving the feeling of a nation out of History, sucked into a spiral of destruction, far from the echoes of the world.

From one war to another

8 and 9 May: collective victory or defeat?

The traditional parade on Red Square commemorating the 'victory' (День Победы) of 1945 took place at the very least in 2023; the authorities had then endeavoured to give it a 'normal' appearance, but it had not really been so: few weapons, no doubt mobilised by the war in Ukraine, had been displayed and the people were kept at a distance. How, moreover, was it possible to celebrate victory when the Russian army on the Ukrainian front was facing great difficulties? Things were very significantly different in 2024, when President Putin was re-elected in March of that year and Russia's positions on the front are now more secure.

9 May is Russia's biggest bank holidays and generally a day of great pride, serious and joyous at the same time. It often coincides with long, sunny days and is not just about the morning parade through the huge Red Square. It was a day of nostalgia and joy for everyone. But the political vicissitudes, the chaos of unbridled privatisations during the transition period and the shock of global economic crises such as that of 2008 never dampened the collective emotion. In the afternoons, families would gather in the public gardens to listen religiously to a few veterans recounting their war to the sound of their guitars. These veterans have all but disappeared, 79 years after the 1945 armistice. On this day, people were happy to wear the orange ribbon with black piping of Saint-Georges, the patron saint of the army, as well as the red poppies - reminiscent of the first flowers to appear on the battlefields of Verdun and the Somme - and the French cornflowers on the lapels of jackets and dresses. The Saint-Georges ribbon was proudly attached to the antennae of the vehicles, forming their flags.

The war in Ukraine inevitably alters our perception of the sacrifices made by the peoples of the Soviet Union. It should also make us aware of a collective defeat that can be summed up as Europe's suicide: Ukraine, which we hope will survive, is already humanely and materially destroyed and reconstruction will take a long time; does the political power in Kiev have the necessary historical depth to realise that tomorrow could be even worse? Europe, which is working to some extent for the King of Prussia in this affair, is also paying a considerable economic price; Russia, by turning its back on its European vocation, which is also part of its history, is embarking on a perilous path towards Asia. Isn't the victory that we would all like to celebrate now a collective defeat?

The room under the vaults in 2025

Whether we like it or not, 2025 will be the Year of Russia, marking the world in a positive or negative way. It is obviously not just a question of evoking a war that is anachronistic and destructive for everyone, particularly for Europe, and which it is high time to put an end to; Nor is it just a question of worrying exclusively about essential long-term energy supplies from and through the country in every direction in the world; it is really a question of ostracising a great civilisation, the receptacle of the Orient and of European culture, with the effect of mentally amputating the continent. Ultimately, there can be no Europe without Russia.

Leo Tolstoy expressed an unbounded understanding of humanity that went beyond Russian patriotism; this was the case in *War and Peace*, particularly in the description of the Battle of Borodino in 1812, a reminiscence perhaps for him of his participation in the Crimean War and the siege of Sebastopol in 1854-1855. His long moral crisis brought him back to his estate in Iasnaïa Poliana, where he was born and where he was to end his life. There he devoted himself to rural life and education, in particular setting up schools for peasant children, who had been freed from serfdom in 1861.

Although Tolstoy's birthplace has now disappeared, the school and the house where he lived can still be found on the vast estate (Usadba). In the master's bedroom is the famous painting by his contemporary Ilia Repine: *'Tolstoy in the room under the vaults'* (1891) representing the room. In an almost monastic setting, Tolstoy appears to be a hard worker, absorbed in intense creative labour, surrounded by tools that reflect both his physical and intellectual activity. It was here that he wrote the beginning of *War and Peace*. Tolstoy, the peasant, the mystic, the inspirer of non-violence, escaped from the world, including his family, on 7 November 1910, to end his days in a final revolt, at Astapovo on the platform of a station near Iasnaïa Poliana. A room under the vaults for supreme freedom...

6 June: a truncated commemoration

Eternal gratitude is naturally due to those who fell on the beaches of Normandy for the liberation of France. But in 2024 there were reasons not to watch the ceremonies marking the 80th anniversary of the D-Day landings and not to listen to the inevitably stereotyped, even piecemeal, speeches.

The 80th anniversary was truncated. The presence of President Zelensky was an implicit recognition of the importance of the fighting against Hitler's armies in Eastern Europe and the immeasurable sacrifices made there, without which the landings in France would probably not have been possible. But the absence of Russia, invited and then disinvited because of a lack of respect for history and confusion with the present, was worse than amnesia; it was quite simply historical manipulation.

In the East, the war against the Nazis was waged by the Soviets and a Red Army that brought together various peoples of the USSR, but Russia paid the heaviest price. What's more, when we talk about the fight against the Nazis, we should not forget the Ukrainian collaboration.

At Babi Yar, near Kiev, more than 33,000 members of the Jewish community were executed in September 1941. It was the first major massacre of the Shoah. Between 1941 and 1944, one million Ukrainian Jews perished in what has sometimes been called 'a land of blood'. In this country, there has been no leader who, like President Chirac, has openly acknowledged the responsibilities of the French state in the collaboration. A country that disguises, or even conceals, its history is in no way a democracy; history is inextricably linked to memory; dictatorships erase the past or distort it.

The 80th anniversary of the 1944 landings was therefore an event that deepened wounds rather than trying to heal them; it reflected a selective, even truncated history, while no voice was raised in the name of integral remembrance and total posthumous justice. 'These two regions are inseparable. In 1944, General de Gaulle decorated the Normandy-Niemen squadron at the Residence of France in Moscow. Prime Minister Dominique de Villepin did the same in 2006 in the same place, with the squadron's heir battalion.

9 March 1945 in Indochina: coup, empires and resistance

The 80th anniversary of 9 March 1945 in Indochina will probably not be celebrated, as it was a tragedy, but we should commemorate this important date in history whose significance went beyond the Second World War.

Continuing its imperialist policy begun in the previous decade, particularly in China, Japan forced the Vichy authorities in 1940 and 1941 to accept its occupation of Indochina; in return, Tokyo pledged to respect French sovereignty. From then on, the policy of Admiral Decoux, the French High Commissioner, was sometimes described by historians as 'wait-and-see' attitude, not to say ambiguous.

Fearing an Allied landing in Indochina, which might have been supported by the French troops there, Japan asked for closer cooperation. When this ultimatum was rejected, Japanese troops staged a 'coup de force' on 9 March 1945, wiping out the French garrisons and administrations. Despite strong resistance, including from French officers and soldiers of Vietnamese origin, several thousand people were killed and tens of thousands locked up.

The Japanese coup in Indochina revealed the ambiguity of alliances or supposed ones between powers, for example between Vichy and Tokyo or between the United States and the Viet Minh, Washington's future implacable adversary in the Vietnam War. It prefigured the end of the French empire in Indochina, which the reconquest efforts of General Leclerc's expeditionary corps never really re-established.
Alongside the military option, the diplomatic route of the Sainteny-Ho Chi Minh agreements was developed (NB: recognition of a free state of Vietnam within the French empire), but these were not respected.
The Japanese empire collapsed in the summer of '45 after Hiroshima and Nagasaki.
Bao Dai's Vietnamese empire, which had declared its independence after 9 March, was short-lived and never counted; it was replaced by the Viet Minh, which also declared independence in Hanoi.

The memory of the French resistance in Indochina must not be forgotten. This admirable resistance was led in particular by 109 French officers of Vietnamese origin (including general Minh), many of whom paid for it with their lives. These officers had been trained in the north of the country at the Tong military school run by General Carbonel. President Giscard d'Estaing took an interest in this French history and the Tong School was officially recognised by Saint-Cyr Coëtquidan Military Academy in the late 1970s.

9 March 1945 was a key moment for several empires, which had been considerable but found themselves on the brink of the Tarpeian Rock. The consequences of not respecting the possible peace with Ho Chi Minh in 1946 were incalculable. The war scenario can never be completely mastered.

Independence Day: revolt of the colonies, freedom, equality

4 July, Independence Day, is an important date for the United States, and one that should also send a message to the rest of the world. On this day, the American people commemorate the Declaration of Independence of 4 July 1776, drawn up principally by Thomas Jefferson and adopted by the country's Continental Congress; 4 July was declared a bank holiday. It is indeed a question of remembering the birth of a nation, and the contemporary American historian Jon Meacham considered (see *The Soul of America*) that an awareness of history is one of the very first duties that should be imposed on every citizen.

John Adams, the second President of the United States after George Washington - and the first to occupy the White House, which was completed in 1800 - is considered to be one of the 'Founding Fathers', who was succeeded by Thomas Jefferson, his Vice-President (NB: he was ambassador to London and Jefferson to France, on the eve of the French Revolution), had a very early vision of '*the emancipation of the enslaved portion of mankind throughout the face of the earth*'. The United States, which should also be a message for the world.

For his part, Pope Francis, speaking before the United States Congress in September 2015, spoke of the democracy deeply rooted in the spirit of the American people; he believed that all political activity should serve and promote the good of the human person and be based on respect and dignity; In support of his argument in favour of freedom and equality, he cited the Declaration of Independence ('*We hold these truths to be self-evident, that all men are created equal, that they are endowed by their Creator with certain unalienable rights, that among these are life, liberty and the pursuit of happiness*').

The American and French Revolutions, liberty, equality and democracy, and the American messianic spirit, all come together in a whole that is difficult to separate, according to this rapid but dizzying historical and philosophical overview. What is the situation today in a world whose profound changes are also leading to upheaval in every part of the globe?

Hiroshima amnesia

'*You didn't see anything in Hiroshima*', the Japanese lover repeats like a leitmotif in Alain Resnais's film based on Marguerite Duras's screenplay. Yet everyone is familiar with the radioactive mushroom cloud that was followed by Nagasaki, whose image has faded, often forgotten, even ignored.

Yet one commemoration follows another, and in 2025 it will be the 80th anniversary of a collective defeat beyond Japan; ritual hymns to peace are raised near the '*Genbaku* dome', the surviving building from the epicentre, which has become an open-air cathedral made of a few steel rods. But is a reconstruction of the tragedy, designed to avert it, even possible? The evidence on the ground is unbearable, so most often it is an aerial view taken from the plane in charge of the sinister task or from an accompanying aircraft. The hitherto unknown explosion did not make a sound on the image, we did not feel the devastating blast and even less the fire spread on the ground like a monstrous sickle. The plane was called *Enola Gay*, after the pilot's mother, and the uranium 235 bomb was *Little Boy*. A mother and a son: how is it imaginable that they could have been symbols of death on a scale previously unimaginable?

It would even be futile to advance rational explanations linked to the phenomenon of war and the strategy that led to this sinister outcome. On 9 August 1945, the day of Nagasaki, Soviet forces entered Manchuria. Was this the price we had to pay to halt Stalin's advance in the Far East? Would it have been too costly in terms of men and interminable to continue with simple conventional means, block by block? Was a stricken and humiliated country justified in wanting to erase the trauma of Pearl Harbor? Could breaking up a hitherto inflexible imperialist power by targeting civilian populations in dozens of entire conurbations continue with impunity? Was total war changing the scale of its means, or rather its nature? Hadn't Tokyo been largely reduced to flames in March of the same year following the deadliest bombing raid of the Second World War? Hadn't there already been the terrible punishments inflicted on German cities in Hamburg in July 1943 during Operation *Gomorrah*, and above all in Dresden in February 1945, when a second wave of air raids quickly followed the first and even targeted the relief efforts for the victims? A provincial, drab-looking, unpopular president whose administration was marked by numerous scandals, he nonetheless went down in history as a major figure in the Cold War.

Hiroshima, mon amour can be understood as a chaotic expression of memory, reflected in strange parallel monologues and a clumsy, because desperate, effort to envisage the reconciliation of peoples. But what remains of Hiroshima in terms of the human and philosophical impact it has had on people's minds? In the Japanese consciousness, the explosion is no longer even identified with the power responsible, but is judged as the supreme Promethean act of fire stolen from the Gods, forbidden until then, committed by a humanity determined to annihilate the very creation that bears it. Hiroshima, martyred, disfigured, is all of us: *'you kill me, you do me good'*, should it remain the ultimate and famous retort?

21

From one international system to another

High-intensity warfare on the European continent, paralysis of the UN Security Council, emergence of new poles of power and fragmentation of the world, questioning of globalisation and rise of populism, threats of a new tariff war: the international system we have known since the end of the Cold War - which was itself made up of only a minimum set of rules and was therefore characterised by imperfections - is unquestionably being called into question. The transition that was taking place before our eyes has taken a more brutal turn that needs to be scrutinised.

The world is facing an 'epidemic' of crises; at least that's the general perception. The term 'crisis' is overused: There was the economic crisis of 1929; the Suez crisis of 1956, which redefined the hierarchy of world powers by highlighting the relative *diminutio capitis* of France and England; the Sudetenland crisis of 1938, which heralded the Second World War despite the Munich agreement; the current Taiwan crisis, against the backdrop of tensions between the United States and mainland China; and the Ukrainian crisis, which is in fact a long-term war rather than a paroxysmal moment of international tension. A crisis, in the strict sense of the term, is a brief episode; it can turn out to be what is now sometimes called a *game changer*, i.e. an event at the root of major economic, military or social transformations.

Crises and the international system

An international system, even one in crisis, is something quite different; it refers to a set of institutions, such as the UN today, and the relationships established between powers. Linking crises and systems can be an interesting approach that sheds light on fundamental changes that are taking place or have taken place in the world. Not all crises have a profound effect on international order. If we look back over the last few years, we can identify a number of moments that correspond to tectonic movements, i.e. deep-seated and lasting changes.

The brutal withdrawal of the Americans from Afghanistan in August 2021, after some twenty years of war preceded by 10 years of Soviet warfare from 1979 onwards, may well fall into the latter category. This episode, which was as spectacular as it was dramatic, had the effect of handing over a whole section of the Afghan population - who had glimpsed Western-style modernisation in the cities - to the implacable rule of the Taliban. It did not put an end to all types of intervention, but undoubtedly to a cycle of classic interventions, based on humanitarian considerations or pretexts. What has come to be known as the 'right of humanitarian intervention' developed and was conceptualised at the United Nations from the end of the 1990s onwards. This landmark development undermined respect for the sacrosanct principle of non-intervention *in matters which are essentially within the domestic jurisdiction of any State* enshrined in the famous paragraph 2, sub-paragraph 7 of the UN Charter.

It should be remembered that in Iraq, during the first Gulf War - which ended with Security Council Resolution 687, which decreed 'inspections' of weapons of mass destruction (WMD) - Security Council Resolution 678 authorised the international community to *use all means* to put an end to the invasion of Kuwait, without the word 'war' being used. This process of implicit authorisation was repeated in the Libyan crisis a few years later.

Closer to home, we should mention the somewhat forgotten AUKUS crisis - an alliance between Australia, the United Kingdom and the United States - aimed at forming an anti-Beijing front in the Indo-Pacific region. In reality, the crisis took place first and foremost between Western powers, since the formation of the AUKUS coincided with France's loss of a 'contract of the century' to supply

Australia with submarines. In this case, it is no longer a question of intervention under the guise of humanitarianism, but of the beginnings of a bloc against China, whereas it was thought that this form of alliance was reserved for a bygone era of the Cold War.

And we cannot fail to mention the crisis, or rather the war, in Ukraine, even if it is difficult to draw definitive conclusions on the spot while it is still unfolding before our eyes and escalating. Nevertheless, it is possible to consider that behind the discourse on the decline of the West and the defence of other values, following the narrative on the *'neo-Nazis of Kyiv'*, it was a Russian post-imperial project that was at stake and which we may finally realise was no longer adapted to the times.

A discourse on method

First and foremost, reference to the past is only of interest if it sheds light on the analysis of contemporary events. Furthermore, building a systems theory may seem excessively ambitious, but we must at least endeavour to produce syntheses, which are the only way to promote understanding of phenomena in a pedagogical approach. Finally, the last main consideration is that while international relations are based above all on interests, what we call 'values' cannot be entirely dismissed either. In the case of France, which often sees itself as the 'homeland' of human rights, it is clear that its foreign policy can ideally only be a combination - and even a subtle and highly unstable mix - of inescapable interests and humanist and universalist ambitions.

The case of the 'liberation' of Kuwait in 1991 is quite enlightening in this respect. France was reluctant to become involved in the coalition, reluctant to wage war and also because of important interests in the region in question, particularly in Iraq itself (see arms supplies, economic relations, Iraqi debt; not forgetting the 'watchdog' role assigned to Iraq vis-à-vis Iran, which on the French side determined the provision of *Super-Etendard* aircraft that enabled Baghdad to strike Iran's oil terminals in the Persian Gulf). This is undoubtedly why President Mitterrand, speaking at the UN General

Assembly in autumn 1990, offered Iraq a final 'perch' by declaring - thereby provoking the fury of the Americans who had already made up their minds - that *'if Saddam Hussein showed - the intention - to withdraw from Kuwait, then everything would be possible'*. Even if it is difficult to draw comparisons, can we not view Germany's reluctance to commit to supporting Ukraine against Russia through the same prism of interests and principles, without forgetting the weight of history?

A changeover in the international system

The moment a permanent member of the Security Council broke away from the principles of the Charter by invading Ukraine, the UN's political system found itself paralysed and even completely called into question. Can the Permanent Five still find some common ground, if not agreement, to tackle issues such as Iran's nuclear programme or proliferation in North Korea? Recent Council debates on the latter issue have given a negative answer. This is particularly worrying and cannot continue without risks for the state of the world.

The first question to ask is this: are we living through a new Cold War? The answer is no. The Cold War was based on the opposition of blocs and the confrontation, if not head-on but rather on peripheral theatres, of the two superpowers, the United States and the Soviet Union. Tensions could have boiled over on several occasions, in particular during the Cuban crisis in 1962 and the Berlin crisis between 1958 and 1961, but the worst was avoided; what was able to 'structure' the system - paradoxically giving it a certain stability - was in fact nuclear weapons; the 'mutually assured destruction' (MAD) and the limitation, under the SALT 1 agreement, of strategic anti-missile systems to a single site on either side, protecting the capitals of Washington and Moscow, ultimately guaranteed the 'balance of terror'.

This system came to an end in 1990/1991. One of the main reasons for this was the break-up of the Soviet Union at the end of the 1980s. Mikhail Gorbachev's priority was to put an end to the dangerous and, above all, ruinous arms race. In his famous speech to the UN

General Assembly on 7 December 1988, he announced the end of the 'Brezhnev doctrine' of limited sovereignty, the leading role of the Communist Party (CPSU) and the Marxist-Leninist doctrine.

The Gulf War of January-February 1991 was also a decisive factor in this development. Its outcome, favourable to the anti-Saddam coalition, led President George Bush Sr to proclaim a 'New International Order', which in practice was a unipolar world dominated by the United States (NB: this was the same order that V. Putin was to criticise in his Munich speech in 2007). With his concept of the 'End of History', the American neo-conservative economist and political scientist Francis Fukuyama set the ideal of liberal democracy as the unattainable horizon for humanity (see *The End of History and the Last Man*).

Multipolar world and multilateral system

It should be noted that the period of American domination - which cannot be said to have come to an end - nevertheless coexisted with the maintenance of a degree of multilateral cooperation within international bodies.

The attacks on the international system began under President R. Reagan. Reagan (1981-1989). In 1987, the UN General Assembly condemned the bombing of Tripoli against Gaddafi. While the American president seemed to be engaged in a crusade against the '*Evil Empire*', the United States questioned its participation in certain international organisations by withdrawing from UNESCO, for example, followed in 1985 by the United Kingdom. It was ubris before its time, the time of the 90s and beyond.

Indeed, while the Security Council was still paralysed in 1988 and, in addition to a financial crisis, was experiencing a real crisis of confidence, the UN experienced a kind of sudden renaissance that benefited its Secretary-General Javier Pérez de Cuéllar. In July 1988, an Iranian civilian Airbus was mistakenly shot down over the Strait of Hormuz by the US Navy; the Iranians took advantage of this tragedy to return to the Council table (NB: in a mirror image of the departure of the Italians from the League of Nations at the time of the Ethiopia affair). This was followed by a comprehensive settlement between Iran and Iraq, the independence of Namibia, the end of apartheid in South Africa and a diplomatic solution to the problem of Cambodia. These sudden developments were facilitated by the end of the Cold War. Among the Permanent Five, Russia appeared to be in decline, while China was still awakening. Faced with Washington and London, was France, the traditional 'troublemaker', and sensitive to a certain non-alignment of Third World countries, going to be in a position in this new context to benefit from a wider margin of manoeuvre and to exist alone? The answer was in fact negative, as was ultimately confirmed by France's participation in the US-led coalition in Iraq. It proved, to borrow an Asian saying, that *you can't put your boat across the current of the river*.

Typology of conceptions of the multilateral system

The existence of a multilateral system, i.e. the cooperation of states in multilateral forums, and the existence of a multipolar world are not phenomena that are necessarily associated and perfectly superimposed, apart from an ideal vision. While we are now witnessing the emergence of a multipolar world, of which the BRICS countries are an illustration, the UN as a political organisation seems paralysed; conversely, multilateral cooperation was possible under the New World Order, under American domination; the agreement of the Five + One (Germany) on 14 July 2015 on Iran's nuclear programme, for example, was possible, but it is inconceivable today.

In the final analysis - even if this classification is obviously artificial - there are four concepts of the multilateral system: *multilateralism of expression* enables states that are small in size and limited in power to find, where appropriate, a broad echo in international fora; *multilateralism of cooperation* gives to states that are economically weak or affected at a particular time a possibility to benefit from the solidarity of the international community; *power-demultiplying multilateralism* concerns medium-sized powers, such as France and the United Kingdom, which have been able to develop and lead networks and thus benefit from thematic or circumstantial coalitions that are broader than their own alliances; *'domination multilateralism'* is reserved for the biggest powers, such as the United States, which are reluctant to accept international cooperation but eventually agree to it because they are the masters of the game. China refuses to be pigeonholed in the latter category because, despite its new-found power, it wants to continue to give the impression that it is 'playing as one'. Is this a reality, or a supreme skill to dominate the system in the end?

Does a system still exist today?

The answer is yes, despite the disappearance of certain regulatory mechanisms, because every lasting reality is ultimately a system. The world, for example, has become less multipolar than the one denounced by V. Putin at the Munich *Wehrkunde* in 2007; for Europe, the concept of 'strategic autonomy' is struggling to make headway, but a direction is emerging; international society, despite a narrative designed to highlight a marked antagonism between the 'collective West' and the 'global South', is not reduced to a confrontation between East and West; the East and the South, like the West, remain diverse and sometimes even fractured; despite a certain resurgence, the new world is not reduced to a confrontation between blocs: it is volatile and is instead made up of 'à la carte' cooperation, which is perfectly illustrated by India's policy, for example in the Indo-Pacific sphere (NB: New Delhi is not in the AUKUS but cooperates with the United States, Australia and Japan in a Four-way configuration; India has been a strategic partner of France since 1998). NATO, which until recently was described as *'brain-dead'*, has been revitalised as a direct result of the war in Ukraine, and has now been enlarged to include Sweden and Finland. The question of Ukraine's membership remains open, but this does not necessarily mean that the Atlantic Alliance will be at the heart of the European security architecture in the future.

The world as it is and as it is not

In the final analysis, it is easier to say what the world is not today than what it is, compared with a system that had shown a certain stability for a few decades. Military nuclear power no longer seems to guarantee the balance of the whole, and we are living in an 'infra-nuclear' context where it is possible to rely on the possession of an absolute weapon to wage war against a State with only conventional means. The world is indeed 'unstructured'. Will we ever be able to speak of 'creative destruction', as some economic theorists do?

The system of international relations has unquestionably become more volatile, as a result of the blocking of its past operating rules, a certain anarchy in relations between states and, above all, changes in the distribution of power. Cracks are being heard on all sides.

As in Hobbes' time, in relation to the state of nature, we will have to rediscover a form of 'social contract' on the scale of humanity as a whole. Isn't the imperial model an anachronistic illusion? Is Deng Xiao-ping's model of a disconnection - and at the same time coexistence - between the economy and the political monopoly of the Communist Party (CCP), which enabled China to achieve double-digit growth, still viable? Is American democracy not under threat, to quote the warnings of Democratic leaders, including President Biden himself? Has Europe not been slowed down, or even shattered, in its attempts at emancipation by the war in Ukraine? Will globalisation be totally called into question, belying Fukuyama's adventurous assertions, or will globalisation retain some of its merits? Globalisation - through the market - has not replaced political order, but it can act as a safeguard against the most extreme tensions (NB: Saudi Arabia's current policy of favouring its post-oil development over certain regional solidarities is an example of this). Don't China and the United States each have comparative advantages (e.g. semi-conductors for the USA, 65% of the world's lithium reserves for China) ? Will Germany, particularly penalised by the war in Europe involving its very important economic partner Russia, not to mention China, seize the moment to 'break certain chains' in a historic *Zeitwende* movement?

Can Russia be ostracised in the long term by Europe, which has so many reciprocal links with it? As for the UN system, some of its mechanisms will inevitably have to be modified and the Security Council will obviously have to be enlarged. The skill of legal experts will not be enough to rebuild a system, but it is also in the most serious moments that qualitative leaps are possible. Didn't the League of Nations emerge from the First World War and the United Nations from the Second in San Francisco in 1945?

Ukraine: law and justice?

Ukrainians often talk about law and justice, and we can hear this complaint due to their deep wounds. International law has been violated, as the UN Secretary General has publicly acknowledged; war crimes have been committed that must not go unpunished. But the organisation of international society is more than imperfect; it remains embryonic and disordered, reflecting a world that is still too much a state of nature. No supranational authority is in a position to enforce, in all circumstances and in all places, rules that are consistent with the civilisation to which we aspire; the United Nations Security Council is only the embryo of an ideal structure, and it is currently paralysed because it requires the unanimity of its members on questions that are not procedural.

The right of pursuit, which Kyiv is currently using on Russian territory, is a matter of self-defence as defined in Article 51 of the UN Charter. The question that arises is all the more that of the effectiveness of the response given that the aims of the operation are unclear. According to Article 51, Ukraine should have *'informed the Council'* of the measures it was taking outside its borders. Was this a diversionary tactic to ease the pressure on Ukrainian fighters in the Donbas? Was it to bolster the morale of the fighters and the population at a time when Kyiv has accumulated reasons for dissatisfaction, not to say failure, since the announced and aborted counter-offensive last autumn? Does the ambition to defeat Russia at home, or at least to undermine its power to the point of destabilising it, still hold sway over the minds of Kyiv's decision-makers?
On this last point, which is the product of long-standing nationalism and the expression of more recent frustrations, we must also understand the questions and even the reluctance of Ukraine's military and financial backers to deliver all types of weapons and to

authorise their use in depth by the enemy. We must never forget the imbalance of power and, in particular, the fact that - although some want to ignore the red lines - we are indeed in the presence of a war between a nuclear state and a non-nuclear state. Moscow, in order to defend its vital interests, could finally 'up the ante' both in terms of mobilising additional troops - which its population is three to four times greater than the Ukrainian population - and in terms of escalating the nature of its military resources.

Such is the harsh reality of a violent and increasingly deregulated world. It should be time once again for diplomacy, which seems to have been extinguished and forgotten, despite some recent tentative steps towards conferences organised without one of the protagonists. It has given way to tacticians with no overall vision and to commentators on military affairs who only speak for themselves. Like the trenches of the Donbas, it's a bit like counting gaiter buttons in the trenches of Verdun more than a century ago, when total war was invented.

The war has already destroyed Ukraine, despite its legitimate and courageous resistance, which is now only allowing it to make marginal territorial gains while being horribly costly in terms of manpower. The Russian nuclear superpower is also like an entangled Gulliver, discovering and identifying its weaknesses, and it cannot help but be worried about its future, particularly its economic and social future. It has cut itself off from a European market which used to provide it with technology and which remains potentially vital for the flow of one of its main resources, gas. As for Europe, which is also suffering from this unprecedented situation on the continent, it is paying, like Germany, a high price symbolised by the sabotage of Nord Stream and the disruption of its traditional energy supplies. Yet it has made major efforts, not to say sacrifices in the case of its less powerful states, to help Ukraine in its quest for survival as an independent nation. But isn't Europe wondering if it isn't working for the King of Prussia? As we know, those who advise are not usually those who pay. The example of the reconstruction of Kuwait, and even more so of Iraq, bears witness to this.

Faced with a war in which there can only be losers, in which the risks of escalation can never be completely ruled out, in which the Northern hemisphere is navel-gazing in the face of the problems and frustrations of the South, and in which Europe is being sidelined from the great creative movement of the world, whose centre of gravity has shifted to Asia, it is high time to pull ourselves together and forget the culture and games of war, to rediscover our identity and our autonomy, without which there can be no promotion of law and justice.

Writing *War and Peace* a few decades after the Battle of the Moskva in 1812 at his estate in Yasnaya Poliana, Leo Tolstoy was able to rise above nationalism and the passions of war by devoting himself to the human aspect of a confrontation that resulted in tens of thousands of victims with no clear winner. International humanitarian law and the law of war had perhaps then germinated in the mind of this universal thinker; Napoleon was to become a Russian hero, while the true victor of Borodino had been designated: humanity as a whole.

The spectre of the BRICS

Paraphrasing Karl Marx's first words about communism in his famous Manifesto published in 1848, we could say that '*a spectre is haunting Europe, the spectre of the BRICS, the spectre of a new, more multipolar world*'. This is the new fear that is plaguing public opinion in the West, paralysing it instead of making it accept the inevitability of the world's major changes and the need to adapt to them by becoming more dynamic.

The BRICS Summit, which has been held annually since its first edition in Yekaterinburg in 2009, and again in Russia this year in Kazan, 800 km east of Moscow, was eagerly awaited. But its impact, at least psychologically, was proving to be even greater than anticipated in the context of the weariness caused by the war in Ukraine, of a sort of rehabilitation of Russia on a major international stage in the face of a West that is often in doubt, somewhat cracked on both sides of the Atlantic, and prey to the languor caused by a fading Democratic administration that will ultimately have failed on all the major international issues since the abandonment of Afghanistan in 2021.

BRIC, then BRICS with South Africa, is now BRICS+ with the accession of four new members (NB: Egypt, UAE, Ethiopia and Iran), not to mention many other states which are still waiting in the wings, such as Turkey, but which are present. The grand organiser of this diplomatic mass, V. Putin was able to express at least three essential messages: that he was not ostracised, and in fact met the UN Secretary-General; from Tatarstan - part of the Russian Federation, predominantly Muslim and industrialised - where the representatives of just under half the world's population and around 35% of the planet's GNP meet, Russia could highlight a peaceful multi-ethnic and multi-religious identity; Russia, driven by necessity and ostracized by Europe in a suicidal move, was pursuing its Eurasian temptation.

But the BRICS are not a bloc in the Cold War sense of the word; it is absurd, for example, to add up the nuclear capabilities of China and India, which have clashed militarily on several occasions. Rather, it is a counter-G7 and confirmation of the emergence of a new world, the more multipolar world - no longer the American-Soviet condominium or the American hyper-power - that France has long been calling for. Rather than fear, we should be opening up grandiose prospects: India, to mention just one country, has been one of France's main strategic partners since 1998.

Eurasia at the heart of the BRICS

There is a Eurasian temptation. In particular, if not primarily, it reflects a questioning of identity, which is not unique to Russia, but is due in general to accelerated modernisation, the effects of globalisation and migrations that have become uncontrolled throughout the world as a result of climate change, wars and global inequalities. Russia is a bi-continental, multi-ethnic, multi-religious and multi-cultural empire, and its Eurasism is as much a protest against the West as an attachment to Asia. The Mongol invasions of 1214 to 1552 - the most dangerous in the history of the Russian nation - came from the East, and the history of Russia, once its territorial expansion had been completed, had always turned towards the West.

Evgeny Primakov's interest in Eurasia was more a matter of circumstance and necessity than belief. Primakov undoubtedly understood better than Putin that post-Soviet Russia - sometimes described as a 'poor power' - no longer had the means to pursue a project in the imperial tradition. He therefore advocated cooperation, which could sometimes be conflictual, but resolutely ruled out the use of force; for him, it was a question of absolutely avoiding a break with the West, which would be contrary to Russia's DNA and to its history of looking towards both the European continent and Asia.

Primakov first conceived of a Moscow-New Delhi-Beijing triangle, which was naturally integrated into his strategic thinking. This project, which was conceptualised in what came to be known as the *'Primakov Doctrine'* in 1998, prefigured the BRICS. But this triangle could also be described as a *'trio of asymmetries'*. China's Belt and Road Initiative, for example, is likely to weaken Russian influence in the region.

Putin has taken on board the foreign policy 'software' of his predecessor at the head of the government, whom he revered for having been an undisputed master of intelligence. In addition to the need for a strong state, the dialectics of the unipolar/multipolar world and the question of not enlarging NATO have brought the current Russian President closer to his mentor.

Neutralisation of Ukraine

It's a truism that Ukraine lies between East and West. It should not forget its history and geography, which destined it, at the end of the Soviet Union, to be a 'buffer zone' or a 'bridge', a more positive term. It benefited from this situation, for example by being virtually subsidised by Russia until 2009/2010, with gas priced at less than $50 per 1,000 m3 at a time when the world price was reaching $250. Tensions in the energy sector clearly preceded the annexation of Crimea, let alone the current war. At the same time, Kyiv could have benefited from its proximity to EU countries, particularly in terms of trade. Geopolitical factors, combined with the negligence of many of its leaders and the divisions within society, have prevented Ukraine from opting for skilful external orientations.

Today's challenge is twofold: the end of hostilities between Russia and Ukraine; the reconstruction of the latter and the normalisation of a relationship with Moscow that is essential for Europe. It is hard to see how the cessation of hostilities - which could even be de facto (frozen conflict), without being formalised (Panmunjom formula), and a fortiori accompanied by a settlement on the status of Ukraine - would be anything other than a 'freeze on image' of sorts, depending on the situation on the ground. As for Russia, the threat of new sanctions, if things did not go smoothly, would not necessarily be effective, as the country has adapted to such a situation; moreover Moscow - in the tradition of an empire with blurred borders (see Transnistria, Georgia) - is not absolutely eager to obtain a formal agreement, unless it ratifies that Ukraine has no vocation to be in NATO or the EU; a Ukraine with uncertain borders would be an insurmountable handicap for it in the perspective of membership of larger entities. The concept of a buffer zone is undoubtedly, in the mind of the Kremlin, a neutralisation on the scale of the whole of Ukraine, the main aim of the war for Russia; it should be noted that neutralisation would not exclude bilateral security guarantees for Kiev from its main supporters.

As for the reconstruction of Ukraine, it is to be feared that Europe, already economically punished by the war, will be made to feel guilty for not having been able to help Kyiv more. Have we ever seen the United States take on such a responsibility, even if it was overwhelming? Just remember Vietnam, Kuwait/Iraq and Afghanistan.

The great Eurasian alliance

Trump, an incomparable actor of the political stage, can only impress, if not arouse admiration, for his personal journey, his energy and his voluntarism. But he is also the reflection of a society - populism being a reaction to an identity crisis -, of a civilisation that is very different indeed from that of Europe, and the exacerbated expression of a world in the throes of transformation. This last development, characterised by the weakening of the rules of the international system, the assertion of the primacy of force over law and the protectionism of the economically powerful, should give us cause for concern and therefore a wake-up call.

The war in Ukraine, which Europe was unable to prevent or put a stop to, was a revelation of the perils that threaten us. At the risk of surprising or even shocking people, the main danger for Europe is not Russia but submission within the so-called Western camp. On the economic front, Trump is no innovator, and we need only recall the application of extraterritorial laws that unfairly hit European companies under Obama. The major cut in Russian energy supplies has impoverished Europe - to the point of threatening Germany's equilibrium - and enriched shale gas suppliers, even to the detriment of the environment. Europeans are now paying three to four times more for their gas than Americans, which is having a major impact on their trade competitiveness. On the security front, Trump is using blackmail with his demands for the share of GNP devoted to defence. In reality, the United States would have no sense in withdrawing from NATO, which serves only one purpose: to dominate Europe.

Evgeny Primakov understood that the weakening of the Soviet Union forced his country to redefine its posture; this was the starting point for a greater interest in China and India that continued and developed into BRIC, now BRICS+. All things considered, Europe should realise that it risks finding itself in a similar situation. Reconnecting with Russia for energy and economic reasons (NB: this country has been a key area of success for major French companies) and even for security reasons (NB: how can we imagine a European security architecture without Russia?) will eventually become a necessity. For its part, while Russia has seen its trade with China grow exponentially, it does not have enough gas pipelines to redirect its flows eastwards; 70% of foreign investment, including technology, came from Europe until the war in Ukraine. As for civilisation, Trump's reaction against wokism is a good thing for everyone, but the United States in the age of the "*techno-industrial oligarchs*" confirms that it is light years away from Europe.

A world of Revisionist powers, without Europe?

Facing uncertainties, we could eventually try to draw up an unvarnished picture of the state of the new world order in the making.

The 'New International Order' was a concept formulated by George Bush Sr. in the early 1990s, when the Soviet Union was disintegrating and the United States had just won the Gulf War. The resulting world was characterised by American 'hyper-power', albeit mitigated by the maintenance of a degree of cooperation within the UN system. During this phase, powers such as China and, above all, Russia maintained their attachment to the UN Charter ('*the whole Charter, nothing but the Charter*'), which, in their view, could not be modified in any way; this applied in particular to the Security Council, whose membership could not be enlarged, let alone the veto mechanism called into question. These powers were described as 'anti-revisionists'.

We have now moved away from this system - which itself succeeded the opposition of the Cold War blocs - as a result of the emergence of a more multi-polar world and the now total paralysis of the Security Council mechanisms, due in particular to the war in Ukraine, which saw a permanent member flout the basic rules of international law contained in the Charter.

The arrival in power of D. Trump could well herald a new era. It is hard to imagine the United States promoting a multilateral system that it feels it can do without. Their withdrawal from several international organisations (e.g. WHO, UN Human Rights Council) already confirms this. Today's world, in its state of nature, is both one of large blocs and of force prevailing over law. Will Trump therefore favour a three-way game with Moscow and Beijing? If so, the changes - introduced by powers that have become true revisionists of the system - would be considerable. Russia has been aspiring for over thirty years to regain its lost power and could live with this new status. For the United States, things are less clear-cut: the Washington-Moscow-Beijing triangle is no longer the Cold War triangle that allowed Nixon to open up to China in the early 1970s. Only China, closely linked to the USA in economic and commercial terms and to Russia for geo-strategic reasons, would be offered a certain - albeit delicate - room for manoeuvre. And what about Europe?

Europe on the verge of a nervous breakdown

The accelerated pace and warm atmosphere of the Russian-American normalisation - as it is taking shape after a first and long telephone conversation between D. Trump and V. Putin made public in February 2025 -, the revelations about the broad outlines of a settlement to the war in Ukraine (NB: specifically excluding this country's accession to NATO and the presence of American soldiers on Ukrainian soil to guarantee peace) have petrified the Europeans, who have been sidelined from these considerable developments, as has V. Zelensky for that matter.

The vibrant voluntarism and all-out disruptive actions of D. Trump since his re-election (see territorial ambitions, tariff war, anti-wokism, reduction of bureaucracy), are sometimes assimilated to irrationality, to erratic and short-lived behaviour, or even to unacknowledged and long-standing compromises with the rediscovered Russian partner. In reality, the world has changed and D. Trump is accelerating the pace of change at breakneck speed; the United States is now undoing what it has long undertaken and Trump is making a U-turn in his country's foreign policy. Since 1991, Washington has never stopped treating the new Russia as if it were still the USSR; the aim was therefore to continue to weaken it, which explains the expansion of NATO as well as the crises on the empire's doorstep, such as Georgia and Ukraine, which was seized as an opportunity. D. Trump has just put an end to this policy, at the risk of breaking a transatlantic bond, by treating Moscow with the language of an ally (see reference to the Second World War; possibility of a presence in Moscow on 9 May; possible reconstitution of the G8). From now on, NATO's role can only be seen in relative terms; the American Secretary of Defence has just stated it bluntly: '*strategic realities do not allow the United States to concentrate on the security of Europe*'; the focus is on China.

D. Trump, who is very un-Wilsonian, is in fact recognising what the international system has become, with a reduced role for international institutions such as the UN Security Council and a more fragmented world in which new powers have emerged. The American president, in the tradition of Theodore Roosevelt's *Big stick*, clearly intends to prioritise dealing with the powerful, whether on economic issues or the fight against terrorism or nuclear proliferation. Did he not just mention the possibility of a summit with Vladimir Putin and Xi Jinping? In this period of global upheaval, Europe's problem is precisely that it is not a power and was not conceived as such. To be one of the 'caimans of the backwater', it would first be required to be truly European.

22

Towards a new Washington, Moscou, Beijing triangle?

While the recent normalisation between Russia and the United States is proceeding apace - the further development of which will depend on how the war in Ukraine is resolved - China remains silent and lurking in the shadows. Voices in the West, which in the end are little more than speculation, are making China the backdrop to the rapprochement between Washington and Moscow and the ultimate objective - if not the main target - for the United States.

In recent years, the international system has undergone accelerated change, with the emergence of centres of power and a minimum of regulation within the framework of the UN. The emerging pattern is not necessarily a real division of the world between the most powerful, but rather that of a new three-way game, distinct by definition from the American-Soviet condominium of the Cold War, and even from the first Washington-Beijing-Moscow triangle of the same period. The opening towards China conceived by R. Nixon and implemented by H. Kissinger in the early 1970s was designed to drive a wedge between the two rival Communist powers of the day and to give the United States greater room for manoeuvre, particularly with a view to settling the Vietnam War. One of the effects of this wide-ranging policy - which led to the recognition of the People's Republic of China following the Shanghai communiqué of 1972 - was also to exert pressure on L. Brezhnev's Soviet Union and to promote major strategic arms control agreements, such as the ABM Treaty on anti-ballistic missiles systems and SALT.

Does the new Republican administration in the United States have such a vision? Are we heading for a new 'Treaty of Tordesillas' to divide up the world, along the lines of the redefinition of relations between Spain and Portugal at the end of the 15th century? Will a minimum of multilateral cooperation within the framework of the United Nations - illustrated by the recent Security Council resolution on Ukraine - be restored? Will the major crises of nuclear proliferation, in North Korea and Iran for example, be brought under control? These are just some of the possible features and prospects for the new world that is taking shape.

The new governance of the world

Votes at the UN: power politics and multilateralism

On 24 February, the third anniversary of the start of the war in Ukraine, the United Nations adopted three resolutions, two in the General Assembly and one in the Security Council. The latter text has far-reaching implications in terms of the functioning and restructuring of the international system.

At the General Assembly, Ukraine and its supporters won only an apparent victory. Indeed, as the votes in their favour on the one hand and the abstentions and negative votes put together on the other tend to balance out, this cannot be considered as a good result by UN standards, but rather as a sign that Kyiv's positions are being seriously eroded. It should be noted that the United States opposed a text that affirmed Ukraine's territorial integrity. At the Security Council, the Russians and Americans voted together on a text prepared by Washington, while the Europeans abstained, London and Paris not vetoing it. It should be noted that China, for the first time, voted with Russia on Ukraine, instead of abstaining.

These procedural convergences between Russia and the United States, if not as regard to the entire substance, paradoxically augur well - at a time when the powers are imposing themselves ever more brutally on the international stage - for a possible return, albeit patchy, to multilateral diplomacy. All things considered, this observation can be compared with the situation that prevailed after 1991 (see Gulf War, end of the Soviet Union) when American domination (see George Bush Sr's New International Order) accommodated the preservation of a minimum of cooperation in international forums.

This sudden shift in American votes at the UN clearly reflects Washington's desire to "keep Moscow on board" as part of its new international strategy. It may have come as a surprise, or even a shock, but if confirmed, it is likely to put an end to the paralysis of the Security Council in recent years.

European nightmare

Europe's rude awakening: on the verge of a nervous breakdown

The accelerated pace and warm atmosphere of the Russian-American normalisation - as it is taking shape after a long telephone conversation between D. Trump and V. Putin -, the revelations about the broad outlines of a settlement to the war in Ukraine (NB: specifically excluding this country's accession to NATO and the presence of American soldiers on Ukrainian soil to guarantee peace) have petrified the Europeans, who have been sidelined from these considerable developments, as has V. Zelensky for that matter.

The vibrant voluntarism and all-out disruptive actions of D. Trump since his re-election (see territorial ambitions, tariff war, anti-wokism, reduction of bureaucracy), are sometimes assimilated to irrationality, to erratic and short-lived behaviour, or even to unacknowledged and long-standing compromises with the rediscovered Russian partner. In reality, the world has changed and D. Trump is accelerating the pace of change at breakneck speed; the United States is now undoing what it has long undertaken and Trump is making a U-turn in his country's foreign policy. Since 1991, Washington has never stopped treating the new Russia as if it were still the USSR; the aim was therefore to continue to weaken it, which explains the expansion of NATO as well as the crises on the empire's doorstep, such as Georgia and Ukraine, which was seized as an opportunity. D. Trump has just put an end to this policy, at the risk of breaking a transatlantic bond, by treating Moscow with the language of an ally (see reference to the Second World War;

possibility of a presence in Moscow on 9 May; possible reconstitution of the G8). From now on, NATO's role can only be seen in relative terms; the American Secretary of Defence has just stated it bluntly: 'strategic realities do not allow the United States to concentrate on the security of Europe'; the focus is on China.

D. Trump, who is very un-Wilsonian, is in fact recognising what the international system has become, with a reduced role for international institutions such as the UN Security Council and a more fragmented world in which new powers have emerged. The American president, in the tradition of Theodore Roosevelt's 'Big stick', clearly intends to prioritise dealing with the powerful, whether on economic issues or the fight against terrorism or nuclear proliferation. Did he not just mention the possibility of a summit with Vladimir Putin and Xi Jinping? In this period of global upheaval, Europe's problem is precisely that it is not a power and was not conceived as such. To be one of the 'caimans of the backwater', it would first be required to be truly European.

A brighter tomorrow

An gusty wind is blowing across Europe. It carries the miasma of a threat supposedly coming from the East and the debris of the cracks in the Western community. Like the Mistral in Provence described by Giono, it ends up taking hold of people's minds, torturing them and driving them mad. By the time the war on the continent had taken hold over the long term, in the manner of 14-18 trench warfare, minds had become numb, mithridatised by American protection. The paradox is that despite the prospect of a cessation of hostilities, or even of a more ambitious and lasting peace agreement, under the blows of Washington, panic has gripped European governments; they are trying to convince public opinion and perhaps above all to make people forget their lack of foresight and vision and their catastrophic management.
Is the threat today greater than it was during the Cold War, which was dominated by blocs and characterised by a balance - in reality

made up of confrontations in peripheral theatres - based on nuclear deterrence? Nothing is less certain. The protagonists are now bloodless: Ukraine has been amputated, destroyed and ruined for a long time to come, dragging us down with it; Russia has been weakened in terms of men and equipment and, as a result of the conflict, has slowed down, if not halted, its efforts to modernise. If Russia were to succeed in loosening the stranglehold of NATO - which was its main objective in the war - its priority would inevitably be to resume this virtuous course, particularly in the face of a China that circumstances have brought closer to it, but which could ultimately prove invasive if not vassalise it.

In reality, President Trump, even if he has not conceptualised such a strategy, could well put an end to the classic East-West opposition. The most objective minds in the West recognise that the post-Soviet transition has not been well managed on their side. The Russian-American agenda drawn up in Riyadh is by no means confined to Ukraine; Russia, for example, has just put itself forward as a possible mediator with regard to Iran's nuclear programme; a debate is under way in Washington on the lifting of sanctions and this is undoubtedly the thrust of the idea of reconstituting the G8, which became the G7 again after the annexation of Crimea. The prospect of a European security architecture that would include Russia - which will take time to establish - is not just a provocative idea devoid of credibility and meaning.

The poetic metaphor of a promising future ('Les lendemains qui chantent'), is a natural contrast to the prevailing pessimism. But we must not forget that these words were spoken by Gabriel Péri, who was shot on Mont-Valérien in 1941 and, in his own words, 'died so that France may live'.

European diplomacy: values and interests

European diplomacy refers as much to the structures in Brussels (see EU High Representative for Foreign Affairs and Security Policy since the Lisbon Treaty of 2007; European External Action Service, EEAS; European Council and Parliament; Common Security and

Defence Policy, CSDP) as to the national policies of the Member States. This is reflected in multilateral forums, such as the UN General Assembly, and in what is known as European political cooperation.

'Values' are part of the DNA of France, which is often described as the 'homeland of human rights'. Its foreign policy is not one-dimensional, i.e. it cannot be based exclusively on international humanitarian law, which it has nevertheless advanced (see the right of humanitarian intervention recognised by the UN at the end of the 1980s); it is in fact the result of a balanced 'cocktail' that takes account of interests.

Values and interests are not mutually exclusive. France's traditional policy in the Middle East is a case in point. The noble objectives of seeking regional peace and stability are also in line with the fundamental interests of a country bordering the Mediterranean.

At a time of economic diplomacy in the face of increasingly tough competition, when governments are supporting their companies, Europe's ambitions are collective in the context of major multilateral negotiations (e.g. EU-Mercosur; EU-China) for which the European Commission receives a mandate from the Member States; on the other hand, this collective action is undermined when companies - particularly the largest ones - and European interests find themselves in competition; However, this competition, which can be fierce, is mitigated by the fact that large companies in strategic sectors (e.g. transport, energy, even space) often have their capital diversified at European level, or even beyond.

The question of how to 'strengthen' Europe is a highly topical one, particularly in the wake of the war in Ukraine, at a time when the European security architecture needs to be redefined and, if necessary, alliances need to be reconfigured. This is the debate on 'Europe as a power', for which the European Community and then the EU were not initially conceived. This is a moment of truth for European diplomacy and for Europe, at a time when the international system is moving towards a division of the world between the major powers, outside the traditional framework of multilateral political structures.

International sanctions: Europe's schizophrenia

Ursula von der Leyen and Christine Lagarde have just jointly sounded the alarm in an editorial column in the Financial Times about Europe's plummeting competitiveness. Among the main causes cited are 'high energy prices' due to 'geopolitical shifts'. The expression of this warning is astonishing coming from the President of the European Commission. She has been a zealous and consistent supporter of sanctions against Russia. Fourteen sets of sanctions have been adopted by the EU, and these were extended a few days ago, despite strong reservations on the part of Member States that are particularly energy-dependent, but which finally relented under pressure from the Commission.

European sanctions do not include gas, but Russian gas no longer reaches Europe via pipelines; the last operating pipeline through Ukraine, which delivered marginal quantities to the continent compared with its past imports (NB: 40% of European gas until the end of 2021), ceased operating on 31 December last year following Ukraine's decision not to renew its transit agreement with Gazprom. On the other hand, Russian LNG is received in some European ports, including in France, and is widely redistributed, but it is under threat of further sanctions. In any case, it is LNG, notably from American shale gas (NB: Europe's leading supplier of LNG with almost 50%), that has largely contributed to replacing Russian gas via pipelines. As a result, Europeans are now paying 3 to 4 times more for their gas than Americans. This is unbearable in terms of competitiveness. Germany, which used to depend on Russian gas imports for almost 50% of its consumption, cannot bear it and is in deep crisis.

We should also mention individual sanctions imposed on hundreds of people, targeted in Brussels in a way that is highly opaque to the public and often based on a lack of serious justification (NB: this has led the European Court of Justice to lift sanctions in some cases).

When it comes to powerful players in the Russian economy or those directly linked to it, Europe has thus deprived itself not only of financial investments and partners, but also of essential intermediaries within civil society with a view to further normalisation with Moscow. The gradual lifting of sanctions against them could provide a significant stimulus to the cessation of hostilities in Ukraine.

The Financial Times Tribune is therefore dizzying because of the gap between a gloomy discourse and the realities for which Europeans themselves are responsible. European schizophrenia is no longer even a disease, it is a suicidal attitude.
Warmongers of all countries, unite!

Friedrich Merz is not yet officially Chancellor of Germany, but he won the recent parliamentary elections (NB: by just a few points over the far-right "Alternative für Deutschland" - AfD). He took advantage of his relative legitimacy to call an emergency meeting of the Bundestag from the previous term (NB: the new parliament resulting from the elections will not take office until after 25 March) in order to proceed with a major constitutional reform that can only be adopted by a two-thirds majority.

The stratagem succeeded and a qualified majority was largely obtained. But the compatibility of the approach, which is certainly in line with the letter of the law but not with the spirit of democracy, is questionable. Indeed a two-thirds majority on the proposed reform would undoubtedly not have been achieved in the new parliamentary configuration.

By virtue of the vote that has just taken place, the federal state and the sixteen Länder will no longer be limited in their capacity to incur debts. F. Merz is planning an investment programme of €1,000 billion, divided more or less equally between military equipment and infrastructure (schools, hospitals, roads, etc.).
According to the future Chancellor, whose coalition has still not been formed, this will be "a first step towards a European Defence Community". This needs to be clarified: initial statements by F.

Merz's initial statements indicate that he could be satisfied with both the American nuclear umbrella and the extension of the French deterrent; during the war in Ukraine, the outgoing Chancellor O. Scholz had a €100 billion defence plan adopted, which was immediately used to buy American F-35 fighter jets, which are responsible for "nuclear service" within NATO, i.e. carrying nuclear weapons.

Germany's massive rearmament project will not necessarily reassure all its neighbours and those who are supposed to be its partners. From a German national point of view - but it is up to the FRG itself to decide on this point - is a great Germany possible without an "Ostpolitik"? After the limits reached by Konrad Adenauer, often referred to as the "Kanzler der Alliierten" (Chancellor of the Allies), great chancellors such as Willy Brandt, Helmut Schmidt, Helmut Kohl and Gerhard Schröder have proved the opposite. Nor is the European out of time - when a ceasefire in Ukraine is within reach - rearmament frenzy any comfort.

The Greenland case: tariffs and borders

The tariff war launched by the United States is, in all its brutality, an attack on free trade, a return to a form of protectionism and a sign that 'happy' globalisation has come to an end. The latter had not only had perverse effects, and general deregulation had also been accompanied by growth and the promotion of the least well-off countries. It is these countries, particularly in South-East Asia (Vietnam, Cambodia, Laos, Burma), that will be hardest hit by the highest taxes (NB: over 40% on all products exported to the United States); American companies that have relocated to markets with lower labour costs will also be targeted.

This general movement is accompanied by a questioning of borders, not in order to abolish them but to establish new ones, whether it be the acceptance of a de facto state of affairs in Ukraine, or plans for Canada or Greenland, or even a nihil obstat on Taiwan. As a result, the economic deregulation that has accompanied the globalisation of trade over the last few decades has been followed by a questioning of the rules by which the international system operates; law and diplomacy have been relegated to second place, and the 'international community' is now 'unstable' in the chemical sense of the term.

Jean Malaurie devoted himself to the Inuit, the most northerly people on Earth, and to their discovery, but he also foresaw the invasion. This invasion began a long time ago and could be accelerated by climate change, the search for new and scarce resources, and the exacerbation of global strategic interests in a world dominated by the greatest powers outside a multilateral framework. Above all, he loved this people of the farthest reaches, beyond even their borders; as soon as it was possible, he travelled to the most northerly regions of Russia with the project of an Academy of the Peoples of the North.

In this context, is there any chance that the legitimate voice of the Greenlandic people, who gained autonomy in 1979 under the sovereignty of Denmark (NB: reinforced by a law in 2009 following a referendum in 2008), will be heard? In the absence of true independence, what is the best formula for the natives, who number fewer than 60,000 inhabitants? Could Europe collectively play a role in ensuring a degree of protection and compliance with environmental protection laws? Shouldn't France, which intends to upgrade its armaments, give priority to resources that guarantee the defence of its maritime area, which is the second largest in the world? Greenland, the old and new frontier, could benefit from this.

23

Alexander's dream

The world's centre of gravity

The world's centre of gravity has already begun to shift towards the Asia-Pacific region, making the war in Ukraine all the more anachronistic in the light of this development.

The New World is therefore developing under the shadow of a large Asian grouping, which is now the most dynamic. The Great Game of the 19th century was characterised in Central Asia by the opposition of the Russian and British empires. The New Great Game, set against the backdrop of China's assertiveness, is unfolding once again in this area - and the Chinese *New Silk Roads* project is an illustration of this - and also beyond. The world's major groupings, in particular the United States and Europe, will be involved, or at least will not be able to ignore it. We must not forget Turkey, four of the five Central Asian republics of which are Turkish-speaking, and which already has a strong economic presence, as well as Korea, which has active minorities there, India and even neighbouring Iran. Russia, whose Central Asia was part of the Soviet Union, has not given up on exerting influence in its former possessions, where it still wields considerable *soft power* thanks to its dual nationality and cultural influence.

Central Asia was the heart of Alexander the Great's power, which has remained the archetype of empires. Referring to this period of antiquity can provide keys to understanding the contemporary world in the area under consideration. Giving in to uchrony is therefore a temptation. What role does war play in the assertion of power? Isn't war, at the heart of regal power, always imposed on the presidents of the greatest power by virtue of a *'Washington manual* that President Obama once spoke of? Didn't the resistance of the Greeks against the Persian power of Xerxes precede what are now known as 'asymmetric wars'? Do military victories guarantee lasting domination, or should we not consider that domination is the result of a hold that goes beyond it and is the affirmation of a civilisation? Beyond autocracies and empires, what is the Orient? 'As Mao Tse-tung put it: *Do not the winds from the East prevail over those from the West?*' And isn't every empire ephemeral and destined to disappear? Alexander, the emperor of emperors, provides some answers to all these questions.

Taking stock of a sparkling young life

In the first weeks of 323 BC, ten years after the start of his campaigns in Asia Minor, which took him as far as the Indus and even within sight of the Ganges, Alexander welcomed us outside the city of Susa, which was the capital of the Achaemenids and harboured fabulous treasures. It was here that he stopped off in 330, after Babylon and before Persepolis, during his glorious conquest of Persia.

The atmosphere is still festive and dazzling. The sumptuous Wedding of Susa in 324 had just been celebrated with Persian princesses, marking a dazzling union with the East. Although Alexander himself had married Statera, the eldest daughter of Darius, as well as another Persian princess, Roxane was still at his side. Alexander was at the height of his glory at the beginning of 323, which coincided in March, during the spring equinox, with the annual celebration for centuries of the Zoroastrian Nowruz.

A sort of circumterrestrial journey has already been completed, and it was a radiant Alexander, with the known world at his feet, but whose features attest to the harshness of the battles and the scale of the task of exercising power, who welcomed us for an exclusive interview. The interview was conducted in Attic Greek, the language of a new empire that had become the largest in the world, and which he generally used with his companions and foreigners.

In response to our questions, Alexander, now known as the 'Great King' since his triumph over Darius, but still often addressed with familiarity by his Macedonian companions, spoke frankly about a wide range of subjects: war and peace, the relationship between the weak and the strong, the divine nature of power, the clash of empires, democracy versus oligarchy, civilising seduction, the legacy of Alexander and the purpose of history.

War and power

Q. - Great King, it's time for an initial assessment now that you've returned to Susa after vast conquests. Your contemporaries did not write about what you did and it is undoubtedly up to you to tell the story. My first question concerns war and the will to power. Were they at the heart of Alexandre's project?

Alexander - We cannot escape our destiny and we tend to reproduce what we have experienced. Philip II of Macedonia, my father, disappeared tragically, assassinated in the summer of 336 along with some of his descendants and relatives. I come from this melting pot where violence was always present.

It was the federal authorities, in particular the League of Corinth, which was capable of achieving Greek unity, that confirmed me in my role as head of the army. They were also the ones who decided on a punitive expedition to Asia against the King of Persia. I thus took up the project conceived by my father. But I did not limit myself to using the traditional weapon of war against a foreign power to establish my hegemony over Greece. What's more, was I not the heir to a house that was supposed to go back to Heracles, son of Zeus? From then on, I could only be part of a divine lineage that obliges me.

But as I often say, I owe it to my father to live, but it is to Aristotle, my teacher, that I owe it to live nobly. War was therefore a natural state of life for me, and I distinguished myself as a young man, surrounded by my father's companions Antipater and Parmenion, first reducing the barbarians on the edges of the Greek world as far as the Danube and the rebellious tendencies of the cities in Attica before engaging in the fight against the Achaemenid Empire. But in the end, philosophical thought tempered this warlike tendency.

It's true that in 330 I set fire to the Achaemenid palace at Persa, which we call Persepolis, but not just to avenge the ravages inflicted by Xerxes during the Second Medieval War. Athens was occupied then, a century and a half ago, and it took the heroism of Leonidas at Thermopylae in 480, followed by the naval battle of Salamines, to save us from the yoke of the foreigner. So if I burnt to the ground the Achaemenid national sanctuary and their riches, it wasn't just out of some Dionysian fury to make amends for the outrage, but to clearly mark the end of a domination. The idea was to signal to the world the collapse of a military, economic and dynastic siege, because strength, wealth and glory had changed sides.

The Washington manual

Q - Great King, didn't this warrior heritage and the memory of conflicts in the 5th century Greek Empire - which was also a golden age - end up constituting a kind of code or manual making it necessary for the King to wage war?

A - Apart from its divine and human origins, war itself is as much a creator of history as it is a victim of it. After the first Persian offensive, which subdued Macedonia, the First Medieval War led by Darius in 490, in response to the uprising of the Greek colonies in Asia Minor, gave us a vital wake-up call.

The Second Medieval War led by Xerxes I in 480 put Greece's existence even more at stake. The forces were unbalanced, while the Persian king was able to mobilise 300,000 men and 1,200 warships - twice as many as our own ships - not to mention 60,000 Greek mercenaries in the service of the Great King. Xerxes forced his way through Thermopylae, despite the heroic resistance of Leonidas, King of Sparta, and occupied Athens and Attica. The narrow passes of Salamines enabled the enemy naval force to be reduced.

In the end, the code of war is also the code of destiny. As Aeschylus put it: *'it was the land and the sea that fought for the Greeks'*, and the weight of the gods' decision in the conduct of human affairs did the rest.

Deterrence from the weak to the strong

Q - Given the initial balance of power, how was it possible to bring about a reversal in favour of the weaker over the more powerful?

A - Eventually, a national feeling united the cities, particularly Athens and Sparta, and this was reflected both at sea and on land. Great figures emerged who made a difference to the threat of autocracy.

Themistocles was the man of Athenian maritime power. He sent Xerxes the false news that the Greeks were fleeing the Straits of Corinth, which led the Persian fleet to enter the narrow passes of Salamis, where it was decimated on 29 September 480. This operation, of unparalleled audacity, was completed by the land victory of the Spartan Pausanias.

The expedition of the Ten Thousand across the Achaemenid Empire, described by Xenophon in the Anabasis, had already been a source of inspiration. It demonstrated that an expeditionary force of Greek soldiers could cross an entire empire, undefeated and with limited losses. We remember the joy of the combatants when they finally reached the sea on their return. The fact that mercenaries in the service of Persia were able to demonstrate such capabilities could lead us to imagine forces that would be multiplied tenfold by a truly national feeling.

After my first battles in Asia Minor, and above all the victory of Issos over Darius III in 333 and the Egyptian campaign of 332-331, seven years of conquests began with a handful of men, beyond fertile Mesopotamia and the Caspian, in Central Asia and across the formidable mountain barrier of the Hindu Kush to the upper Indus near Kashmir and the Punjab. Only 40,000 infantry and 7,000 cavalry left Syria in 331.

But we have replaced the weakness of numbers, faced with the inexhaustible multitudes of a continental empire, with endurance, fighting strength and mobility. The Macedonian phalanxes abandoned their heavy armour and cumbersome shields for long spears; the cavalry was unrivalled in its daring, well-versed in lightning-fast counterattacks; Alexander wanted to set an example; he didn't entrust war to satraps; he waged it himself, and he could even have died at the Battle of the Granite. In the end, it's possible that my pilgrimage to the site of Troy, in memory of Achilles, protected me.

Peace and war between nations

Q - Are military victories a guarantee of lasting peace?

A - My order was based on the use of force, which it legitimised. As soon as my spear was planted for the first time on the Asian shore of the Straits by a privileged man, favoured by the gods, the project of a new type of empire was launched.

But while the triumph of arms is often a permissive condition for a return to more peaceful times, it is not necessarily a sufficient one. Themistocles, the great man of the Second Medieval War, suffered the vicissitudes of the political life of the cities; he was finally ostracised and died in exile in Asia Minor. It was not until thirty years later, with the Peace of Callias in 449, that the autonomy of the cities and the demilitarisation of the western coasts of Asia Minor were secured.

Military victories were not enough, and the army of conquest was also able to transform itself into an administration. Macedonian officers were established as new satraps with reduced garrisons, without any real change to the previous system of local administration, which had proved its worth. Oligarchies were sometimes replaced by democratic regimes, which won popular support. The restitution of tributes responded to aspirations for regional governance. Finally, the cult of Alexander began to spread during his lifetime in a new polytheistic universe, and this solidified the whole.

Cutting the Gordian knot

Q - Can we consider that large-scale warmongering, as well as a legitimate reaction to external aggression, express the essence of a great leader? Was cutting the Gordian knot an illustration of this?

A - The triple value of Gordion, in the heart of Anatolia, as a road junction, military post and supply point explains the bold decisions I took. They are also in line with my conception of politics and power. This is a noble matter, consisting of clearly defining a line of direction and expressing the will to act; one cannot exist without the other: there is no point in setting goals if you don't have the energy to achieve them; wanting is pointless if you don't know in which direction you want to go. This virtuous combination is the nobility of the job and it must be shared by all those who have faith in me.

The eagle that landed in front of Gordios, announcing the Empire, is undoubtedly a replica of the Delphic eagles charged by Zeus with determining the location of the omphalos. An ancient tradition promised Asia to whoever could untie the complex knot attaching the yoke to the tiller of the chariot of the founder of the dynasty. So I cut the knot with my sword and fulfilled the divine prediction. From now on, instead of the stone symbolising the centre of the world, my position will indicate its centre of gravity. It will be where I am.

History, philosophy, spirituality

(At this point in our interview, Alexander suddenly stands up. He was immediately surrounded by his bodyguard, who led him away, and he left us alone in his sumptuous tent while - according to the belief of his new subjects - he himself went to a temple to perform oriental rites of ablution and divination as befitted the Great King who had supplanted Darius. Alexander returned about an hour later, giving the impression of a changed man - if we can still use that term - even more concentrated, less accessible and more inclined to monologue. It is a more serious Alexander who resumes the discussion at the point where it had been interrupted).

The Persian fortress

Q - How did you approach Persia, known as an impregnable bastion? Was it just another conquest or were the stakes higher? And what was the main significance of all this? A major uncertainty still persists as to the meaning of your conquests: was it a question of imposing the Hellenic world on the Persian Empire or did the East finally conquer Alexander?

A - The future of the world was at stake in this particularly difficult undertaking. As I said in 331: *'just as two suns cannot rise at the same time, two kings cannot hold the sceptre of the earth together'*. The approaches have prepared my troops. We crossed the most terrible deserts made of black volcanic sand. We even passed through a place called *'the mouths of hell'*, a sort of crater from which flames have been emanating day and night since time immemorial. The sulphur and furnace were followed by icy winds.

But the reward came later in Babylon, Susa and Persepolis. In these high places, the simple, no-frills protocol of the Macedonian monarchy met with the lavish ceremonial and rules of the Achaemenid court. The sacking of Parsa, which was delivered to the flames, was a catharsis in memory of the infamies suffered on our own soil, as far away as Athens in the heart of Attica, and of the profanation miraculously contained at Delphi, and not an explosion of rage at the munificence of an East that appeared superior to the Greek world.

A belligerent mood and greed for riches were replaced by a fascination for a mythical unknown. The East thus revealed to us realities beyond appearances. In Babylon - which I entered in 331 and which was five times the size of Athens - the hanging gardens and their water supply by means of complex norias were not simply a display of luxury, wealth and voluptuousness. As with the spiral towers known as '*ziggurats*', access to the upper levels was in reality a representation of the journey to heaven. In Pasargadae, the holy city near Persepolis, I honoured the tomb of Cyrus, with whom, according to Herodotus, '*no Persian ever considered himself worthy of comparison*'.

The grand design of the discovery of a mysterious Orient was strengthened, but it is still a mirage and remains hidden. In 327, in Bactria, I married Roxane, whose name means 'light', and who is now pregnant for the second time. This union of races, to which the gods have successively entrusted the domination of the world, was not the result of a simple alliance; it was ultimately the embodiment of the supreme ideal of my politics. Many years ago, I refused Darius his daughter's hand in marriage. I told Parmenion, a companion of my father Philip II who was inclined to be a temporiser, who urged me in October 333 to accept the offers of the Great King, including his daughter: '*I would accept them if I were Parmenion*'. But Alexander was no longer the Macedonian.

The wedding in Susa, celebrated a few months ago, demonstrated once again that the undertaking was something else. It was a question of making a mark on people's minds and expressing a lasting fusion of East and West. My officers, who married Persian princesses, and ten thousand of my soldiers, who followed their example with Asians, will see their descendants spread over the centuries. I myself set the example by finally marrying Statera, the daughter of Darius, as well as Parysatis, a descendant of Artaxerxes.

Since the battles of Issus and Granico, I have built an empire amid the clash of arms and the cries of the slain, but also through the construction of cities and temples dedicated to the gods. Alexander was finally won over by the East as soon as he made his pilgrimage to the oasis of Ammon. He became a great king by refusing money, an alliance pact and finally the daughter of Darius, before marrying her nine years later. He also married a form of government. This is the legacy I will leave to my epigones, Ptolemaus and Seleucos. Vast territories, in Persia and even more so in Syria and Egypt, would be dominated for centuries by Hellenism. But the nature of Hellenism would also have changed, as demonstrated by the development, even after me, of an art that was the product of a fusion of Greek and Asian influences.

Aristotle, the mentor
Q - Aristotle, your tutor, was a mentor, but you became Great King. What will history remember of Alexander, of his conquests, of the size and nature of the Macedonian imperium, of his aura among so many peoples, of Roxane? And will there even be an Alexander legacy?

A - In the end, it's all down to the teachings of my master Aristotle. We can talk about domination and the influence of the Macedonian imperium, but there is another dimension to this. In the end, my empire will only survive me through the seduction it will continue to exert. In the East, history becomes legend. Alexander, the conqueror of the East, was also conquered by it. A confrontation of opposing extremes ultimately created a superior synthesis, a source of progress for humanity.

Every morning, as I climb a mound in the early hours, I smell the winds. The north-easterly winds are still dominant and outweigh those that carried me from Macedonia. But they will probably never take me back to the mother country. I quickly realised that Greece would not fertilise the East in any lasting way, but that Alexander would become the messenger of an East that he would make comprehensible and attractive for centuries to come. The ubris of Dionysus would prevail over the solar perfection of Apollo. Human reason would give way to the power of the gods.

I was careful not to destroy everything because I wanted to build and seduce, but in the end I was captivated by a whole that surpasses us and is itself adorned with so many attractions. Much will also depend on the time I am given, because only Alexander can accomplish this work. So I wonder about tomorrow: will the dream of a universal empire still be alive after me, centuries from now? Will it be the ambition of a new Great King?
Power, myth and divinity

Q - But isn't your divine nature a guarantee of perpetuity?

As far as my own cult is concerned, it was in line with Hellenic polytheism. It enabled me to establish moral authority first over the Greek colonies and then beyond. But I was never worshipped in my own homeland and my fellow soldiers were always reluctant to practise *proskynesis* by bowing down to me. In the East, the divine is linked to the living, in other words to power; both can disappear together.

Q - But, Great King, isn't the whole universe bowing down to you in this year 323 ? Is it not your ambition to continue the great conquests, interrupted since 325, throughout the entire Oekumene ?

It is true that my multi-racial army of the Indus represented the apogee of my forces, three times as many infantrymen and twice as many cavalrymen at the start of my conquests. In the end, these conquests were part of a world of chaos from which we had to emerge in order to enter the world of ideas. This is the true *Oekoumene*. In fact, it was this latter superiority that made the Greeks so strong. In addition to the Macedonian phalanx, which was a military innovation, we were victorious thanks to geometry, mechanics, physics and astronomy. Breadth of thought and precision of calculation went hand in hand.
In doing so, we thought we were increasing man's freedom in order to restrict the arbitrariness of the gods. But wasn't Prometheus chained up in the Caucasus for stealing fire from the sky? The struggle between man and the gods will be eternal until they are reconciled. Although I have tried to put an end to the great conquests, will this point of culmination be reached? Perhaps the East has shown me the way: mystical ecstasy and attachment to the essence of things prevail over the search for appearances; wisdom is preferred to pure knowledge. It's important that the light never goes out, and the real intoxication is that of the infinite.
A ride into eternity

(Alexander stood up, putting an end to the conversation. A horse is brought to him, no longer the faithful Bucephalus he had tamed in his youth and which accompanied him to Bactria in 326. A few riding companions accompanied him, while Roxane's retinue was already heading for Susa. Alexander set off for a mysterious destination.

Those around him mention a sacred place. Could it be a new oasis at Siwah, where the oracle of Ammon had confirmed his divine birth and predicted world domination and infinite victory? Does victory always have to be renewed in a quest for the absolute? There are whispers that it could be Nisa or Nysai, whose namesake recalls cities founded on the fringes of the empire whose very name was derived from that of Dionysus, a deity who was ultimately terribly human.

Be that as it may, Alexander was due to travel to Babylon in the spring of 323. This is where it all really began, where the Macedonian discovered monumental splendour, commercial prosperity and Dionysian exaltation, where he gained a foothold on the soil of an empire that he succeeded in supplanting and whose legacy we can expect to illuminate the centuries).

Epilogue

A baroque world half-grave, half-voluptuous

Seen from the West, we live in a world that could be described as Baroque, a world of violence but also of uncontrolled pleasure and exaggerated freedom, with no limits on so-called societal transformations. The Baroque world was historically linked to the Counter-Reformation, and was a revolt against austerity, alienation from nature and, in short, against a form of conservatism; this intellectual and artistic uprising led to decorative exuberance and an explosion of the senses. In this way, the movement was also the expression of an unstable world in counterpoint to classicism; we now live in a time when the international system is extremely volatile, when societies are freeing themselves from all rules by wanting, for example, to control - in a Promethean way - both the beginning and the end of life, which is not without comparison with this historically dated great moment in European civilisation.

The essence of Baroque

The essence of Baroque from the sixteenth to the eighteenth centuries is fundamentally an opposition between light and shade. Lightness alternated with the sumptuousness of dark pieces when it came to music. The approach is half grave, half voluptuous, in the tradition of the great figures of the Italian Renaissance of the *Quattrocento*, such as Lorenzo de' Medici, also known as *The Magnificent*. It is true that we often cultivate a love of the shadow, like Xerxes in the famous Largo *Ombra mai fu* (the shadow never was) from Handel's opera. But it's all in vain, because the light can also impose itself on us, in spite of ourselves.

Finally, the Baroque was resolutely optimistic. Light triumphs, for example over the Queen of the Night, the embodiment of evil ('*a vulture with the voice of a nightingale*'), in Mozart's *The Magic Flute*, a Masonic opera par excellence reflecting a de-Christianisation before its time, but imbued with spirituality with the cult of Isis and Osiris inherited from Egyptian antiquity. The High Priest Sarastro concludes the opera with the obvious wisdom that 'the rays of the sun chase away the night' (*die Strahlen der Sonne vertreiben die Nacht*). The initiatory journey takes us from star-studded night to sun-drenched day. Power, bravery, love, of course, but associated with virtue, work, the arts, friendship, truth and, finally, harmony (*Macht, Tapferkeit, Liebe/Tugend, Arbeit, Künste, Freundschaft, Wahrheit und Harmonie*), to the sound of the protective flute, are the guiding thread and the key concepts and landmarks of existence.

Reformation and Counter-Reformation

Paradoxically, the Counter-Reformation, a frenzied movement directed against Protestantism, ended up restoring religious orders, if not order, and the Jesuits were among the most active within this general movement. But in this baroque world, the Catholic Church - but we could also talk about the centrifugal forces within Islam, right up to its most extremist expression - is undoubtedly at a moment that is similar to that of the Protestant Reformation. There are even some similarities with sixteenth-century Germany.

At the time, it was a question of dealing with the dysfunctions of the Roman Church (cf. the debauched 'curetons'; popes behaving like sovereigns, such as Leo X, a sumptuous patron of the arts and son of Lorenzo the Magnificent) in a climate of profound economic and social disorder (see the Peasants' War of 1525). We should mention Thomas Münzer - one of the religious leaders of the Peasants' War and one of the great protagonists of the Reformation - as much as Martin Luther, who in the end sided with the powerful ('*Dear lords, stab, slaughter, slit throats*') and put an end to revolutionary Protestantism. The main inspiration behind the Reformation movement was the need to return to the origins of Christianity, in other words, to the Scriptures (see '*the true treasure of the Church is the Holy Gospe*', according to the Wittemberg theses). For Luther, the author of these theses posted on the eve of All Saints' Day in 1517, *'a Christian is the master of all things and subject to no one'*, which is an affirmation of free interpretation (*sola fide*), if not of free will.

The European crisis of conscience

We need to re-read Paul Hazard and his work *La Crise de la conscience européenne* (1680-1715) published in 1961 (The European crisis of conscience). The great tipping point in European civilisation is analysed at the end of the reign of Louis XIV. The seventeenth century loved constraints, dogma and authority, whereas the eighteenth century hated them, says the author; divine law was opposed by natural law; a class society was replaced by the principle of equality; the century of Bossuet was succeeded by that of Voltaire. Man became the measure of all things, but today we would have to speak of individualism and even abysmal egoism; after the society of duties, it's the society of rights that we pull out of our pockets like a lethal weapon. The lack of coherence of the new times lies, at least in the West, in the search for total freedom, without the slightest hindrance, guaranteed at the same time by the protection and comfort of a traditional order that has disappeared.

In its frantic search for happiness, Europe has also forgotten that it is no longer alone in the world; the West as a whole is having difficulty accepting these new realities. Instead of a stable world, we should be talking about turmoil without a compass. Blaise Pascal said that *'man's greatest misfortune is that he does not know how to rest in his room'*. If Racine could confine himself to Paris, this has become inconceivable in an age of travel and migration.

The question of ultimate purpose is no longer asked. The fear of God has disappeared and the Vatican, even for Catholics, since it refers mainly to a Europe with Christian origins, is sometimes perceived as much as a non-governmental organisation (NGO) as the heart of the most powerful religion in the world. Spirituality has not entirely disappeared, nor will it ever do so, but is it not located outside the churches and sometimes even against them?

The tip of the iceberg

If we are talking only about France, it no longer has the primacy of the Grand Siècle on the scale of the European continent, or even the world. In its time, France asserted itself after an Italy that was no more than a land of orange trees and ruins (see Goethe and his nostalgia for Italy: '*Kennst-du das Land wo die Zitronen blühen? im dunklen Laub dis Goldorangen glühen*' - Do you know the land where the lemon trees bloom? The dark foliage glows with orange-yellow). At Versailles, the centre of the world, the waters were harnessed by spectacular basins and fountains, but everything has been transformed into a movement that seems uncontrollable.

On a more down-to-earth level, promises, as always, are only binding on those who believe them. Who would oppose the announced increase in purchasing power for the majority? To raising the standard of living and quality of life by working relatively less, without raising taxes? Who would not dream of an ideal world, with no pandemics, no major climate disruption, no energy dependency and no war on our borders threatening our continent?

Genuine, reasonable choices must take all these dimensions and variables into account. They will also have to ascertain the identity of those who find themselves - and sometimes even hide - behind their champion, promoting or wishing to promote ideas that may be contrary to the values of the Republic, in the days of *wokism* - no longer the sole preserve of American university campuses - and anti-Semitism that we thought belonged to a bygone, ignominious and tragic era.

This does not mean that we should despair of politics, which is indispensable to societies and must remain a noble activity: ideally, it should express a will and a direction; one cannot exist without the other. It is the destruction of politics that leads distraught peoples to extremes. Political discourse and those who support it must be highlighted and sometimes unmasked - in view of the constant need to build - and never be considered as just the tip of an iceberg.

Reformation and Counter-Reformation clash today, in a great clash, within societies as well as on the international scene where a new deregulated and multipolar World is emerging. Nietzsche distinguished between the Apollonian spirit - made up of rationality and light, symbolised by the French mind - and the Dionysian spirit - made up of impulses and passions but also of depth - characteristic of German thought and sensibility. But is such a mental separation still valid in Europe, or is it not becoming necessary today with the clash of civilisations?

Baroque accompanied the Counter-Reformation, but it also preceded Classicism, of which France was the most dazzling incarnation in the Grand Siècle. *'Classicism is a mastered romanticism'*, said André Gide. The great movement of history is therefore pendular and cyclical, but the revolution of the person that will succeed the cult of the individual will always be possible, and it will once again be able to transform the universe.

Palm Sunday, 1st May 2025

Appendix

Interview with the author (16.11.2024):

From the imbalance of terror to the reinvention of diplomacy

What motivated you to write 'Imbalance of Terror' at this particular moment in history?

This book is a logical follow-up to a previous work, 'Journal d'Ukraine et de Russie' (Diary of Ukraine and Russia), published in the summer of 2022, whose subtitle was 'Crises and a changing international system'. This was an analysis of the changes that have taken place in the international system as a result of major international crises, such as the withdrawal from Afghanistan in the summer of 2021, the crisis between the United States and France over security in the Pacific - caused by Australia's abrupt termination, under pressure from Washington, of the contract to sell French nuclear submarines to Australia. in addition to the distrust shown towards France, the formation of the new AUKUS alliance between Australia, the United States and the United Kingdom, the beginnings of an anti-Beijing defence system, was a signal of hostility towards China. And of course there was the war in Ukraine.

This high-intensity conflict has continued ever since, and 'The Imbalance of Terror' has resulted in particular from the opposition between Russia, a nuclear power, and Ukraine, a conventional power, albeit supported by a broad coalition of states that are also members of NATO and include three nuclear powers. The balance of terror of the Cold War, during which nuclear weapons paradoxically ensured a degree of stability in the system, has been replaced by a more volatile overall situation. This was the starting point for this new book, which is by no means limited to questions of military strategy.

You describe the erosion of nuclear deterrence as a worrying phenomenon. What current factors make you fear that this balance of terror may be called into question?

During the war in Ukraine, the nuclear issue was raised on several occasions, more than subliminally but admittedly unofficially, particularly on the Russian side. According to specialists, military nuclear power has continued to be managed in a very 'classic' way and high-level contacts, particularly between high-ranking military personnel, have never ceased between the nuclear superpowers, the United States and Russia. But such references would have been unimaginable during the Cold War, apart from the climactic moment of the Cuban missile crisis in 1962.

Furthermore, it should be noted that the evolution of the world towards greater multipolarity has been accompanied by trends towards increased nuclear proliferation, both horizontal (see the number of countries involved) and vertical (see the sophistication of the means used). To what extent is North Korea, which is in the news, under the 'control' of China and Russia? Where does Iran stand in relation to the nuclear 'threshold', i.e. mastery of the manufacture of the weapon? If we are talking about Iran, what are the risks of proliferation on a regional scale in the Middle East region? (see, for example, the long-term ambitions of Saudi Arabia).

You see the Ukrainian crisis as a global watershed. In your view, does this conflict mark the end of an era in international relations? Is it still possible to return to the old order, or have we definitively entered a new geopolitical dynamic?

It's still too early to say that the war in Ukraine was a global turning point. It appears to be a conflict of the old order, anachronistic even by Cold War standards: The war in the Donbass was trench warfare, reminiscent even of the confrontations of the First World War in 14-18; the term 'high intensity' refers to the armoured vehicles and artillery of the Second World War; it is true that this war has also been perceived as a post-modern, robotic conflict, for example with the increasingly massive use of aerial drones, not forgetting the naval drones used in the Black Sea.

Everything will depend on how the crisis is resolved. Will an agreement be formalised beyond a de facto ceasefire? A broad, long-term agreement on a new European security architecture might prove premature and be reserved for another stage; but in any case it would raise the question of Ukraine's status: will it be subject to a form of military 'neutralisation' ? Will a true status of neutrality even be envisaged, which would not exclude defence capabilities but would certainly exclude participation in any type of military alliance? This point is certainly, in the Russian view at least, the real issue at stake in the war in Ukraine, if it was not Moscow's main objective at the outset of the war enterprise, failing to achieve it by other means, notably diplomatic or by putting pressure on the Ukrainian governments. Such an interpretation would mean that, from Russia's point of view, this was not a conflict over territory, with the exception of regions occupied by Russian-speaking communities turned towards Moscow.

In a multipolar world where alliances are becoming more 'à la carte', as you put it, what risks does this present for the more vulnerable players, such as small nations or international organisations?

Multipolarity and multilateralism are not identical concepts, but neither are they necessarily mutually exclusive. Depending on how we interpret the existence of a world dominated by new poles, the spread of power would be to the detriment of a single international system, dominated politically by an organisation such as the UN, despite its limitations.

This could be the phase we have entered. For its part, the G7 on the Western side, originally an economic forum - which enabled Russia to be added to a G8 that functioned until the annexation of Crimea in 2014 - has turned into a kind of political directoire, as demonstrated by the most recent summit in Hiroshima, where current conflicts were discussed.

The BRICS, now BRICS+ since the recent summit in Kazan, are a kind of counter-G7; a sign of political ambition, the Secretary-General of the United Nations was invited to attend; although the latter was present rather like a cousin in the style of Brittany, there is no structural incompatibility between the regional organisations and the United Nations, and such cooperation is moreover provided for in the Charter.

What is certain is that we will not be able to do without some form of centralisation of the political organisation of the international system at some point, unless we accept deregulation without safeguards, in other words a world in the state of nature as described in Thomas Hobbes' Leviathan ; I am not talking here about the specialised institutions of the UN or the various economic agencies in particular, but about a form of global political governance.

From this point of view, the UN must be reformed or, at the very least, its operating mechanisms must be transformed - and here we are thinking of the famous 'veto right' of the current permanent members of the UN Security Council - and the Security Council must be enlarged to better reflect the state of the world. It is then that multipolarity and multilateralism can be brought closer together, if not superimposed.

You describe the weakening of international law and the decline of diplomacy in conflict resolution. What approach do you think could be taken to restore diplomacy to its regulatory role?

Part of the answer lies in resolving the issue of enlarging the Security Council, as mentioned earlier. Such a reform, which has been talked about for over twenty years, has been put off for too long for many complex reasons. At the end of the 90s, India, a natural candidate - publicly supported at the time by France, Germany, Japan (NB: at the time the 2nd largest contributor to the UN) and 'a major African country' - carried out nuclear experiments, as did Pakistan. Moreover, any candidacy is bound to give rise to counterclaims: if we are talking about Germany, for example (NB: long described as an 'economic giant' but also a 'political dwarf'), Italy - whose presence on the international stage is now more assertive and which retains a great diplomatic tradition - cannot fail to see its exclusion from the closed club as a *diminutio capitis*. The fact that the new French Foreign Minister has just mentioned France's support for the idea of 'two African states' in the Council is a clear indication of the renewed topicality of the issue of enlargement in the wake of the war in Ukraine.

But the answer cannot be limited to the question of institutional mechanisms. We also need to talk about the international context. Apart from the question of the end of the war on the European continent - which seems to affect the system more than the conflicts in the Middle East (NB: Russia and a fortiori China have remained relatively aloof) - what will be the policy of the new American administration? What will happen in the coming years to Sino-American relations, which could have the effect of 'structuring' the system on their own? What's more, sometimes all it takes is one major event to tip the balance in one direction or the other. At the end of the 1980s, when the Cold War was not over and was partly responsible for it, the United Nations was paralysed, discredited even, in a way that was completely unfair to the Secretary-General at the time, the Peruvian Javier Perez de Cuellar, a very fine diplomat. All it took was the resolution of the Iran-Iraq conflict, followed by the independence of Namibia, the settlement in Cambodia and the end of apartheid in South Africa, to completely change the mood and the situation in New York; this development was of course greatly facilitated by developments in the Soviet Union under Gorbachev, which led the USSR to cooperate in the Security Council. Today, the focus is mainly on Ukraine and Iran/Middle East, and to a lesser extent on the Formosa Strait and Taiwan, which is a longer-term issue.

The rise of populism is another central theme in your book. How is this phenomenon linked to the current major international crises, and what consequences might it have for democracies ?

Although it's not a central issue, it's one that can't be ignored, and it's often in the headlines, from Brexit to Trump's MAGA, to name but a few in the Western world. It is better to talk about populisms than populism as a single, one-dimensional phenomenon. All the more so since populists themselves generally insist on national specificity.

My analysis is that populism is closely linked to a common quest for identity, but that it expresses itself in different forms: non-interventionism, protectionism, sovereignism, even nationalism. It reveals itself from one region of the world to another: from the American Middle West to Prime Minister Modi's Hindu India, from a Russia returning to an imperial project based on history and orthodoxy to certain parts of Europe contesting a federalist drift away from the control of nations and peoples. Populism may be seen as a danger to democracy, but it exists in countries with diverse political systems, from Indian 'democracy' to Russian autocracy, from Europe with its wide variety of political systems to the United States with its strict presidential system. Conversely, depriving populist movements of any expression can also be contrary to democracy and even paradoxically dangerous for it.

*** As a diplomat, you have certainly observed global power games at close quarters. What moments or experiences in your career have had the greatest impact on you and perhaps influenced your approach in this book? ***

It's naturally tempting to think of several moments over several decades of diplomatic life. My first diplomatic post in East Berlin, behind the wall rather than in front of it, in an atmosphere worthy of the famous film 'The Lives of Others' (das Leben der Anderen), could not have given me a better feel for the realities of the Cold War; on the other hand, the appearance in December 1988 of Mr. Gorbachev's rock-star appearance at the UN General Assembly - announcing a unilateral reduction of Soviet military forces by 500,000 men and their withdrawal from certain countries in the Socialist camp, including Poland and the GDR - preceded its disintegration. At the same time, following S. Hussein's invasion of Kuwait in August 1991, the Security Council negotiated a series of resolutions sanctioning Iraq and paving the way for a military operation against that country, thereby ushering in a more unipolar world dominated by American hyper-power. It is from this period that the world is in the process of emerging with what is known as multipolarity.

But I could also talk about the Middle East, where I witnessed the height of French influence in Syria and the influence we were able to exert in the region, not just for ourselves but in favour of peace, which is also in our overriding interests as a country bordering the Mediterranean; or Central Asia, which is often overlooked but of considerable strategic importance, and where the new 'Great Game' of the 21st century will be played out.

You describe transnational threats such as digital surveillance and terrorism, which often fall outside the traditional diplomatic framework. What solutions do you envisage to deal with these problems more effectively?

There are specialised bodies and organisations to deal with these issues, but traditional international, regional (see the Five Eyes of Western intelligence) or bilateral cooperation remains relevant. For example, the attack on a Moscow concert hall in March 2024 was the subject of a prior warning from a Western source to the Russian authorities. This illustrates that security cooperation sometimes survives tensions between states and that it can even be an important reason for bringing them closer together or attempting to do so (see France's efforts at one point to re-establish cooperation - which was very effective - with Syria in the fight against terrorism; but it was unable or unwilling to draw the political conclusions from this in its relations with Bashar al-Assad's regime).

In your conclusion, you call for international cooperation to manage global crises such as climate change. Do you think that current governments and institutions are ready for such cooperation, or should we expect a major restructuring of the international order?

We have undoubtedly experienced a certain 'eclipse' of diplomacy in recent years, and the war in Ukraine immediately springs to mind to explain the phenomenon. Climate change is one of them, but we could also mention nuclear non-proliferation, the persistent challenge of development and migration, all major issues that cannot be resolved in isolation.

Diplomacy will have its day again. It was defined by P. Renouvin and J.B. Duroselle, masters of international relations, as *'relations between political communities organised within the framework of a territory'*. It is therefore like a natural breath of air dating back to time immemorial and known in Mesopotamia as well as between Greek city-states, before being formalised in the Italian *Quattrocento*. The great diplomatic traditions endure, even in countries that are not necessarily at the forefront of the international scene, such as Italy and Turkey, heir to the Ottoman Empire. It is true that diplomats need a major project to truly flourish; its conception responds to fundamental national, regional or global interests, and its implementation is up to them, calling on all the resources of their experience and culture, in a process that is sometimes akin to artistic craftsmanship. Today, diplomacy has also become economic or cultural, in the service of what is known as soft power. Diplomacy is eternal: without being inappropriately humorous, it is also one of the 'oldest professions in the world', but it must be constantly reinvented.

Index

A

Aeschylus : 346

Afghanistan : 9, 33, 39, 66, 67, 69, 93, 94, 123, 127, 128, 130, 132, 160, 161, 162, 163, 164, 174, 178, 184, 189, 194, 199, 202, 236, 283, 315, 325, 327, 359

Africa : 41, 62, 84, 120, 126, 143, 144, 145, 146, 147, 148, 150, 151, 234, 287

Agrippina (Nero) : 298, 299

Airbus : 29, 31, 129, 151, 152, 318

Alexander (the Great) : 36, 297, 302, 303, 342, 343, 344, 347, 348, 349, 350, 351, 353

Alawites : 54, 58, 159, 303

Algeria : 102, 103, 153, 154, 155, 156, 157, 158, 159, 249, 254, 268

Allison (Graham) : 59, 180, 182

Alstom : 115, 116, 117, 118, 120, 129

Annan (Kofi) : 62, 63

Appeasement : 13, 71, 83, 157

Apple : 152, 181, 182

Arabelle (turbine) : 114, 115, 117

Assad (Bashar) : 49, 50, 51, 54, 304

AUKUS (Indo-Pacific) : 138, 165, 179, 315, 320, 359

Autonomy (European strategic) : 20, 42, 77, 78, 83, 165, 181, 234, 299, 320

B

Baker (James) : 225, 226

Bandoeng (conference) : 126, 143, 217

Baroque : 291, 354, 358

Berdiaev (Nicolas) : 221

Berdymuhamedov (President) : 33, 126, 131

Berlin (Quadripartite Agreement) : 175

Berlin (Wall) : 153, 160

Biden (Joe) : 39, 47, 59, 108, 119, 139, 153, 181, 184, 186, 187, 188, 191, 192, 193, 194, 195, 196, 197, 198, 199, 201, 202, 204, 242, 321

Black Sea : 17, 18, 124, 170, 229, 361

Blanc (Pierre-Louis) : 29

Blinken (Antony) : 21, 39, 181, 186, 195

Braudel (Fernand) : 160

Brazil : 143, 203

Brezhnev (Doctrine) : 318

BRI (Belt and Road Initiative) : 137, 222, 326

BRICS : 15, 153, 222, 319, 324, 325, 326, 328, 362

Brink (André) : 145

Brochand (Pierre) : 29, 30

Budapest (Protocol) : 43, 232
Buffer zone : 42, 230, 235, 236, 327
Burns (William) : 181, 195
Bush (George Jr.) : 67, 174, 189, 192, 226, 253
Bush (George Sr.) : 11, 30, 189, 190, 203, 204, 227, 318, 329, 334

C

Carter (Jimmy) : 34, 185, 190, 206
Caspian Sea : 45, 123, 125, 127, 131, 134
Caucasus : 90, 93, 94, 123, 131, 171, 172, 173, 352
Chateaubriand (François-René) : 198, 289
Central Asia : 24, 30, 67, 93, 97, 122, 123, 124, 125, 126, 127, 128, 129, 130, 131, 134, 136, 139, 140, 141, 163, 171, 172, 173, 174, 219, 223, 231, 232, 283, 287, 342, 346, 365
Chiang Kai-shek : 66, 178, 209, 213, 214, 215
China : 11, 12, 13, 14, 15, 21, 23, 32, 34, 38, 41, 66, 76, 93, 94, 97, 104, 105, 107, 111, 113, 119, 122, 123, 124, 125, 126, 127, 130, 132, 133, 134, 135, 136, 137, 138, 139, 140, 141, 142, 143, 151, 152, 161, 163, 166, 170, 172, 177, 178, 179, 180, 181, 182, 190, 191, 195, 196, 199, 202, 207, 208, 209, 210, 211, 212, 213, 214, 215, 216, 217, 218, 219, 220, 221, 222, 223, 224, 233, 234, 239, 240, 287, 293, 294, 299, 310, 311, 314, 316, 319, 320, 321, 325, 326, 328, 329, 330, 331, 332, 333, 335, 336, 337, 342, 359, 360, 363
Chirac (Jacques) : 50, 52, 54, 260, 265, 304, 309
Chou En-laï : 80, 208, 209, 216, 217
CIS (Commonwealth of Independent States) : 92, 124, 131, 172, 229
Clinton (Bill) : 34, 47, 195, 196, 241
Clinton (Hillary) : 202
Cold War : 11, 12, 13, 15, 19, 20, 24, 64, 66, 70, 74, 101, 110, 114, 123, 137, 143, 151, 170, 175, 177, 182, 183, 204, 221, 225, 227, 313, 314, 316, 317, 319, 325, 329, 330, 332, 336, 359, 360, 363, 364
Condominium (American-Soviet) : 11, 12, 75, 81, 325, 332
Crimea : 28, 41, 79, 82, 98, 173, 226, 232, 233, 234, 235, 308, 327, 336, 361
Crisis (global economic and financial) : 90, 94, 113, 117, 120, 318
CSTO (Collective Security Treaty Organisation) : 124
Cuba (missiles crisis) : 18, 20, 59, 60, 61, 70, 147, 166, 175, 180, 217, 317, 360
Cyrus (the Great) : 7, 283, 284, 350

D

Daesh : 35, 46, 55, 173
Decision (Essence of) : 59, 180
De Gaulle : 18, 26, 29, 71, 78, 121, 155, 158, 166, 175, 243, 244, 249, 262, 267, 268, 274, 292, 305, 309
De Klerk (Frederic) : 146
Deng Xiao-ping : 178, 207, 208, 209, 210, 212, 216, 217, 321
Despotism (Enlightened) : 89, 99

Deterrent : 42, 48, 61, 77, 230, 238, 281, 302, 340
Donbas : 20, 40, 69, 73, 76, 78, 83, 138, 226, 322, 323, 360
Dresden : 313

E
Eisenhower (Dwight) : 36, 66, 166, 178
Erdogan : 51
Eurasia : 76, 124, 129, 139, 219, 220, 221, 224, 325, 326, 328
EU (Commission) : 94, 100, 102, 103, 104, 107, 108, 114, 119, 142, 227, 230, 244, 235, 327, 336, 337, 338
Ethiopia : 30, 32, 146, 147, 319, 325
Europe : 12, 13, 14, 15, 17, 18, 20, 21, 26, 28, 34, 38, 39, 40, 41, 42, 53, 54, 57, 66, 68, 69, 70, 71, 72, 76, 77, 78, 79, 83, 84, 85, 92, 94, 96, 98, 99, 100, 101, 102, 103, 104, 105, 107, 108, 109, 110, 111, 112, 114, 115, 119, 121, 123, 124, 125, 126, 128, 129, 130, 131, 132, 135, 137, 138, 140, 141, 142, 151, 153, 155, 159, 161, 163, 164, 165, 166, 167, 168, 169, 170, 171, 172, 173, 175, 176, 178, 179, 181, 182, 194, 196, 200, 201, 202, 203, 204, 206, 207, 211, 213, 216, 217, 218, 220, 221, 222, 224, 226, 227, 230, 233, 234, 235, 236, 237, 238, 242, 244, 245, 246, 248, 251, 257, 268, 272, 276, 277, 279, 281, 288, 299, 300, 301, 307, 308, 309, 314, 320, 321, 322, 323, 324, 325, 326, 327, 328, 329, 330, 331, 333, 334, 335, 336, 337, 338, 339, 340, 341, 342, 354, 356, 357, 358, 361, 363, 364

F
FAO (Food and Agricultural Organisation) : 144, 145
France : 26, 28, 29, 32, 33, 35, 37, 39, 41, 42, 43, 44, 48, 49, 50, 51, 52, 53, 54, 55, 63, 66, 68, 71, 77, 78, 81, 83, 91, 100, 101, 102, 103, 109, 110, 111, 114, 115, 118, 125, 129, 144, 145, 148, 153, 154, 155, 157, 158, 159, 164, 165, 166, 167, 168, 169, 170, 172, 173, 175, 176, 178, 200, 202, 203, 207, 209, 211, 216, 218, 228, 230, 231, 232, 234, 243, 244, 245, 247, 248, 249, 250, 251, 252, 253, 254, 256, 258, 259, 266, 267, 268, 269, 272, 274, 276, 277, 278, 279, 281, 284, 285, 288, 289, 290, 292, 304, 308, 309, 311, 314, 315, 316, 319, 320, 325, 336, 337, 338, 341, 357, 358, 359, 362, 363, 365
Fossil (fuels) : 100, 110, 112
Francis (Pope) : 276, 280, 289, 290, 291, 292, 293, 294, 295, 296, 297, 312
Frozen (conflict) : 40, 42, 230, 235, 237, 327

G
Gaidar (Egor) : 228
Gazprom : 92, 101, 111, 115, 229, 338
General Electric : 117
Germany : 53, 54, 63, 77, 102, 103, 105, 108, 110, 111, 115, 129, 152, 153, 155, 156, 167, 176, 179, 181, 183, 184, 221, 225, 237, 238, 242, 255, 275, 278, 279, 317, 319, 321, 323, 328, 338, 339, 340, 355, 362
Giscard d'Estaing (Valéry) : 27, 37, 311

Georgia : 67, 69, 93, 94, 97, 174, 200, 201, 213, 226, 230, 235, 249, 327, 331, 334
Glienicke (bridge) : 183
Golan (Heights) : 44, 46, 50, 51, 180
Gorbachev (Mikhail) : 79, 85, 86, 88, 146, 225, 227, 228, 229, 280, 317, 363, 364
Great Game : 122, 123, 129, 136, 141, 163, 172, 173, 342, 365
Group (of 77) : 143
Gulf War : 11, 19, 38, 60, 107, 190, 204, 228, 240, 280, 315, 318, 329, 334
G7 : 34, 41, 141, 228, 234, 325, 336, 361, 362

H

Hadrian (Emperor) : 171
Haile Selassie : 148, 149, 150
Harris (Kamala) : 184, 185, 186, 187, 188, 189, 190, 191, 192, 193, 195, 196, 197, 202, 206
Heartland : 133, 219, 221
Hezbollah : 44, 45, 46, 48, 49, 59
Hiroshima (G7) : 41, 141, 234, 361
Hiroshima (Nagasaki) : 18, 160, 179, 300, 310, 312, 313
Hobbes (Thomas) : 17, 20, 21, 321, 362

I

ICC (International Criminal Court) : 205, 239, 240
India (Pakistan) : 63, 66, 76, 104, 113, 119, 127, 132, 136, 137, 143, 151, 152, 153, 161, 162, 178, 182, 203, 204, 216, 275, 283, 320, 325, 328, 342, 362, 364
Imbalance/Balance (of Terror) : 14, 19, 359
Infra-nuclear : 20, 70, 321
Iran : 13, 21, 29, 30, 33, 38, 45, 46, 47, 48, 54, 55, 58, 59, 61, 71, 72, 93, 107, 109, 113, 119, 120, 123, 131, 132, 136, 161, 165, 176, 196, 223, 224, 282, 283, 316, 317, 319, 325, 333, 336, 342, 360, 363
Iraq : 30, 51, 52, 55, 60, 62, 102, 189, 190, 194, 236, 244, 253, 315, 316, 317, 319, 324, 327, 363, 364
Islam : 49, 127, 173, 275, 280, 284, 286, 287, 293, 301, 302, 303, 355
Israel : 29, 44, 45, 46, 47, 48, 50, 51, 56, 59, 61, 71, 72, 111, 186, 196, 240, 241, 280
Istanbul (talks) : 41, 234
ITAR : 32

J

Japan : 63, 101, 113, 152, 178, 179, 180, 181, 182, 209, 213, 214, 215, 216, 221, 230, 294, 310, 312, 320, 362
Jefferson (Thomas) : 190, 311
Jesuits : 213, 292, 294, 355
Jobert (Michel) : 27
John Paul II (Pope) : 51, 279, 280, 281, 291, 293

K

Karaganov (Sergei) : 75, 76, 77, 80
Kazakhstan : 32, 124, 125, 127, 128, 129, 131, 134, 136, 141, 172, 173, 227
Kennedy (John F.) : 60, 61, 166, 189, 198
Kerry (John) : 81, 195
Kirienko (Sergei) : 118
Khodorkovsky (Mikhail) : 85, 88
Khrushchev (Nikita) : 60
Kissinger (Henry) : 12, 13, 27, 61, 332
Korea (North) : 13, 21, 46, 65, 176, 186, 223, 224, 317, 333, 360
Kuwait : 60, 190, 236, 315, 316, 317, 324, 327, 364
Kurds : 51, 54, 55, 304
Kursk : 72, 73, 74, 77, 112, 160, 236

L

Lavrov (Sergei) : 21, 79, 80, 81, 82, 83, 84, 85, 98, 128
League (of Nations) : 30, 52, 53, 64, 65, 319, 322
Lebanon : 47, 48, 49, 50, 52, 53, 59
Long March (Mao's) : 32, 37, 209
LNG (Liquefied Natural Gas) : 100, 102, 103, 104, 105, 106, 108, 109, 110, 111, 338
Louis XIII : 288
Louis XIV : 64, 288, 356

M

Malraux (André) : 210, 243
Mandate (of France) : 49, 58, 304
Mao Tse-tung : 37, 133, 207, 208, 209, 210, 211, 212, 214, 216, 217, 343
Margerie (Christophe de) : 103
Marseillaise : 36, 37
Meacham (Jon) : 197, 311
Medvedev (Dimitri) : 80, 82, 90, 92, 93, 96, 97, 98, 110, 113, 116, 118, 125
Merkel (Angela) : 132
Middle East : 15, 17, 21, 24, 32, 38, 41, 45, 46, 47, 48, 49, 52, 59, 62, 72, 81, 160, 177, 183, 184, 186, 195, 199, 282, 304, 337, 360, 363, 365
Mitteleuropa : 153
Mitterrand (François) : 25, 33, 50, 52, 54, 55, 129, 145, 228, 249, 250, 255, 260, 263, 265, 268, 304, 316
Modi (Prime minister) : 122, 151, 153, 203, 204, 364
Mondale (Walter) : 190
Moulin (Jean) : 243
Mozart (Wolfgang Amadeus) : 276, 277, 355
Multipolar (world) : 15, 20, 107, 221, 222, 223, 318, 319, 324, 325, 326, 358, 361
Munich (1938) : 20, 71, 82, 138, 249, 314, 318, 320

Musk (Elon) : 40, 205

N

Nabiullina (Elvira) : 92
Narychkin (Sergei) : 82, 118
NATO : 39, 42, 43, 55, 62, 66, 67, 70, 83, 85, 94, 108, 127, 164, 166, 169, 174, 177, 178, 181, 182, 184, 196, 196, 200, 201, 222, 223, 225, 226, 230, 231, 233, 234, 235, 236, 237, 238, 242, 279, 320, 326, 327, 330, 331, 334, 335, 336, 340, 359
Naval Group : 165
Neutrality : 43, 124, 128, 231, 232, 280, 361
New International Order : 11, 19, 203, 204, 318, 329, 334
New Start (Treaty) : 195
Nixon (Richard) : 11, 12, 27, 61, 166, 190, 330, 332
Notre-Dame (of Paris) : 281, 289, 290
Nord Stream : 100, 104, 107, 108, 110, 111, 114, 115, 119, 323
Nowruz : 283, 284, 287, 343
Nuclear-generated (electricity) : 112
Nye (Joseph) : 34

O

OAU (Organisation of African Unity) : 147
Obama (Barack) : 47, 67, 174, 181, 187, 189, 191, 192, 194, 195, 196, 198, 219, 253, 328, 343
Oppenheimer (Dr.) : 18
Oslo (Convention) : 204, 241, 242

P

Pacific : 138, 139, 165, 178, 179, 182, 188, 192, 315, 320, 342, 359
Palestinians : 47, 48, 241, 304
Palmyra : 35, 50, 159, 302, 303
Paolo (Dall'Oglio) : 305
Paris (2024) : 33, 34, 35, 36
Patrushev (Nicolai) : 82
Pearl Harbor : 178, 215, 313
Pelosi (Nancy) : 187
Peskov (Dmitri) : 80
Pompidou (Georges) : 27, 175, 218, 262, 263, 272, 274
Pope : 40, 44, 51, 275, 276, 277, 279, 280, 281, 288, 289, 290, 291, 292, 293, 294, 295, 296, 297, 312, 355
Populism : 19, 202, 203, 204, 314, 328, 363, 364
Powell (Colin) : 60
Power of Siberia : 104, 220
Primakov (Evgeny) : 82, 135, 137, 176, 220, 221, 222, 326, 328

Putin (Vladimir) : 13, 20, 42, 45, 67, 74, 75, 77, 79, 80, 82, 84, 86, 88, 90, 91, 92, 94, 96, 97, 98, 105, 113, 116, 117, 118, 122, 130, 131, 132, 133, 134, 135, 136, 138, 140, 151, 173, 174, 176, 183, 184, 185, 219, 221, 222, 223, 224, 225, 230, 236, 237, 240, 307, 318, 320, 325, 326, 330, 331, 334, 335
Putsch : 27, 79, 84, 85, 86, 87, 88, 198, 229

Q

Qaeda (Al) : 46, 50, 161
Quai d'Orsay : 22, 23, 24, 25, 26, 27, 28, 29, 52, 144, 240, 242

R

Rafale (aircraft) : 70, 78
Reformation : 275, 354, 355, 358
Rémond (René) : 216, 267
Rolls-Royce : 152
Romania (Moldava) : 84, 166, 167, 168, 169, 170, 171, 249
Rosatom : 115, 116, 118, 119, 120, 125
Roxane : 343, 350, 351, 353
Russia : 11, 12, 13, 14, 15, 18, 19, 21, 30, 32, 34, 35, 38, 40, 41, 42, 43, 44, 45, 46, 49, 51, 61, 65, 67, 68, 69, 72, 73, 74, 75, 76, 77, 79, 80, 81, 82, 83, 84, 86, 87, 88, 90, 91, 92, 93, 94, 95, 96, 97, 98, 99, 100, 101, 102, 103, 104, 105, 106, 107, 108, 109, 110, 111, 112, 113, 114, 115, 116, 117, 118, 119, 120, 121, 122, 123, 124, 125, 126, 128, 130, 131, 132, 133, 134, 135, 136, 137, 138, 139, 140, 141, 142, 143, 151, 161, 163, 167, 168, 171, 172, 173, 174, 176, 181, 182, 183, 184, 185, 186, 195, 200, 201, 203, 204, 205, 214, 216, 219, 220, 221, 222, 223, 224, 225, 226, 227, 228, 229, 230, 232, 233, 234, 235, 236, 237, 239, 243, 244, 252, 254, 279, 280, 286, 287, 293, 300, 306, 307, 308, 309, 316, 317, 319, 321, 322, 323, 324, 325, 326, 327, 328, 329, 330, 332, 333, 334, 336, 338, 339, 341, 342, 359, 360, 361, 363, 364, 365

S

Saakashvili (Mikhail) : 94
Sanctions : 83, 88, 94, 100, 102, 103, 106, 107, 108, 109, 110, 111, 131, 140, 142, 145, 205, 232, 233, 235, 237, 327, 336, 338, 339
Schmidt (Helmut) : 102, 238, 340
Schuman (Robert) : 28
SCO (Shanghai Cooperation Organisation) : 136, 138
Sechin : 118
Secretary general (United Nations) : 62, 63, 64, 177, 322
Security Council (UN) : 11, 13, 15, 19, 24, 29, 30, 38, 40, 48, 51, 52, 60, 61, 62, 63, 64, 65, 66, 81, 82, 102, 106, 109, 137, 138, 152, 176, 177, 204, 224, 239, 241, 314, 315, 317, 318, 322, 329, 331, 333, 334, 335, 362, 363, 364
Siberia (Power of) : 101, 104, 115, 136, 142, 220
Siemens : 113, 117, 119

Silk Roads (BRI) : 123, 126, 139, 141, 161, 172, 342
Simonian (Margarita) : 79, 98
Skolkovo (Innovation city) : 80, 96
Sobyanine : 118
Soft power : 33, 34, 36, 68, 119, 123, 124, 131, 172, 342, 366
Soong : 211, 212, 213, 215
South Africa (apartheid) : 107, 145, 283, 319, 363
South China (Sea) : 139
South (Collective) : 17, 21, 80, 99, 120, 132, 143, 144, 159, 160, 173, 177, 217, 222, 320, 324
Space X : 32
Staël (Germaine de) : 7, 58
St Petersburg (Economic Forum) : 23, 35, 93, 117
Suez (1956) : 20, 115, 129, 165, 314
Supreme Court : 165, 191, 239, 244, 245, 246, 247, 256
Sun Yat-sen : 208, 212, 213, 214
Syria : 35, 45, 46, 47, 49, 50, 51, 52, 53, 54, 55, 81, 159, 190, 194, 244, 253, 288, 301, 302, 303, 304, 347, 351, 365

T

Taiwan : 17, 34, 137, 138, 139, 196, 208, 215, 293, 314, 341, 363
Taliban : 39, 130, 160, 163, 194, 244, 315
Tanizaki (Jun'ichirō) : 215
TAPI (gas pipeline) : 132, 162
Terror (Balance/Imbalance) : 14, 18, 19, 74, 75, 317, 359, 360
Thales : 31, 32, 33, 129
Thucydide (trap) : 180, 182
Tocqueville (Alexis de) : 251, 252
Tolstoy (Leo) : 308, 324
Total : 102, 105, 109, 114, 129, 132
Troubles (Time of) : 98
Trump (Donald) : 11, 13, 14, 39, 70, 166, 176, 181, 182, 185, 186, 187, 188, 190, 191, 192, 193, 194, 195, 196, 197, 199, 200, 201, 202, 203, 204, 205, 236, 237, 239, 245, 328, 329, 330, 331, 334, 335, 336, 363
Turkey : 50, 51, 54, 55, 61, 66, 119, 136, 178, 184, 325, 342, 366
Turkmenistan : 31, 32, 33, 45, 124, 125, 128, 129, 130, 131, 132, 134, 136, 162, 172, 231, 232

U

Ubris : 61, 204, 205, 298, 318, 351
Ukraine : 11, 12, 13, 15, 17, 18, 19, 20, 21, 24, 34, 38, 39, 40, 41, 42, 43, 45, 47, 60, 61, 64, 65, 67, 68, 69, 70, 72, 73, 74, 75, 76, 79, 82, 83, 84, 85, 86, 89, 90, 92, 96, 97, 98, 99, 100, 102, 103, 105, 108, 109, 110, 111, 112, 114, 119, 120, 122, 124, 127, 130, 131, 133, 134, 135, 136, 137, 138, 139, 140, 153, 164, 166, 167, 168, 169, 170, 172, 174, 176, 177, 181, 182, 184, 185, 186, 195, 196, 199, 200,

201, 204, 206, 219, 220, 223, 224, 225, 226, 227, 229, 230, 231, 232, 233, 234, 235, 236, 237, 238, 242, 243, 279, 299, 300, 306, 307, 316, 317, 320, 321, 322, 323, 325, 326, 327, 328, 329, 330, 331, 332, 333, 334, 336, 337, 338, 339, 340, 342, 359, 360, 361, 363, 365

UNIFIL : 48, 49

United States : 11, 12, 13, 14, 19, 23, 27, 34, 36, 39, 41, 42, 43, 59, 63, 66, 67, 70, 72, 76, 77, 78, 81, 83, 94, 101, 103, 105, 109, 110, 111, 119, 123, 126, 128, 134, 139, 140, 142, 151, 152, 153, 161, 163, 165, 166, 174, 176, 178, 179, 180, 181, 182, 183, 185, 186, 187, 188, 189, 190, 191, 192, 193, 195, 196, 197, 199, 200, 201, 203, 204, 205, 208, 209, 213, 214, 215, 218, 219, 221, 224, 231, 233, 234, 236, 237, 239, 240, 242, 243, 244, 245, 246, 252, 253, 299, 310, 311, 312, 314, 315, 317, 318, 320, 321, 327, 328, 329, 330, 331, 332, 333, 334, 335, 340, 342, 359, 360, 364

UNO (United Nations) : 13, 15, 24, 29, 38, 48, 61, 62, 63, 64, 66, 81, 82, 109, 122, 124, 137, 139, 143, 177, 180, 232, 241, 315, 322, 333, 362, 363

V

Vatican (Holy See) : 84, 276, 277, 279, 280, 289, 291, 292, 293, 356

Versailles (Treaty) : 240

Veto (right of) : 106, 362

Vietnam : 12, 38, 61, 104, 146, 166, 179, 182, 189, 193, 196, 205, 217, 236, 242, 243, 243, 294, 310, 311, 327, 332, 340

W

Wehrkunde : 20, 138, 249, 320

WFP (World Food Programme) : 144

X

Xi Jinping : 14, 126, 133, 134, 136, 138, 140, 141, 181, 207, 211, 331, 335

Y

Yeltsin (Boris) : 86, 88, 90, 94, 221, 227, 228, 229

Z

Zaporijjia : 74, 112

Zelensky (Volodymyr) : 38, 40, 138, 167, 226, 309, 330, 334

Zimbabwe : 145, 146

Zorgbibe (Pr. Charles) : 27, 61, 259, 261

Zyuganov : 91, 221